PRAISE FOR ROBERT MOSS'S *THE THREE "ONLY" THINGS*

"Readers will be pleased and inspired by Moss's reinterpretation of the world."

— *Library Journal*

"The pioneer of a dream-interpreting technique called Active Dreaming, Australian-born Moss believes that the Three Only Things can connect with extraordinary sources of direction, healing, and energy. Writing about dreams, Moss is eloquent and authoritative, a wise teacher."

— *Publishers Weekly*

"Robert Moss, a great storyteller and master of the practical, shows us how to reclaim this side of our life. In our demanding, challenging world, we ignore this book's vital message at our peril."

— Barbara Montgomery Dossey, PhD, RN,
author of *Holistic Nursing: A Handbook for Practice*

"What Robert Moss does — again and again and with such clarity and greatness of heart — is to remind us that magic is a breath away and that everyone has the capacity to tap into the heritage that is truly ours. Everyone and anyone can lift the lid on their life — we can all find our soul's purpose and live it fully and with heart."

— Manda Scott, bestselling author of the Boudica novels

"If I could say 'only three things' about it: intensely engaging; a source of clarity on the deeper truth that guides us all; and truly inspiring — a must-read."

— Robert Hoss, MS, author of *Dream Language* and
executive officer, International Association for the Study of Dreams

the *SECRET*
HISTORY *of*
DREAMING

the SECRET HISTORY of DREAMING

ROBERT MOSS

New World Library
Novato, California

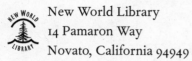 New World Library
14 Pamaron Way
Novato, California 94949

Text design by Tona Pearce Myers

Library of Congress Cataloging-in-Publication Data
Moss, Robert.
  The secret history of dreaming / Robert Moss.
      p.   cm.
Includes bibliographical references and index.
ISBN 978-1-57731-638-1 (hardcover : alk. paper)
  1. Dreams—History. I. Title.
BF1078.M66 2009
154.6'309—dc22   2008033009

First printing, January 2009
ISBN 978-1-57731-638-1
Printed in Canada on 100% postconsumer-waste recycled paper

g New World Library is a proud member of the Green Press Initiative.

10 9 8 7 6 5 4 3 2 1

For Marcia, who saw and believed in this book
twenty years before it was written

❦

CONTENTS

INTRODUCTION

❧

FIELDS OF DREAMING

The imaginal life is central to the human story, and should be central to the writing and teaching of history. The world of imagination nourishes humans and leads them to action. A history without imagination is a mutilated history, a history of the walking dead.

— JACQUES LE GOFF, *The Medieval Imagination*

Our project was fraught with peril. The ground we hoped to explore was untouched. No one had sifted through or even identified useful source materials . . . . We had to clear away the brush, stake our claim, and, like archaeologists approaching a site known to contain riches too great to be systematically explored, settle for excavating a few preliminary trenches.

— GEORGES DUBY, ON THE MAKING OF *A History of Private Life*

I

Dreaming is vital to the human story, central to our survival and evolution, to creative endeavors in every field, and quite simply, to *getting us through*. This book addresses the central importance of dreams, coincidence, and imagination as secret engines in the history of all things human.

It may be that, just as babies rehearse for walking and talking in dreams before they have developed the corresponding physical abilities, humanity rehearses for new phases in its development through dreaming. We are on the edge of grasping what this might mean when we talk about ideas that are "in the air." We see one facet of it when we learn that artists and science fiction writers have frequently anticipated new technologies by decades or centuries.

If I were writing in French, I might call this book an essay in *l'histoire de l'imaginaire*, a field pioneered and passionately advocated by the great French medievalist Jacques LeGoff. But the word *imaginaire* does not translate comfortably into English. It refers to the "imaginal realm," a dimension beyond the physical that is the precinct and playground of *true* imagination, a creative realm that may be the seedbed of our great discoveries and innovations, and even the origin of events and situations that are manifested in the surface world. Indigenous peoples call it the Dreamtime or the dreamworld. We go there when we go dreaming, which may or may not involve going to sleep.

In modern Western societies, we think of dreams as sleep experiences. But for many cultures, dreaming is fundamentally about waking up. In the language of ancient Egypt, the word for "dream" is *rswt*, which means "awakening."[1] The implication is that, in much of ordinary life, we are in the condition of sleepwalkers, following programs and routines. In dreams, we wake up. This may happen during sleep, or in a twilight state of reverie, or in a vision or meditation or shamanic journey, or through the dreamlike play of coincidence and symbolic "pop-ups" in the midst of everyday life — all of which may be viewed as modes of dreaming and may provide experiences that can be reviewed and honored in the manner of dreams.

To uncover the real history of dreaming, we need to read scenes from other times with the patience and intuition of a *CSI* technician. We need to flag and tag as evidence all sorts of clues and sources that previously may not have been recognized as relevant. We need to situate dreaming activity in its social and cultural context. Above all, we need to imagine ourselves inside the scene, as vividly as basketball great Bill Russell did when he replayed games inside his head — and then go beyond the mental replay into a deeper play.

"Dream archeologist" is my name for the kind of investigator who is able to read all the clues from a scene in another time, *enter* that scene, and then bring back new discoveries that will stand up to cross-examination. While archeology is often understood to be the science of unearthing and studying antiquities, the root meaning of the word takes us deeper: it is the study of the *arche*, the first and primal, chief and essential, things.

There are three essential requirements for the dream archeologist. The first is mastery of a panoply of sources, along with the ability to read between the lines and make connections that have gone unnoticed by specialists who were looking for something else.

Second, the dream archeologist must have the ability to locate dreaming in its context — physical, social, and cultural. For example, to understand the dream

practices of the Mayoruna Indians of Amazonia (known as Cat People), we need
to know that, in the typical sleeping arrangement, you climb into a hammock
woven from vines and tied at one end to the center pole of the communal hut,
as are all the other hammocks. If you go to bed alone, you'll pull down the center pole and all the other hammocks. You have to agree with at least one other
person that you'll go to bed at the same time. So sleep and dreaming are shared
experiences from the moment you decide to go to bed.[2]

We need to understand the imaginal space, as well as the physical space,
within which dreaming experiences take place. Certain cultures instruct or
even command dream travelers to journey within a fixed imaginal geography.
For example, in his fieldwork among a Nahuatl-speaking people in Mexico,
anthropologist Timothy Knab was encouraged by his mentors to locate his
remembered dream experiences within an Otherworld, or Underworld, known
as Talocan. If there's a lot of water in a certain scene, that means he's traveled
to a Water World on the east side of Talocan. If there are mostly women, that
means he's gone to the House of Women to the west of Talocan. As the outsider
is drawn deeper into the communal mind of his hosts, he begins to find himself
dreaming inside their shared landscapes.[3]

Third, the dream archeologist must develop the ability to enter a different
reality and experience it from inside. "One cannot conduct fieldwork in another
person's dream," says anthropologist Roger Ivar Lohmann.[4] While this may
seem to be common sense, it is a view that dream archeologists are going to test.

Through the arts of conscious dream travel, active imagination, and
"mutual visioning," we can enter other times and gain firsthand knowledge of
conditions there that we can then research and verify — and in doing so may
help both scholars and practitioners go beyond what was previously understood.
We can reclaim the best of ancient traditions and rituals in authentic, helpful,
and timely ways.

As we enter deeper levels of past and future history, we may be able to re-
envision the linear sequence of events from the standpoint of metahistory, an
understanding that transcends linear time. We can enter the life situations of
personalities in the past or future who may be related to us in various ways —
as ancestors or descendants, as members of our larger spiritual families, as
embodied aspects of ourselves, or as counterpart selves actually living in other
places and times. And we can experiment with direct communication with personalities living in other times, for mutual benefit, in *their* "now" time as well
as the spacious Now of the Dreamtime.

II

Here's an overview of where this venture in dream archeology is going to take us:

In the opening chapter, we learn that, among indigenous peoples, dreamers are speakers for the earth and travelers between the worlds. They connect us with the web of life in an animate universe, with the ancestors, and with the needs of the whole. In the language of the Iroquois, they also help us "not to let our minds fall" from the memory of the deeper world in which human life has its origin and its purpose.[5] Dreaming is concerned with maintaining and renewing bridges to a deeper and higher reality and with opening paths for soul and its healing.

In chapter 2, we study passages from the interweaving history of dream interpretation and divination from before Artemidorus to Freud. Across most of history, no firm distinction has been made between looking for clues to the future in dreams and reading signs in other ways — from the flight of birds or the fall of runes or yarrow sticks. We'll find that ancient dream interpreters often did more than decode symbols. They offered rituals to turn away the dark energy of an evil dream, to guard the dreamer's psychic space, and to tame and redirect a future event. The best were able to *enter* a client's dreamspace to find out what was going on there. In the Bible story of Joseph, we see that the ancient dream interpreter's role is not confined to reading the future from a dream; he must help determine what is to be done. We'll study how Freud, while rescuing dreams from nineteenth-century psychiatrists who denied they had meaning, shifted dream interpretation from prediction to personal psychohistory — and how, in insisting on a narrowing doctrine of what to look for in dreams, he may have tragically missed a potentially lifesaving health warning.

In chapter 3, we examine the role of dreaming in the world's major religions. "The greater part of humanity receives its knowledge of God from dreams," wrote a second-century bishop. Dreaming is at the root of the mythologies and religions that have guided humanity's path. For many peoples, our existence on the planet is itself the product of the dream of a creator god. Dreaming is central to the birth and development of the *historical* religions — those that teach an extraordinary, unrepeatable revelation followed by an irreversible forward movement according to a divine plan — as well as all the others. We'll find that the Bible is a book of dreams and visions, and that it was a vision, followed by a dream, that made Christianity the religion of the West. We'll explore the tremendous importance of dreaming in the world of Islam, as a source of prophecy, a mandate for authority, and the means of entry to the "isthmus of imagination," the place where "divine history" — the greater drama beyond the surface dramas of our lives and our world — unfolds.

Dreaming is central to the history of medicine and the practice of healing. In chapter 4, we enter the world of ancient Greek physicians who used dreams in diagnosis, and we travel into the experience of healing in the dream temples. In the precinct of a healing god (or later, a healing saint) you are assisted in dropping your old mind-set and opening to the direct experience of healing during sacred sleep. You leave with a story that is bigger than and different from the one you were living before, and if you wish to continue your healing, you'll find ways to carry that story and create with its power. In the epilogue we'll explore how imaginal healing is reemerging as a central facet of twenty-first-century medicine, helped by scientific research demonstrating that the body and brain do not distinguish between a thought and an action.

In chapter 5, we enter the world of writers dreaming. From priestess-scribes in ancient Mesopotamia to Stephen King or Neil Gaiman, writers have always known that dreams are central to literary creation and provide a cornucopia of material for stories and novels, scripts, and poems. We'll take a close look at how Graham Greene worked with his dreams almost every day of his marvelously productive life. We'll go on a wild ride with some of the many Russian writers who were inspired by dreams, used dreams in key scenes in their books, and lived lives that were often as crazy and flamboyant as any dream. We'll discover that when they are truly "on," many writers work in a state like conscious dreaming, and we'll study how they get themselves there.

In all times and all fields of endeavor, dreaming has helped humans get by and get through the challenges of life. In chapter 6, we look at this theme through six windows. We'll find that, among the Founding Fathers, there were dedicated dreamers, in more sense than one. We'll investigate a dream experience that led directly to one of the biggest oil strikes in history, changing the history of the Middle East and the world. We'll learn how, in one modern European country, dreams are shared in almost every household and are used by farmers to read the weather and by fishing skippers to find the fish. We'll see how dreams fuel the imaginations of rock composers and performers, and how athletes and sports coaches run "inner movies" to prepare for an event. We'll explore the role of dreaming — and above all the ability to enter a place of imagination — in the history of scientific creativity.

Part 2 is devoted to the biographies of six remarkable individuals who can be described as masters of the Three "Only" Things, in the sense that dreams, coincidence, and imagination powered their achievements and steered their lives and, through them, the lives of many others.

In chapter 7, we enter the world and visions of Joan of Arc. Her tragedy is the good fortune of historians of the medieval mind and of visionary experience. Dutiful notaries at her first trial preserved remarkably detailed and seemingly accurate transcripts of her own testimony, and that of witnesses, that contain vital clues to how and where she received her visions, was able to see into the future, and could seize the minds and hearts of rough men in iron and rally a broken and defeated people and their dissipated feudal lords against their invaders. We'll learn from the documents about the importance of trees in her visionary experience and may sense continuity, beneath the language of Christian revelation, with the practices of the ancient women tree-seers of Europe. We'll discover how *practical* clairvoyance — Joan's ability to see across time and space to scout the enemy's position or discern the outcome of a skirmish — enabled her to win the trust of brutal warlords who normally would have had no use for an illiterate peasant girl except in bed. Where the documents cease to speak, I have dared to speculate on some of the mysteries of her extraordinary life: notably on tree-seeing, the "king's secret" that she shared only with the weak dauphin she made king of France, and on how a running deer may have enabled her side to rout the English in a decisive battle.

In chapter 8, we travel to Madrid in the time of the Spanish Armada. Since women are absent from so much of the history written by men, it is remarkable that — thanks in part to the Spanish Inquisition — the record of no fewer than 415 dreams of a young woman called Lucrecia de León survived. Her dreams were prized by powerful men, who had them transcribed before her arrest because she had a gift for seeing the future and discovering what was going on behind closed doors. Her dreams were exploited as sources of military intelligence and as political propaganda, in a time when dream visions were still greatly respected. Some of them were painted; others were performed as theatre for high society in the town house of a dowager duchess who may also have been an English agent. The beautiful dream spy of Madrid was also a young woman of healthy appetites; as we follow her dreams, we won't want to miss the tide of sexual longing on which they travel.

In chapter 9, we go to Maryland's Eastern Shore in search of the real Harriet Tubman. She is an iconic figure in American history: the most successful "conductor" of the Underground Railroad, which helped escaping slaves find freedom before the American Civil War. Yet the secret of Harriet Tubman's achievement has rarely been told. She was a dreamer and a seer. In her dreams and visions, she could fly like a bird. Her gift may have been associated with a near-death experience in her childhood, in which an angry overseer threw a lead weight that laid open her skull. We'll learn from her that great gifts sometimes come with our wounds. Harriet herself said she inherited special gifts — including the ability to travel outside the body and to visit the future — from her father, who "could always predict the future." Her father's people came from West Africa, and we'll explore the possibility that West African traditions of dream tracking lived on in her. We'll also look at the influence of the first, fiercely brave and inspiring, itinerant black women preachers, whose example may have helped Harriet develop the power to transfer her vision. She could sing courage into people's hearts.

In chapter 10, we ride the river of Mark Twain's life. He lived by coincidence, and he noticed. A remarkable run of coincidence prevented him from becoming the first cocaine dealer in North American history (that's a snapper but not a joke) and gave him the riverboat job from which his pen name and some of his best inspiration came. He staged experiments in "mental telegraphy." He was an avid and prolific dreamer, whose personal experiences convinced him that we are time travelers in dreams, able to interact with personalities from different times. In one of his later stories, he wrote, "In our dreams — I know it! — we do make the journeys we seem to make, we do see the things we seem to see."[6] His rhyming life is a fascinating specimen of how coincidence, dreams, and imagination can shape a creative life.

In chapter 11, we study the adventures in dreaming and coincidence of two intellectual giants, Carl Jung and Wolfgang Pauli. In a twenty-five-year creative friendship, the psychologist and the physicist goaded each other to step beyond the boundaries of their disciplines and develop a working model of a universe in which mind and matter are constantly interweaving. Pauli played a seminal role in Jung's development of his theory of synchronicity. Pauli became celebrated not only for his contributions to quantum physics but also for the "Pauli Effect": in his presence, *big* things tended to blow up. We'll explore the mystery of Pauli's "Chinese woman," an alluring dream figure misunderstood by Jung and Pauli himself until she stepped out of his dream life and into the world at the center of a revolution in science.

In chapter 12, we enter the tremendous imagination of Winston Churchill. He had the great gift of being able to transfer a vision that could grip the imagination of a whole people and rally it to action, even against seemingly insuperable odds. We'll find that, while Churchill was always a man of action, his greatest strength lay in his imagination. In his mind, past and future battles and dramas moved like floats in a Renaissance pageant. He had the gifts of a seer: he foresaw "weapons the size of an orange" that could destroy great cities, decades before the atom bomb.[7] He was forever tracking *alternate* histories, studying the outcomes of different choices. He was fascinated by time travel. His own ability to travel into the future extended to predicting, years in advance, that he would die on the same day as his father, January 24.

History is about the future as well as the past. In the epilogue, we explore why our society may find it necessary, as well as desirable, to become a dreaming culture again. We need to revive the skills of the dream seer to avoid being constantly blindsided by unexpected disasters for which our governments and risk analysts leave us hopelessly unprepared. We need vision in leadership. We need to imagine our own healing, live more creatively, and make sure our children are getting a dream education. We want to revive the skills of the Waymakers — the ancient Polynesian navigators — who knew that the way to cross a thousand miles of uncharted sea is to listen to the many voices of earth and sea, and to grow a vision of our destination strong enough to bring it toward us.

III

Dreaming has inspired scientists. What does science have to tell us about dreaming?

One of the most important discoveries is that, in modern urban society, few people sleep the way most humans did for all of our evolution before the introduction of artificial lighting. For hundreds of thousands of years, humans thought that what the pushers of sleep meds promise — an uninterrupted night of seven or eight hours' sleep — was an unnatural and undesirable thing.

Experiments by a team led by Dr. Thomas Wehr at the National Institutes of Mental Health in Bethesda, Maryland, have supplied compelling evidence that our technology has ripped us from our natural cycle. Deprived of artificial lighting for several weeks, the typical subject evolved the following pattern: lying awake in bed for an hour or two, then four hours sleep, then two to three hours of "non-anxious wakefulness" followed by a second sleep before waking for the day's activities. One of the most exciting findings in Wehr's study involved the endocrinology of the night watch. The interval between first sleep and second sleep is characterized by elevated levels of prolactin, a pituitary hormone best known for helping hens to brood contentedly above their eggs for long periods. Wehr concluded that the night watch can produce benign states of altered consciousness not unlike meditation.[8]

Wehr and his team put their subjects on the Paleolithic plan, without alternatives to electrical light such as candles or fire or oil lamps. The Paleolithic two-sleeps cycle wasn't only a Stone Age phenomenon; it was characteristic of how people spent their nights until gas lighting and then electricity became widespread. A seventeenth-century Scottish legal deposition describes a weaver as "haveing gotten his first sleip and awaiking furth thairof." Sleep historian Roger Ekirch says, "until the modern era, up to an hour or more of quiet wakefulness midway through the night interrupted the rest of most Western Europeans" — and presumably most other people — and that "consolidated sleep, such as we today experience, is unnatural."[9]

This may help explain the extent to which so many of us in our urbanized society are out of nature and out of touch with dreaming. "Segmented sleep" was the norm for our ancestors until quite recently, as it remains for some indigenous peoples today. Like Virgil and Nathaniel Hawthorne, the Tiv of central Nigeria speak of "first sleep" and "second sleep." They wake at any time during the night and will talk to anyone in the hut who is also awake — often about their dreams.[10]

Most interesting, the intermediate state the French called *dorveille* was widely regarded as an excellent time to birth new ideas. In 1769, the artful London tradesman Christopher Pinchbeck advertised a device called a "Nocturnal Remembrancer," a parchment tablet inside a box with a slit to guide the writing hand in the dark to enable "philosophers, statesmen, poets, divines and every person of genius, business or reflection" to secure the "flights and thoughts which so frequently occur in the course of a meditating, wakeful night."[11]

It is possible that in our modern culture, through our suppression of ancient and natural circadian cycles, we have rendered ourselves "disannulled of our first sleep, and cheated of our dreams and fantasies."[12]

While our modern sleep patterns may interfere with our awareness of night dreams and our ability to share them, new technologies for imaging brain activity tell us we are dreaming at night nonetheless — maybe dreaming all night long — and that some of the brain's behaviors during sleep dreams are curiously similar to those associated with creative flow in other states of consciousness. The new science of dreaming suggests the following:

- Almost everyone dreams, every night — even those who have suffered massive brain injury.
- Humans who conform to the modern sleep pattern average six dreams (or dream sequences) every night, whether or not they remember them.

- While many researchers continue to associate dreaming with the rapid-eye-movement (REM) state of sleep discovered in a Chicago laboratory in 1953, there is growing scientific evidence that dreaming — or at least some form of "mentation" — is going on all through the night.[13]
- During creative states of the waking brain — as when jazz performers enter a riff of improvisation — its behavior is quite similar to that of the dreaming brain.[14]

"A type of spatial and temporal binding underlies dreaming that is analogous to the perceptual binding thought to underlie waking consciousness."[15] While cognitive neuroscientists are notorious for dismissing dreams as nonsense, even within that mind-field recent studies support the idea that dreaming plays a critical role in growing learning skills and consolidating memory. "Dreaming about newly learned material enhances subsequent recall of that material," report Tore Nielsen and Philippe Stenstrom.[16]

The neurobiology of sleep and dreams are not a major focus of this book. There are excellent resources available for those who want to know more about this, ranging from Andrea Rock's very readable and accessible *The Mind at Night* to the hard-core technical papers collected in the three volumes of *The New Science of Dreaming*, edited by Deirdre Barrett and Patrick McNamara.

While brain science tells us important things about the quality of our reception, it no more tells us how our dreams are made than pulling apart a television set can show you how and where a movie is produced and how it travels from a network to your screen.

Having confessed that this book does not offer a history of the neurobiology of dreaming, I should mention that it is also not a history of modern dream psychology, though it does contain a close examination of some aspects of the theories and methods of Freud and Jung. There are excellent books available that survey many of the approaches to dream analysis and dream appreciation that have been developed over the past century. We have already noted that, for most human cultures prior to the modern era — and for many non-Western cultures today — dreaming is less about personal psychology than about prediction and transpersonal experience, and in this book we follow the mainstream of lived experience over the centuries rather than what the theorists have to say about it.

We should note a very troubling thing about dreaming and psychology in our contemporary academies. Undergraduate psychology students, at least in the United States, find little or no indication in their textbooks that dreams mean anything at all, and they learn that imagination is worthless or a pit of deception. Here is one alarming report from the front: American psychology majors learn that "dreams are meaningless by-products of brain processes. This is taught by every textbook in introductory psychology used in our department over the past decade." The source is Roger Knudson, a psychology professor in the Midwest. He reports that not only are dreams dismissed in the standard psychology curriculum but also the imagination is denied or disparaged. In the same psychology texts, "imagination is mainly a source of error in memory and therefore is not to be trusted. Most introductory textbooks do not have an entry for imagination in their index; but if they do, it almost always refers to a section on errors in memory."[17] The problem appears to be systemic.

History is what historians — and those who hire them or influence them — say it is. E. H. Carr, writing from a very different perspective, pointed out in *What Is History?* that, despite the old saying, facts really don't speak for themselves. "The facts speak only when the historian calls on them. . . . A fact is like a sack — it won't stand up till you've put something in it."[18]

In this book, I have called on the kinds of facts that are often left on the margin in the telling of history, or left out altogether, to the detriment of our understanding of the forces that drive our lives and our world. It didn't used to be so. Read Plutarch's works on the lives of the Greeks and Romans, and you'll find he gives the same importance to dreams and coincidence that he gives to the chronicle of "factual" events, understanding that life's dramas are played out in more than one reality. Read the great Muslim historian Ibn Khaldun's fourteenth-century introduction to world history, the *Muqaddimah*, and you'll find he begins by describing dreaming as one of the six essential conditions for a human society, as important as climate, geography, and food supply. One of my aims in this book is to help renew our understanding that dreaming is a vital *understory* in the human odyssey — past, present, and future — and to incite others to restore it to its rightful place in the study of history.

No matter how deep and wide he prospects, and how much he is guided and helped by specialists and native guides, any digger's ability to cover more than a small part of such vast and rich territory is limited. I hope I have turned over enough of the ground, and exposed a sufficient glint of the greater treasures below, to inspire many other scholars and dream archeologists to dig deeper, until they lay bare the buried cities of the imagination.

PART ONE

❧

SECRET ENGINES
OF HISTORY

Without history there can be no psychology.
— C. G. JUNG, *Memories, Dreams, Reflections*

The past is never dead. In fact, it's not even past.
— WILLIAM FAULKNER, *Requiem for a Nun*

"Explain all that," said the Mock Turtle.
"No, no! The adventures first," said the Gryphon
in an impatient tone: "explanations take such a
dreadful time."

— LEWIS CARROLL,
Alice's Adventures in Wonderland

CHAPTER I

❧

EARTH SPEAKERS
AND DREAM TRAVELERS

The angel —
three years we waited intently for him
closely watching
the pines the shore and the stars.
One with the plough's blade and the keel of the ship,
we were searching to discover the first seed
so that the ancient drama could begin again. . . .

We brought back
these carved reliefs of a humble art.

— GEORGE SEFERIS, *"The Angel"*

ou find the villages of the Temiar when a shady path through the rain forest opens out onto a field of hill rice or a clump of man-high tapioca plants. This people of the Malaysian rain forest live in the old way, by slash-and-burn agriculture, moving their thatched houses when their fields get tired. They live very close to their land. Their stilt houses are walled with bamboo poles laid horizontally, with gaps between them. There are also gaps between the bamboo slats of the floors. Earth and trees are always visible. No solid boundary is set between human settlement and the natural world.

It is not surprising that, in this setting, people have an intimacy with the earth that colors and informs their dreams. They believe that everything is alive and conscious, and that in dreams human spirits, traveling outside the body, encounter spirits of plants and animals and mountains and rivers. There is great power in these encounters, especially when a tiger or a tree gifts the dreamer with a song that later can call in its energy for healing. A song of this kind, received in a dream and freighted with the power to summon an animal guardian, or wake a mountain, is called a *norng*, which literally means a "road" or pathway. The kind of path that can get your body safely through the forest or guide a soul to where it belongs.

I learned about the Temiar through the beautiful work of American musicologist and anthropologist Marina Roseman, who not only has recorded their dream songs but also has sung in the women's chorus when healers have sung over a patient. I have listened to her recording of a tiger dream song. It is thrilling. Above the tapping of bamboo sticks, you hear the gravelly voice of the tiger as he rises from a nap to become an ally in healing, by driving away a disease spirit or lending his own fierce vitality to a sick person.

One of the songs Roseman translated reveals the process of acquiring a healing song from a plant spirit. A man had been seeding and tending keralad plants, patting and shaping the earth around the roots. In the time when the keralad came into flower, he smelled its fragrance strongly inside a dream. After releasing its odor, the plant took human form and announced a spiritual connection with the dreamer: "It is you that I want." As a human, the plant now began to sing, giving the dreamer a new song for healing. Notice the stages in this process, which proceeds like the natural growth of fruit and flower. You make a connection in the natural world by getting your hands in the earth, seeding, and weeding. The plant releases its odor. Then its spirit morphs into human form, initiates conversation, and finally produces the song.[1]

For peoples who live close to the earth, like the Temiar, dreaming is a way to communicate with the earth and all that shares life on it. Everything is alive. Everything will speak to you — and speak *through* you — if you will pay attention. Dreaming is not only about what goes on in the night; it is also about being attuned, at every turning, to the speaking land.

I once met a wonderful woman called Freida Jacques, who at that time had served for twenty-seven years as the mother of the turtle clan of the Onondaga, the keepers of the central fire of the Six Nations of the Haudenosaunee, or Iroquois. The clanmother told me, "I don't dream so much in the night anymore. My head is getting full of the junk food of American culture. I dream like this: I've been asking myself whether I should make a trip out West. And at that moment, I see a hawk flying west, followed by three geese flying in arrowhead formation. I get my message, from the arrow pointing west in the sky."

Indigenous dreamers not only listen to the earth; they also speak for it and seek to sustain the web of connection between humans and the whole. I think of my friend Ed Harkins, a Vietnam vet of mixed Native American heritage who now lives in the Cascade foothills of Washington State and works with a wilderness school, following the trails of cougars and bears, the flight of eagles and ravens, and the cycles of the salmon and the salal berries. After the disastrous oil spill from the *Exxon Valdez* tanker in Alaska, Ed sat at a favorite spot on Puget Sound, thinking of all the harm that had been caused to the fish, the whales, and the sea. "Without much thought, I put a short prayer into the waters of the Sound by offering my hand to the waters, expressing my atonement for what had happened there. It was a short prayer to the creatures of the sea and the birds affected by that spill, asking for their forgiveness."

Afterward, as he drove home through heavy traffic, he heard deep pulsing sounds reaching to him through the highway noise. It took him a while to figure out what he was hearing. Late that night, in his den, he heard the sounds again and suddenly realized they were the song of whales. "A pod of gray whales appeared in my mind's eye. They were calling to me while clapping their long side fins, expressing gratitude for my humble prayer for forgiveness."

When I picture that man offering his hand, with his prayer, to the waters, I wonder whether the day will come when there is no one left who will speak to the powers of nature and ask forgiveness for what humanity has done to other forms of life on the planet. If that day comes, then as described in indigenous prophecy, humanity's time on earth will be over.

The view of most indigenous peoples is that, when we dream at night, we are either traveling or receiving visitors. They recognize multiple aspects of soul or spirit, some of which have great mobility during sleep and dreaming.

When I moved to a farm on the edge of traditional Mohawk Iroquois country in the mid-1980s, I started dreaming of a woman dreamer and healer of long ago. When I approached Iroquois elders to help me understand these dreams, one of them told me matter-of-factly, "You made some visits and you received some visitations."

The Chiquitano of eastern Bolivia believe a human has three souls, called the breath soul, the blood soul, and the shadow soul. During dreams, while the breath soul stays with the body, the blood soul (*otor*) can wander a little. The shadow soul (*ausipis*) can make longer journeys, leaving the body and the blood soul far behind. In the morning, it returns and gives the other souls an account of its adventures. The longer journeys of the shadow soul produce memories of *big* dreams in which the dreamer enters other realms and other times.[2]

For many indigenous peoples, dreaming is a highly social activity, in several senses. You go places and meet people when you travel in your dream body; they may be people in the next village or campsite, or beings in another world.

You also have *interactive* dreams in which you meet and share adventures with other dreamers. Dreaming is also social in the sense that you talk about your dreams, maybe with whoever is stirring in the same cabin or the big house in the middle of the night, and you help each other figure out what went on in the dream and what you need to do. Among the Canelos Quichua of Ecuador, husband and wife sleep on either side of the center of the house, and take off on their dream travels from their respective sides. They frequently wake during the night and talk about their experiences. They may agree to return to a certain dream place and continue an adventure together.[3] However, there are some dreams that are so powerful or so dark you'll hold them secret or share them only with specialists — shamans or medicine people or your favorite grandmother — who know about these things.

It is not unusual among indigenous dreamers for two or more people to find themselves, like the Canelos Quichua, having adventures together inside the dreamspace. An interactive dream experience may be felt to have greater objectivity. If more than one person has experienced it, then there is a stronger reason to believe in what happened, or what could happen in the future, as revealed by the dream. The Dine (Navajo) medicine woman Walking Thunder recounted that she and her husband dreamed the same night of buying a new car. In both their dreams, they had an accident after leaving the dealership. Trusting that a future event they had both dreamed was likely to take place, they decided to postpone buying the new car for a month, shifting the time frame beyond the one exposed in the dream, and had no problems.[4]

Let's be clear about this: for peoples living on the edge of survival, dreaming is a highly practical matter. A good dreamer is also a good hunter or fisher, one who finds the game or the catch ahead of time. A Chukchi fox hunter explained that he always knew when a fox was in one of his traps, because the night before he found it he always dreamed of being attacked by a wild and beautiful red-haired woman. Sometimes she mauled him and ran away. Whenever he managed to subdue her and have sex with her, he woke certain that he would find a fox in his trap; by his account, he was never disappointed.[5] Jivaro hunters also believe that having sex with an attractive woman in a dream promises a good hunt; after such a dream, they'll set off at first light.[6]

A widespread practice among ancient and indigenous peoples is to open contact with spiritual guides and allies by seeking a dream at a special place in nature. Such a vision quest at puberty is an essential life passage in many traditional cultures. Among the Ojibwa of North America, a boy approaching manhood might be instructed to perch in a "nest" — a platform set high in the branches of a tree — for several days and nights, inviting an encounter with a *pawagan*, or dream visitor. Sometimes the boy's vision quest is supported by an adult male beating a drum. In one classic account, a *pawagan* appeared to a boy in human form and told him, "You are strong enough now to go with me." The visitor started dancing. As he danced, he turned into a golden eagle. The boy looked down at his own body and saw that it too was covered with feathers. The great eagle spread its wings and soared into the sky. The boy, in eagle form, followed.[7]

A strong working relationship with a *pawagan* is considered essential to personal health and success. The initiatory encounter typically includes directions for future meetings. The *pawagan* might show the dreamer another place in nature where they could make contact again. This might be a place inside a rock, where they could meet in a secret chamber. This rock might be small enough to carry in a pouch.

The practice of ancient and indigenous dreamers very often includes establishing such stable locales in the dreamspace, where dreamers and beings at home in these realms can rendezvous and have further adventures. Master shamans will test apprentices by giving them a few clues to a place of power in the Dreaming, and then ask them to travel by these landmarks and go beyond them into territory *not* described. On their return, the apprentice dreamers are then required to describe, in convincing and accurate detail, places known to the adepts but not revealed to the novices in advance. If their descriptions are accurate, the elders know the apprentices have been where they were sent and have fulfilled their assignments.

Dreaming into the Aboriginal Dreamtime

Aboriginal Australians believe that we dream our way into this world, and dream our way out of it. "We talk to the spirit child before a baby is born," naturopath and traditional healer Burnham Burnham explained to me. If the father-to-be is a dreamer, he is frequently the one who first meets the spirit child in dreams. These dream encounters often unfold at places of water that exist in the natural world — a billabong, the shallows of a river, a waterfall — where the spirit child plays with its own kind and is not confined to a single form. It can appear as a kingfisher or a platypus, as a fish or a crocodile. The dreamer may have to negotiate with the spirit child, giving it reasons for coming into a human body. Finally, the dreamer plays soul guide, escorting the incoming spirit to the mother's womb.

On the way to death, the soul guide appears from the other side. Departed loved ones and ancestral beings who are at home in the Dreamtime come calling, in dreams, to prepare a dying person for his or her journey. When the spirit leaves the body in death, these guides from the Dreamtime escort it along the roads to the afterlife, which may involve a sea crossing, descent through a cave, and/or the ascent of a magical tree whose roots are in the World Up Top.

Aboriginal dreaming is an antidote to Freud, who wrote that the dream "has nothing to communicate to anyone else."[8] The first Australians know that dreaming means everything and is a highly social activity. We meet other people and other beings when we go dreaming, and sharing dreams is not a matter of puzzling over obscure texts but a means of developing practical wisdom, community guidance, and grand entertainment. Among nomad communities, listening to a dream by the campfire or over a morning cup of tea is better fun than going to the movies, and the dream may run the whole gamut from romance to horror, from Star Trek to soaps.

The five-hundred-plus Aboriginal tribes of Australia share this understanding: a dream is a journey. When we dream, "the spirit goes on walkabout," says Nungurrayi, a wise woman of the Kukatja, a people of the Western Desert. A powerful dreamer, she explains, is a person who knows how to open the *tjurni*, travel — in spirit — to interesting places, and bring back a "good story."[9] *Tjurni* is usually translated as "womb" or "abdomen." For anyone familiar with chakra work, it may be helpful to think of it as the second chakra. The dream journey is powered by the same energy that is discharged in sex. The female dreamer opens her womb or vagina; the male dreamer projects a magical cord from his penis or testes and uses it to climb to another realm.

If you know that your dream is a journey, or a visitation by another dream traveler, then you are unlikely to be interested in the kind of analysis that reduces dream experiences to a list of symbols and then interprets what the symbols mean. When traditional Aborigines share dreams, they want to know *who*, *when*, and *where*. Who was that sorcerer I saw pointing the bone at me? Who was that person who came to my camp and wanted sex with me? Where is the cave where the dream ceremony took place? When will the car break down?

When you know that a dream is a real experience, then you want to clarify the information in order to figure out what to do with it. Maybe you'll want to tell that dream of the sorcerer all over the camp to scare away the actual sorcerer, as anthropologist Sylvie Poirier saw done in the Western Desert. Maybe you'll get together with your dream lover (if the experience was pleasant) or find a way to prevent that person from intruding on your psychic space (if it was not). Perhaps you'll travel to the dream cave and celebrate a ritual to confirm and honor what has already taken place in the Dreaming. Maybe you'll get your car fixed before it breaks down.

The Yolngu of northeast Arnhem Land view dreams as a field of interaction between the living and the dead. This can be helpful when the encounter is with the higher spirit of the departed, or a benign ancestor, but dangerous when the contact is with the lower aspect of the departed, known as the *mokuy*. The Yolngu are very clear about something that is almost hopelessly confused in contemporary Western society: the need to distinguish the different nature and destiny of at least two aspects of soul or spirit that survive the death of the body, and to handle them accordingly.[10]

Aboriginals look to dreams as the place of encounter with spiritual guides and sacred healers, who often appear as totem animals but may come in many other forms. Since the missionaries arrived, Aboriginal dream visitors have often included Jesus and the angels. A Yolngu woman dreamed that the Hero Sisters — the mythic founders of her people — came to her dancing, resplendent in lorikeet feathers, and were joined by a smiling Jesus Christ. Together, they showed her a place of power, used for a fertility rite in earlier times, that had been forgotten by her community and urged her to make it a place of worship again.[11] One of the messages of the dream seemed to be that, if we go to the living heart of religion, there need be no conflict between traditions.

Aboriginal Australians are well aware that dreaming can be active: you can decide where you are going to go, and you can go consciously. You can travel across time and space or into other dimensions. You can rendezvous with other dreamers and embark on shared journeys. Shamans receive their calling and much of their training in this way.

The first Australians do not live under the illusion that it is necessary to go to sleep in order to dream. They dream with a *living* landscape in a way that baffles urbanized, deracinated people. Everything in that landscape is alive and conscious, every place has its Dreaming. "Nothing is nothing," as they say on the Cape York Peninsula; everything means *something*.

The powers of the Dreaming are closely tied to the land. You can find them only if you are endowed with what the native people of the Kimberley Plateau of northwestern Australia call *kurara*, the power to "talk to the land." Otherwise, as when the mysterious, mouthless Wandjina figures of the Kimberley appear to those who do not hear inner voices, the landscape is mute.

You might listen to the kingfisher, which is good at spotting ghosts. If the kingfisher calls out *ekwe, ekwe, ekwe*, you must watch out for a malevolent ghost that could bring illness or even death.

In the speaking land, for those who can hear, some places speak louder and stronger than others. Four thousand years ago, at a site called Eagle's Reach in the Wollemi National Park, an easy drive from Sydney, Aboriginal rock artists created stunning images of composite beings — human figures with the heads of birds, and therianthropes that are half-man and half-kangaroo. They recall the gods of Egypt and the shape-shifters of the Lascaux and Alpine caves. To touch these images is to draw in their power through the skin — a power that may be too much for the uninitiated to handle — and engage directly with the energies of the Dreamtime.

Let's be clear: there is the Dreaming, or the Dreamtime, the realm of gods and ancestral beings, and then there is everyday dreaming. The two interweave but are not the same. The Kukatja, in common with many other Western Desert tribes, use the word *Tjukurrpa* for the ancestral Dreaming, but a different term — *kapukurri* — for personal dream experiences.

Dreamtime is creation time, and stories of the Dreamtime often tell us about the origin of things. But Dreamtime is not long ago; in Dreamtime it is always *now*. Aborigines call Dreamtime the "all-at-once." Dreamtime is the seedbed of life, the origin of everything that is manifested in the world. It is not separate from the physical world; it is the inner pulse of the land.

The science of the twenty-first century may help us grasp the Paleolithic science of the earth's oldest ongoing tradition. Dreamtime may encompass the six (or seven) hidden dimensions of the physical universe posited by superstring theory. Dreamtime is the multidimensional matrix in which three-dimensional reality floats. By entering Dreamtime, we may be able to reach into the quantum soup of possibilities from which the events of the three-dimensional world bubble up.

A crisis of illness may open the gates of the Dreaming. I learned something about this in childhood. At age nine, in a Melbourne hospital where I underwent an emergency appendectomy, I left my body and found myself drawn down into what seemed to be a world inside the world. I was welcomed by very tall, pale beings who raised me as one of their own. I seemed to spend a whole life with these people, becoming a father and grandfather, until they laid my body to rest — and I found myself yanked back into the body of the nine-year-old kid in the hospital and learned that I had lost vital signs for a few minutes and everyone had been worried that I had checked out.

Many years later, I encountered an Aboriginal artist from Arnhem Land who said that, whenever he got sick, he went to live with the "Mimi spirits" until he got well. In painting and sculpture, the Mimis are depicted as very tall and skinny. They are said to be more ancient than the Rainbow Serpent and to live inside rocks. They come and go through what my Celtic ancestors might call the "thin places," blowing on crevices in the rocks to open doorways to and from their hidden worlds.

Though I have lived outside my native Australia for most of my adult life, something of the Dreaming seems to live in me, and creatures of the Dreamtime sometimes cross the ocean to call me back. At very important passages in my life and the lives of my family members, a sea eagle I remember from boyhood in Queensland has come into my dreamspace and flown me back to Australia. Once the sea eagle launched me on a journey that led to a Dreaming place of the Mununjali of southern Queensland. When a "spirit man" of the Mununjali heard my dream as the result of a "chance" encounter in Beaudesert, he led me to the exact place of power, on a bend of a muddy river, that I had previewed in the dream.

Our dreams may lead us into the Dreaming and into ways of seeing and knowing that were shared by *all* our ancestors. In this way, our dreams may open the way for cultural soul recovery and the healing of the relations between our kind and the natural world.

Dreaming Like an Egyptian

The ancient Egyptians understood that in dreams our eyes are opened. Their word for dream, *rswt*, comes from the root word meaning "to be awake." The hieroglyphs that spelled out *rswt* were followed by a sign known as a "grammatical determinative" and depicted as a wide-open eye.

The Egyptians believed that the gods speak to us in dreams. As the Bible story of Joseph and the pharaoh reminds us, they paid close attention to dream messages about the possible future. They practiced dream incubation for guidance and healing at temples and sacred sites. They understood that, by recalling and working with dreams, we develop the art of memory, tapping into knowledge that belonged to us before we entered this life journey and awakening to our connection with other life experiences.

The Egyptians also developed an advanced practice of conscious dream travel. Trained dreamers operated as seers, remote viewers, and telepaths, advising on affairs of state and military strategy and providing a mental communications network between far-flung temples and administrative centers.

They practiced shape-shifting, crossing time and space in the dreambod-
ies of birds and animals. We can see this in all the depictions of the *sem* (or *setm*)
priest — a specialist in guiding astral travel, notably the journey to the afterlife — who wears a leopard skin, and in the bull's-hide kilt worn by the pharaoh
in rituals to marry the worlds, as well as in the spells for becoming a bird,
recorded in the Papyrus Ani, better known as the Egyptian Book of the Dead.
We may guess that the theriomorphic gods of Egypt, who may wear the head
of a ram or a falcon or a cow or a crocodile, were born from a primal level of
African shamanic experience.

Through conscious dream travel, ancient Egypt's "frequent flyers" explored
the roads of the afterlife and the multidimensional universe. It was understood
that true initiation and transformation takes place in a deeper reality accessible
through the dream journey beyond the body.

In early dynastic times, it seems, a true king of Egypt, one of whose praise
titles was "Lord of the Two Worlds," was expected to be able to travel between
the worlds. In the earliest version of the *heb sed* festival, conducted in the
pharaoh's thirtieth year, the king was required to journey beyond the body,
and beyond death, to prove his worthiness to continue on the throne. Led by
Anubis, the guardian of astral travel and the gates of the afterlife, the pharaoh
descended to the Underworld. He was directed to enter death, "touch the four
sides of the land," become Osiris (the god who dies and is reborn), and return
in new garments — the robe and the spiritual body of transformation. The
palace tombs and pyramid texts of Egypt were about more than funerary
arrangements. Recent scholarship suggests that Egyptians traveled beyond the
gates of death while very much alive, not only to bring back firsthand knowledge of the afterlife but also to enter into sacred union with the gods and
enthrone their power in the body, and so acquire the spiritual and sexual
potency to marry the worlds.[12]

The dream guides of ancient Egypt believed that the dream journey might
take the traveler to the stars — specifically to Sirius, the "moist land" believed
by Egyptian initiates to be the source of higher consciousness, the destination
of advanced souls after death, and the home of higher beings who took a close
interest in earth matters.[13]

When we look for ancient sources on all of this, we are challenged to decode
fragmentary texts, some collated over many centuries by pious scribes who jum-
bled together material from different traditions and rival pantheons. Wallis
Budge complained that "the Egyptian appears never to have relinquished any
belief which he once had."[14] We gaze in wonder at the Egyptian picture-books

displaying the soul's journeys and ordeals after death — and the many different aspects of soul energy that survive death — and quickly realize that, to understand the source of such visions, and the accuracy of such maps, we must go into a deeper space.

In Hellenistic times — the age of Cleopatra — dream schools flourished in the temples of Serapis, a syncretic god who melds the qualities of the gods Hades, Osiris, and Apis, the divine bull. From the second century BCE, we have papyri recording the dream diaries of Ptolemaios, who lived for many years in *katoche*, or sacred retreat, in the temple of Serapis at Memphis. Ptolemaios was the son of Macedonian colonists, but like ancient Egyptians he was called to the temple by a dream in which the god appeared to him. He seems to have lived for years as a full-time dreamer, and his dreams guided him not only in his spiritual practice but also in handling family and business matters beyond the temple walls.[15]

We have an account of a dream from the same period that provided military intelligence. In 168 BCE, in the midst of a war between the successors of Alexander, a priest called Hor sought an interview with the pharaoh's cavalry commander. The priest told the general he had dreamed of the goddess Isis walking on the sea, accompanied by Thoth, the god of writing and the moon. When the gods reached the Egyptian harbor of Alexandria, Isis announced, "Alexandria is secure against the enemy." The general was skeptical about this dream information, despite the alleged presence of the gods. To the best of his knowledge, Alexandria was in imminent danger from the invading army of Antiochos IV Epiphanes. But before the end of the month, Antiochos withdrew from Egypt, leaving Alexandria untouched. The general then sent the priest, with a letter of commendation, to report in person to King Philometer; Hor was plainly a dreamer to be trusted.[16]

In this later period, the Egyptian priests who specialized in dreaming were called the Learned Ones of the Magic Library.

Egyptologists tend to evince a high degree of professional caution in discussing the practice of dreaming in ancient Egypt, which is understandable given the florid versions circulated by some occultist groups that claim to be the legatees of an ancient mystery tradition whose rituals and grades of initiation centered on temple wall paintings of the twenty-two images of the major arcana of the Tarot. We'll take a middle path between the caution of the Egyptologists and the fantasies of the ceremonial magicians.

Those who write from true imagination can take us where historical data cannot, into the Magic Library. To my mind, the most intriguing — and ironically, some of the more reliable — published sources on the Egyptian way of dreaming are three books that have been classified as fiction. Two are ancient works; the third is a novel that was very popular in the 1930s but is waiting to be rediscovered by a new generation. Apuleius (who was almost certainly an initiate of the Eleusinian mysteries) chose the mask of a comic novel for *The Golden Ass, or the Transformations of Lucius*, in which Isis speaks directly to humans in dreams, travelers encounter each other in the dreamspace, and dreamers are coached for future events before they manifest. In another ancient tale, *The Romance of Alexander the Great*, the author known to scholars as pseudo-Callisthenes describes the practice of a sorcerer-king of late Egypt, Nectanebo, who fights battles long-distance and visits others in dreams (not always, alas, for the most evolved purposes).

Joan Grant's book *Winged Pharaoh* (first published in 1938) takes us into the possible reality of the first dynasty and the dream training of a king's daughter who becomes co-ruler of Egypt. As Grant explains in a memoir, the book came to her through "far memory" of a possible past life. After a short visit to Egypt, she was shown a collection of Egyptian scarabs in London. When she took the oldest in her hand, she saw vivid scenes of the time and place from which it had come, and then began talking *as* Sekeeta, the dreaming princess of her story.[17]

We are dealing here with a visionary narrative that transcends the categories of fiction and nonfiction. The best word to describe it is *mythistorema*, the Greek title of a collection of poetry by George Seferis. The term could be translated as "mythic history" but (like Seferis) I prefer to use a single word, "mythistory," to describe a true history of something that may or may not have happened but always *is*.[18]

The most fascinating element in Joan Grant's mythistory is the description of a dream school that operates within the temple of Anubis. When she is a small child, Sekeeta's mother gives her a tiny statue of Anubis — represented as a black hunting dog — and a little painted house for it to live in, and tells her that Anubis is the bringer of dreams to small children. When she is a few years older, Sekeeta meets her dream teacher, a priest of Anubis. Her training begins in the dreamspace when he shows her an open lotus flower and tells her that, just as the lotus opens its petals to the sun, she must learn to open the gateway of soul memory to reflect the light. When the scene is played out in waking life the next day, she recalls her dream, which is confirmation to both of them that she is ready to begin her training.

She learns to go scouting in dreams to find lost objects, look into the future, observe things happening at a distance, and discover what is going on behind the scenes. Suspicious of a foreign ruler who is visiting the court, she embarks on a dream journey to his country — flying to her target like a bird — and brings back a very detailed and disturbing report that she shares with the pharaoh, her father.

At the age of twelve, she becomes a full-time student at the dream school, taking up residence in the temple of Anubis. She sleeps on a bed that has Anubis heads carved at head and foot. Beside the bed she keeps a wax tablet, and her first task each morning is to record her dreams. Every morning she goes to the priest of Anubis and tells him what she has recorded. Some days she must also carry out assignments he has given her *inside a dream* — for example, to bring him a certain flower, or bird feather, or colored bead. Through practice her memory is trained and sharpened.

After three years, she undergoes advanced training. On the night of each full moon, she sleeps in total darkness in a room that has been psychically shielded. She undertakes many assignments, visiting distant places and bringing guidance and healing to people on both sides of death. She recounts her dream travelogues to her teacher and he confirms her experiences, adding further details and sometimes suggesting follow-up missions. Frequently in her dream travels, she encounters people who have died and are confused about their condition. She meets a man who had been murdered in a wineshop on Crete, and who refuses to believe he is dead. Her teacher encourages her to go to the dead man again, gently help him awaken to his condition, and guide him in the right direction on the paths of the afterlife.

At this point we come fully alive to the intimate connection between dreaming and dying well, and the reason why Anubis is such an appropriate patron of dream travel. As every schoolchild knows, Anubis, most often portrayed as a human figure with the head of a jackal or black dog, is a guardian of the otherworld who watches over tombs and mummies and guides souls of the departed to the Hall of Osiris. But Anubis's significance goes much deeper. As psychopomp, or guide of souls, he is the patron of journeys beyond the body (which is why he is invoked to guard those who have left their bodies under trauma or anesthesia), and *everyone* journeys beyond the body in death and dreaming, with or without instruction.

As Sekeeta's training in the dream school deepens, she takes on more and more work as a psychopomp. One of the most movingly realized scenes in the book is one in which Sekeeta helps a grieving widow who has been crushed by the drowning deaths of her husband and son. Sekeeta advises the woman that she can meet her loved ones in dreams. The woman insists that she does not dream. Sekeeta gently insists that, nonetheless, she would like the woman to be open to a dream experience with her loved ones. That night, Sekeeta goes out — as a conscious dream traveler — to reintroduce the grieving woman to her husband and son. She enters the woman's dreamspace, and finds her sobbing over the dead bodies of her loved ones, frozen in a past scene of trauma. With the power of her focused intention, Sekeeta bathes the widow in light and lifts the "cloak of grayness" that is preventing her from seeing her husband and son as they now are. There is a loving reunion, and Sekeeta skillfully guides them to a beautiful parklike setting where they can share happy times together.[19]

This episode is a wonderful glimpse of what compassionate psychopomp work is all about. While it is unlikely that the idea will receive widespread endorsement in the academic field of Egyptology, it seems entirely plausible that skilled dreamers in ancient Egypt did things this way.

DREAMING THE SECRET WISHES OF THE SOUL

Long before the first Europeans arrived, the Woodland Indians of North America taught their children that dreams are the single most important source of both practical and spiritual guidance.

We have a remarkable source for the dreaming practices of the Iroquois and their neighbors at the time of first contact, in the reports of Jesuit missionaries collected and translated in the seventy-three volumes of the *Jesuit Relations*. Though sometimes blinkered by religious intolerance and fear of demons or sorcery, the Jesuits were keen and intelligent observers. One of them, Father Joseph-François Lafitau, the superior of a mission near Montreal, has been viewed as the father of modern anthropology. Culling the Jesuit reports for clues to the dreaming practices of the First Peoples of North America at the time of first contact is a fertile exercise in dream archeology, and was one of my passions for several years. Since I have discussed the Iroquois dreaming traditions in previous books, I'll confine myself to a brief summary here.[20]

The first business of the day in an Iroquois village was dream sharing, as dreams were messages from the spirits and the deeper self and might contain guidance for the community as well as the individual. The early Iroquois believed that, in dreams, we routinely travel beyond the body and the limits of time and space, can visit the future or the past, and may enter the realms of the departed and of spiritual teachers on higher levels.

Dreaming was a survival tool. In the depths of winter, the community looked to powerful dreamers to scout out the location of game and to negotiate with the animal spirits to provide sustenance for the people. For the Iroquois, dreaming is also good medicine. The Mohawk word *atetshents*, which literally means "one who dreams," is also the term for a doctor or shaman.

The early Iroquois were not fatalists about the futures perceived in dreams, for they developed rituals and practices designed to divert — or reinforce — future episodes observed in dreams. By enacting part of a dream, under controlled circumstances, they might be able to prevent the dream from manifesting fully in the future.

A dream of impending disaster or tragedy that felt close to fulfillment in physical reality might inspire radical enactment; for instance, a Mohawk warrior who dreamed that he was captured and fire-tortured to death by his enemies once arranged for his fellow villagers to bind him and burn him with red-hot knives and axes — but not to kill him.[21]

The Iroquois recognized that the spirits sometimes send certain individuals "big dreams" with major revelations about the soul's purpose and the environment. While big dreams may contain information of vital importance to the dreamer's personal health or physical survival, many of these powerful dreams seem to be directed at benefiting the community as a whole. This is why, among Iroquoian traditionalists, the first business of the day for the whole community was to share and tend to important dreams.

Father Paul Ragueneau wrote in 1648, "The Hurons believe that our soul has desires other than our conscious ones, which are both natural and hidden, made known to us through dreams, which are its language. When these desires are accomplished, the soul is satisfied. But if they are not, the soul becomes angry. Not only does it fail to bring the body the health and well-being it might otherwise have done, but often it even revolts against the body, causing various diseases and even death. So most Hurons pay careful attention to their dreams! If, for instance, they have seen a javelin in a dream, they try to get it; if they have dreamed that they gave a feast, they will give one on awakening. They call this secret desire of the soul expressed by a dream, *ondinnonk*."[22]

It was a social duty to help dreamers read the language of the soul, as revealed in their dreams, and take appropriate action. If someone experienced a particularly troubling or obscure dream, a strong dreamer, an *atetshents*, might be consulted on its meaning. Sometimes, if a dream seemed to contain a warning of impending death or disease, the whole community would become involved in unfolding and enacting the dream.

Two centuries after the missionary reports collected in the *Jesuit Relations* were written, Iroquois elders told ethnologist Harriet Converse that you can lose your soul if you won't listen to what your soul is telling you in dreams. The punishment for failing to heed repeated dream warnings is that the "free soul" may abandon the dreamer, leaving him to live out his life on earth as one of the walking dead, "bereft of his immortal soul."[23]

The early Iroquois regarded someone who was not in touch with his or her dreams as the victim of serious soul-loss. A specialist might be called on to bring the lost dreams — and the missing vital energy — to the sufferer.

Honoring dreams, in early Iroquois tradition, required action. Ragueneau explained, "They say that these feasts are given to oblige the soul to keep its word. They believe the soul is pleased when it sees us take action to celebrate a favorable dream, and will move faster to help us manifest it. If we fail to honor a favorable dream, they think this can prevent the dream from being fulfilled, as if the angry soul revokes its promise."[24]

THE DREAMER AS SOUL CATCHER

To honor and care for the soul, it may be necessary to find it and bring it home. Among indigenous peoples, the diagnosis of soul-loss accounts for many symptoms of illness, depression, low energy, and misfortune. One of the primary functions of the most proficient dream traveler, the shaman, is to journey to the realm where a lost or captive soul is to be found, catch it, and put it back in the body of the victim of soul-loss. The story of the Nishan shaman is one of the great tales of the dream traveler as soul catcher and soul restorer.

The story is told by the fires of the Daur Mongols and neighboring peoples of Manchuria. In addition to the oral traditions, there is a written version collected by Russian ethnographers before the Bolshevik Revolution. *The Tale of the Nishan Shaman* is the one great surviving text of Manchu literature. By harmonizing the different voices, we can reclaim the extraordinary experience of a shaman who is a woman and a dreamer, and who uses her gift to rescue souls, even from the Underworld. It begins like this:

A rich boy is out hunting. They call him Sergudai. He kills animals without reverence, for sheer pleasure. Sometimes he does not even bother to send his retainers to take the hides and the meat. He revels in running down a mature female reindeer; her antlers are bigger than those of the males. He kills her with his arrows, and laughs.

The animal spirits complain to Irmu Khan, the Lord of Death, that the order of things has been disturbed. The death lord sends his shadow to strike down the boy hunter and carry his soul down to his inner keep in his sunless domain.

The boy's father, a wealthy headman called Baldu Bayan, is inconsolable. A stranger tells him there is a powerful shaman who lives on the Nishan River and who could bring back his son. Bayan is skeptical; the local shamans are greedy charlatans and the stranger is a hunchback in rags. Then the stranger performs a disappearing act on a many-colored cloud, and Bayan understands — whether or not he was dreaming — that his message came from a very special source.

So the father sets out in quest of the shaman. People describe her house, on the east side of the river. When he comes to the western shore, Bayan looks over the water and sees a pretty young woman doing the wash. She is wearing a simple, unbelted dark blue gown, the year-round garb of any other ordinary woman. But when he swims his horse across the river, he greets her with respect. "Elder Sister, are you the shaman?"

"Not me," she tells him. She directs him back across the river, to another house. When Bayan recrosses the river, the people over there tell him that he has been deceived. Shamans are tricky.

Bayan crosses the river for the third time and confronts the young woman he now knows to be the Nishan shaman. "You are a powerful shaman. Can you bring back my son?" She must consult her guardian spirits, her *onggors*. They can take many forms. They promise their help. She must also ask permission from her mother-in-law, because she is living with her husband's clan and is required to conform to their rules, shaman or not. She has been a widow for some time and may be older than she looks. The mother-in-law says she can go.

Her personal name, as noted in the Manchu version of the tale, is Teteke. But most people who tell her story call her simply "the Nishan shaman," as if to release her from personal and family circumstances.

The shaman's fee is agreed upon. The Nishan shaman gathers her professional tools — her drum, her robe, her headdress — and follows Bayan back to his home, where the son's body is laid out. She knows that her work will require a long journey to where no normal person would choose to go. Her safety requires an assistant who is a powerful drummer and singer, strong enough to propel her along the roads of the Underworld — and, above all, to bring her back. She names the man she must have, Sunny Anggu. There's an edge of excitement when he is named; we sense that they know each other body and soul.

When Sunny arrives, the Nishan shaman gets ready to journey. She is unrecognizable now as the girl with the wash, resplendent in her long, fringed coat of skins, hung with bells and horsetails, with a bronze mirror hanging over her heart. In her own language, the mirror is called the "soul vessel," a place to capture and carry a soul. She pounds her skin drum while Sunny echoes her beat. She is cantering, galloping, turning to the left, her feet almost noiseless in her high reindeer boots. A deerskin fringe flutters over her face, hiding her eyes. The antlers of her headdress, bursting from a spray of feathers, sweep back and forth.

She dances until there is foam on her lips, until she crumples into a dream as deep as death, her drum over her face. "She dies," they say.

The hoofbeats do not slacken or tire. Her assistant is riding his drum, sending her the power. The steady beat helps her to make out a road in the chaos of fog and sourceless shadows. The road brings her to a river. The Lame Boatman is on the other side. He is a hard bargainer. She has to promise more than is easy before he comes for her in his dugout canoe.

There are more crossings, more negotiations, and many tests of her courage before she descends at last to the inner keep of Irmu Khan. She sees the soul of the boy hunter playing with a youngster she knows to be the child of Death. None of her ancestral guardians can help her now. She must raise a cry from her heart and her gut that can reach all the way to the nest of the heaven bird that is her strongest ally. In some lands, they call him the Garuda. The shaman's cry spirals up from the depths of the Underworld. In the Middle World, her assistant echoes it. The cry rises up the World Tree and rouses the Garuda from his nest. The great bird unfolds his long form and swoops down. At the shaman's direction, he folds himself tight enough, like a projectile, to penetrate the fortress of Irmu Khan, snatches up the boy hunter, and delivers him to the shaman, who places the soul in her mirror.

Now she is racing back up the confusing, murky roads from the lower depths, pursued by Death's servitors. Her animal guardians can help her now, blurring her trail, leading pursuers in the wrong directions.

Her greatest test is in front of her. From a mob of hungry spirits twittering like bats, a man's shape separates and becomes gruesomely familiar. It's her ex-husband. He often dragged her down when he was still living, beating her if the milk was sour or his meal was late, chasing after other women. But he wants her now, desperately. "Take me with you," he implores, alternately cajoling and threatening. When she explains that there is nothing to be done for him — his body rotted long ago — he tries to hold her in the Underworld by laying a guilt trip on her, then by brute force. She has to fight him and silence him. "She stamps on his face and his mouth" to stop the words that are draining her strength and resolve.

She stops by a kind of registration office and bargains hard for a good long lifespan for Sergudai, the soul in the mirror. She has a moving encounter with Omosi-mama, the "divine grandmother" who "causes leaves to unfurl and the roots to spread properly," who is the giver of souls and protectress of children. We learn that it was Omosi, no less, who ordained that Teteke would become a great shaman.

The Nishan shaman loses so much energy during all of this that she might never make it back, except for the pull of the drum. Sunny is beating harder and faster, calling her back. Now she is riding his beat, back to her prostrate body. When she rises in that body, she finishes her job by fanning the boy hunter's soul from its vessel — the bronze mirror — back into his own body. The Nishan shaman has dreamed strong enough to rescue a soul even from the fortress of Death.[25]

No such feat goes unpunished. The Nishan shaman is not allowed to enjoy her triumph for long. In one telling, her fame spreads to the emperor himself, who summons her to cure his wife. But the shaman is so long gone on that journey that the emperor has her buried in chains, in disgust. In another version, the Lord of Death complains to the High God about the arrogance of this intruder in his realm, and together they beat the stuffing out of her. In the Manchu text, her late husband's mother brings the equivalent of legal action against her for failing to bring the ex-husband back. The shaman is forced to relinquish the tools of her trade — the antlers and the mirror, the robe and the drum — and to give up her lover, the indefatigable drummer. She becomes just another of the drab "work women" in her village, bound to the routines and taboos of her husband's people. In this last version we encounter a perennial theme in the history of women.

The Nishan shaman is not a solitary figure in the history of shamanism, especially in this part of central Asia. The Chukchi say, "Woman is by nature a shaman."[26] Among the Manchus, most shamans were women. There is strong evidence that, under the Shang dynasty in China (1766–1122 BCE), again most shamans were women. Barbara Tedlock's beautiful book *The Woman in the Shaman's Body* has helped to restore the grossly underreported history of women in this field.[27] For the Nishan shaman, as for women of power in other cultures, the only way to recognized authority is to dream stronger than others, to become at home with the uncanny, and to risk herself in a soul journey from which most men would flinch. A woman with gifts like hers will be sought after in an emergency, but the guardians of the conventional order will pull her down as soon as they can once the crisis is over.[28]

BRITAIN'S LADY OF THE DREAMWAYS

The ancient dreamers of Britain did not leave written accounts of their practices. The druids knew Greek but did not keep records. Their power was so feared by the Romans that, in 60 CE, their legions made the crossing to Mona, the island of the dreamers, through a druid mist and began the destruction of the sacred groves. Tacitus reports, "On the beach stood a serried mass of arms and men, with women flitting between the ranks. In the style of Furies, in robes of deathly black and with disheveled hair, they brandished their torches; while a circle of druids, lifting their hands to heaven and showering imprecations, struck the troops with such awe at the extraordinary spectacle that, as though their limbs were paralyzed, they exposed their bodies to wounds without an attempt at movement."[29]

With great effort the Roman governor, Suetonius Paulinus, rallied his men to attack this "band of females and fanatics," and at last they hewed their way through. "The next step . . . was to demolish the groves consecrated to their savage cults." Paulinus had to leave his work unfinished because of the campaign launched by the warrior queen Boudica, whom he finally defeated and drove to suicide in the Midlands. The Romans invaded Mona again eighteen years later, this time using "native auxiliaries" who were good swimmers to stage a surprise attack, and they completed the destruction of the island of dreamers.[30]

The Roman assault on the druids and their groves testifies to deep fear; the Romans were usually quite tolerant of the religions of conquered or allied peoples. In the epilogue, we'll explore how the gifted Scottish novelist and shamanic teacher Manda Scott has helped to bring the dreaming of Boudica's time alive for modern readers. Here we'll engage in a more modest exercise in dream archeology to discover that among the ancient goddesses of Britain is a patron of dreaming, and that a tale in the *Mabinogion* reveals the understanding and practice of dream reentry and tracking.

In ancient Britain, Elen is a patron of roads and journeys, especially the dream journey. In a lovely image painted by Chesca Potter, the lady is depicted wearing green — and a huge rack of antlers — as she looms before the gates of the Otherworld, including a dolmen arch and through it, a rainbow.[31] In the great cycle of Welsh epic poems known as the *Mabinogion*, Elen calls a king to her in his dreams, and he finds her embodiment in the physical world when he learns to use his dreams as a map and to follow their roads. Here is the story of the king's dream road to Elen:

A great king is out hunting with his men, in the heat of the sun, when he is overcome by the sudden urge to nap. His men make a tent for him with their shields, set up on spears, on the slope beside the river, and at once the king is away, in his dream floating rather than riding toward a mountain upstream that seems to touch the sky.

Beyond the mountain, he comes to a great plain, and beyond this a great harbor, where he crosses a bridge made of ivory to board a ship that speeds him to a beautiful island in a western sea. He surveys the whole land and enters a castle, where he finds two handsome young men playing a board game that is something like chess but has different plays and much greater stakes. Beyond them, a white-haired man with an air of majesty is enthroned in a chair embellished with the figures of twin eagles, fashioning new pieces for the game.

On a throne in front of the royal game-maker sits a woman who shines like the sun, lovely in her flowing white garment and red-gold clasps and armlets and necklaces flashing with jewels. She rises to greet the traveler, and they are joined in an embrace that claims the king's heart. They fit together, as one, on her throne.

When the noise of the world pulls him out of his dream, the king's vital energy stays in it. His soul has been claimed. He wants only to go back inside his dream and live with his beloved. His followers become troubled when he no longer joins their pleasures or speaks in their councils. When they confront him, warning him that some say the king is no longer fit to rule, the king tells his dream. The wise ones of the kingdom confer. They advise him to send his men out to search the world for three full years to find the woman of his dream. Perhaps the hope that she can be found will enable the king to keep enough of himself in his body to perform his duties. Nobody questions that the dream woman exists. She is *somewhere*, because the king finds her there whenever he dreams.

The searchers go out, and they fail in their mission. Now the advisers have a better idea: the seekers decide that, if the king returns to the place of his dream, and sets out from there in the direction he traveled in his dream, perhaps he will recognize the landmarks of his dream and they will take him to the lady who shines like the sun. The king delegates thirteen envoys to try to make the journey on his behalf. They find the mountain that touches the sky, and the ivory bridge to the ship that takes him to the western island, and the castle where young men play a game while a kingly man makes new pieces . . . and the woman who shines like the sun. She is not impressed by their rank and power. She will not go with them. If their king wants her, he must come and pay court to her himself.

So the king takes the road of his dreams and finds the woman sitting with her royal father as he makes pieces for a game that is no ordinary game. The golden-haired woman leaps into his embrace. They make love that night, and are married, and the king shares his power and his possessions with her as she directs. Just as she gave the king a road to her in his dreams, it is now the pleasure of this Lady of the Ways to make roads across the land.

This is a simple telling of the central part of a wonder story from a Welsh story cycle.[32] In the *Mabinogion*, the story is called "The Dream of Maxen." King Maxen is the emperor of Rome, and the dream woman who becomes his queen is Elen of Britain.

Scholars discuss the history that has been shape-shifted in this tale. Most agree that a Magnus Maximus, a Spanish general in the armies of Rome who was stationed in Britain and raised to the purple by his men in 383 CE, most closely resembles Maxen, although there are huge differences between their careers. While Maxen wins all his battles and is confirmed as world emperor with the help of Elen's unbeatable brothers, Magnus Maximus was defeated and killed by his fellow soldier-emperor, Theodosius, after briefly usurping the empire of the west.

It is mythistory, rather than literal history, that is being transacted here. Caitlín Matthews helps us to swim in its deeps in her splendid book *King Arthur and the Goddess of the Land*.[33] When we do this, we may discover, like the king, a way to bring the soul back into the body and marry the worlds.

The map is inside the dream. The road brings love and healing and power in the physical world, but to follow it you must become a traveler in two worlds.

When the trackers, and then the king himself, go back to the place of the dream, they travel inside a dreamscape. The mountain as high as the sky is no worldly mountain, and the bridge of ivory is no ordinary gangway, but they are quite real. The most important part of the journey to the beloved of the soul — who is also a goddess of the land and, in this version, the sovereignty of Britain — is a dream journey.

The board game in the story is highly significant. It is called *gwyddbwyll* (goodbowl) in Welsh, *fidhchell* among the Irish. As played in the ordinary world, it involved a smaller set of pieces representing a king and his bodyguard, who had to flee across the board — fighting to cover their retreat — while pursued by a much larger invading force under its own king. The player with the weaker force wins if he can get his king to safety across the board.

However, it seems that the game played in the dream is not confined to these rules. It is clearly a Game of the World. Others have dreamed something like

it: You are surveying an array of miniature figures, maybe little dolls or toy soldiers, that suddenly come alive. Then you can choose to move them around at
will, or shrink yourself to their scale and enter their dramas. This, perhaps, is
how gods or other beings at home in a multidimensional reality see the conflicts
and dramas of men. It may be that this is also how events that will later manifest in the physical world are initiated.

The dreams of the *Mabinogion* suggest that for early Europeans, as for other
ancient and indigenous cultures, dreaming is traveling, and the best way to grasp
the gift of a dream is to reenter the territory it reveals. This is very different from
modes of dream interpretation that slice and dice dreams into symbolic fragments and try to explain these one by one. Nonetheless, because dreams are often
mysterious, and many dreamers have difficulty coming and going within their
mists, there has always been a demand for interpreters.

CHAPTER 2

✦❦✦

INTERPRETERS AND DIVINERS

I think that in general it is a good plan occasionally to bear in mind that people were in the habit of dreaming before there was such a thing as psychoanalysis.

— SIGMUND FREUD

The occurrence of important events in any city or country is generally preceded by signs or portents, or by men who predict them.

— NICCOLÒ MACHIAVELLI, *Discorsi* 1:56

Divination is the effort to see into the future or discern the divine will. It has never been out of style.

The oldest and most effective forms of divination are those in which you look very carefully at what the world is telling you. You have a question on your mind and you pick up a stone, or examine the bark of a tree, and see what patterns they suggest to you that may hold an answer. The women seers of the German tribes, who gave Roman commanders plenty of trouble, liked to find pictures and hear voices in running water. Plutarch writes, "Their holy women used to foretell the future by observing eddies in the rivers, and by finding signs in the whirling and in the noise of the water."[1] When the Romans themselves needed guidance on whether the divine will was favorable or unfavorable to a certain undertaking, they sent their augurs up onto Capitoline Hill to monitor the behavior of birds.

From very early times, humans have constructed divination kits to limit to manageable numbers the answers the world could give them, that could be read according to an agreed upon and teachable method of understanding. African diviners carry pouches containing stones and pieces of bones and other objects and artifacts that represent certain themes or outcomes. They can be cast as lots, like runes, to make a story.

The world's great divinatory systems, such as China's I Ching, West Africa's Ifa, and Europe's Tarot, are more than tools for fortune-telling. In their design, the hexagrams, the *odu* (the patterns or "books" of Ifa divination), and the cards bring together symbols representing all the forces and processes at work in the world, including those that emanate from a deeper world. The magnitude of the design is clear in the oldest text of the I Ching, from Mawangdui, China, where it is written that the ancient sages "drummed" the patterns of heaven and earth into the hexagrams. Such patterns give form to the ever-shifting dynamics of manifestation. The world is before you, with all of its players marshaled in finite numbers adapted to the finite understanding of humans: the sixty-four gua, or hexagrams, of the I Ching, the sixteen master *odu* and 240 derivative patterns of the Ifa diviner, and the seventy-eight cards of Tarot.

A reading is designed to show what forces and factors are at play in a given moment of time, and which are absent. For a devoted reader of one of these systems, what is *missing* from the field may be as significant as what is present. If you do a daily card reading, for example, and you find that a certain card or suit never seems to show up, you will want to ask yourself why that element or power is absent from your life. A recurring pattern of absence may be comparable to a medical test that reveals, for example, that you do not have enough iron in your body.

Great readers, using any of these systems, rely on memory, intuition, and a gift for recognizing resemblances. Phenomenal memory is required to learn and carry the poetic oral recitations that hold the possible meanings of Ifa. A great *babalawo* ("father of the mysteries," the title of the Ifa divination priest) may carry in his head a hundred poetic stories about each of the *odu*, and will scan his memory banks during a reading to see which of these, in which combinations, are relevant to his client in that moment. A great reader of the I Ching will remember, as coins or yarrow sticks reveal a hexagram, not only the commentaries of past masters that he has memorized but also incidents that followed when a certain hexagram came up before. In the presence of the Hanged Man, the Queen of Cups, or the Seven of Swords, a great Tarot reader may wander through a personal memory palace where each of the rooms holds a living history of each of the cards — its transformations, its consequences — and where there is a great room in which the cards move together and interact, as in a medieval pageant with its mystery plays.

Intuition may involve courting, or at least being receptive to, the guidance of past masters. In China, for many generations the yarrow stalks preferred for casting the I Ching were plucked from the gravesites of previous masters, including Confucius. The *babalawo* recognizes that certain *odu* not only feature the ancestors or the orishas (the gods and demigods of the Yoruba) but also may announce their irruption into the space. When the pattern of Ogun, the iron lord of justice and retribution, is revealed, everything comes to a stop while his praise-names are chanted. Those who work deeply with variants of Tarot based on Kabbalah or the work of Western esoteric orders may come to feel they are in contact with the intelligences of some of those who traveled before them on these roads.

In all cultures, attitudes to divination range from superstitious credulity to impatient skepticism. The most pragmatic approach may be the one the great Roman statesman and advocate Cicero attributed to his brother Quintus in a celebrated treatise in which he argues both *for* and *against* divination: *eventa non causae* — pay attention to "outcomes, not causes." If it works, use it.[2]

The universally recognized source of divination is dreams. The dream interpreter is never likely to lack business — even in a society that disparages dreams — because people *know* that their dreams are important, but need help in three important ways: to figure out the meaning of dreams, to determine appropriate action to be taken, and to disperse or ward off bad energies that may be operating during the night.

Aristotle maintained that "dream-pictures, like pictures on water, are pulled out of shape by movement."[3] Hence we need help with the meaning of dreams because their shapes are distorted. An older and more popular view was that we need help in discerning the origin and nature of dreams because not all of them speak truth. Some dreams may be deceptive messages dispatched by evil spirits or manipulative magicians the Greeks called "dream senders" (*oneiropompoi*).

Again, we may need help in reading dreams because, as Artemidorus maintained, "the gods love to speak in riddles," sometimes to test us and to goad us to expand our understanding. Aristotle and Artemidorus agreed that the prime requirement for a dream interpreter was a gift for noticing resemblances. "The interpretation of dreams is nothing other than the juxtaposition of similarities," wrote Artemidorus.[4] Our earliest records of the work of a dream interpreter come from ancient Mesopotamia. Here the person you asked for help with your dream was called the "questioner." On clay tablets from Assur and Nineveh, the questioner is usually a woman.[5] The title suggests that she puts questions to the dreamer but also, more fundamentally, to the dream itself. Who or what was speaking in the dream? Is the dreamer's recollection reliable? Where did the dream experience take place? What part of the dreamer — a higher part of the soul or a lower one — was active in the dream? Is the female entity — who was "as high as the sky and as wide as the earth" — who appeared to that young man in Kish truly the great goddess?[6] What was the context of the dream? For example, was the dreamer sleeping in a special hut built from reeds that was used for dream incubation after ritual purification? Or was he sleeping off a bender?

A Mesopotamian term for an obscure or mysterious dream is "a closed archive basket of the gods." Picture a woven basket used for carrying a set of clay tablets. The role of the questioner is to lift the lid and help read what is in there. One technique she might use in doing this, suggests the cuneiform decoder Scott Noegel, is to record the dream and look for visual as well as auditory puns in the patterns that emerge as she scores the clay with a reed or wooden stylus.[7] That image, from five thousand years ago, seems strangely modern: the dream as text, the dream reader looking and listening for puns.

But we are in a world different from that of modern analysts. Literacy is still a rare skill, and the questioner uses the magic of writing. But she also brings other tools to bear. She may seek a second opinion through one of many systems of divination, which range from reading the stars to examining the entrails of a sacrificial animal to noticing what is coming into view in the landscape in a given moment — the cry of the boatman, the wind bending the reeds. In Mesopotamia, as in most human cultures, dreaming was understood to be close kin to divination. The famous Assyrian dream book in the library of King Ashurbanipal — brought to Nineveh in 647 BCE from the house of an exorcist of Nippur — was stored with the omen tablets, the largest category in the royal collection.[8] Among ordinary folk as well as in royal palaces, across most of history, dreamwork has never been separated from other ways of reading the sign language of life.

In Ur or Uruk, the questioner may decide to go beyond the dreamer's imperfect recollection of a dream into the fuller dream *experience* by transporting herself to the place where the dream action unfolded and asking questions inside that space. What would that mean? There's a clue in a tablet that describes the questioner as "one who lies at a person's head." An Oxford scholar suggests that "the method was to lie beside the sleeper in the hope of intercepting or sharing the dream as it entered his head."[9]

Dreams may suggest or require action, so one of the crucial roles of the dream interpreter is to counsel on what is to be *done* with a dream. When in the Bible Joseph is called on to interpret Pharaoh's dream, he does not stop with telling

him that the dream parables of the fat and starving cattle, and the full and withered sheaves of grain, foreshadowed seven years of plenty followed by seven
years of famine. He gives Pharaoh an action plan.

Joseph suggests that Pharaoh appoint a wise viceroy and impose a new tax
during the seven years of plenty to fill the granaries against the coming time of
famine. Pharaoh decides that Joseph himself is the man for the job. He is given
an Egyptian name, meaning "God Says He Is Alive,"[10] and married into
Egypt's highest nobility, to the daughter of a priest of Ra.

The role of the dream diviner may also involve suggesting apotropaic
practices for preventing bad dreams and dispelling any negative residue from
an unwanted dream. The New Kingdom Dream Book (the Chester Beatty
papyrus, inscribed in the thirteenth century BCE) contains a most interesting ritual for turning away the negative energy of "bad" dreams and the psychic forces
at play in them. The first part of the ritual involves cleansing the dreamer by
rubbing his face with bread soaked with beer, herbs, and myrrh. The second
part requires the dreamer to tell his dream to Isis, addressed as "Mother." The
act of telling the dream to the Great Mother is held to disperse its evil. In the
Gardiner translation of the papyrus, Isis says, "Come out with what you have
seen, in order that the afflictions you saw in your dreams may vanish." The ritual ends with a triumphal cry from the dreamer that he has dispelled an evil
dream sent against him and is now ready to receive pleasant dreams. "Hail to
thee, good dream that is seen by night or day!"[11]

In Mesopotamia, an evil dream would be transferred to a lump of clay that
was placed in a river and allowed to dissolve in the power of water.[12] In ancient
India, when King Asoka (third century BCE) was troubled by a bad dream, the
priests assisted him in ritually saluting the four directions and imploring the gods
to help avert any evil effects of the dream.[13] A manuscript from Tun-huang, in
central Asia, on the Great Silk Road (c. 800 CE) describes practices for trans-
ferring the energy of bad dreams to physical objects such as pieces of wood or
bits of earth that are then destroyed or dispersed.[14] Such practices reflect a belief
— widespread in human history — in the *manifesting* power of dreams. A dream
may be like a storm cloud ready to burst. When it's that close to discharging,
you can't simply wish or talk its effects away; you must provide it with a safe
channel that will carry its energy away.

In Homer's *Odyssey*, we first learn, with Penelope, about the two gates of
dreams: the Gate of Ivory and the Gate of Horn. Dreams that come through the
Gate of Ivory are "dangerous" and might not be manifested; dreams that come
through the Gate of Horn are clearer and may be embodied in events. The

difference seems to be a matter of clarity rather than deception. Carved ivory is totally opaque; polished horn is translucent.

The gates reappear in *The Aeneid*, but Virgil changes their characterization in his account of Aeneas's descent to the underworld to visit his dead father, Anchises. Now dreams that come through the Gate of Ivory are designated as false, while those that come through the Gate of Horn are said to be true. This becomes a standard distinction for centuries in the minds of Westerners raised on the classics.

But there is a mind trap in Virgil's story. Anchises sends his son back from the Underworld through the Gate of Ivory. Is the poet hinting that our ordinary experience of reality is the false dream?

Let's explore the approach of the Greek whose name was synonymous with dream interpretation long after he wrote his *Oneirocritica* in the second century, in the time of the philosopher-emperor Marcus Aurelius, who thanked his dreams for divine guidance, and the great physician Galen, who used dreams for diagnosis.

RIGHT AND WRONG WAYS TO HAVE DREAM SEX WITH YOUR MOTHER

It's doubtful even Freud considered as many ways for a man to have sex with his mother as Artemidorus described in the most famous book on dream interpretation prior to Freud. Sex in the missionary position, which Artemidorus, as a good pagan, called "according to the precepts of Aphrodite." Sex from behind. Standing up. Sex with mom on top. Oral sex. "Other positions invented for wantonness, licentiousness and intoxication." It goes on for pages in the *Oneirocritica*, "The Interpretation of Dreams," from which, seventeen hundred years later, Freud borrowed his title but certainly not his approach.[15]

In no case does Artemidorus interpret any of these incest dreams literally. Sex in these dreams is not about sex. Nor, it seems, does it have anything to do with personal psychology, though it may speak of family dynamics. "Many a man has dreamed as much," Jocasta told Oedipus.[16] Artemidorus presumably knows the Oedipus tragedy better than Freud, but he has never heard of an Oedipus complex. It does not occur to him to investigate infantile fantasies or wish fulfillment, or even to ask in what sense a dreamer may want to "screw his mother." And he never raises the question of whether the mother figure in a dream could be an aspect of the dreamer himself.

He wants to go beyond the surface content of the dreams to their concealed, or latent, meanings. Any resemblance to Freud begins and ends here. Artemidorus is interested not in psychology but in prediction. An incest dream — like all other dreams in his book — must be decoded to reveal a message for the dreamer about a future event. The Greek interpreter's decryption machine is calibrated. The exact meaning of a man's dream of incest with his mother will depend on many things: on how they are doing it, first of all, and then on whether the mother is living or dead and on the dreamer's circumstances, including his health, the state of his finances, and his travel plans.

Artemidorus starts with the simplest, in-your-face version of the incest dream. The dreamer is having frontal sex with his mother, who is still alive. This could portend rivalry and conflict between the dreamer and his father, if the father is alive. However, dreaming of frontal sex with your mother is lucky if you hold public office or are seeking power, because it suggests you will possess your mother country. Frontal penetration is also lucky for artisans and tradesmen, because the Greeks call a person's trade his "mother."

If you have been estranged from your mother, a dream of frontal sex with her means you'll be friends again. If you are living in different countries, you'll be reunited. If you are sick, you'll probably recover, "since nature is the common mother of all things and we say that the healthy are in their natural condition."[17]

It's not so good to have sex with your mother in other positions. If you're taking her from behind, she is looking away from you, which means that anything good she represents is turning its back on you too. Sex with her while standing up is unlucky, "for men use this position when they have neither bed nor mattress," implying straitened circumstances.[18]

Watch out if your mom is on top. Mother Earth lies on top of the corpse in the ground, so this could portend death, depending on your health at the time of the dream. "I have observed that sick men regularly die after this dream, whereas those who are in good health spend the rest of their lives in comfort doing whatever they want." If your mother is dead, sex of any kind with her is risky, since this may mean you are going to have "intercourse with the earth."[19]

Adding sexual improv to incest is not likely to turn out well. The worst of all versions is fellatio with your mother; "this signifies to the dreamer the death of children, the loss of property and grave illness."[20]

Artemidorus is not writing about dreams in a vacuum, cooking up some kind of ancient drugstore dictionary. It was his lifelong passion to travel the cities of the eastern Roman empire, starting with his hometown, the great temple city of Ephesus, and listen to dreams and those who sought to interpret them, watching carefully to see the events that followed a particular dream. His statement that a man's dream of incest with his mother is favorable for someone seeking power was in no way exotic in Greco-Roman times; this was a general opinion, and some famous men had made historic decisions based on it. On the eve of his decision to cross the Rubicon (which marked the frontier between Gaul and Italy) and march on Rome, Julius Caesar was torn by indecision, foreseeing the horrors of the civil war his action would unleash. Plutarch tells us, "That night he dreamed that he was committing incest with his own mother."[21] The dream was interpreted to mean that Caesar would take possession of his mother country. Caesar's enemies had an understandably jaundiced view of the dream, calling him by the Roman version of a street name familiar today.

Freudians haven't been able to cope with Artemidorus's treatment of incest dreams. On Freudian principles, overt dreams of sex between parents and children aren't supposed to be possible; the sexual desires involved are so horrifying they should never get by the dream censor. One Freudian tried to dismiss Artemidorus on the grounds that his incest dreams are "psychologically implausible": such dreams practically "never occur" in clinical and anthropological experience. But this ignores the fact that many famous men in Greco-Roman history, from Hippias to Julius Caesar, dreamed of sex with their mothers — and understood that these dream messages were about something other than sex.[22]

What did Freud make of Artemidorus's incest dreams? We don't know, because he never read them. Freud's knowledge of Artemidorus was confined to an abridged German edition by a translator who prudishly deleted these pages. It is an amazing irony in the history of psychology that Freud — celebrated for his description of infantile sexual fantasies, especially the Oedipus complex — missed out on the incest dreams in the ancient book from which he borrowed the title of his own most famous work.[23]

Artemidorus states his general objective at the start of his book. He wants to make a rational and effective case for divination, based on his personal experience and the case studies he has collected. Second, he wants to offer a practical and original guidebook that any intelligent reader can use. He gives his credentials in his opening pages: "I have not only taken special pains to procure every book on the interpretation of dreams, but have consorted for many years with the much-despised diviners of the marketplace. . . . In the different cities of Greece and at the great religious gatherings of that country, in Asia, in Italy and in the largest and most populous of the islands, I have patiently listened to old dreams and their consequences."[24] He declares, "Everything has been the result of personal experience, since I have always devoted myself, day and night, to the study of dream interpretation."[25]

Artemidorus proceeds to distinguish different types of dreams. A fundamental difference is between *oneiros*, which he defines as a dream that "indicates a future state of affairs," and *enhypnion* — stuff "in sleep" — which "indicates a present state of affairs," ranging from the state of your digestion to your desire to be with your lover to the haunting images of things you fear. People who lead "an upright life" try to discipline themselves to avoid being "muddled" by the fears and desires reflected in such sleep experiences, which are the stuff of much modern dream analysis. In the *Oneirocritica*, Artemidorus is interested only in dreams that reveal the future, and only in those that do this through allegory rather than by literal depiction of possible scenes and events. Allegorical dreams are "those which signify one thing by means of another."[26]

"The mind predicts everything that will happen in the future."[27] Artemidorus gives several examples of precognitive dreams that presented future events in an entirely literal way. A man dreams of a shipwreck, and then his boat is wrecked and he narrowly avoids drowning, as in the dream. Another man dreams he is wounded in the shoulder by a friend in a hunting accident, and again the dream is played out exactly.

If it is possible to dream the future with this kind of clarity, why do we need allegories? Artemidorus gives two reasons. First, we may lack the experience to understand a future event perceived in a dream — for example, because we have not yet encountered a person or situation featured in the dream. By presenting us with a puzzle to figure out, the allegorical dream gives us a *rational* way to access what the larger mind knows about things to come. Second, the kind of dream dramas Artemidorus describes can bring an emotional charge that leads to action: "it is the nature of the *oneiros* to awaken and excite the soul by inducing active undertakings."[28]

Artemidorus also notes that, while the gods do not lie, they do like to speak in riddles. This is because "they are wiser than we and do not wish us to accept anything without a thorough examination." He gives the example of a man who dreamed that the god Pan told him his wife would poison him via his best friend. But it was the relationship that was poisoned, when the wife proceeded to have an affair with the friend.[29]

Thus Artemidorus sets very clear boundaries around the field of dreams he explores in the *Oneirocritica*. He is going to show us how to decode allegorical dreams in order to discern the future. He is well aware that other kinds of dreams require other kinds of dreamwork; he wrote about other types of dreams in books that have not survived, in addition to writing a book about augury, or, in the original meaning of that word, divination by bird-watching.[30] This approach is completely different from that of Freud, who postulated that all dreams have equal status and are formed by the same mechanisms.

Artemidorus recognized that every dream may be unique. The snake in your dream is not the same as the snake in mine. To read the meaning of a dream symbol correctly, one must know the dreamer's identity, position in life, habits, and medical condition. "You must examine closely the habits of men before the dream.... You must inquire carefully into them."[31] Suppose you dream you are made of silver or gold. If you are a slave, this means you'll be sold; if you are poor, you'll become rich; if you're already rich, you'll be the victim of plots, because everyone will be out to get your money.[32] One must also question the dreamer's *feelings* about a dream.

Artemidorus observes that we dream the future for others as well as for ourselves. Sometimes we receive a dream message for someone else: "Many dreams come true for those whose characters are similar to the dreamer's and for his relatives and namesakes." Artemidorus gives the example of a woman who dreamed she was married to a man who was not her husband. He observes that work with this dream could proceed in several directions, including exploring the possibility that it warned of death: "marriage and death signify each other because the circumstances surrounding a marriage and a funeral are similar."[33] This association, it turns out, was on the right track, but it was the dreamer's sister, not the dreamer herself, who "married death" after the dream.

Artemidorus kept in touch with his clients after consultations and, apparently, believed that divination through dreams benefits the whole community. This carries a burden: "If a man dreams that he has become a prophet and has been celebrated for his predictions, he ... will take upon himself, in addition to his own anxieties, those of others."[34]

Artemidorus wanted to raise dream divination to the level of an applied science. In the view of one modern scholar, Christine Walde, he succeeded. "The more complex aspects of divination — which is the attempt to investigate the connections underlying fate and the cosmos through natural and artificial means — constituted both an ancient mode for mastering life and a way of gaining knowledge or insight that, in the context of its time, can in no way be dismissed as irrational; at most, it might be considered extrarational." Artemidorus devised a "demystified" approach to divination that "provides the standardized conditions that scientific distance requires" and "an imposing reservoir of knowledge about things in the world and their interdependence."[35]

The Dream Seer of Alexander the Great

Let's examine the role of one dream diviner in shaping world-historical events. The diviner's name is Aristander, and he is a Merlin figure in the story of Alexander the Great (356–323 BCE). He was at Alexander's side throughout the astonishing campaigns that made him the master of Persia and Egypt and carried his army all the way to India. Aristander left clearer footprints than the later Merlin, and as we track them we discover that his deepest magic was a double gift of vision: through dreams and portents, he could read the patterns of what *wanted to happen*, and he could communicate his insights with a drama that helped drive men to action.

Aristander was in the Alexander story before Alexander got there. King Philip of Macedon dreamed that he sealed the vagina of his beautiful wife, Olympias; the figure of a lion was stamped on the wax of the seal. Other interpreters feared trouble in the marriage, but when Aristander was called in, his reading was reassuring. He told Philip his queen was pregnant — you don't seal up an empty container — and predicted that the boy she was carrying would be a lion in strength and courage.[36]

All we know of Aristander at this point in his career is that he came from Telmessus in Caria, a city renowned for its diviners, and already had the confidence of the Macedonian royal house. After Alexander inherited the kingdom at age twenty, Aristander reappeared as one of his intimate counselors. There are nineteen passages in the ancient sources in which we see Alexander's seer doing his stuff, which includes watching birds, interpreting dreams, reading the entrails of sacrificial animals, and monitoring the sign language of the world. We catch glimpses of the *mobilizing* effect of the kind of seership that convinces people that the gods and/or the powers of nature are on their side. There's a cheerleading quality to some of Aristander's predictions, but he also delivers warnings, one of them involving a plot against Alexander's life.

On one occasion, as Alexander's army marched through Pieria, the home of Orpheus and the Muses, it was observed that a cypress-wood statue of Orpheus was sweating, and this made Alexander's men uneasy. Aristander gave a confident reading: since Orpheus was a patron of music and song, the sign meant that Alexander's achievements would be such that musicians and poets would sweat to compose praise-songs worthy of them.[37]

Like other ancient seers, Aristander paid very close attention to the behavior of birds. During the siege of Halicarnassus, a great walled city in what is now southwest Turkey, Alexander took a nap in the middle of the day. A swallow fluttered around him, chirping noisily. When the king brushed at the bird, sleepily, with his hand, she perched on his head and would not leave him until he was wide awake. Alexander immediately called his seer to explain the sign of the swallow. Aristander told him it was a warning that someone close to him was plotting to betray him, and that the plot would soon be uncovered.[38] The incident led Alexander to take action that resulted in the exposure and arrest of one of his trusted Companions, formerly the commander of the Thessalian horse, who was plotting with the Persians to kill him.

Aristander's dreamwork with Alexander helped encourage him in the long and grueling siege of the Phoenician city of Tyre, during which the defenders came up with an especially nasty weapon; they heated sand in bronze cauldrons until it was almost incandescent, then poured it over the attackers from the battlements. Months into the siege, Alexander dreamed that Herakles stood atop the walls of Tyre, beckoning for him to come. Aristander told him that the dream meant that the siege would succeed, but at the cost of immense effort comparable to the labors of Herakles.[39] In another dream, Alexander saw a satyr mocking him from a distance. When Alexander went for him, the satyr ran away, and the king could catch him only after a long chase. Aristander's reading of this dream is an ancient example of finding the meaning of a dream by listening for puns. Broken into two words, *sa tyros* means "Tyre is yours."[40] The reading of victory was fulfilled after Aristander confirmed it by studying the entrails of a sacrificed animal.

It is probable that Aristander was with Alexander when he journeyed across the desert to the temple oracle of the god Ammon at the oasis of Siwa in what is now Libya. Lost in the desert when a guide became confused, Alexander's party was led on the last stage of the journey by twin snakes (according to Ptolemy) or twin crows (Plutarch). What exactly was transacted between the Macedonian king and the god with ram's horns is a mystery; Alexander wrote to his mother that there were "secret affairs" he would tell only to her. It is all but certain that, when he was hailed as pharaoh in the temple of Ammon, he was recognized as an incarnate god. From this point on, as Alexander marched east, easterners prostrated themselves before him, to the disgust of Macedonians and Greeks, who did not like humans being converted into gods until *after* death.

The night before the great battle against the Persians at Gaugemala (Camel House), Aristander spent hours with Alexander in his tent performing "magical rituals," scouting the possible future by his own methods, and helping to work up a tactical plan.[41] Alexander then slept soundly for a few hours. The host assembled by Darius, the Persian king of kings, outnumbered Alexander's force by at least ten to one. Alexander's plan involved an element of deception: he would deploy his forces so the Persians would be lured into attacking his deceptively weak flanks, giving him a chance to drive through their center. But his first need, on the morning of battle, was to fire up his men, who could see the formidable odds they were facing. As he spoke to the army, Aristander rode up, resplendent in a white robe and a gold crown, and pointed to an eagle that soared, on flat wings, over Alexander's head and then flew straight toward the enemy. Alexander's men were fired up by this portent of victory. His battle plan was a brilliant success, copied later by generals such as Marlborough, Winston Churchill's ancestor.[42]

Later, when the Macedonians were camped far to the east near the Oxus (Amu Dar'ya) River, a crew digging a trench struck something Europeans had never seen before. As a thick, greasy black liquid spurted into the air, soldiers rushed to alert Ptolemy, one of Alexander's Companions (who later founded an Egyptian dynasty and dreamed up a new god). Ptolemy hurried to tell Alexander, who called on his seer to explain the meaning of the "black spring." Aristander said it portended much labor, but victory after hard work. Alexander's men had struck oil. However far Aristander could see, he was probably unable to foresee what oil would mean to the world long after Alexander.[43]

GOVERNING BY THE I CHING

When we turn to China, we find that divination was central not only to the career of a great individual but also to the conduct of state policy over millennia. For thousands of years, the I Ching, or Book of Changes, was a basic tool of government.

The emergence of the I Ching is wrapped in legend and mystery. By tradition, it was the ancient Dragon Emperor, Fu Tsi, who noticed patterns in the cracks of turtle shells and distinguished these patterns as the eight trigrams that are the root of the I Ching. Later, the "King of Writing," Wu Wen, amplified the system, giving it sixty-four hexagrams, and Confucius ordered and numbered the arrangement.

Archeology suggests the I Ching underwent an evolution over some four thousand years. Under the Shang dynasty, shamans read auguries in the cracks that appeared in the bones of animals used as burned offerings. It was believed that, as the appeals of humans traveled upward in the smoke, messages and warnings from higher powers came down. The relation between patterns of cracks and subsequent events was noted, and cracked bones were kept in preliterate "archives." Later, turtle shells were substituted. They provided a larger surface, and their shape was thought to resemble the dome of heaven above and the square fields of earth below. With the coming of the Bronze Age, turtle shells were cracked with bronze pokers. Patterns corresponding to later events began to be marked with simple symbols suggesting fire or flood. From these symbols, Chinese writing emerged. Under the Chou dynasty — before the supply of turtles was exhausted — shamans and diviners began to record the code of the I Ching on strips of bamboo tied together with silk ribbons. And the first books of China emerged.

The I Ching hexagrams are stacks of six lines, broken or unbroken, variations on a binary code. The unbroken lines are *yang*, the broken ones are *yin*. When you read the I Ching, you work simultaneously with three kinds of imagery: the patterns of the hexagrams, the pictures contained in the Chinese ideograms that name them, and the poetic lines of the commentaries. Sometimes the visual image is right there in front of you in the shape of the hexagram. Hexagram 20, Guan ("Watching"), for example, is shaped like a watchtower.

The Great Treatise, one of the earliest long commentaries on the I Ching, maintains that the Book of Changes contains "the measure of heaven and earth," and that if we place ourselves in exactly the right point in its revolutions, we move in synchrony with the workings of the universe and can help to shape events on every scale through our conscious participation. The Great Treatise suggests that not only can we learn from the I Ching how to meet every event in the right way, but also we may be privileged "to aid the gods in governing the world."[44]

The oldest copy of the I Ching known to us is one of two books buried with the Marquis of Tai at Mawangdui around 175 BCE, intended to function as his companions on the journey to the afterlife; the second book was the Taoist masterwork the *Tao te-ching*. The Mawangdui text hints at a shamanic source for this system of divination: the sage "drums the movements of all under heaven" into the hexagrams, "drums them and causes them to dance."[45] The I Ching "knows the reasons for light and dark."[46] There is a hint of the observer effect working on a human scale. Reading the Book of Changes "strengthens beings and *fixes fate*" (italics added).[47]

One of the earliest reported uses of the I Ching to guide affairs of state involves the rise and fall of imperial dynasties. Toward the end of the Shang dynasty, the brutal and wayward oppression of the ruling tyrant, who was goaded on by a dissipated concubine, had grown intolerable: he forced respectable women to take part in sexual orgies and had his victims chopped into mincemeat or roasted alive. The Duke of Chou, known to history as King Wu, emerged as one of the resistance leaders. In 1048 BCE, he gathered an army and marched to the ford of Meng, where he was met by forces led by eight hundred princes. He boarded a boat to cross the river, but called off the army's advance when a huge and vigorous white fish jumped into his boat and then jumped out again. The princes wanted to continue with the campaign. King Wu told them, "You know nothing of Heaven's decree."[48] King Wu knew that a white fish was a symbol of Shang; he took the appearance and escape of the strong white fish on the river as a sign that the tyrant of Shang dynasty was still too strong to be defeated in open battle at that time.

King Wu continued to gather his forces and assembled a larger army at the same point on the river two years later. The king reviewed the hosts and declared that he had received double confirmation — through divination with the aid of the I Ching, and from his dreams — that their cause would prosper. "It would seem that Heaven by means of me is going to rule the people. My dreams coincide with my divinations; the auspicious omen is double. My attack on Shang must succeed."[49]

He was correct. The army of Shang was routed; the tyrant fled to the palace he called the Stag Tower — the scene of many orgies — put on his finest robes and jewels, and burned himself to death. The victor founded the Chou (or Zhou) dynasty.

For many centuries after the fall of Shang, both turtle-shell and yarrow-stick readings and the careful observation of natural phenomena and spontaneous synchronicity were used by the rulers of China for guidance on important undertakings. The chronicles known as the *Zuo Zhuan* contain detailed descriptions of many castings of the I Ching to guide the wars and marriages of the house of Qin in the seventh and sixth centuries BCE.

Let's jump forward to the time of the Manchu dynasty. K'ang-hsi was a scholar-emperor of the Ch'ing (or Manchu) dynasty who ruled China for over sixty years, from 1661 to 1722, surviving wars, rebellions, and numberless intrigues. He was a man of science and reason who personally attended to many details of government without getting overwhelmed by those details. Dissatisfied with the quality of graduates from the all-important civil service examinations, he personally graded hundreds of exam papers while campaigning under a military tent.

Unimpressed by his generals' handling of river pirates, K'ang-hsi issued exact and savvy directives on the recruitment of agents, the deployment of special forces, and the need for rulers to have personal knowledge of the character and motivation of the enemy: "To learn about pirates you need more than official reports — you can question pirate leaders in person, as I did. . . . You can employ captured pirates themselves as advisers, or use them to take messages to their fellows and induce them to surrender. . . . One needs, too, to examine the type of person who is a pirate."[50]

From his own writings, we can track this emperor's study of the Book of Changes and the decisions he made based on specific readings. In 1680, K'ang-hsi embarked on a "preliminary reading" of the Book of Changes with three counselors. *They devoted three days' study to each hexagram.* Four years later, they went through the hexagrams all over again. The emperor noticed that his diviners were placing some issues in the category of "things there was no need to discuss" for fear of offending their master — for example, the sixth line in hexagram 1, Ch'ien: "Arrogant dragon will have cause to repent." K'ang-hsi instructed that *nothing* would be off-limits in the discussion of a reading. A warning against arrogance was especially important, since "arrogance means that one knows how to press forward but not how to draw back . . . something about winning but nothing about losing."[51]

In 1683, after the capture of Taiwan, the emperor discussed hexagram 56, Lu — "Fire on the Mountain" — with his diviners: "The calm of the mountain signifies the care that must be used in imposing penalties; the fire moves rapidly on, burning up the grass, like lawsuits that should be settled speedily. My reading of this was that the ruler needs both clarity and care in punishing: his intent must be to punish in order to avoid the need for further punishing."[52] Here the emperor's reading is based on considering the natural qualities of the two elemental trigrams, Mountain and Fire. Be calm like a Mountain and look on things from a higher perspective; be quick and decisive in cleansing, like Fire.

The emperor gives us excellent guidance on the need for a ruler to be open to receiving unwanted messages: "My diviners have often been tempted to pass over bad auguries, but I have double-checked their calculations and warned them not to distort the truth: the Bureau of Astronomy once reported that a benevolent southeast wind was blowing, but I myself calculated the wind's direction with the palace instruments and found it to be, in fact, an inauspicious northeast wind; I told the Bureau to remember that ours was not a dynasty that shunned bad omens."[53]

He insists that we make our own fate and should "urge on Heaven in its work": "Things may seem determined in our lives, but there are ways in which man's power can help Heaven's work. . . . We must urge on Heaven in its work, not just rely on it. . . . In our own lives, though fixed by fate, yet that fate comes from our own minds. . . . If you do not perform your human part you cannot understand Heaven's way."[54]

Late in his reign, he celebrates the Book of Changes in these words: "I have never tired of the *Book of Changes* and have used it in fortune-telling and as a source of moral principles; the only thing you must not do, I told my court lecturers, is to make this book appear simple, for there are meanings here that lie beyond words."[55]

Given the great Chinese respect for the ancestors, it is not surprising to find that work with the I Ching traditionally involves invoking and discerning the spirits. As noted earlier, the yarrow stalks most valued for early divination were found growing on the graves of past teachers and masters of the I Ching, including Confucius. In the seventeenth century, a prince decided that a recent divination was confirmed when his entourage found a yarrow plant with fifty stalks (the number used for divining) growing right on Confucius's grave. Early translator James Legge reported that he himself had seen yarrow growing on the grave of Confucius. It was widely believed that, when a good diviner in the right state of mind is doing his or her stuff, there is communication with ancestors who will guide the reading.

The Great Treatise states that the I Ching is to be used to discern the spirits. "The escape of the soul brings about change. Through this we come to know the conditions of outgoing [*shen*] and returning [*kuei*] spirits."[56] When the Chinese were faced with events that could not be rationally explained, they often attributed them to the operations of two very different types of spirits. The *shen* is a higher, spiritual aspect of soul. The term is also used for gods and deified mortals. On painted and embroidered hangings in the tomb of the Marquis of Tai, where the oldest copy of the I Ching was found, the *shen* spirit is depicted as a gorgeous, human-headed bird. In life — according to the medical treatise of the Yellow Emperor — the most important aspect of *shen* resides in the heart. After death, the *shen* ascends to the spirit world and may join the ranks of the wise ancestors who counsel and protect the living.[57]

The *kuei*, on the other hand, is a hungry, restless ghost that roams the world bringing misfortune, illness, and death. *Kuei* include spirits of individuals who were not properly buried or who are trapped between the worlds by their evil natures and accumulated misdeeds. They may be manipulated by malevolent sorcerers. Vampirelike, they seek to drain the energy of the living. In traditional

China, numerous protective rituals and talismans were devised to keep *kuei* out of the home.

One of the traditional functions of the I Ching was to provide a diagnostic of the condition of spirits in the psychic environment. Reading the Book of Changes is central to health and healing in the old Chinese way, because it holds up a mirror to emotional, spiritual, and psychic forces at play and suggests the means to make the proper balance and to repair soul loss. It was believed that, in itself, the Book of Changes could offer defense against the intrusions of ghosts and psychic attackers. G. Willoughby-Meade relates a story in which the scholar Wu fights off hostile sorcerers with his copy of the Book of Changes. When he strikes his psychic attackers with it, they become paper dolls that he then cages inside the book.[58]

Since Richard Wilhelm produced the first accessible translation that provides practical instruction for doing readings, the I Ching has become the property of the world. As Beverley Zabriskie observes, "Although assembled in alien and distant times, the hexagrams offer images and analogies for common external mishaps and internal disjunction: frustration over a flat tire, or . . . the searching of the soul."[59] There is even more: there is the chance, in the constant shifting of the Book of Changes, to catch the possible movement between alternate event tracks, even parallel worlds. The shape of hexagram 61, Zhong Fu ("Inner Truth"), resembles that of an open heart, the possibility of seeing through to the core of things. When Juliana casts this hexagram in Philip K. Dick's visionary novel *The Man in the High Castle*, the protagonist's reality begins to shift, and he sees a more desirable world, a world where Hitler did not win. Dedicated readers of the I Ching, like careful students of synchronicity, may grasp that to see something for what it is can change *everything*.

THE DREAM DIAGNOSIS DR. FREUD MISSED

Dreams have meaning and they can be interpreted. Dreams exhibit the same kind of creativity and poetic consciousness that is at play in art and literature. And they may be the trace elements of a universal language of signs and correspondences that humans once could speak before the darkening of their minds.

These ideas all come from Freud, from the 1900 edition of his *Interpretation of Dreams* and from a chapter on symbols that he added in 1914.[60] The ideas are ancient, yet at the end of the nineteenth century they were a fresh wind in the stale consulting rooms of psychiatrists who maintained, like some later neuroscientists, that dreams are meaningless epiphenomena of somatic processes.

Unfortunately, Freud promoted other aspects of his dream theory into a rigid dogma that tried to confine the meanings of dreams to a very narrow band of understanding. While he seemed to respect the individuality of dreamers by asking for their personal associations with dream images, he tried to shunt interpretation along a certain track. He insisted, almost to the point of monomania, that dream symbols are all about sex. Thus, opening an umbrella is always about having an erection, a woman's hat is a genital organ, a necktie is a penis, and "stairs and going upstairs in dreams almost invariably stand for copulation."[61] Really? What about going to a higher or lower level in life, in the sense of personal development of social status or job description? What about scouting out a building you haven't visited yet? Freud's obsession with sexual symbolism is spoofed hilariously in the film *The Umbrellas of Cherbourg*, where every time an umbrella is raised or the cork of a wine bottle is popped — nudge, nudge — we know that Guy and his girl are getting it on. Also central to Freud's dogma was the notion that the overt content of a dream is a subterfuge by the editing mind, which seeks to repress the latent content, which usually involves embarrassing infantile fantasies and wish fulfillment.

Freud parted company radically with the ancient dream interpreters by dismissing the idea that dreams reveal the future. On the contrary, he insisted, dreams stem from the dreamer's past, starting with day residue and extending back — under the veils of repression — into early childhood. Dreams are not predictions; they are psychosexual biographies.

The flaws in Freud's approach were dramatized by two revealing incidents. The first, quite famous, led to the rupture of his relationship with his most gifted apprentice, C. G. Jung. The second, which has somehow escaped most of the legion of students and biographers of Freud, is tragic and suggests that Freud may have paid a terrible price for ignoring both the premonitory and the somatic aspects of dreams.

A *big* dream of Jung's that Freud was utterly unable to analyze by his system contributed to their breakup and Jung's emergence as leader of an original school. In a many-storied house in his dream, Jung becomes conscious that there is a floor below the ordinary bourgeois level on which he is living. When he starts to explore it, he finds a darkened floor with medieval furnishings and, below that, a beautifully vaulted Roman cellar and, down below that — when he lifts a stone slab by a ring — a primal cave with scattered bones and pottery and two skulls.

Jung shared the dream with Freud when they were traveling together. The only way Freud could deal with it was to persuade Jung to twist it until it became an example of Freud's theory that what lies below the manifest content of dreams is a repressed desire, which in this case (because of the skulls) must be a death wish. Who did Jung want to see dead? Poor Jung, still in awe of his teacher, was obliged to identify his new wife (with whom there were absolutely no problems) and his sister-in-law as the people against whom he must be carrying a death wish. He confessed this knowing it was a lie, because he knew Freud felt personally helpless and menaced by anything that escaped the narrow mind-traps of his theory.

The lie brought Jung to realize both the wrongness of his mentor's approach and his need to break with it. Far from being agents of repression, dreams open a space that is free of waking repression and denial. "To me," Jung wrote, "dreams are a part of nature, which harbors no intention to deceive, but expresses something as best it can, just as a plant grows or an animal seeks its food as best it can." Jung's dream of the many-storied house was of huge importance, since — by his own account — it led him for the first time to the concept of the collective unconscious. It brought him alive to the rich ancestral geography — the "structural diagram of the human psyche" — that becomes accessible in dreaming.[62]

But Jung had to make the break with Freud before he could make his decisive breakthrough. After the house dream, he was coached for their parting of ways by another dream, in which he saw Freud as the peevish ghost of an Austrian customs official fading to nothingness while a different guide — a Grail knight in flashing armor — appeared to the dreamer.

The most famous of all the dreams Freud analyzed was one of his own, the Irma dream. In *The Interpretation of Dreams*, he gives a lengthy account of this 1895 dream and his work with it. In the dream, he inspects the mouth of a patient called Irma and discusses her condition with several doctors.[63]

His work with this dream, by Freud's own account, led him to invent psychoanalysis. He wanted a "marble tablet" with the following inscription to be placed at the house where he analyzed the Irma dream:

IN THIS HOUSE, ON JULY 24TH, 1895,
THE SECRET OF DREAMS WAS
REVEALED TO DR. SIGM. FREUD[64]

The tragic irony is that, in all his work on this dream, Freud may have missed a health warning that could have saved his life. Dr. José Schavelzon, a cancer surgeon who is also a psychoanalyst, has concluded after a careful review of Freud's personal medical records that the Irma dream contained an amazingly exact preview of the precise symptoms of the oral cancer that would kill Freud twenty-eight years later.

The night before the dream, Freud received a visit from a junior colleague, "Otto," with whom he was in the habit of sitting up playing tarok (a card game related to Tarot) and smoking cigars. They discussed the case of "Irma," whom Freud had been treating for hysteria. Freud was irritated when Otto reported, "She's better, but not quite well."[65] He spent part of his evening writing up Irma's case history.

He then dreamed that Irma arrived in a large hall where he was receiving guests. He immediately took her aside and told her, "If you still get pains, it's really only your fault." She was pale and puffy and told Freud she was suffering dreadful pains, especially in her throat: "It's choking me." Freud was alarmed and began to fear he had missed "some organic trouble" in his approach. He took Irma to a window and peered into her mouth. He had a hard time getting it open, because "she showed signs of recalcitrance, like women with artificial dentures." When he got a good look inside, he found very disturbing symptoms — "a big white patch" inside the mouth on the right side and "extensive whitish grey scabs." Freud gave an oddly specific description of these scabs; they reminded him of "the turbinal bones of the nose."

In the dream he called for a second opinion on his patient. His senior colleague, Dr. M., appeared, looking pale and clean shaven, and repeated Freud's examination. He gave a positive prognosis: there was certainly an "infection," but "the toxin will be eliminated." Another medical colleague, Leopold, was less confident; he found that infection had spread to the patient's left shoulder, and that there was "a dull area low down on the left."

The dream scene became a medical gathering. Freud's associate Otto was there too. All four doctors — including Freud himself — had no doubt of the origin of the patient's illness. Otto had given her an injection of "a preparation of propyl, propyis . . . propionic acid . . . trimethylamin." Freud saw the formula for the last chemical printed in heavy type, underscoring its importance. He concluded his dream report: "Injections of that sort ought not to be made so thoughtlessly. . . . And probably the syringe had not been clean."[66]

In commenting on his dream, Freud began by noting that he had been thinking and writing about his patient the night before. Yet this left the content of the dream totally mysterious to him, since his actual patient did not have symptoms anything like the ones that concerned him in the dream. "Constriction of the throat played scarcely any part in her illness. I wondered why I decided upon this choice of symptoms in the dream but could not think of any explanation at the moment."[67]

Freud wondered whether Irma, in his dream, was actually a stand-in for another patient, who had experiences of choking. Freud's analysis wandered off through many other associations. When he pondered the names of the chemicals in his dream, he recalled a conversation in which a colleague suggested that trimethylamin might be an element in sexual arousal. This carried him away into "Freudian" thoughts about the probable source of hysteria in sexual frustration.

He wrapped up his interpretation of his Irma dream by declaring that it was a textbook example of wish fulfillment in dreams. He had been jarred the night before by Otto's suggestion that his patient had not been fully cured. In his dream he'd had his "revenge" on Otto by establishing that her pains were Otto's fault, not his own.

In all his discussion of substitution — how a dream character may stand in for another person or several other people — he paused for only a heartbeat to consider the possibility that the real patient might be the dreamer himself. He wondered whether the "scabs" that resembled nasal structures could be a warning to him about the possible effects of his excessive use of cocaine, but moved briskly on from that thought without considering other substances and their possible effects.

Twenty-eight years after the Irma dream, Freud's oral surgeons were looking at the precise symptoms he had dreamed — in Freud's own mouth. Early in 1923, a surgeon performed an excision of a cancerous growth resembling the "big white patch" on the right side of Irma's mouth "at the right anterior palate."[68]

In a series of surgeries and treatments over the next fifteen years, Freud's doctors worked to excise "proliferative papillary leukoplakia" inside his mouth resembling the unusual "scabs" in the 1895 dream. His many surgeries produced further scabs.[69]

In the Irma dream, the patient had difficulty opening her mouth. After Dr. Pichler performed radical surgeries on Freud late in 1923, Freud — like the patient in his dream — had to wear "dentures," actually a removable prosthesis. Because Freud developed lockjaw during his multiple surgeries, there was often difficulty inserting the prosthesis. Toward the end of his life, there were times when he "could not open his mouth."

Dr. Schavelzon suggests that the reference to structures of the nose in the 1895 dream report may have been a preview of Freud's condition after surgery that left the nasal cavity visible from the oral cavity.

What about all the doctors who figure in the Irma dream? Stripped of their pseudonyms, they were medical colleagues who gave Freud differing advice on his smoking habit. "Dr. M," who gives a cheerful but wrong prognosis for the patient, was actually Dr. Joseph Breuer, a friend and mentor who was persuaded by Freud — despite Breuer's misgivings — to drop his opposition to Freud's heavy cigar smoking.

"Leopold" was a "slow but sure" medical colleague who had cautioned that smoking could contribute to serious diseases.

"Otto" was Oskar Rie, a friend who shared Freud's taste for cigars and may have brought him a gift of cigars the night before the dream.

Whether Freud's dream doctors represented aspects of himself — or their actual personalities and positions — their role in the dream held up a mirror to the dreamer's behavior and attitude. Unfortunately, he was able to see in that glass only darkly.

Freud thought the syringe (the German word also means "squirter") was a penis, and that the cure for the patient's symptoms was sexual intercourse. But a "dirty syringe" could also be a nicotine delivery system — one of the cigars Freud was almost certainly smoking the night before. All the chemicals named in the Irma dream are found in cigar smoke. Though trimethylamin is not regarded as a carcinogen, when mixed with nitrites in an acidic environment (such as the smoker's mouth) it can be "nitrosated" into a very toxic carcinogen, dimethylnitrosamine (DMNA).

The evidence suggests that Freud's dream gave him a rather exact picture of both the origin and the histology of the oral cancer that subjected him to a painful and protracted death.[70] Although Freud became interested in the idea that dreams can contain messages from the body, he missed this one — unlike Jung, who gave up smoking because of a dream.

An important question for our understanding of the nature of diagnostic dreams is whether the Irma dream may have contained a warning message from inside Freud's cellular system, as it was at the time of the dream. In other words, could the Irma dream have been a tumor marker? It is possible that a single affected cell could trigger a dream, sending a distress signal out via neighboring cells, or via the endocrine system, that was shaped into a dream by the production company in the brain.[71]

Freud may have paid an enormous penalty for forcing his own dreams to run along narrow-gauge rails of interpretation. Since the bigger story of the Irma dream resonates heavily in dream interpretation, it seems appropriate that the pseudonym Freud chose for his patient means "universal."

DREAMING IN OLIVE OIL

Most people across most of history have grown up with traditional beliefs about the meaning of different signs and dream symbols. Though these may sound completely silly to outsiders, they may work perfectly well — in focusing and harvesting practical guidance — if your belief is fully engaged.

I have business friends on Bainbridge Island in Washington State who were told by their Taiwanese housekeeper that it's good luck if a bird poops on your roof. The man was skeptical, having been educated as an engineer. On the morning he was hoping to float a major new venture, he noticed a bird pooping on the roof of his house. His deal went through triumphantly, and in the evening he confessed to his housekeeper that her system apparently worked.

"It's better luck if a bird poops on your head," she told him, straight-faced.

The next time he had a big deal in the works, his wife caught him outside, waving his arms at the birds, coaxing them to "come and shit on my head."

One of my favorite places in Troy — the down-at-the-heel city in upstate New York where I lived in the 1990s — was a family-owned Italian grocery story called De Fazio's. The owners had emigrated from Sicily many decades before. Through the open door of their kitchen, you could often watch them making sauce and sausage by hand. Josephine De Fazio had snowy white hair and a songbird in her heart.

Mrs. De Fazio loved to talk about dreams. She had a way of interpreting dreams that had come down from mother to daughter for generations in Sicily. Dogs in dreams are good (depending on how they act); dead chickens are always bad; horses are "devils."

"I dreamed I was sweeping up the dirt. I was cleaning, cleaning, cleaning, all night long. That's good. Dirt in dreams is good, as long as you're cleaning it up."

Once when I came into the store, Josephine grabbed a crumpled five-dollar bill off the pegboard behind the counter. "Go on, take it," she urged me. "I knew it was yours because nobody else keeps their money as messy as you."

How many storekeepers have you met who would do something like that?

I was back in De Fazio's the next day for tomatoes and garlic; they always had the very best. Josephine sang out, "Thank you! We know you did it."

"Did what?"

"After I gave you the five and you left, I went out on the sidewalk and found a crisp new hundred-dollar bill."

She proceeded to deliver one of the laws of manifestation: "What goes around comes around. It's God's truth."

CHAPTER 3

ꙮ

DIVINE DREAMING

The greater part of humanity receives its knowledge of God from dreams.
— TERTULLIAN (C. 210 CE), *On the Soul*

Our God admonishes us in many ways, by heavenly signs, by the warnings of the prophets, and he wills that we understand even by the visions of sinners.

— BISHOP AMBROSE OF MILAN TO THE EMPEROR THEODOSIUS (390 CE)

Dreaming is at the root of the mythologies and religions that have guided humanity's path. It is central to the birth and development of the *historical* religions — those that teach an extraordinary, unrepeatable revelation, followed by an irreversible forward movement according to a divine plan — as well as all the others.

GODS DREAMING HUMANS, HUMANS DREAMING GODS

For many peoples, our existence on the planet is itself the product of the dream of a creator god. In the mind of India, Vishnu is dreaming this world, which will continue until he ends the dream and disperses his dream characters — including ourselves. The god sleeps on a great serpent whose name is Endless. The serpent drifts on the great Milky Ocean. Through the exotic features — the threefold, undulating movement of the dreaming god, the serpent, and the ocean — the passage may evoke, among those raised on the Bible, the flow of the second verse of Genesis, where "the spirit of God moved upon the face of the waters."

While Vishnu sleeps, his mind generates dreams, and this is the stuff we and our world are made of. "The pure Vishnu principle is the source, the plan, of life.... World planning is the work of Vishnu."[1]

Another version of a god dreaming up a world comes from the Guajiro, a forest people of South America. For the Guajiro, the universe was born when the creator, Maleiwa, became aware that he was dreaming. He did not come to this awareness unassisted. His helper was an intriguing being called Apusanai, whose function is to set up the matrix within which dream experiences take place. Apusanai not only performed this operation for the creator; he performs it for every human. So whenever we go dreaming, it is possible that — on our own scale — we may enter into the manifesting power of the first conscious dreamer, the creator god.[2]

In the cosmogony of the Makiritare, a shamanic people of Venezuela, the high god Wanadi created his own mother through dreaming. First he projected a double that entered the physical world. The double "just sat there in silence, thinking, dreaming, dreaming. He dreamed that a woman was born. . . . He made his own mother." Then Wanadi entered her body in the form he had dreamed.[3]

That story may provoke us into thinking more deeply about what is really going on in divine-conception dreams like the famous dream of Queen Maya that heralded the coming of her son, Siddhartha, who became the Buddha. In approaching Maya, we don't want to miss the fact that in Sanskrit her name means "illusion," not merely in the negative sense but in that of the play of images that brings things — even worlds — into manifestation. Maya dreamed of a six-tusked elephant, "white as the snow-capped mountains," that entered her body by the side. Priests were summoned to interpret the dream, and predicted that she would give birth to a spiritual being who would change the world. On the night of conception, according to some early texts, she slept apart from her husband. Though the queen was not a virgin, up to this point she had been childless, and the birth of Siddhartha was certainly an extraordinary event. He is sometimes described as exiting his mother's body through the side, without surgery and without harming her. Some versions suggest that the six-tusked elephant not only represents the spiritual power of the Buddha but also is the spiritual begetter of the coming Buddha.[4]

Humans Dream the Gods

In the ancient world, dreaming was "a nightly screening of the gods," who might show themselves in many forms. Greeks reared on Homer knew that gods may enter a dreamer's space in the guise of a friend, as Zeus appeared to Agamemnon, and as Athena appeared to Nausicaa and Penelope. It was widely understood in the ancient Mediterranean world that, when gods want to show themselves without subterfuge, they will often adopt the forms that human hands and imaginations have given them. They often appear in reports of Egyptian and Greco-Roman dreams in the shapes of their temple statues. The statues come alive in the dreams, as they were sometimes thought to do in ritual processions. This is a less "primitive" notion than we may at first understand. "Human kind cannot bear very much reality," as T. S. Eliot wrote, and it is especially hard for humans to bear the reality of the more-than-human showing itself in untempered form. Think of the terror that seizes Arjuna, in the Bhagavad Gita, when Krishna conforms to his request to reveal himself in his cosmic form, as the maker and devourer of worlds. Think of the people of Israel begging Moses to speak to God on the mountain on their behalf; the divine glory looks to them like a devouring fire.[5]

In the consecration of Hindu temples today, the gods are invited through prayer and *pujas* to take up residence in the statues that have been made to house their energies. For ancient dreamers, the "breathing statues" of the gods are the preferred forms in which to encounter gods. Sometimes we are fortunate to find among the surviving texts, clues to the birth of a god-form in the ancient mind. Serapis, who became an immensely popular god in the early Christian centuries and the personal deity of Antonine emperors, was born from the dreams of a Macedonian prince of Egypt.

The Macedonian general Ptolemy Soter inherited the kingship of Egypt from Alexander the Great and founded a dynasty whose most celebrated member was Cleopatra. The Egyptian priests gave the following account of Ptolemy's dream, according to Tacitus. When Ptolemy was engaged in building walls and temples for the newly founded city of Alexandria, "he dreamed that he met a young man of remarkable beauty and more than human stature, who instructed him to send his most trusty couriers to Pontus to fetch a statue of himself. This, he said, would cause the kingdom to prosper.... The same youth appeared to ascend into heaven in a blaze of fire."

Ptolemy discussed his dream with Timotheus, a priest of the Eleusinian mysteries, who in turn talked to travelers who knew Pontus, on the Black Sea. They thought the statue in Ptolemy's dream might be a colossal figure of Jupiter Dis — known to the Greeks as Hades or Pluto, the lord of Death and the Underworld — that had been erected at a Greek colony on the Black Sea called Sinope.

"Just like a king," Ptolemy did not rush to act on this information, showing himself "keener on pleasure than religion." He was now visited by a terrifying dream vision, in which the radiant being showed himself in wrath, promising that Ptolemy and his kingdom would be ruined unless he obeyed the directive of the first dream. Ptolemy then sent envoys with gifts to the ruler of Sinope, who initially refused to part with the statue. Three years later, terrified by menacing dreams of his own that were reinforced by plague and other worldly disasters, he finally shipped the god's statue to Alexandria.[6]

The god was renamed Serapis — a name that evoked both the sacred Apis bull of Egypt and Osiris, the dying and renewing god.[7] The statue of Serapis became the hub of a vast temple complex, the Serapeum, where one of the greatest libraries of the ancient world was assembled and where people came very specifically to dream. As in the temples of Asklepios, dream incubation was practiced for healing in the precincts of Serapis. But a *kathodos*, or temple student, at a Serapeum might also be trained in dreaming as a discipline in his own right.[8]

From Ptolemy's dreams, a syncretic religion emerged that appealed to Greeks, Egyptians, and other residents of the eastern Mediterranean. The new cult was highly successful and soon recruited Roman emperors.

When Vespasian visited Alexandria, a blind man threw himself at his feet, shouting that Serapis had appeared to him in a dream and told him that he would be cured if the emperor spat in his eyes. A second petitioner, also guided by a dream of Serapis, wanted the emperor to tread on his withered hand. Vespasian laughed and refused these requests, until his physicians told him there was some chance the "royal touch" would work. The imperial spit and the imperial foot were delivered, and both men were cured.[9] Understandably intrigued, Vespasian decided to inspect the Serapeum. Alone in the inner sanctum, he encountered an Egyptian called Basilides, though he knew this man to be at his home eighty miles away — a fact the emperor confirmed by sending riders to check. The emperor accepted the phenomenon of Basilides's bilocation as a "divine vision," proof of the god's ability to "carry men wherever he pleases."[10] Serapis was well on his way to becoming the personal deity of Roman emperors. A later emperor, Caracalla, had his hair styled in the distinctive "Serapis mode" and called himself "Lover of Serapis."

Serapis quickly assumed the attributes of a universal deity who is powerful but not remote, accessible to everyone in dreams. Aelius Aristides observed, "Everyone calls upon you as a helper on every occasion, Serapis."[11] In his first oration, Aristides declared, "The deeds of Serapis are those by which the life of mankind is saved and administered." Serapis possessed the powers of all the gods: "some men worship him in place of all the gods, and others believe in him as being a special universal god for the whole world, in addition to those gods in whom they believe in any given circumstance."[12]

Flights of the Lonely Swan

The earliest Indian references to dreams, in the Rig Veda (c. 1200 BCE), aren't cheery. They involve scary things — being robbed, being attacked by a wolf, being raped — that can spill over into waking reality. The verses include formulas of protection designed to turn away the evil seen in a dream. "If someone I have met, O king, or a friend has spoken danger to me in a dream to frighten me, or if a thief should waylay us, or a wolf — protect us from that, Varuna."[13]

The Upanishads describe four states of awareness: waking, dreaming, dreamless sleep — all natural and available to all — and a transcendent state of identity with the divine, which requires illumination. Dreaming gives us a glimpse of the god who creates us by dreaming us into existence.[14]

In the Great Forest Book, one of the oldest Upanishads, from the seventh century BCE, the dream state is one of "emitting" (*srj*), a word that can also mean the ejaculation of semen. The dreamer "emits," or projects from himself, "joys, happinesses and delights[,] . . . ponds, lotus pools and flowing streams, for he is the Maker."[15]

In the Great Forest Book, the dreamer moves between the worlds like "the lonely swan," flying in and out of the nest of the body.[16] He is godlike in his ability to create in the dreamspace: "In the state of dream going up and down, the god makes many forms for himself, now enjoying himself in the company of women or laughing or even beholding fearful sights."[17]

A Sanskrit name for dream travelers, *kamacarin*, means "those who can transfer themselves at will." The literature and sacred writings of India are a treasury of tales of dream travel clearly grounded in experience. The Yogavasistha, a vast Kashmiri compilation, is one of the richest troves. In these narratives, dream travelers find that time is elastic. You may live a hundred years in a dreamworld and return to find that only a day has passed in ordinary time.

What is experienced in the dreamworlds is real and has real consequences in the traveler's waking world. Spiritual apprenticeship and initiation can take place in this way. A king called Lavana applied his mind to offering, inside a dream, the elaborate sacrifices required at a royal coronation. He supervised three Brahmins actively performing the required sacrifices while a fourth acted as witness to the correctness of the proceedings. In this way, Lavana accomplished work of "royal consecration" that normally involves twelve years of effort, suffering, and sacrifice. However, the gods made him suffer in another way — and learn, in the process, about the human condition and the connection between the life experiences of different personalities in different circumstances.

Lavana is seated in splendor on his throne, drinking a warm cup of mulled wine, when a wandering sage appears, leading a magnificent horse. When the king turns his attention to the horse, he finds himself mounting it and galloping off across plains and desert. He is unable to check the horse until his foot catches in a dangling vine and he is pulled out of his stirrups. Broken in body, he is dying of hunger and thirst when a dark woman — an untouchable, lowest of the low in India's caste system — finds him. When he begs her for food and water, she agrees to save him on the condition that he accompany her to her village and marry her. The king agrees. He spends a lifetime among the untouchables, raising children and working in the cemeteries among the bodies and ghosts of the dead. When he dies, his corpse is thrown on the funeral pyre. In that instant, the king is jerked out of his dream as his head nods forward onto his chest. The mulled wine in his cup is still warm.[18]

There are more complex versions of this story. In one of them, a Brahmin ascetic dreams he is an untouchable who dreams that he is a king. The ascetic is standing in a river meditating, with the water up to his chest. His awareness is drawn into the life of an untouchable who enters a city, where he is hailed as the new king. After several years, old companions recognize him and he is dethroned as an unclean impostor. At the end of his life, his body is thrown on the funeral pyre. As it burns, he finds himself back in the Brahmin's body he left standing in the river.[19]

In another Hindu story, Markandeya is a human being who is curious about what is real. He tries so hard to see beyond the obvious that one day, without meaning to, he falls out of the mouth of Vishnu, the dreaming god. He now discovers that he has spent his whole life inside the body of the god. Now that he's out there, he has a cosmic vision of the structure of the universe; he sees that everything he knew is contained within the body of the dreaming god. But this vision is too much for him; it inspires him with a trembling awe that easily shifts to terror. It's too much for him, even though he is an evolved soul, an adept. So he climbs back through the mouth of Vishnu, back into the world contained in the god, and as Markandeya resumes his life there, he starts to forget what he saw beyond it.

Ayurvedic physicians maintain that we are deluded if we believe we are fully awake and conscious in our everyday lives. At all times, we are actually in a state of dreaming. Enlightenment and healing become possible when we awaken to the reality that we are continually dreaming.[20]

Sweets for Tara

"Without dreams there would be no Buddha and no Buddhism," is the conclusion drawn from a recent scholarly study that incorporates a wealth of newly translated texts.[21] We have already seen that Buddhism starts with the dream of a queen. The dreaming goes on.

For Buddhists, as for others who believe in reincarnation, conscious travel into past life experiences may be a way of "burning karma." The ideal is the *tathagata* (literally, one "who has come in truth"), who is able to recollect all of his or her previous incarnations without succumbing to the emotions they might arouse, and without drawing metaphysical conclusions.[22] A technique for dissolving karma and for transcending time is to practice traveling backward "against the fur": back through the womb, into previous lives — and the space between lives — perhaps all the way back to the first irruption of life in the world, to the border between time and no-time.

Especially in Tibetan Buddhism, dream yoga is a practice for raising and focusing consciousness and a training ground for death and the afterlife journey. A ninth-century Tibetan Buddhist text instructs that, in order to have a good dream, you should offer the goddess Tara the "three sweets of sugar, honey and molasses." To meet the goddess, you approach sleep while reciting her eight-syllable mantra. Be sure to lie on your right side, in "the posture of the sleeping lion," which leaves the heart unrestricted. "From the sky Tara will spread a cool ray of light rising from her heart. . . . Her hands are strong like an elephant's trunk . . . pouring down streams of nectar which fill up one's heart."[23]

Today, the Dalai Lama recommends another ritual for attracting divine dreams. During the Kalachakra ceremony, he distributes *kusha* grass, explaining that this is to encourage "unmistaken, clear dreams." Placed under both the mattress and the pillow of the sleeper, the grass will also "clear away pollutants so your mind will be clear." This ritual, too, instructs you to lie on your right side, in the lion position, and to pay attention only to dreams that occur around dawn.[24]

Milarepa (1040–1123) instructed his disciples to report their dreams. "Remember your dreams tonight and report to me tomorrow. I will then interpret them for you."[25] He cautioned his followers to cleanse their minds of "habitual thoughts" that would carry over into the dreamspace and confine the dreamers to deceptive and illusory experiences. He interpreted a rich and complex dream of his chosen heir, Gambopa, explaining that it foreshadowed Gambopa's future role as a great teacher. Milarepa cautioned his followers not to assign excessive importance to dreams, which partake of "the illusory nature of all beings. Yet he congratulated Gambopa for dreaming true: "Your dreams were marvelous, wondrous omens foretelling things to come."[26] And he delighted in recounting his own numinous dreams portending the growth of his lineage. "Last night I dreamed that an eagle flew from here to Weu and alighted on the top of a precious gem. Then many geese flocked around it. . . . They dispersed in different directions, each goose again gathering about five hundred more companions."[27]

Central to Tibetan Buddhism (and also the Vaishnava, or Vishnu-centered, branch of Hinduism) is the practice of unearthing sacred texts by visionary means. These sacred books are called *termas*; they are "earth treasures" or "mind treasures" concealed in unlikely places in this earth and beyond it, in a stone or tree, at the bottom of a lake, in the cloud realm, or in the underworld of the Naga serpents, where Nagarjuna, a central figure in Mahayana Buddhism, was required to travel. Many of the *termas* are attributed to tantric masters said to have hidden their core teachings in realms of mind and imagination, where they can be discerned only by an adept — a *tertön* — who has expanded his consciousness to a sufficient level.[28] The most famous of the *termas* is the Tibetan Book of the Dead, describing transits through the *bardo* zones of the afterlife. A *terma* text called the Four Treatises, said to have been written in Sanskrit around 400, and which is attributed to the Medicine Buddha, was recovered psychically in the eleventh century; it contains a list of dream meanings relevant to medical practice.

Dreaming before and after the Fall

It's been said that there are no dreams in Paradise, because heaven and earth are still one.[29] We don't need to dream our way back if we are already there. In the Garden of Eden, Adam sleeps while his rib is removed to fashion Eve, but we are not told whether he dreamed. Nonetheless, many great minds, Jewish and Christian, have been fascinated by the possibility that Adam dreamed before the Fall. A Gnostic sect claimed to have a full account of Adam's visionary experiences during that sleep in the Garden, presumably collected by some process of psychic retrieval like that practiced by the Tibetan *tertön*.[30]

Milton's Puritan imagination was inflamed by the idea of dreaming in the Garden. In *Paradise Lost* his Eve is first tempted by Satan in a manipulated dream, after he slips by the careless guardian angels.

> Squat like a toad, close at the ear of Eve,
> Assaying by his devilish art to reach

The organs of her fancy, and with them forge
Illusions as he list, phantasms and dreams. (IV.800–804)

By contrast, Adam's dream in the Garden is a true one, prophetic and divinely inspired. He sees the temptation of the forbidden fruit and feels a "sudden appetite / To pluck and to eat" (VIII.308–309), but wakes before he succumbs. His dream has shown him the circumstances of the Fall, but he is unable to prevent its manifestation.

Let's return to the source. In Genesis and the early books of the Old Testament, dreams are valued after the Fall as sources of restored communication with God and as means of prophecy. Sometimes they provide a mandate or mobilize a leader to action. True dreams come not only to the Israelites but also to their enemies.

When Sarah is taken to the house of King Abimelech, God speaks to him in a dream and warns him that she is married and that the king should not touch her (Gen. 20:3). This is an example of a dream exposing the true nature of a situation and providing counsel.

The Lord appears to Solomon at Gibeon, soon after Solomon has assumed the throne, and asks what he wishes. Solomon asks for an understanding mind. God is pleased, and Solomon becomes the wisest person in the world (1 Kings 3:5–12). If a king can receive the gift of divine wisdom in a dream, cannot we — if we, too, choose wisely?

God's promise to Aaron and Miriam echoes across long centuries: "If there will be a prophet among you, I will make myself known to him in a vision, I shall speak with him in a dream" (Num. 12:6–8).

The story of Joseph in Genesis, briefly noted in chapter 2, introduces the world's most celebrated dream interpreter. In an Egyptian jail, he successfully interpreted the dreams of two fellow prisoners: the baker would be hanged, the royal cupbearer would be restored to Pharaoh's favor. These predictions were fulfilled. Back in his old job, the cupbearer heard Pharaoh complain that he was troubled by evil dreams. In one of these dreams, Pharaoh sees seven fat cows devoured by seven lean ones. In the second dream, he watches seven full sheaves of grain consumed by seven withered ones. These dream events are played out on the banks of the Nile, on whose annual inundation the life of Egypt depended.

The cupbearer remembered the dreamer in jail who had accurately predicted the outcome of his dream. Joseph was brought before Pharaoh to hear the king's dreams. He advised that the two dreams were one and the same; they predicted seven years of plenty followed by seven years of famine. "The reason why Pharaoh had the same dream twice is that the event is already determined by God, and God will shortly bring it about" (Gen. 41:32).

If we can see the future, we may be able to change it for the better. "It is not to distress men that God foreshadows to them what is to come, but so that forewarned they may use their sagacity to alleviate the trials announced when they befall," Joseph instructs Pharaoh in a later version of the story.[31] Joseph did not stop with an interpretation of Pharaoh's dreams. He suggested an immediate action plan. Pharaoh should appoint a wise viceroy and impose a new tax during the seven years of plenty in order to fill the granaries against the coming time of famine. Pharaoh decided that Joseph himself was the man for the job.

The Joseph story is also a fine example of one of the rules of coincidence: for every setback, there's an opportunity. If his jealous brothers had not sold him into slavery, and had a woman scorned not gotten him thrown into prison with her false charge of attempted rape, he would never have become prince of Egypt.

Daniel's fame as a dream interpreter is second only to Joseph's, and dream books popular in the Middle Ages were named after him. The *way* he discovered the dream Nebuchadnezzar would not tell is more interesting than what he said about its content. The story is familiar: the Babylonian king is troubled by a dream, and summons all the interpreters in the land to tell him what it means. The snag is, he won't tell them the dream. They protest that they can't interpret a dream he will not share. The king is adamant: he'll have all of them put to death unless someone can discover his dream and its meaning.

This situation puts Daniel's head on the block, along with that of the famous magi of the Chaldees, since Daniel has a reputation as a dream reader among the Jews who are living in captivity in Babylon. Daniel asks his friends to support him in praying for help from "the God of heaven." "The mystery was then revealed to Daniel in a night vision" (Dan. 2:19).

Daniel goes to the palace and tells Nebuchadnezzar in vivid detail "the dreams and the visions that passed through your head as you lay in bed." As Daniel speaks, the king recognizes his dream. It involves a composite statue with a golden head, a silver torso, a bronze belly, iron legs, and feet of clay. A stone flies through the air and shatters the clay feet. The statue falls apart, its pieces diminish to the size of "chaff on the threshing-floor" and are blown away by the wind, while the stone grows until it becomes a great mountain which fills the whole earth (Dan. 2:31–36).

Daniel explains how this dream foretells the rise and fall of great empires. Scholars suspect that some political propaganda was slipped in here by the hand of a second-century author who had watched a succession of empires come and go, and who hoped for the downfall of another. However much of this story is legend, the nature of Nebuchadnezzar's challenge, which may escape modern readers, would have been readily grasped in the ancient world, especially in Mesopotamia. You don't fully trust someone to interpret your dream unless that person is capable of entering your dreamspace. Daniel appears to have practiced what in Active Dreaming we call *tracking*: entering someone else's psychic space in order to bring back information and guidance.

He was not operating alone. As the seventh-century bishop Isidore of Seville observed, "Daniel was worthy to know, by an angel revealing it, the sacraments of the mysteries."[32] We soon learn that Daniel has a special working relationship with Gabriel, who is the archangel of dreams for Jews, Christians, and Muslims alike.

Dreaming with Gabriel

Gabriel's name first appears in scripture when he explains a troubling vision that Daniel does not understand. The archangel shows himself in the form of a man. But when he comes closer, Daniel is seized with fear and awe and falls prostrate on the ground (Dan. 8:13–16). When Gabriel comes again to explain a prophecy about the restoration of Jerusalem, he "swoops" on Daniel in "full flight" (Dan. 9:22).

The name Gabriel is a composite of two Hebrew words meaning "man" (*gever*) and "God" (*El*). As Rabbi Joel Covitz comments, "Gabriel brings man to God and God to man, thus divinizing man and humanizing God."[33]

In the Talmud, Gabriel figures as an angel of justice, smiting the hosts of Sennacherib with a sharpened scythe. He is also an interpreter between nations, fluent in languages. In Jewish tradition, Gabriel is sometimes identified with the nameless voice that told Noah to prepare the Ark, and the invisible force that prevented Abraham from sacrificing Isaac, and the voice that spoke to Moses from the burning bush.

The Jewish mystical text the *Zohar* identifies Gabriel both as the Master of Dreams and as the angel who mentors the soul before birth. In this conception, the bringer of dreams is also the source of the soul's knowledge of its destiny and its place in the order of creation.

In the Christian story, Gabriel is the angel of the Annunciation. He appears to Mary to announce the coming of the Christ, as he formerly appeared to Zacharias to announce the coming of John the Baptist. He visits Joseph in a dream to reveal the identity of the divine child. He returns in another dream to warn the family to flee from Herod's persecution.

As we shall see, the whole of Islam hangs on Gabriel's relationship, as dream guide, with the prophet Muhammad.

In Kabbalah, Gabriel is associated with Yesod (Foundation) and the sphere of the Moon. In the Western Mystery traditions, his color is blue and his element is water.

My favorite account of Gabriel is from Rumi. The great Persian mystical poet put himself inside the scene in which Mary first encountered the archangel and found that (of course) she was terrified. Alone in her room, Mary saw a "heart-ravishing form." It "rose up before her from the face of the earth, bright as the moon and the sun."

She trembled with fear. She was naked and feared that her body would be ravished by this amazing power. She was so scared she jumped out of her skin, trusting herself to the protection of God. She was practiced in "flight to the unseen." "Seeing this world to be a kingdom without permanence, she made a fortress of the presence of God" — and sought shelter in that fortress now.

The angel spoke to her. "I am the true messenger of the Presence. Do not fear me." As he spoke, a pure light flamed from his lips, like a candle, and spiraled up to the star Arcturus.

"You flee from me from the seen into the unseen, where I am lord and king. What are you thinking? My home is in the unseen. What you see before you is only a portrait. Mary, look closely, for I am difficult to grasp. I am a new moon and a yearning in the heart.

"You seek refuge from the one who is your refuge. You confuse the Friend of your soul with a stranger. You flee from the Friend you seek. Don't choose sorrow when what is before you is joy."

Now the angel *breathes* the Holy Spirit into Mary. The divine Word, traveling on the breath of compassion, penetrates her to her core. "The Father speaks the Word into the soul, and when the Son is born, each soul becomes Mary."[34]

DREAMING UP CHRISTIANITY

To understand the birth and triumph of Christianity as the religion of the West, we must grasp its imaginal history, which was driven by world-changing and world-revealing dreams and visions.

Through dreams and visions, according to the Bible, Jesus's mother and father learned the identity of the extraordinary being who was coming to join the family. Without a visitation from the archangel of dreams, Joseph might have believed the rumors that Mary had had sex with another man (the favorite suspect being a Roman soldier called Pantera) and cast her out, giving the world a different story.

The vision of a star guided the Magi to Bethlehem, and their dreams persuaded them not to return to Herod with the location of the wonder child, enabling the holy family to escape into Egypt and thus saving the life of baby Jesus.

The star of the Magi is about more than an astronomical or astrological phenomenon, though it is likely there was one of those. Ephrem the Syrian maintained that the Magi had encountered a star angel.[35] According to the *Chronicle of Zuqnin*, a text found and quoted by Marco Polo, twelve of *the* Magi — the priest-magicians of the ancient religion of Persia — climbed a sacred mountain every year to watch for portents of the coming of the Sayoshyants, the World Redeemer. On the crucial night, a new star appeared. A beam of light descended from the star. A divine being appeared within the pillar of light and instructed the Magi to go to Bethlehem. Each of the Magi perceived the luminous messenger in a different way: as a radiant child, as a youth, as a "humble and ugly and afflicted man," as a crucified man.[36]

A no less famous vision, on the road to Tarsus, turned a Jewish tax collector who was hostile to the Jesus cult into a passionate and effective proselytizer for the new faith. Saul (who now became Paul) was caught up into the "third heaven" and could not say whether he was "in the body or out of it" (2 Cor. 12:2–4).

Three days after Jesus's execution, the vision of him radiantly alive at the place of his burial provided evidence of his promise of life beyond death. Only the women could see him at first. Then the sight and senses of the men were opened.

The interlocking visions of the Roman centurion Cornelius and the apostle Peter, supported by synchronicity, turned a Jewish sect into a world religion. Cornelius was a centurion in the Italian cohort of the garrison of Caesarea, the great harbor city and capital of the Roman province of Judea. We can almost *smell* Caesarea when we know that one of its signature exports was garum, a fish sauce made from decaying herrings, heavily spiced, that was a great favorite in Rome.[37] We can picture Cornelius, with the centurion's vine stick of office, leading the bodyguard of the Roman prefect, who may still have been Pontius Pilate. Cornelius's name, which means "of the horns," belonged to a patrician Roman family. Someone who knew Latin would recognize that the following adventure involves a "horned man," which is of more than casual interest given the near-universal association between horns and spiritual power in the ancient world.

We are told in Acts 10 that Cornelius was a "devout man" who "prayed continually" and gave alms to Jews. An angel appeared to him in a vision and told him to send men to Joppa — the port of Jerusalem, thirty miles to the south — to the house of a tanner near the sea, to fetch "a man named Simon who is also called Peter" (Acts 10:5–6).

Cornelius did as he was told. He sent two servants and a soldier to find Peter. As they entered Joppa, Peter was up on the flat roof of the tanner's house, praying. He got hungry and asked for food. While his meal was being prepared, "he fell into a trance." He saw the heavens open and something like a huge tablecloth descend. On the cloth were all kinds of animals and birds and "crawling things of the earth." A voice said to him, "Get up, Peter, kill and eat!" (Acts 10:11–13).

This horrified Peter, since many of the animals were unclean from a Jewish perspective and, in Leviticus, specifically forbidden as food items. Yet the vision and the directive were repeated three times. He was then told that three men were looking for him, and that he should accompany them "without misgivings" (Acts 10:20).

By one of those fine coincidences that power the Acts of the Apostles, Peter went downstairs and met Cornelius's messengers. When he accompanied them to meet the centurion at Caesarea, Cornelius received him as a divine emissary. Peter said that through his vision "God has shown me that I should not call any man unholy or unclean" (Acts 10:28). He began to preach the message of Christ to the gentiles in the centurion's house, and as he spoke, "the Holy Spirit fell upon all those who were listening to the message" (Acts 10:44). Peter decided that the water of baptism could not be denied to those "who received the Holy Spirit just as we did" (Acts 10:47). Cornelius became the first gentile to be baptized as a Christian.

The Dream Visions That Made Christianity the Religion of the West

Three centuries later, the vision of a Roman emperor, unfolded in a dream, made Christianity the religion of the West. A great historian described this episode as "an erratic block which has diverted the stream of human history."[38]

The year is 312, and the Roman Empire is divided between four "tetrarchs," senior and junior emperors of the East and the West. Constantine has marched through the Alps at the head of an army that includes legions from Britain formerly commanded by his father, Constantius. Constantine's men have proclaimed him "Augustus" (senior emperor) of the West. All along his route, he has been greeted with pagan honors. He is marching on Rome, now ruled by the usurper Maxentius, who has defeated two previous challengers in the past five years. The city is believed to be almost impregnable behind its strong walls.

Constantine, marching south from Milan along the Via Flaminia to do battle for Rome, has a vision and a dream. There are two accounts of it from Christian apologists Lactantius and Eusebius.

Writing within four years of the event, Lactantius — the future tutor to Constantine's son — reported that Constantine had seen a dream "on the eve of battle" and was ordered in this dream to inscribe the "heavenly sign of God" on his soldiers' shields. The historian Robin Lane Fox maintains that the sign was a "staurogram," an upright cross with a loop at the top; this appears in Christian papyri from 200.[39]

Writing after Constantine's death (twenty-five years after the vision), the church leader and historian Eusebius claimed to have heard the emperor tell his own version "on oath." By this account, Constantine felt the need for divine support as his enemy resorted to pagan spells and sacrifices in Rome. He prayed to the supreme deity to reveal himself and "stretch forth his hand."[40]

On their march, Constantine and "all the troops" saw a "sign of the cross" in the noonday sky inscribed with the words "By this, conquer." The Latin version, *in hoc signo vinces*, is familiar today as a fraternity motto, but the words seen by Constantine and his men were actually in Greek: *en touto nika*. Constantine went to bed wondering what the sign meant. That night he was visited by the figure of a radiant young man bearing the same symbol, who ordered him to "use its likeness in his engagements with the enemy."[41] Constantine was encouraged by one of his advisers, a Spanish bishop called Ossius, to identify this being as Christ.

Constantine instructed his craftsman to make a standard bearing the cross he had seen. This was not the Calvary cross, or an equal-armed cross, but the Chi-Rho, formed from the intersecting Greek letters that appear as an *X* with a *P* through the center. These were later assumed to be the first letters of the Greek word for "Christ," but the Chi-Rho monogram was better known in Constantine's day as the abbreviation used by scribes for the word *chreston*, "good," a mark that indicated something especially important in a text.[42]

Constantine gave Eusebius a private viewing of the standard, which had been adorned with gold and jewels and a banner with pictures of the emperor and his children — evidently fashioned long after the dream. The first version was presumably a wooden cross.[43]

While Maxentius had held off two previous attackers behind the safety of Rome's massive walls, he now proceeded, inexplicably — unless you believe in divine intervention — to lead his troops out of safety and across the Tiber to face Constantine on open ground. After his defeat, he drowned in the river near the Milvian Bridge, either by falling into the water in full armor or by riding into the river to seek his own death.

For Constantine, as for his contemporaries, "the proof of a god is best found in his protection."[44] Constantine proceeded to exempt Christian clergy from the burdens of civic office, a huge privilege previously accorded only to exceptional individuals and certain Egyptian priests. He explained himself by saying that Christian prayers were intimately connected with the safety of the state.

The depth of the emperor's conversion has been debated. Some even suggest that he was never quite sure that there was any difference between Christ and Helios, the sun god. In 324, new coins struck in Antioch in honor of his defeat of Licinius show him receiving power from the sun god, described as his *comes*, his soul "companion" or genius. After lightning struck the Coliseum in 320, pagan rites of divination were held, and Constantine instructed that they should be repeated if lightning struck another public building. The emperor continued to call himself pontifex maximus and delayed baptism until his deathbed.

Lane Fox sets a sermon against the coins. The sermon — the "Oration to the Saints," appended by Eusebius to his biography of Constantine — weaves pagan literary sources and Bible references into an apologia for Christianity. Lane Fox has compared this sermon to royal letters sent out at the same time and contends that it was written by Constantine. Lane Fox argues from circumstantial evidence that it was delivered on Easter Friday 324 at a church council at Antioch.[45]

Whatever the depth of Constantine's personal belief in Christianity and familiarity with scripture, there is no question about his munificent patronage of the church, his support for the Catholic bishops in their struggles against heresy, and his effort to make the Catholic Church dominant among the many religions of the empire. He did not ban the old religions — the army was still overwhelmingly pagan — but within a few years of the persecutions of Diocletian's time, he had advanced church interests to the point where Christianity had clearly emerged as the religion of the Roman Empire and was set to claim a monopoly on religious life.

The Bishop of Dreams

You have direct access to sacred knowledge, in your dreams. Your dreams are a personal oracle that reveals the future and helps you prepare for it. Don't let anyone tell you what your dreams mean; get rid of dream dictionaries. Pay attention to signs from the world around you; know that everything in the universe is interconnected and constantly interweaving. Use your imagination. What you grow there will be stamped on your world and on your soul — on the energy body in which you will travel to another life after death.[46]

Amazingly, these insights come from a fifth-century bishop of the church. His name was Synesius of Cyrene, and his treatise *On Dreams*, composed around 405, is one of the wisest books ever written on dreams, coincidence, and imagination. Synesius was a most unusual bishop. In his life and work we find — alas, only briefly — a confluence between the best of the ancient *practice* of philosophy and the new religion of the Roman Empire.

Synesius was a Greco-Roman aristocrat who could trace his pedigree back to the founders of Sparta, seventeen hundred years before him. He lived on a great estate in Cyrene, part of modern Libya, enjoyed the pleasures of both the hunt and the study, and chuckled over the fact that rural folk in his area still thought "the king of the world" was Agamemnon.[47]

He received the best education possible in his time, in Alexandria, in the school of Hypatia, the extraordinary woman scientist, mathematician, and Neoplatonist who strode the streets of the world-city in her philosopher's cloak surrounded by eager students. It was in Alexandria that Synesius experienced his first and deepest conversion, when he found "the eye of the soul" within him opening to reveal the sacred depth of the universe. His consciousness expanded to give him the clear vision of the One beyond the many. He saw the reality behind the forms of religion. In his quiet hours, he dedicated himself to the "mysteries without rites" devoted to awakening the divinity within the human that corresponds and coincides with the divinity within and beyond the cosmos.[48] He was a convert to philosophy as it was understood in the Greco-Roman world: the love and practice of wisdom.

It was in Alexandria, around 405, that Synesius, recently married, wrote his treatise *On Dreams*.[49] In it he makes it clear that his discussion of dreams is grounded in personal experience. Dreams had guided him in the hunt, showing him how and where to find the game. Dreams had led him to "swarms of wild beasts that have fallen to our spears."

He had been guided by dreams when his city sent him to Constantinople to plead for favors from the emperor. In a hothouse of political intrigue, his dreams helped him tell friend from foe and alerted him to hostile intrigues in which his enemies hired "ghost-raising sorcerers" to attack him by black magic. The dream oracle "helped me in the management of public office in the best interest of the cities, and finally placed me on terms of intimacy with the Emperor."

His dreams had contributed to his success as a writer and orator. The dream source "frequently helped me to write books," correcting his style, and helping him prune archaic Attic expressions — products of his love of old books — from his essays and poems.

Synesius explains in his treatise that dreams are "personal oracles." We want to claim authority over our own dreams and reject anything and anyone who tries to come between us and the dream source. "We ought to seek this branch of knowledge before all else; for it comes from us, is within us, and is the special possession of the soul of each one of us." The dream oracle speaks to us wherever we go. "We can't abandon this oracle even if we try. It is with us at home and abroad, on the field of battle, in the city and in the marketplace."

Dreams are our common birthright. They belong to rich and poor, to kings and to slaves. The dream oracle turns no one down because of race or age, status or calling. Even the worst tyrant is powerless to separate us from our dreams — which may hold the key to his overthrow — "unless he could banish sleep from his kingdom."

"Dream divination is available to all, the good genius to everyone," explains Synesius. It is no wonder that dreams show us the future, because dreams are experiences of soul and "the soul holds the forms of things that come into being."

Synesius dismisses dream dictionaries — popular in his time, as in ours — with admirable vigor. "I laugh at all those books and think them of little use." General definitions don't work because each dreamer is a different mirror for dream images — some are funhouse mirrors, some are made of various materials. *Big* dreams do not require interpretation; their meaning is in the experience of the dream itself. Dreams that are "more divine" are "quite clear and obvious, or nearly so," but come only to those who live "according to virtue."

Steeped in Homer, he can't avoid mentioning the scene in the *Odyssey* where the Gates of Horn and Ivory are described. In Synesius's view, both Homer's Penelope and legions of commentators and borrowers failed to understand that dreams, in themselves, are never false. Penelope assumes that there are true dreams and deceptive dreams "because she was not instructed in the matter." Deception arises through false interpretations, not false dreams. If Penelope had understood the nature of dreaming better, "she would have made all dreams pass out through the Gate of Horn. . . . We should not confuse the weakness of the interpreter with the nature of the visions themselves."

He recommends setting an intention for the night. "We shall pray for a dream, even as Homer prayed. And if you are worthy, the god far away is present with you. . . . He comes to your side when you sleep, and this is the whole system of the initiation."

Synesius also stresses the value of keeping a dream journal and of writing and creating from dreams. "It is no mean achievement to pass on to another something of a strange nature that has stirred in one's own soul."

He urges us to keep a "day book" for our observations of signs and synchronicities as well as a "night book" for dreams. "All things are signs appearing through all things. . . . They are brothers in a single living creature, the cosmos. . . . They are written in characters of every kind." The deepest scholarship lies in reading the sign language of the world; the true sage is a person "who understands the relationship of the parts of the universe."[50]

Five years after writing his essay *On Dreams*, Synesius was persuaded by Theophilus, the Patriarch of Alexandria, to accept the bishopric of Ptolemais. It seems that he was baptized at the same time, rather late in the day according to our common understanding of what is involved in becoming a bishop of the church.

Synesius's entry into the episcopate was a political, rather than spiritual, event. The influence of his wife — whom he loved deeply — may have been important; she was presumably Christian, since Theophilus was at their wedding in 403. Winning an aristocratic philosopher to the church was a coup for the Patriarch; though Christianity had become the religion of the empire, the old houses were still keeping their distance. For Synesius, assuming the rank and responsibilities of a bishop was both a case of noblesse oblige and an accommodation of the movement of history. In 399, the Serapeum — the great temple complex of Serapis at Alexandria — had been destroyed, and the might of the Roman Empire was now being used to stamp out pagan practices. The new god was fast supplanting the old ones.

In theological language, Synesius joined the Christians through *adhesion* rather than through the transformative experience of a full conversion.[51] But we can trace some possible lines of convergence between his philosophy and the Christian message. He believed in One divinity behind the many forms of the divine. He wrote of the "fall" of the soul from a state of knowledge and truth. He believed that in times of darkness a saving power may be sent to rescue humanity from itself and its deceivers. His essay *On Providence* depicts a world dominated by dark forces whose purpose is to drag humans down and destroy them if they reach for the light. Behind the surface events of history is the struggle between the higher instincts of humanity and the darkness within and around it. The power of light in humanity runs down at the end of the great cycles of history and must be restored periodically. But sometimes, when humans are in extremis, divine intervention may take place before the end of a cycle, to keep the game in play.[52]

If Synesius had lived long enough to learn the end of his mentor, Hypatia, he would have been left in no doubt that the darkness was rising. Though Hypatia's students included Christians, the fanatical Cyril, who became bishop of Alexandria in 412, saw her as a magnet for pagans. His violent diatribes against her helped to inflame a mob, led by a church lector, that pulled Hypatia from her carriage one night. In their collective dementia, these frenzied fundamentalists dragged her into a church called the Caesarium, tore off her clothes, and flayed her alive with sharp-edged shells. Then they butchered her body and burned the pieces to ashes.[53]

In such a world, Synesius offered the means of communicating with a higher realm and of bringing gifts from it into everyday life. He taught that the realm of imagination is "the hollow gulf of the universe" where the soul is at home. Imagination is "the halfway house between spirit and matter, which makes communication between the two possible."[54] The soul travels in this realm in dreams.

For Bishop Synesius, dreaming was everyday church. It was also a way of entry into the real world. According to Synesius, the dreamer does not return to reality when he awakens; dreaming, he is already there.

The Challenge of Dreamers for the Early Church

It has been widely assumed that, by the time Synesius was writing, around the end of the fourth century, the church triumphant was in the process of driving dreaming underground. People who claim a direct line to the sacred are a challenge to religious authority, and in the early Christian centuries the leaders of schismatic movements — Montanists, Gnostics, Donatists — had claimed that their mandate came from dreams and visions. The workings of the Holy Spirit were now unwelcome, according to E. R. Dodds, who has suggested that "from the point of view of the hierarchy the Third person of the Trinity had outlived his primitive function."[55] Yet, in suggesting that people in all walks of life could have divine dreams, and that they needed to be heard, Synesius was not a lone voice in the church. Around the time he was writing his treatise on dreams, a more orthodox bishop, Ambrose of Milan, instructed the Emperor Theodosius that "our God admonishes us in many ways, by heavenly signs, by the warnings of the prophets, and he wills that we understand even by the visions of sinners."[56]

In a remarkable study of dreaming and religious authority in early France, Isabel Moreira demonstrates that dreams and visions were still central to the lives of Christian communities and were heard by princes of the church (and the other kind). And, despite Peter Brown's suggestion that the locus of visionary authority moved to the "holy man" (the "only professional in an age of amateurs") in the period,[57] there is plenty of evidence that everyone was dreaming up a storm, and that the dreams of sinners as well as saints were heard. Gregory of Tours noted that "drunkards" were prolific dreamers in his area and witnessed magnificent sights in their visions.[58]

The church never managed to establish effective criteria for determining whether a dream or vision was to be trusted. Efforts to determine that the truth of dreams depended on the merit of the dreamer did not prosper — first because heretics could be very holy people, and second because "drunkards" and "sinners" were constantly reporting important dreams. Saint Martin of Tours thought he was able to tell that a demon was impersonating Jesus in a dream when the Christ figure showed up wearing a purple robe and a diadem. This could not be Jesus, according to Martin, because the true Jesus would come in "the dress and appearance of his passion," bearing the wounds of the cross.[59] Maybe this worked for Martin, but other holy people in the early Middle Ages (like Radegund) saw Christ richly dressed and believed in these visions of Christ the King.

So there was constant tension in the early church's relations with dreamers. The church could not proscribe a mode of direct experience of the sacred that contributed hugely to its own early growth, was sanctioned by scripture, and was endorsed by leading church figures — not only by heterodox figures like Tertullian and Synesius but also by no less than Pope Gregory the Great. But the risk remained that spiritual dreams could inspire a new heresy or undermine established authority, religious or secular.

Little by little, church-approved dreaming was brought closer and closer to the cult of the saints. Those who communed with the saints in their dreams were believed to be tapping immense sources of power and healing.

The vision of Anselm became a celebrated example of the ability of the dreamer to draw power from a higher realm to correct earthly affairs. The second Norman king of England, William II, also known as William Rufus, was a rapacious, brawling, big-bellied lout who earned a lot of opposition, including that of the great scholar Anselm, the Archbishop of Canterbury. He forced Anselm into exile.

In 1100, Anselm had a vision in which he saw the "saints of England" asking God to deal with the Norman thug on the throne. God summoned Saint Alban, the first martyr of England, into his presence and handed him a flaming arrow. Saint Alban took the arrow, promising to make it "an avenger of sins." In Anselm's vision, the saint threw the arrow and it came down like a fiery comet.

Around the same time, William Rufus was struck by an arrow while hunting in the New Forest; he fell from his horse, mortally wounded, and died the same night. Before the news reached Anselm, the archbishop had already offered a thanksgiving mass, packed his bags, and started his journey back to his cathedral, confident that the arrow fired in his vision had actually reached its mark, flying from the realm of the Aevum (the dimension between the world of time and the world of eternity) into the king's domain. As he rode into Canterbury, Anselm received word that the king had been killed by an arrow. The story spread across Europe that the cleric Anselm had the power to destroy kings through his prayers and visions — perhaps a desirable reputation for a leading churchman in a time of constant power struggles between church and state.

This account of Anselm's vision comes down to us from a chronicler known as Matthew of Westminster. Modern scholarship suggests that the author may have stretched his facts more than a little. It appears that, at the time of the king's death, Anselm was in France — and did not return to his see until after five years of bargaining and jockeying with William II's successor, Henry I.

According to other chronicles, William Rufus had his own premonitory dreams — in the most terrifying one, he saw blood spurting from his body until it darkened the sky.

On the morning of his death, the king received a warning from another dreamer that he took very seriously. Robert FitzHammon brought William Rufus word that a monk had dreamed that he saw the king trying to bite off the legs of a figure of Christ on the cross. In the monk's dream, the Christ figure came alive and smashed the king to the ground. The king lay under Christ's feet, belching fire and smoke from his mouth until the air was dark.

These horrific images weighed heavy on the mind of the king, arousing deep fear. Maybe in some obscure way the king recognized a very personal message in the part where he self-combusts under the trampling feet of an angry Lord. Spontaneous combustion has been a known phenomenon among alcoholics for as long as humans have been able to make alcohol, and William II drank hugely.

The Norman king's response to the monk's dream reveals the power attributed to the dreamer in these times. William Rufus ordered FitzHammon to give the monk a hundred shillings and "bid him dreame of better fortune to our person" — seeking to change the future by changing the way others dreamed it.

He may have sensed that his offer came too late. The chronicler Holinshed reports that the king could not shake the sense of oppression that came with the dream report. Instead of riding out to the hunt at dawn, as was his custom, he lingered in his palace and did not leave for his date with Saint Alban's arrow until after a very boozy lunch.[60]

French medievalist Jean-Claude Schmitt observes that, in the Middle Ages, dreams were recognized as "an immediate recourse to a supernatural legitimacy source."[61] Hence dreams were of the highest political importance, and there was constant tension over rival readings and experiences of dreaming.

Few dreamers might be able to call down arrows of divine wrath against an unsatisfactory ruler, but medieval culture allowed some dreamers the power to criticize the monarch by disseminating unflattering dreams. Thus the monk Wetti of Reichenau was able to circulate a quasi-pornographic dream in which Charlemagne was genitally tortured in a way that matched his reputed sexual exploits.[62]

DREAMS OF ISLAM

The extraordinary importance of dreaming and dream interpretation in the history of Islam is brought home by two medieval Arabic books. The first is an immense biographical dictionary prepared by a certain al-Khallal in the fourth century. Titled *The Classes of the Dream Interpreters*, it contained life histories of no fewer than seventy-five hundred people who were renowned as dream interpreters. It reflected both the profusion of dream interpreters in the Muslim world and a deep awareness of other traditions, especially Greek, Jewish, and Indian.[63]

The second book is the *Muqaddimah* of Ibn Khaldun, the introduction to a universal history composed in 1377. Ibn Khaldun was an extraordinary philosopher of history, with a searching, far-ranging mind. Five centuries before Darwin, he offered a theory of evolution, daring to suggest that, in the course of life on earth, lower forms have always had a tendency to evolve into higher forms. "The last stage of each group becomes the first stage of the next group.... The higher stage of man is reached from the world of the monkeys."[64] Humans, in turn, may evolve to the level of angels; so far only prophets are at home in this realm.

The *Muqaddimah* opens with six long essays defining the stage on which history is played out, covering, for example, the influence of climate and geographical features in human affairs, the human need for community, and the nature of group consciousness.

His sixth essay is the most arresting and arousing. It is devoted to "the various types of human beings who have supernatural perception either through natural disposition or through exercise, preceded by a discussion of inspiration and dream visions."[65] Ibn Khaldun argues that human history unfolds in engagement with suprahuman forces, and that a key requirement for civilization is the presence and activity of individuals who are alive to the hidden order of events and who can mediate between humanity and higher powers. Such people include dreamers as well as prophets.

"God created man in such a way that the veil of the senses could be lifted through sleep, which is a natural function of man. When that veil is lifted, the soul is ready to learn the things it desires to know in the world of Truth." All human beings have shared something of this experience. "Every human being has, more than once, seen something in his sleep that turned out to be true when he awakened. He knows for certain that the soul must necessarily have supernatural perception in sleep." What is possible in sleep "is not impossible in other conditions, because the perceiving essence is one and its qualities are always present. God guides towards the truth."[66]

We cannot grasp the true nature and causes of events unless we study the "inner side" of history, which involves the workings of coincidence as well as dreams and imagination. Inner and outer causes are always at play together in the world. "Chance" (*al-bakht*) and "coincidence" (*al-ittifaq*) are names we give to "unknown causes."[67]

Here, then, is a view of history in which dreaming is central to everything. The historian who seeks to understand both the inner and the outer logic of events should not rest content with studying how others dream and talk about dreaming; he must take up the *practice* of dreaming. Ibn Khaldun describes how he practiced dream incubation: by announcing what he wanted to learn during the night and reinforcing his intention by reciting certain formulas known as "dream words." The results, by his account, were gratifying: "With the help of these words, I have myself had remarkable dream visions, through which I learned things about myself that I wanted to know."[68]

Up to the present day, all branches of Islam have been characterized by a deep reverence for dreams and visions (which are rarely differentiated), and the "true" dream vision (*al-ruya*) has often been a mandate for political as well as spiritual power. We will track the origins of the Islamic affinity for dreams in two directions. First, we will explore how the religion of Islam was born through dreams and visions, especially the "night journey" of the prophet Muhammad in the company of Gabriel, the archangel of dreams, known to the Muslim world as Jibril. Second, we will explore the *ground* of dreaming in Islamic visionary experience. Fundamental to Islam is the understanding that there is a hidden realm where "true dreams" take place. These are either journeys of the soul that take the dreamer to the hidden realm, or visitations by authentic guides who come from that realm. The most luminous description of this hidden realm — "the isthmus of imagination" — is in the writings of the medieval Sufi philosophers Ibn 'Arabi and Suhrawardi.

There is a well-known hadith (a saying attributed to the prophet Muhammad) which states that "dreaming is one-forty-sixth part of prophecy."[69] Such a minuscule part of something may not sound like a big deal, but only because we do not understand the context. According to his wife, Aisha, *all* Muhammad did for the six months prior to the *lailat al-mir'aj*, the heavenly journey from which he returned with the content of the Koran, was dream. That journey made him the Prophet. He lived for twenty-three years after that tremendous night of revelation. Six months is $\frac{1}{46}$th of twenty-three years. In this context, to say that dreaming is "one-forty-sixth part of prophecy" is to say it is of the most fundamental importance; it is the key to and precondition for prophecy.

By tradition, the Koran is the gift of a tremendous dream vision, in which Muhammad tours many higher worlds — including the paradisiacal "garden worlds" — in the company of Gabriel. Gabriel of the "140 pairs of wings," dictates the Koran, *sura* by *sura* (chapter by chapter). It is Gabriel who escorts Muhammad on his Night Journey (*mir'aj*) to gain personal knowledge of the higher worlds.

Gabriel brings Muhammad an extraordinary ride, the Buraq, sometimes depicted as a mule with a woman's face. Like the human mind, the Buraq is restive and must be calmed by the angel before it can carry Muhammad through the many worlds. They fly to Jerusalem, swift as thought. They ascend to higher realms from the Dome of the Rock. They explore successive heavens — some say seven, others nine — where Muhammad interviews spiritual masters who once lived on earth, as well as planetary angels.

Gabriel parts company with Muhammad at the Lote Tree of the Farthest Boundary. The Lote Tree is unlike any tree known on earth. It marks the outer limit of the realm of images; beyond this, the intellect may not go.

When Muhammad returns to his body, he finds that water from the jug his mystical steed kicked over during its takeoff is still spilling onto the floor of his cave. His travels through all the heaven worlds have taken less time than is required to empty a jug of water.

Sura 8 of the Koran, "The Spoils," recounts two of Muhammad's personal dream experiences, which gave him courage in the midst of his battles. Sura 12 retells the story of Joseph in Egypt, stating that Joseph's skill in interpreting dreams — especially dreams of the future — is a sign of God's favor.

As a leader and military commander, Muhammad often exhibited the powers of a seer or remote viewer. Asked about the progress of a certain caravan, Muhammad shifted his perception — "the veil being lifted" — and announced that it would arrive in the morning; it did.[70]

Muhammad started the day by asking his companions if they had dreams for him to interpret. In the hadiths (the reported sayings and actions of the Prophet), there are numerous references to dreams and dream interpretation. In Bukhari's collection of the hadiths, Aisha, Muhammad's wife, says that the beginning of his "divine inspiration" came in "true dreams in his sleep," and that "he never had a dream but that it came true like bright day of light."[71]

Beyond Muhammad's own story, dreams played a critical role in the emergence of Islam. A companion of the Prophet, Abdullah ibn Zayd, dreamed the Adhan, the five-times-daily Islamic call to prayer, at a time when Muhammad and his followers were seeking a way of defining their new faith in contradistinction to the calling horn of the Jews and the bell of the Christians.

Powers of seership and mental telegraphy were also ascribed to caliphs, the commanders of Islam after Muhammad. When the caliph Umar Khattab was reading scripture, he entered a state of vision (*muktashafa*) and saw that the enemy had prepared an ambush for Sariya, one of his generals, who had been sent with an army to Nihazar. He called out to his general, "Go to the mountain!" Across the miles, Sariya heard the message, seized the high ground, and won his victory.[72]

In traditional Islamic dream interpretation, dreams are divided into three categories. The "true dream" (*al-ruya*) is a dream inspired by God or his Prophet and is an experience of a higher aspect of spirit or consciousness. The evil or deceptive dream is inspired by Shaitan, the Devil. Then there is the great profusion of dreams, void of any real importance, that reflect the confused, desire-driven wanderings of the *nafs*, a lower aspect of consciousness.

Suhrawardi is very clear on the point that we cannot understand dreams without grasping which aspect of the dreamer is active in the dream. "Some are true and some are false," depending on whether the *nafs* or the higher *ruh* soul is dominant during the experience. Dreaming is traveling, so the fact that the dreamer can see things at a distance in space or time is in no way surprising: "after separation from the body, the soul [*ruh*] knows even of the small things heard and seen in this world."[73]

A dream is most likely to be a true one when the Prophet makes an appearance and the dream message is congruent with the teachings of the Koran and the hadiths. In one hadith the Prophet says, "Whoever has seen me in a dream, then no doubt, he has seen me, for Satan cannot imitate my shape."[74] However, for some of the shaykhs this is as problematic as alleged appearances of Jesus or the saints were for medieval Christian clerics: who can tell for sure whether the dream visitor is what he seems to be?

In practice, in much Islamic dream interpretation this is left to the presumed authority, a religious leader. In a wonderful study of a contemporary Muslim community in Egypt that keeps a collective book of "true dreams," Amira Mittermaier describes the central role of the religious leader in determining which dreams are true and what they mean.[75] However, when dream interpretation is based on authority — and dreams are highly valued — the potential for the abuse of power and the practice of mind control is immense. Think what it means if your spiritual leader is Osama bin Laden, and he is interpreting your dreams for you, as bin Laden was doing for members of Al-Qaeda prior to 9/11.

The hadiths contain this statement on telling dreams: "A dream rests on the feathers of a bird and will not take effect unless it is related to someone." Taken literally, this would mean we should tell our good dreams but be very careful about telling our bad ones, in case the telling helps to manifest what is seen. In any event, we should be careful about whom we choose as our dream confidants — "Tell your dreams only to knowledgeable persons and loved ones" — and be very wary of those who may use our dreams against us.

The hadiths contain fearsome warnings that those who lie about their dreams will suffer fearsome penalties. Here is what lies ahead for someone who invents a dream report: "Whoever claims to have had a dream in which he says he saw something he did not shall be ordered [in Hell] to tie a knot between two barley grains, and will not be able to do so."[76] Now *that* comes from a culture where people think dreams really matter! Where a dream can confer authority — even that of a king or prophet — it is necessary to warn off false dreamers.

In the world of Islam, dreaming is understood to be a doorway for interaction between the dead and the living. The common formula that introduces many Muslim dream reports — "somebody came to me in my dream" (*atani atin fi l-manam*) — often refers to a visitation by the dead. There are many reports of agreements between friends that whoever dies first will contact the survivor from the other side. The "Book of Dreams" (Kitab al-Manam) of Ibn Abi Dunya (d. 894) contains accounts of three hundred dreams of the dead. Ibn Sirin (d. 728), a revered Muslim dream interpreter whose books are still in wide circulation, declared, "Whatever the deceased tells you in sleep is true, for he stays in the world of truth."[77]

In the early Arab world, there was a practice of incubating dream encounters with the dead by sleeping near their tombs.[78]

The dead provide tours of Paradise, which includes black-eyed maidens and palaces for those who live and die the approved way. In the Muslim dream books, the fortunate dead often appear wearing green and crowned with light. It is stressed again and again that the dead are aware of the living, eager to receive news of them — and are directly affected by actions of surviving friends and family members.[79]

The Isthmus of Imagination

The Arabic word for "interpretation," *ta'bir*, literally means "crossing over." The truest dream interpreter (*mu'abbir*) is one who "crosses over" from the limited images of the remembered dream to deeper levels of meaning and the fuller dream experience.[80] If he is deep and wise enough, his imagination may even travel to the realm of images where the dream experience took place.

When we approach the great visionary philosophers of medieval Islam, we find ourselves in the presence of extraordinary minds that could cross over at will into true realms of imagination. They have given us a geography of nonordinary reality, and an insight into the power of the imagination to create and reshape worlds, that is of immense contemporary value.

Here we'll briefly examine the visionary explorations of two medieval masters, Suhrawardi and Ibn 'Arabi. They share the understanding that imagination is a "creative magical potency" that gives birth to forms in more than one world.[81] The universe itself begins when God imagines (or dreams) it. The Realm of Images — *alam al-mithal* — is the "place of apparition" of spiritual beings. "It is also the place where all 'divine history' is accomplished" — the place of the greater drama beyond the surface dramas of our lives and our world.[82]

The Persian master of imagination Shihabuddin Yahya Suhrawardi was born in northwestern Iran between 1153 and 1155. He was judicially murdered by the doctors of Sharia law at Aleppo in 1191, when he was in his midthirties. His philosophy of "illumination" and his vivid descriptions of the Realm of Images were founded on his own visionary journeys, which began on a night when he had exhausted himself struggling with intellectual problems. He fell into "a dreamlike ecstasy" and found himself "wrapped in gentleness; there was a blinding flash, then a very diaphanous light in the likeness of a human being. I watched attentively and there he was: helper of souls, Imam of wisdom, whose form filled me with wonder and whose shining beauty dazzled me." This radiant guide said, "Awaken to your self, and your problem will be solved."[83]

Later Suhrawardi explained that this encounter had taken place not in his room but in a shining city called Jabarsa, located in the *alam al-mithal*, the realm of true imagination. "The encounter with suprasensory reality" may come through divine visitation, but the heart of the practice is astral travel. The adept's physical body becomes "a tunic which he sometimes casts off and at other times puts on." He puts on another body — a "robe of auroral light" to travel to higher realms, and "if it pleases him, he can manifest himself in whatever form he chooses."[84]

The Realm of Images has countless cities, including Jabarsa and Jabalqa, each of which has a thousand gates. Its mixed population includes many beings that are quite unaware that God decided to create an experiment with a life-form known as humanity on a planet called Earth.

Ibn 'Arabi (1165–1240) was born in Spain, the son of an official of the Muslim ruler of Murcia. He met many Sufi masters in Andalusia and wrote about their practices in an early work. He left Spain for Tunis when he was thirty, was guided by a vision to make the pilgrimage to Mecca, and traveled widely in the Middle East before settling in Damascus. His own great visionary "opening" — which he called "the shining of the full moon" — came in his youth in Spain when he was still "beardless," and all his important work flowed from that.

For Ibn 'Arabi, imagination is the "isthmus" (*barzakh*) between body and spirit and between being and nothingness.[85] To travel this realm requires discipline, practice, and discernment. The imagination works through "embodiment" (*tajassud*). Higher beings become visible and intelligible through the forms that the imagination helps give them, as happened with the Prophet, who said, "I saw my Lord in the form of a youth." According to a hadith, Gabriel used to come to the Prophet in the shape of a beautiful young man he knew. The plastic work of imagination is "to embody that which is not properly a body."[86]

To help those of us whose imaginations lie dormant in ordinary life, God has given us dreams. According to Ibn 'Arabi, "The only reason God placed sleep in the animate world was so that everyone might witness the Presence of Imagination and know that there is another world similar to the sensory

world."[87] In certain kinds of sleep, "the soul travels like a king in his royal treasury." It visits the Treasury of Imagination, which is full of scenes and images
that are generated both by sensory memories and by "the form-giving faculty"
of creative imagination itself. "Imagination in sleep is the most complete and
general in existence, since it belongs to both the [adept] and the common people."[88] "The clearest access shared by all human beings to the nature of existence
. . . is our own imagination, especially dreams."[89]

The world itself requires interpretation just as a dream does. As we grow
in understanding and step beyond the veils of ignorance, we come to know that
"all of existence is sleep and its wakefulness is sleep." What we think is reality
is a mundane dream. When, through dreaming and imagination, we step
through the curtain of our consensual hallucinations and get *out there*, we enter
into the deeper reality. The Realm of Images is *more* real, not less real, than our
physical existence. The curtain that prevents us from seeing and experiencing
it has been placed over us by — ourselves. Ibn 'Arabi insists: God did not place
the veil between him and us; we did. "He placed no veil upon you but yourself.
You are the curtain over yourself."[90]

The scholar who did the most to bring the work of these Islamic masters of
imagination to the West, Henry Corbin, entered, in a dreamlike way, the field
that would become his life's work. He was a student at the École Practiques des
Hautes Études in Paris when one of his professors, Louis Massignon, came back
from Tehran with a lithographic copy of Suhrawardi's major work, the *Kitab
Hikmat al'Ishraq*. Corbin did not yet know Arabic, but when he mentioned that
he had heard something about Suhrawardi, his professor gave him the Arabic
text, saying, "I think there is in this book something for you." That something,
for Corbin, proved to be "a lifelong companion." After he mastered Arabic, he
translated Suhrawardi's book under the title *Le livre de la sagesse orientale*.[91]

Corbin struggled through the thickets of language to help us grasp the idea
that creative imagination, for the masters he interpreted, centers on the operations of *himma* — the power and perception of the heart. It is *himma* that works
wonders of manifestation by firing and fueling the active imagination. It signifies "the act of meditating, conceiving, imagining, projecting, ardently desiring."
It carries "the force of an intention so powerful as to project and realize a being
external to the being who conceives the intention." *Himma* is the mode of creative imagination — charged by the deepest passion — that has the power to
create objects and produce changes in the outer world.[92]

Sufi philosophers liked to quote an example from Sura 27 of the Koran, involving Solomon and the Queen of Sheba, to show how this works. Solomon asks whether one of his companions can produce the queen's throne before she arrives. For Asaf, this is no problem. He applies his *himma*, and the throne dematerializes in Sheba and manifests before Solomon and his court.[93]

At age seventy, Corbin wrote, in the spirit of Suhrawardi and Ibn 'Arabi, that "to be a philosopher is to take to the road, never settling down in some place of satisfaction with a theory of the world."[94]

When he first journeyed to Iran, Corbin described it as "a country the color of heaven." It may have been one of the mercies of his personal history that he died the year before Ayatollah Khomeini and other fundamentalist mullahs seized power.

CHAPTER 4

❦

THE ANGEL THAT TROUBLES THE WATERS

For an angel went down at a certain season into the pool, and troubled the water; whosoever then first after the troubling of the water stepped in was made whole of whatsoever disease he had.

— JOHN 5:4 (KING JAMES VERSION)

The healing pool of Bethesda is famous. Its name has been borrowed by countless hospitals and medical centers, and by a town in Maryland that is a bedroom community for Washington, D.C. One of the distinctions of Bethesda, Maryland, is that it has one of the longest subway escalators in the world. To come off the bright street and be confronted by that steep descent into darkness is very much like looking into the mouth of the Underworld. Bethesda, we'll find, is the right name for the entry to the underground, as well as the hospitals.

The first medical guide written in America was titled *The Angel of Bethesda* after its author, the learned New England minister Cotton Mather, had a vision of an angel "whose face shone like the midday sun."[1] You can view a splendid winged version of the angel of Bethesda in Central Park in New York City, looking very much like an angel of the Lord is supposed to look.

You may have heard of him, as I first did in Sunday school, in the King James version: "For an angel went down at a certain season into the pool, and troubled the water; whosoever then first after the troubling of the water stepped in was made whole of whatsoever disease he had" (John 5:4).

His presence explains the "multitude" of the sick, the lame, and the impotent who are gathered around the pool at Bethesda, in the hope of being healed, when Jesus arrives and performs one of his best-known miracles. Jesus cures a lame man by telling him to get up and walk. The man had been waiting by the pool for years in the hope that someday he would manage to get in first when the waters were troubled, but the moment had always been snatched from him.

In modern revisions of the New Testament, the angel of Bethesda disappears. The whole verse that presents him has been excised from the New Revised Version, the New American Bible, and the New Jerusalem Bible; you'll find it only in a footnote in minuscule type. The learned justification for this blue-penciling is that John 5:4 is missing from the earliest Greek manuscripts of the Gospel of John and contains expressions that do not conform to the Johannine style.

Without the angel, the mystery of why a multitude is waiting for the troubling of the waters is unexplained. Are all these people simply convinced that the waters of Bethesda have healing properties that are augmented when they gush more strongly from the nearby spring that feeds them? We can't understand what is going on until we grasp that, before textual scholars deleted the angel, early Christians had deleted a pagan god who was literally born from dreams and who healed through dreaming.

The French scholar Antoine Duprez made a careful study of the archeological evidence from Bethesda and suggests there were at least three stages of religious activity around the Pool of Bethesda. The earliest evidence is a complex of pools and grottos from the second century BCE. This was likely a place of sacred healing, but the evidence does not tell us in whose name it was conducted. The structures of that time were destroyed, along with much of Jerusalem, in 70 CE. They were replaced by a sanctuary of the healer-god Asklepios-Serapis, a composite deity. This sanctuary was replaced in turn in the fifth century by a Christian church commemorating the miracle of John 5. In the tenth century, the Crusaders built yet another church, dedicated to Saint Anne, on top of all the above.

Who was first worshipped at the site? Duprez argues that, given the popularity of the Asklepian religion in Syria, Palestine, and Egypt in Hellenistic times, it is entirely likely that a healing temple was operating at the gates of Jerusalem, near the Roman garrisons.[2]

Against this backdrop, textual analysis of John 5 suggests that a creative editor took an older miracle story and relocated it at Bethesda, the site of a popular pagan temple of healing (just as churches were often built at pagan places of power) in an effort to claim the glamour of the old religion for the new one. In this analysis, John 5 is the first testimony to the struggle between primitive Christianity and the religion of the healing gods, which centered on dreaming at places of power where prayer had been valid.

The double attribution of the old healing temple at Bethesda to both Asklepios and Serapis is revealing. In the testimonies of those who were healed in his sanctuary, Asklepios is praised as a kindly and gentle god, one who carries the sufferer from wild oceans of pain and despair into safe harbor.

There is nothing cozy about Serapis. He is lord of the Underworld as well as a healing god. He is born from the dreams of a Macedonian prince of Egypt. His first image — the one that stays and grows — is that of a Hades figure from the fierce eastern edge of the known world, a lord of death and of the fertile dark. His crown is a cylindrical grain measure symbolizing the fact that, like seed, unless we die into the earth we cannot be reborn.

Into the whirling centrifuge of his composite forms, he draws the attributes of Osiris, the Egyptian god who is forever dying and coming again, and that of the Apis bull, who is both primal sexual power and the necessary sacrifice. Yet he remains, first and last, the lord of the Underworld, as Aelius Aristides made clear when he eulogized Serapis in his first public speech: "After the necessary termination of life he remains as ruler for mankind. . . . Our fate is to go at his side from him to him, from home to home."[3] You enter his precinct in hopes of mercy, but you are not there unless you know fear. "When mindful of Serapis, man is filled at the same time with joy and fear. For he is both the most generous and the most terrifying of the gods, and he inspires a profitable fear in mankind."[4]

Now *there* is an angel that could trouble the waters.

DREAM DIAGNOSTICIANS

Before we explore the experience of dreaming yourself well in the precincts of the healing gods, let's look at what dreams meant in the practices of the best physicians of Greco-Roman times. We'll find that people whose names are all but synonymous with rationality and empirical methods were inspired by dreams, that they respected the direct healing that might come through divine dreams, and that they worked constantly with their patients' dreams to diagnose their complaints and identify the correct treatments.

Aristotle was skeptical about many aspects of dreams, but he respected their diagnostic value and observed that the most successful physicians paid close attention to patients' dreams. Throughout the Hippocratic corpus — the large body of ancient medical texts attributed to Hippocrates, the great early physician from whom the oath of our medical profession is derived — the diagnostic value of dreams is recognized again and again.

The author of the Hippocratic treatise *On Regimen* (fourth century BCE) tracks dreams that foreshadow physical symptoms and reveal their progress. He maintains that in sleep "the soul becomes its own mistress" and is able to tour its bodily residence without distractions. In the morning, it leaves the dreamer some pictures from its nightly tours. To read the diagnostic meaning of these souvenirs, we must recognize that inside the body is a whole world. Thus earth, in a dream, may represent the body as a whole. A river may be the blood, a tree (for a man) or a spring (for a woman) the reproductive system. For the author of *On Regimen*, dreams of the dead may refer to food one has eaten, "for from the dead come nourishment and growth and seed."[5]

Let's look at the dreamwork of two Greek physicians who were renowned in the Roman empire of the second century: Rufus of Ephesus and Galen.

Rufus means "red-blond"; probably that was the color of his hair. Rufus the physician studied and practiced medicine in Ephesus, a thriving Greek city on the coast of Asia Minor famed for its "breathing statue" of Artemis as the great goddess, sprouting many breasts like ripe fruit. He wanted to master every aspect of medicine and anatomy. Forbidden to dissect human cadavers, he cut up monkeys and pigs. He described the difference between diastolic and systolic blood pressure. He wrote medical texts on kidney ailments, diseases of the joints, optics, and the symptoms and treatment of the plague. He was an empirical scientist and a humanist. He prescribed sexual intercourse as a remedy for depression. He is said to have treated all his patients, whether patricians or slaves, with equal care.

Today's physicians would do well to follow his counsel on how to interview patients. "One must make inquiries about sleep; whether or not the patient was sleeping; what his habits were with regard to sleep and wakefulness; and whether he has had any visions or dreams. From these answers a doctor can make his inferences." Rufus cited a number of case studies to make his point that on no account should the physician "neglect these matters."[6]

Myron the Ephesian was a wrestler seemingly bursting with good health. But he dreamed he spent the night thrashing and sinking in a horrible black marsh. He told his dream to his trainer, but the trainer dismissed it, pushing Myron into an intensive workout. Halfway through the session, the wrestler developed shortness of breath and heart palpitations. Soon he lost control of his limbs, could no longer speak, and died before help could be found. "It seems to me he would not have died," Rufus commented, "if he had had a knowledgeable trainer" who had arranged suitable medical treatment based on the dream, which indicated the need for "a massive evacuation of blood."[7]

In another case, a patient told his physician he was frightened by recurring dreams in which a powerful black man tried to choke him. The doctor was baffled by these dreams until his patient developed "a fierce bleeding from the nostrils."[8]

Galen (128–210) was one of the greatest scientists of his time and a pioneer of scientific methods of experiment. He was a prolific author in many fields, ranging from psychiatry to linguistics and from pathology to mathematics. He was court physician to Marcus Aurelius and was able to influence the most powerful men in the Roman Empire. He doctored gladiators and enjoyed their company. He wielded his sharp mind like a scalpel and a digging tool and was in many ways the model of Greek rationalism. Second only to Hippocrates, Galen is the most important person in the rise of Western medicine.

He owed his career and, by his own account, his life to dreams of a god. He was born in Pergamon, a highly civilized Greek city renowned for its library of two hundred thousand parchment books and its Asklepieion, a huge temple complex devoted to the healing religion of Asklepios. Galen's father, Nikon, was one of the top architects in the city. He initially opposed his son's desire to study medicine, until his mind was changed by "vivid dreams" of the god.[9] When he was twenty, Galen wrote, "Asklepios, god of my fathers, saved me when I had the deadly condition of an abscess."[10] The god directed him to perform a surgical procedure, to open an artery in his hand between his thumb and forefinger.

Galen wrote some of his medical books under the direction of Asklepios. When he was at the height of his career, the god cautioned him not to go on an eastern campaign with Marcus Aurelius. He may have won the emperor's indulgence, because Marcus Aurelius paid attention to appearances by gods in his own dreams; the emperor thanked the gods for granting him (Marcus Aurelius) "assistance in dreams" and especially for showing him "how to avoid spitting blood and fits of giddiness."[11] Later in Galen's writing career, Asklepios reproached him in a dream because he had not completed a treatise on the optic nerve; he then pushed himself to finish this work.[12]

As he recorded medical case histories, Galen paid close attention to the appearances of the god in diagnosing and prescribing for different ailments and to instances when the god facilitated direct healing. He was in no way superstitious. It would have been irrational, from his perspective, not to work with a friendly god who could fix the parts other medicine could not reach — and who demonstrated this again and again.

The surviving text of Galen's essay *On Diagnosis from Dreams* shows his no-nonsense approach. He explains that dreams can provide accurate diagnosis because, during sleep, the soul travels inside the body and checks out what is going on. He notes the need to distinguish a somatic dream of this kind — for which he uses the word *enhypnion* — from other types, such as those that originate in waking thoughts and actions and the prophetic dream (*oneiros*). He is especially interested in dream weather, believing that an excess of moisture or dryness, of heat or cold, in a dream indicates the action that must be taken to balance a patient's "humors," or vital energies. He notes as a cautionary example an instance when a dream warning was missed: a patient's dream that one of his legs turned to stone was interpreted symbolically instead of literally. "This dream was interpreted by many skilled in these matters as a reference to the man's slaves. However, contrary to all of our expectations, the dreamer became paralyzed in that leg."[13]

Galen prided himself on his ability to use his observation and intuition to diagnose both emotional and physical problems. Called to treat a woman who was suffering from insomnia, he noticed that her pulse became wildly disturbed when the name of a handsome dancer, Pylades, was mentioned, but remained unaffected when he mentioned the name of a rival dancer. Galen diagnosed love-sickness.[14]

And then there are the dreams where the god appears in order to prescribe and cure. Sometimes he does this by issuing prescriptions that might puzzle even the most adventurous physician. In a case reported by Galen in his *Outline of Empiricism*, a sick Thracian came to the temple at Pergamon in response to a dream, and had a deeper dream encounter with Asklepios. "The god then ordered [the Thracian] to take a daily potion of the snake drug and to anoint his body externally with it. The disease, within a matter of days, turned into leprosy. And this disease, in turn, was healed by the drugs the god prescribed." Galen adds, "I confidently began to use the snake drug copiously, in the manner described by the god. They call it theriac antidote. Moreover, I also used theriac salt, which by now many prepare by burning live snakes, together with certain drugs, in a new earthenware vessel, to which they also add snake food. I myself removed the heads and the tails of the snakes."[15]

One of the benefits of divine dreams, according to Galen, is that patients are more willing to comply with directions from a god than from a regular doctor. "In Pergamon we see that those who are being treated by the god obey him when on many occasions he bids them not to drink at all for fifteen days, while they obey none of the physicians who give this prescription."[16]

The god may also offer a prescription that addresses the whole person rather than merely the symptom. Galen believed that this approach was at the heart of healing. In one of the most striking fragments from his works (many of which perished in a fire in the Temple of Peace — of all places — in Rome) he states, "We have made not a few men healthy by correcting the disproportion of their emotions." Asklepios now appears as a power that restores balance in a life. He ordered some "to compose comic mimes and certain songs," and others to take up vigorous exercise including hunting, horse riding, and martial arts to "arouse passion when it was weak" and to restore "measure" in the patient.[17]

We don't want to miss the *place* of healing in Galen's city of Pergamon, which was also well known to his contemporary Aelius Aristides. The Asklepieion was on the southwestern edge of the city and was approached through a long colonnade. Those seeking health of body and mind entered a courtyard whose central feature was a white marble pillar adorned with the snakes of Asklepios. Beyond it, they moved through an arch into the sacred precinct. In it stood the round temple of Telesphoros, the Finisher, an enigmatic figure sometimes described as the son of Asklepios but depicted as a hooded dwarf whose name and image carried the sense of nearness to death: he was the Finisher of human affairs. On the subterranean level of this temple, patients were immersed in purifying baths, and rites of dream incubation took place.[18] A passage led to the sacred well, and what went on here may give us a further clue to the mystery of Bethesda.

Aristides tells us that "this well is the discovery of the great magician who does everything for the safety of mankind." For many it "is like a drug." By bathing in it, the blind recover their sight; by drinking from it, many are cured of chest trouble and regain "the breath of life." The lame get up and walk. Some who drink from the well become prophetic. "For some merely drawing up the water has been like a means of safety."[19]

No surprise, then, that Galen not only reports dreams as clinical data but also invokes Asklepios when he administers medical treatment, as he did with these words for an emperor: "Be gracious, blessed Healer, you who made this remedy; be gracious and send your always gracious daughter Panacea to the Emperor, who will offer pure sacrifices for the freedom from pain which you can grant."[20]

In the Temple of Dream Healing

Let's go to a sanctuary of dream healing. Isn't it time? There were more than two hundred of these temple complexes around the Mediterranean littoral from Palestine to Spain. They included the great temples at Epidauros and Pergamon and the complex the Romans built on a boat-shaped island in the Tiber to house the Greek god they brought on a boat — in the shape of his "breathing likeness" — and naturalized under the Latin name Aesculapius. The religion of the healing gods flourished for a thousand years, until the church finally succeeded in suppressing it (while stealing from it) in the fifth century.

The four-part journey that follows is closely based on the testimonies of those who dreamed with Asklepios and Serapis, on the descriptions of ancient travelers like Pausanias, and on archeological reports. Quotations and case descriptions are drawn from several centuries of inscriptions and parchment dream books. But let's simply imagine we are journeying to the healing temple about the same time that the Gospel of John puts Jesus at the healing pool at Bethesda.

The Approach

You are called to the temple of healing. Your dreams may have told you to come, or you may be driven by desperation: you are suffering in body or mind, and nothing you have tried has fixed you or relieved your pain. Maybe you feel as if the spring within you — the one that used to wind you up and keep you going — is broken. Maybe you have lost your *big* dream, your sense that your life has meaning and purpose. So you take to the road, as many others have done, in hopes of finding yourself once you find a god you can talk to.

The road is not easy. It will take persistence and courage to reach the dream temple. There are people who will do anything to stop you. They will mock you and try to beat you up and rob you of whatever is still yours. The hazards of the journey may be the first step toward your healing. You have left the familiar grooves of your life. You have a chance of becoming the protagonist, rather than a victim or an extra, in your own life drama.

Shifting Expectations

The boundary stones of the precinct of healing alert you that you are about to enter sacred space. Over the outer gate, you may find an inscription cautioning you that only those with a "clean mind" may enter "the fragrant temple." You are being challenged to open to the experience of *metanoia*, the changing of the mind. You may not yet grasp that, unless you drop your old mind-set and your past history, as a snake sheds its skin, you will never truly enter the temple. You will be helped to learn this, and to slough off the old skin, through a period of preparation that starts with ritual cleansing.

You are bathed in the waters of a sacred spring. Perhaps you are immersed in the sea for the deep cleansing of salt water. "The god delights most of all if what is most godlike within ourselves is clean."[21] You put on fresh clothes: the simple white garment of a neophyte — someone who does not claim to have the answers — would be best.

You make your offerings to the healing god. Food is always welcome, especially food that the snakes and dogs of the temple precinct would enjoy. The dogs will be panting and padding around you hopefully if you have brought meat or perhaps a trussed chicken or rooster to be sacrificed, which is what Socrates sent to Asklepios.

You'll be given lots of time to look around, and this part of the preparation is vitally important because it is going to shift your understanding of what is possible. One of the first things you notice is that you have entered an orchard of body parts. Replicas of eyes and kidneys, ears and intestines, hang from walls and ceilings. These votive offerings testify to healings that have already taken place. If you can read, you can inspect fuller testimonials: the inscriptions carved on stelae (marble pillars) set up in the courtyard.

Some of these narrative testimonials are wonderfully personal. The god has a kindly bedside manner and he *talks* to you: "I struck up a conversation with the god," one visitor testifies.[22]

In some of the older testimonials, the god performs oneiric surgery. He rips open your chest or your abdomen, rinses and heals your organs, and sews you up, whole and renewed.[23] He cuts your eyeball and your sight is restored. He tells you to get up and — even if you were previously paralyzed and had to come here on a litter — you stand up and you walk, and you are healed.

He corrects chronic conditions like infertility, blindness, lameness. People come to him with problems for which there is no medical cure available. A woman who was barren for five years gives birth to a baby who immediately gets on its feet and goes to a fountain.

He works wonders, but he also issues prescriptions — some weird, some perfectly ordinary — and he tells you what you can do for yourself, through diet and exercise and creative expression. It seems he always wants you to make a story, and he gives you a bigger story to tell than the one you were trapped in before you came here.

All these testimonies and replica body parts are on display to help you understand that you are in a place where prayer has been valid. Whatever doubts you are carrying, whatever self-defeating mantras you are still inclined to recite in your head, the evidence around you is helping you shift your expectations. You are starting to *expect* healing.

Let's make Asklepios, who is older than Serapis (though not as old as his father, Apollo, who was first hailed as Paian, the Healer), the owner of this sanctuary. You are still in the outer temple, taking in the sights and learning from them.

You pause in front of the statue of the god. It is fashioned from gold and ivory. The god is well muscled and larger than human size. He was human once, the son of the god Apollo and Coronis, the crow woman. You know some of the story. As a boy, Asklepios was taught medicine by Chiron the centaur, a being half human and half animal. Chiron is the model of the wounded healer: he bleeds from a wound inflicted by an accident, a wound he can never heal.

To become a god, Asklepios had to die and be reborn. In his great compassion, Asklepios, as a human, expanded his healing practice to include raising the dead. Zeus struck him down with a thunderbolt. In death, he was transfigured, becoming a god who appears to humans in dreams and visions. Certainly you know a story like this.

The breathing likeness of the god is enthroned and has a dog at his feet. Asklepios is inseparable from his dogs; it's said that in infancy he was nourished by a dog. If you have a wound or a rash and are very lucky, right now one of the temple dogs might come to you and heal you with his friendly slobber. Serapis is often depicted with a dog as well, always a black dog. On a coin now in the Museum of Fine Arts in Boston, it is Cerberus, the black dog who guards the gates of the Underworld, who lies at Serapis's feet.

Asklepios holds his hand over the head of an enormous snake. He has raised the serpent energy yet manages to control and contain it. Truth comes with goose bumps. Are you feeling them yet? There are live snakes in the grass around you. You will spend tonight in an incubation listening to the snakes of Asklepios slithering around you in the dark. The "health-giving snakes," Statius called them.[24] What part will the snake play in your healing? You sense its connection with the earth, and the gifts and challenges of the fertile dark. You can't miss the raw sexual vitality it suggests. Do you know yet that you are here to claim the snake's power to shed your old skin?

You are not done with looking. There are images carved on the throne of the god. One of them shows the hero Perseus beheading the snake-woman Medusa. Medicine may be poison, poison may be medicine, as it was for the Thracian Galen treated with a drug derived from a snake and theriac salt.

You may be drawn, or guided, to a *tholos*, a beautiful round building of white stone. On its airy, light-filled upper levels, there are wall paintings that suggest beauty and leisure and entertainment. But you feel a strangeness here, the sense that something is looking at you from the other side of the painted scenes. A wineglass is raised, and through the glass you see a woman's eyes staring at you.

Below the airy upper level of the *tholos*, there are deep underground chambers, maybe even a labyrinth. By the flickering light of oil lamps, you see darker paintings and the enigmatic image of the hooded dwarf called the Finisher. Beyond the commonsense prescriptions and the bedside manner, you are in a place where it is understood that sacred healing travels close to Death, and the passionate clarity that intimacy with Death can bring.

Your emotions are now fully engaged. Hope and fear struggle within you, like writhing snakes. You may be taken to the nearby theatre to sit on a seat cut into the living rock of the hillside and let your emotions be purged through the catharsis of deep tragedy. But you won't be left in the tragic mode. Afterward, you'll blush and honk and chortle as bawdy comics claim the stage, one of them flapping a fake phallus as long as his body.

With the lighting of candles, you are made ready to enter the Abaton, the "forbidden dormitory" of the god — forbidden to those who have not undergone the necessary preparations.

You join in hymns and invocations to wake up the god and engage his attention. "*Egreo Paian Asklepios!*" "Wake, Asklepios the Healer!"

You sing his praises. "From sharp-sighted Death you rescued many who had advanced right to the gates of Hades whence none return."[25]

Your expectations are running high. You join the voices that call for the power of healing: "Healer of all, come, blessed one!"

You feel the shift in the night air as the chorus of voices responds, "*Megas o Asklepios!*" "Great is Asklepios!"

The Healing Night

Your bed for the night in the womblike space of the darkened chamber is an animal skin. A lambskin is always acceptable and comfortable, but you may need to lie on the skin of an animal that has shared your dreaming or your life odyssey in a deeper way. You may even lie on the skin of a lion, though if you presume to do that you must be ready to face the trials of Herakles, who had to earn his lion skin.

As you enter deeper into the night, maybe you'll want to add your own statement of intention to the ritual formulas. Aristides addressed Asklepios like this: "You in your kindness and love of man, relieve me of my disease and grant me the health that is required for the body to serve the purposes of the soul." Now *that* is a creative way to invite the benign intervention of a god of healing! From the viewpoint of a god or angel, a human who asks for help to serve "the purposes of the soul" must be rather more interesting than one who is just ringing changes on "Gimme" (as in: "Heal my liver" or "Cure my baldness" — something people actually wished for at Epidauros). However, Aristides, as a gentleman of late antiquity, could not resist slipping in a further wish: "And grant me a life lived with ease."[26] You'll probably spend most of the night drifting and nodding between sleep and waking, and some of it in that fruitful intermediate state where the big encounter often takes place.

"I seemed almost to touch him," wrote one supplicant. "Halfway between sleep and waking, I perceived that he was there in person. I wanted to open my eyes but I was anxious that he might leave. I listened and heard things, sometimes as in a dream, sometimes as in waking vision."[27] The god heals through the awesome power of his presence, by a wordless energy transfer.

The god may perform oneiric surgery. Interestingly, Aristides received this from Serapis rather than Asklepios: "It seemed to me that Serapis, in the form of his seated statues, took some sort of lancet, and made an incision around my face, going somehow under the gum itself in the root of the lips[,] . . . removing and purging refuse and changing it to its proper state."[28]

He also heals by telling patients to stand up and claim their power. He commands a man who has been crushed by chronic headaches to stand up straight and make the physical moves of an athlete.[29] Like the angels of the Bible, and like Jesus at Bethesda, he is forever telling people, "Get up!" In the Abaton of Epidauros, he gave this command to a man named Hermodikos, who was "paralyzed of body." He not only told the paralytic to get up and walk but also ordered him to go fetch something much heavier than a sleeping mat. Hermodikos did as he was told. He searched the hillside for the largest boulder he could carry and set it up in front of the Abaton as a testimonial to his dream cure.[30]

This is not only a god who gives orders; he's a god you can talk to. Asklepios may begin his night visit by discussing the price of his services, as any physician might do in a society where there is no standard pay scale. "What will you pay in order to be healed?" he asks a young man who is in agony with a kidney stone. "Ten dice," the youth proposes. The god is entertained by the implied gamble. In the morning, the young man is cured, and we can safely assume that he adds ten dice to the god's endowment.

The god proposes lifestyle changes, and he offers prescriptions. Some of these are plain common sense: eat more vegetables if you are constipated, gargle for a sore throat. A man vomiting blood is told that eating pine nuts with honey will help, and it does. Sometimes the god prescribes potions that a pharmacist of the time could fill without raising an eyebrow. Sometimes his prescriptions are a little more exotic (make a poultice of wine and ashes from the god's altar; eat partridge stuffed with frankincense) or require you to embody your belief in miracles (touch the base of his statue and then touch your eyes to cure blindness). Sometimes his remedies are very earthy indeed: get some exercise, get in the water (or stay out of it), change your diet, purge.

You have been programmed to see the god in his approved form, as an animated version of the statue in the courtyard of the sanctuary. But he may come in the shape of one of his animal familiars, as a snake or a dog or a bull. He may send another member of his family. One of his daughters, Hygeia or Panacea, may come to embrace or to tend you. The god may break free from the forms the sculptors have given him.

"The cult statue appeared to have three heads and to shine about with fire, except for the heads," wrote Aristides. In his vision, the worshippers stood before the shining, three-headed form, ready to sing the paian, the hymn of praise for the divine healer. The living statue gestured for them to leave, but motioned for Aristides to stay. Thrilled by this honor, the dreamer shouted out "the One," saluting the god. And the god responded, "It is *you*." Aristides wrote that this experience was "greater than life itself, and every disease was less than this, every grace was less than this. This made me able and willing to live."[31]

Something tremendous is going on here. We see what a scholar of the Epidaurian inscriptions describes as "the value of worship as a focusing lens for the inner life, making hopes and emotions external and actual."[32] But this vision goes far beyond that. When the god who appears to Aristides steps out of his standard form, he shows the dreamer he is more than a projected consensual hallucination; he is real. Then the god reveals to the dreamer that, at the same time, he is in no way external to the dreamer's own identity. He is both in there and out there. You think there's a contradiction? Go dream on it, as Jung did when confronted with the interplay of the psychic and the "psychoid." The gods we can talk to don't stay in boxes any longer than we do.

The Morning After

The morning after the night in the Abaton, stories are told and action plans are devised. The storytelling component is crucial. "For each of our days, as well as our nights, has a story," wrote Aristides in the book he composed from his dream journals and titled *Sacred Tales*.[33] And he described how an illness went into remission as he composed a long poem about the marriage of Coronis and Apollo.[34]

If you have received healing, you'll want to honor that and express your thanks. You may add to all those hanging miniatures in the orchard of body parts. You may host a feast to be shared with the god and his temple assistants. You may create or commission a work of art, an ode, a comic mime, or a theatrical production. The gods of healing love drama and other forms of entertainment, so anything you do in that line will be welcome.

You may have dream prescriptions to be filled or to be discussed. You may feel the need to check the remedies of the god against the counsel of regular doctors.

Galen observed that Asklepios was the doctor who helped patients to manage their "heat" by bringing it safely to boil or by reducing it. His methods were sometimes shocking to conventional thinkers. On a bitterly cold January night, when Aristides was weak and frail, wracked by a host of maladies, the god ordered him to take a cold plunge in an icy river. Aristides's doctor was initially skeptical but came to agree that the god was the chief physician, and that the patient should follow the dream prescription. He swam in the cold river. "When I came out, all my skin had a rosy hue and there was a lightness throughout my body." During the rest of the day and night, he felt "continuous warmth" of body and mind and "continuous pleasure."[35]

Aristides also listened to the god, rather than the doctors, when he was troubled by a "tumor" that grew very rapidly until a monstrous swelling extended from his groin to his navel. Several different physicians offered different advice. One wanted Aristides to take unspecified drugs; another wanted to "cauterize" the swelling, perhaps with quicklime; another gave the opinion that the patient was beyond help. In their nightly dialogues, Asklepios told Aristides he must simply soldier on and let the disease run its course. Eventually, he gave Aristides the formula for an astringent, heavy on salt, that helped relieve the swelling. When the swelling was completely gone, Aristides was left with horrible folds of loose skin that the doctors wanted to cut off. Again, the god counseled the dreamer to let nature run its course, and eventually advised that rubbing eggs on the skin wouldn't hurt. At the end of all this, according to Aristides, his body was unblemished. Modern physicians speculated that his "tumor" was actually an omental hernia, a condition that could bring excruciating pain, but could clear up through a natural progression.[36]

The early Christian apostles found that the healing gods were formidable rivals. Justinus noted that, when the gentiles were told that Jesus performed healings and raised the dead, "they brought forward Asklepios."[37] One way round this was not to attack the old gods head on but to play on resemblances. Justinus said, "We propound nothing new and different from what you believe regarding those whom you esteem sons of Jupiter.... Asklepios, who, though he was a great healer, was struck by a thunderbolt, and ascended to heaven."[38]

Appropriation of the powers and methods and sites of the older gods proved smarter than controversy. This may go deep, if Morton Smith is correct in his contention that some of the earliest images of Jesus Christ were portraits of Asklepios that had been appropriated and renamed.[39]

Patricia Cox Miller observes that Asklepios "lived on in the cult of the saints."[40] There is a spectacular example in the cult of Saint Thecla of Seleucia, which lay on the Mediterranean coast of what is now Turkey. According to legend, Thecla was converted by Paul, who inveighed against the great healing temples of Ephesus and Pergamon. She was actually born from the imagination of the author of a second-century Christian romance, a work derided by the early church father Tertullian as pure fiction. Despite her dubious origins, she became hugely popular as the patron saint of a dream incubation center, healing by appearing in dreams of the sick who slept in her church, and by working miracles.[41]

TROUBLING THE WATERS

Whatever else goes on in the precinct of a healing god or saint, you leave with a story that is bigger than and different from the one you were living before. If you wish to continue your healing, you will find ways to carry and create from that story.

In one of his most powerful passages, Aristides described the experience of initiation by means of a cosmic vision of the Angel That Troubles the Waters. When he revealed himself in his cosmic form, Serapis was as terrible to Aristides as was Krishna when he unveiled himself in the same way to the archer on the field of battle: "There were ladders, which delimited the region above and below the earth, and the power of the god on each side, and there were other things, which caused a wonderful feeling of terror, and perhaps cannot be told to all.... Serapis is able to carry men wherever he wishes."[42]

We want to know more about the secret of Bethesda, and the Angel That Troubles the Waters. We can go there as dream archeologists. Here's a glimpse of what we might find:

You are at the pool in the time of Jesus, when Rome rules this part of the world. Notice how you are dressed. The place stinks of rotting flesh (lepers are here), feces, and unwashed linens. You may want to sniff a sachet containing sweet-scented herbs, a kind of potpourri. You give a wide berth to the many dubious practitioners peddling charms and readings to the credulous. You notice sacrificial lambs being led through the nearby Sheep Gate for rituals at the great temple of Jerusalem. You recognize the bright white light carried and transferred by the genuine healers among the packs of charlatans. One of them, whose light blazes very strongly, may be the Christ or one of those infused with his power.

You go down the steps, beneath the colonnade, taking care to avoid the desperate hands of those who reach for you from all sides, hoping that by touching some part of you, in your present form, they might receive a healing.

You may picture a loved one who is challenged by illness walking with you toward the healing waters.

There are chthonic daimons at the pool that become larger and stronger as the hot spring bubbles up from deep below. The pool is not inviting. It may remind you of hot baths or hot tubs that have been used by too many people, who have left their effluvia behind. The waters are unclean, and they reek of sulfur.

But with the rushing of the waters, a portal opens, and there is now no doubt that this place is a mouth of the Underworld. With the rushing of the waters, you gain a sense of the rushing of bulls. Serapis is also the Bull of the West. You may receive the impression — memory or imagination? — of the bulls carrying people beneath the waters, into the afterlife. Many have died here, some swallowed by the waters. There is healing at this place, but it might be the healing that comes through physical death. This is a gate into the Great Below. You sense you are recognized and you are welcome.

This has become a part of my own story. Make it part of your own if it speaks to you. The important thing is to *choose* your story and make sure it is big enough to live and die in, until you find an even bigger one.

We are reminded by Aristides's account — of his recurring cycles of illness, dreaming, and recovery through creativity — that one episode of healing may be far from definitive. It may be hard for us to identify with Aristides, with all his quirks and his vanity. Yet we learn something from the way his illnesses drove him to new acts of creation and new depths of vision and initiation.

The larger theme is brought out brilliantly by Thornton Wilder in his version, titled *The Angel That Troubled the Waters*. In this short play, Wilder gives us a physician waiting by the pool, hoping to be released from an unnamed malady and a "fearful flaw in my heart." When the water moves, an angel refuses to let him enter the pool. "Without your wound where would your power be? It is your very remorse that makes your low voice tremble into the hearts of men. The very angels themselves cannot persuade the wretched and blundering children on earth as can one human being broken on the wheels of living. In love's service only the wounded soldiers can serve. Draw back."[43]

The power of healing comes through the wound. If the physician is healed, he will lose his power to heal others. Aristides was a speaker and writer, not a doctor. Yet creative expression was his mode of healing and brought gifts to others, as when his eloquence persuaded the emperor to provide earthquake relief for the city of Smyrna on a scale that led the town fathers to erect a statue to Aristides and proclaim him the new founder of the city. We can find many analogues for Aristides's recurring cycles of illness and creative rebound in the dreaming of writers, to which we now turn.

CHAPTER 5

❧

FROM THE DREAM LIBRARY

Literature is nothing other than a directed dream.

— JORGE LUIS BORGES, *Doctor Brodie's Report*

The raw sexuality of her call to her lover is wild and shocking: "*Plow my vulva!*" He plunges into her like a "wild bull." When they couple, he is the green life of all growing things and she is the Queen of Heaven. He is Dumuzi and she is Inanna.

But she is called to go down into the dark places and travel a terrifying path of ordeal and initiation. When she returns, transformed, to the surface world, she finds that her man has forgotten her and is playing king of all he surveys. Her angry curse sucks the light out of his day. Now Dumuzi dreams that everything turns against him. Trees are uprooted, his hearth fire is doused, his drinking cup is thrown down, his shepherd's crook is taken away. A fierce raptor seizes a lamb from his sheepfold, and he knows that something fearsome and unforgiving is coming for him.

The churn lies silent; no milk is poured.
The cup lies shattered; Dumuzi is no more.
The sheepfold is given to the winds.

Death is coming for him, and his only hope lies in the love and feminine wisdom of his younger sister, Geshtin-anna. She is a reader, "a tablet-knowing scribe" who knows the meaning of words and of dreams.

She tells him, "Your demons are coming for you." She helps him hide, but in the end he cannot escape his own demons. He is overpowered by them and carried in the talons of a raptor down to the realm of Inanna's dark double, the Queen of the Underworld, and into his own cycle of death and rebirth. Grieving, both Inanna and his constant sister, drumming like shamans, will seek him in the lower world. And they will make a deal by which Geshtin-anna will take her brother's place in the Underworld for half the year, giving him time up top with the goddess in her sunnier disposition. But that is a later story in the cycle of Inanna.

The Dream of Dumuzi is the oldest recorded dream. It was written in Sumer nearly five thousand years ago, scored with marks on baked clay that look like the tracks of a very thoughtful sandpiper. Almost certainly, it was written by a woman. We can't miss the fact that the first dream interpreter on record is a woman who can read and write, the "tablet-knowing scribe."

Geshtin-anna becomes the goddess of dream divination (and of wine). Her consort, who is depicted with serpents shooting up from his shoulders, has an awkward-looking name, Ningishzida, which is worth inspecting closely. Chastely translated by previous generations of scholars as "Lord of the Upright Tree," it actually means "Lord of the Erect Penis" or "Lord of the Hard-On." Those Mesopotamians knew a thing or two about sexual arousal in dreams and how real magic rides on sexual energy.[1]

The Dream of Dumuzi, unclothed in its beauty and terror in a modern translation by Diane Wolkstein, is great writing, and it takes us where great writers do not fear to go: into the inner chambers of the heart, into the demon-haunted mind, into the mysteries of death and rebirth. Thanks to its survival, we can say without hesitation that one of the first uses of writing — which was invented in Sumer — was to record dreams, and that one of the great things that emerged from recording dreams — at least five thousand years ago — was literature. Writers have *always* been dreamers.

Dumuzi was king of Uruk, not far from Ur, the most famous city of the Sumerians and the one from which Abraham set out to found a new people. So Bert States is doubly correct when he says "dreaming is the Ur-form of all fiction."[2]

States suggests that storytelling springs from the same "skill" that allows us to produce dream narratives.[3] He compares the mental state of the creative writer to that of a lucid dreamer: "Just as the lucid dreamer is slightly awake, slightly *outside* the dream, while being largely *inside* it, so the waking author is slightly asleep, or slightly *inside* the fiction while being largely *outside* it."[4] Many fiction writers (including me) would attest to the accuracy of this description. It probably applies to creative minds from many fields operating in a flow state of relaxed attention or attentive relaxation. In this state, as Samuel Beckett wrote of Proust, the writer may also be, for the moment, "an extratemporal being."[5]

Dreams provided both energy and inspiration for literary creation. As a boy, Aeschylus (born 525 BCE) was sent to watch over ripening grapes in a vineyard.

When he dozed off, Dionysus, god of wine and drama, appeared to him and gave him instructions for a new kind of theatre. Prior to this, ancient Greek drama was rather static ritual, with a single actor on stage and a chorus that did not interact directly with him. Aeschylus was inspired in his dream to introduce a second actor; this was the birth of Western theatre. He went on to write ninety plays, although only seven are extant.

"Poetry is always the result of flooding," a young poet told Stefania Pandolfo as she journeyed among rural Moroccan villagers for whom dreaming and poetry are vitally important and always interweaving. A real poem bursts from an emotion that is inundating, overwhelming — until it finds creative release.[6] The most respected poet in the area, one Sheikh Mohammed, was alien to poetry until he dreamed of a flood. The dream came at a time of personal trauma, when he was close to despair. Previously a violent man of action, he had managed to blow off his right hand in a gun accident. He dreamed the river was coming down in flood, its front like a mountain, carrying along everything it encountered in its path, trees and carrion and debris. Instead of fleeing, he stood there in the dry riverbed, watching and waiting. Then he opened his mouth and swallowed the flood and everything borne along by it. He recounted the dream to his mother, and she told him that he had become a poet. This became his life's calling.[7]

From the priestess-scribe who wrote Dumuzi's story to Stephen King and Neil Gaiman, writers have always found that dreams provide wonderful material for stories and novels, scripts and poems. The dream may provide the rough first sketch of a theme or a plot or a character, with everything still to be worked out and delivered — perhaps with the help of subsequent dreams — over a considerable period of time. The dream may have the structure and detail required for a finished story or poem (but is unlikely to be "finished" in the sense that it is truly good writing before the raw report has been shaped and polished). The dream may be inserted in a narrative and attributed to one of the characters (as I did in the case of Nikolsky, my boozy KGB philosopher, in my novel *Moscow Rules* and as Graham Greene did in the case of Querry in *A Burnt-Out Case*). The dream may be delivered as a story without a frame: Franz Kafka delivered a nightmare in *Metamorphosis* while insisting, in the tale, that the man who turned into a giant bug was not dreaming.

The literary dream has been used as a plot device in many ways. It may take the reader into the inner life of a character. It may set up critical narrative tension — for example, between a character's desires and his conscience, a central theme in Dostoyevsky's fictional dreams.

The dream can be used as an architectural device to open and frame a story that may be anything but a dream; the medieval *Roman de la Rose* is a classic example, from an age when dreams were greatly respected. The classic Chinese novel *The Dream of the Red Chamber* opens with a goddess creating a mountain from 36,501 pieces of stone, one of which — rejected — is a speaking rock whose complaint is heard by two immortals. The rock is gifted with a very mobile life, in different forms, in the mortal world — known to gods and immortals as the Red Dust — and elsewhere.

Writing and dreaming are closely related in daily *practice*. Writers who keep journals and record their dreams are giving themselves a warm-up, flexing the creative muscles that will work on the larger project. Writers who don't record their dreams with any regularity nonetheless rise from sleep with their heads full of words — as Dickens related in a letter to a certain Dr. Stone[8] — that are pressing to come out.

A writer's dream may help "break up the great fountains of the deep" (a phrase Mark Twain used repeatedly), releasing the power of long-buried memories or bringing into consciousness ideas that have been growing in the preconscious or the deeper unconscious for years or decades. This is how Aslan came to C. S. Lewis, giving him the key to Narnia. As "Jack" Lewis recalls,

> The *Lion* all began with a picture of a Faun carrying an umbrella and parcels in a snowy wood. The picture had been in my head since I was about sixteen. Then one day, when I was about forty, I said to myself: "Let's try to make a story about it."
>
> At first I had little idea how the story would go. But then suddenly Aslan came bounding into it. I think I had been having a good many dreams about lions about that time. Apart from that, I don't know where the Lion came from or why he came. But once he was there he pulled the whole story together, and soon he pulled the six other Narnian stories in after him.[9]

Finally, it is in dreams and flow states that writers come into contact with inner helpers. Robert Louis Stevenson communed with his "Brownies" while in states of reverie, and gave them the credit for accomplishing more than half his literary work. Yeats spoke of the "mingling of minds" that can bring assistance,[10] in a creative venture, from intelligences that seem to belong to other times or other dimensions. Milton described the source of his inspiration as

> my celestial patroness, who deigns
> Her nightly visitation unimplored,

And dictates to me slumbering, or inspires
Easy my unpremeditated prose. (*Paradise Lost* IX.21–24)

Milton spoke of "being milked" after his nights of inspiration, as — totally blind by the time he composed his most famous work — he dictated to a scribe.[11]

When they are truly "on," many writers experience the sense that they have entered a creative partnership with a larger power, a power the ancients used to call the genius or the *eudaimon* (the good demon). We'll see how some writers have developed the ability to enter a certain kind of imaginal space — call it the Dream Library — where such encounters are easy.

DREAMS INTO STORIES, STORIES INTO DREAMS

I dreamed of conversing with Roger Caillois in French before I started reading him, and I sought out his published works to honor my dream. I found that he was a wonderfully gifted French dream explorer and literary adventurer, a friend of the Surrealists, a student of games and myths, and a traveler in the realms of stones and minerals. He edited a remarkable anthology titled *The Dream Adventure*, which sows many fertile ideas about the relationship between dreams and story. The anthology has three parts. The first is a lively introduction by Caillois distinguishing two fundamental approaches to dreams — that of those who wish to interpret dreams, and that of those who wish to enter and explore the dreamspace itself (which is vastly more exciting and creative).

Next comes a selection of dream experiences from classical Chinese texts, many of which show the influence of Taoist modes of soul journeying. In one of the Chinese tales, a man on his way home is shocked to hear his wife partying with strangers inside a temple. He grabs a loose tile and hurls it, breaking plates on the table and scattering the revelers. When he returns home, he finds his wife rising from her bed, chuckling over a funny dream in which she was partying with strangers in a temple, then interrupted by someone throwing a tile that broke the crockery. "This then," Po Hsing-chien (776–827) concludes, "is a case of dreaming spirits being encountered by a waking person."[12]

In another Chinese tale, P'o Sung-ling's "The Painted Wall" — written long before *Through the Looking Glass* or the film *What Dreams May Come* — a man called Chu enters a picture and marries the beautiful maiden he admired in it. Recalled to the other side by his companions' shouts, he turns and sees that the maiden in the picture now has the topknot of a married woman. How can this be? A priest responds, "Visions have their origins in those who see them."[13]

The third, and major, section of *The Dream Adventure* is devoted to dream-inspired short fiction. As all good writers know, while many dreams come fully shaped as stories or scripts, it can be a challenge to turn dreams into *effective* fiction. If we start by revealing that the action takes place in a dream, we may set the reader at a distance, losing the magical "just-so" quality of an actual dream experience. So some of the most dreamlike fiction may never mention the word "dream." Caillois has hunted with great skill for stories in which dreaming is an integral and thrilling part of the action.

One of my favorites is a switcheroo (whose title in this collection is "The Distance") by Argentine Julio Cortázar. In this chilling story, Alicia Reyes dreams again and again, with increasing vividness and detail, of a sad woman with broken shoes on a bridge in the cold of Budapest; people beat her, and she is miserable and alone. When she marries, Alicia persuades her husband to take her to Budapest, where she's never been. Out walking, she finds herself drawn to the bridge she saw in the dream. In the middle of the bridge is the sad woman with the broken shoes. They embrace and Alicia knows ecstasies of joy. As they separate, she begins to scream — because she sees the smartly dressed form of Alicia Reyes, hair slightly mussed by the wind, walking confidently away.... They have switched bodies.

Another of my favorites is "The Brushwood Boy" by Rudyard Kipling, who was no stranger to the possibilities of dreaming. In Kipling's story a boy and a girl who have never seen each other in waking life start meeting each other in dreams, and have high adventures that often begin at a pile of brushwood near an ocean. As the years pass, they continue to meet and adventure in their shared world, which defies the laws of ordinary reality. Decades after the first of these dreams, they meet each other in waking life, recognize each other, and come together as a couple.

I do not know what inspired Kipling to write this tale, through perhaps I should, since I once lived in a house in East Sussex that he visited which was just over the hill from the setting that inspired "Puck of Pook's Hill." I *do* know that the premise of "The Brushwood Boy" — that in dreams we may live continuous lives, shared with others — is quite correct and (if better understood) would transform our consensual notions of reality. I know this because one of my soul sisters and I started meeting each other in the dreamspace when we were nine years old, more than three decades before we met in waking life — and have been sharing adventures in parallel realities ever since.

DREAMING IN GREENELAND

When I first traveled to Paris as a foreign correspondent, early in the 1970s, the office secretary made a reservation for me at the Saint James & Albany, which turned out to be twin hotels — very handsome Right Bank townhouses — separated by a quiet courtyard with a fountain and flagstones and flowerbeds and shade trees. It struck me that the courtyard between the twin hotels was a liminal space, ideal for intrigue and trespass of various kinds — for games involving lovers, or spies, even players from different worlds.

I later discovered, to my great delight, that Graham Greene had similar feelings and had made this location a part of Greeneland, the fictive world of his novels. He used the courtyard of the Saint James & Albany as the setting for a hilarious scene in *Travels with My Aunt* in which two women, meeting by chance, discuss the lovers with whom they tryst in secret in each of the twin hotels — and then, when M. Dambreuse arrives with his wife and children, discover that their lovers are the same man.

Graham Greene led many lives, but first and last he was a writer, with a professional writer's discipline. Through his many intrigues, both personal and political, he managed to sit down almost every day from 7 AM to 9 AM — on a verandah in Tahiti or a cottage in Brighton — and knock out his quota of five hundred words, and he did this for seventy years, producing a steady stream of popular novels and essays. A crucial part of Greene's practice was to write down his dreams. He started keeping a dream journal when he was sixteen. He often reported his dreams in letters to lovers and friends. Over the last twenty-five years of his life, he recorded his dreams with great faithfulness — though in fiendishly difficult handwriting — in notebooks that are now in an archive in Texas. His last literary project was to edit a selection of his dreams for a posthumous collection he titled *A World of My Own*.

The interweaving of Greene's dream life with his other lives makes a fascinating study, for which the primary source materials are unusually extensive. We see how a man who chose to live on the dangerous edges of the world was able to create — richly and repeatedly — from the borderlands of dreaming. We can track many different modes in which a writer can create from dreams, from receiving the initial idea for a story, to solving a problem during sleep, to bridging a narrative gap, to dreaming deep into a character's life.

As a young boy, Greene had psychic dreams, often involving death by water, a prospect that terrified him. On the night the *Titanic* sank, when he was just seven, he dreamed of a shipwreck and a man in oilskins bent double beside a companionway under the blow of a great wave.[14]

He was miserable at school — nothing unusual in the life of a creative and sensitive individual — and ran away when he was sixteen. This was highly embarrassing for the family, since Graham's father was headmaster. They decided to send him to London to be psychoanalyzed, which was still a novel idea in 1920, especially for a teenage boy. The analyst selected, Kenneth Richmond, had no formal training; he was a writer with spiritualist leanings who followed an eclectic approach. While Greene was boarding with him in Lancaster Gate, Richmond instructed him to write down his dreams. In midmorning sessions, Greene was expected to tell a dream and then give his associations to the key images while the analyst merely listened. When Greene did not recall a dream, he made something up. The whole experience — which he later described as the happiest six months of his life[15] — laid the foundation for his literary career by training him to write from dreams and invent stories. And the frequent presence of well-known writers (including Walter de la Mare, another avid student of dreams) in the Lancaster Gate house encouraged Greene to think of becoming a writer.

Kenneth Richmond's beautiful wife, Zoe — about whom Greene had mildly erotic dreams — thought Graham was clairvoyant, "a natural medium." While in Lancaster Gate, Greene dreamed of a ship going down in the Irish Sea. That same night, just after midnight, the *Rowan* sank in the Irish Sea.[16]

In some of his precognitive or clairvoyant dreams, Greene found himself in the situation of one of the victims. At age twenty-one, he dreamed of another shipboard disaster in which he was being ordered to jump overboard from an upper deck. He later read the news of a terrible wreck in a storm off the Yorkshire coast in which the captain ordered his men to jump into the violent sea, and all but two were drowned.[17] Greene speculated that "on an occasion like this there must be terrific mental waves of terror, and my mind seems to be particularly attuned to the terror of drowning wave."

His youthful psychic ability to dream his way into someone else's situation resembles his mature ability as a novelist to dream his way into his characters' lives. Later in life he observed that "sometimes identification with a character goes so far that one may dream his dream and not one's own."[18]

In one of his scary dreams from the Lancaster Gate period, he was pursued by sinister Chinese agents. He took shelter in a hut with an armed detective. Just as he began to feel safe, he looked at the hand grasping the revolver and was horrified to see that his supposed protector had "the long nails of a Chinaman."[19] That dream may have been a life rehearsal foreshadowing the games of spy and counterspy he would later play as an officer of Britain's Secret Intelligence Service and a lifelong friend of the notorious mole Kim Philby.

Later dreams rehearsed him for the illness and slide into alcoholism of his longtime lover Catherine Walton. He wrote to Catherine in 1957 about a strange dream in which he found her in an awful boardinghouse, "very ill in your bones." The dream began to play out in Catherine's life and body seven years later.[20]

But here we'll focus on how Greene's dreams influenced his writing. He said that two of his novels, *It's a Battlefield* and *The Honorary Consul*, both started with dreams. Greene also dreamed the plots and characters of entire short stories. One of these dream-inspired tales involves the surreal situation of a leper who calls on the doctor who has consigned him to a public hospital, to beg for more discreet private treatment, only to find that the doctor's house has been turned into a casino for the night. In the dream, Greene seemed to be the doctor.[21]

When he was writing *A Burnt-Out Case* — which drew heavily on his diary of a trip to the Congo — Greene came to a point in the plot where he was stuck. Then the author dreamed of himself in the role of his character Querry and found he could insert his dream "without change" in the novel, "where it bridged a gap in the narrative which for days I had been unable to cross."[22]

Greene made it a habit to solve writing problems in his sleep, noting that it is not necessary to remember the content of a dream in order to receive a dream-inspired solution. "When an obstacle seems insurmountable, I read the day's work before sleep.... When I wake the obstacle has nearly always been removed: the solution is there and obvious — perhaps it came in a dream which I have forgotten."[23]

He harvested some of his personal dreams and assigned them to characters in his novels. Separated from his lover Catherine, Greene dreamed that he discovered she had slept with four other men (apart from her complaisant husband, Lord Harry Walton). In the dream he took revenge by having sex with another woman in front of her. After a spat, they came together. He adapted this dream for a scene in *The Comedians*.[24]

In another dream, reflecting his lifelong preoccupation with religion, Greene gave a lecture on the theme that God evolves, as well as man, and that behind their apparent duality God and Satan are one. He later made use of this theory in a passage in *The Honorary Consul* where his character explains that God has a "night-side" as well as a "day-side"; the night-side will wither away ("like your communist state, Eduardo") as God and man both evolve.[25]

Graham Greene was a man of mystery who had much to hide in his private life and in his engagement with the worlds of power and espionage. At the very end of his life, his official biographer was still pleading for clarity on his relationship with Kim Philby. "I am my books," Greene told journalists when they tried to probe his identity.[26] He generally referred to himself in the third person, as "one," not "I."

He became well known for espousing left-wing causes, yet cautioned that "the writer should always be ready to change sides at the drop of a hat. He speaks up for the victims, and the victims change."[27]

For Greene the great mystery, at the end, concerned what follows death. He thought — and dreamed — about this all his life. He was greatly affected by a series of dream encounters with his father after his death. Charles Greene, once the aloof headmaster of the school Graham had hated, died during World War II while Graham was in Sierra Leone "running ineffectually a one-man office of the Secret Service." In one of the cock-ups typical of Greeneland, Greene received the telegram announcing his father's death before he received the previous telegram telling him his father was seriously ill. For many years afterward, Greene dreamed that his father was shut away in a hospital out of touch with his wife and children. This was not Charles's situation in his physical life; until the end, he had stayed at home with his wife, who gave him insulin shots for his diabetes. The dream story changed — and its meaning became clearer — when Greene dreamed his father appeared at a turn in the road as he was driving with his mother, and flagged him down. His father jumped into the back of the car with a joyful smile and announced happily that he had been released from the hospital that day. Greene wrote to his mother, "Perhaps there is some truth in the idea of purgatory, and this was the moment of release."[28]

Later, Greene had a disturbing dream suggesting he might be extinguished after death because of his lack of belief. "I had been aware of people I had loved who called me to join them. But I had chosen, by my lack of belief, extinction. A great black cone like a candle extinguisher was to be dropped over my head."[29] But he did not go out like that. He left sure of continuing life, ready for new travels, regretting only separation from the last woman to share his life, Yvonne Cloetta. A week before his death, knowing it was at hand, he said to Yvonne in the hospital at Vevey: "It may be an interesting experience; at last I shall know what lies on the other side of the fence."[30]

Toward the end, he made this note in Yvonne's "red book" of their conversations: "Perhaps in Paradise we are given the power to help the living. I picture Paradise as a place of activity. Sometimes I pray not *for* the dead friends but to dead friends, asking their help."[31] Yvonne recalls that "he worked every morning, as he always did, right up to the end, on his book of dreams."[32] Evidently he came to believe that through dreams (as one of his characters said in *The Confidential Agent*) "there was something in the warring crooked uncertain world he could trust beside himself."[33]

Things Happen in Russia
That Don't Happen on Earth

*In Russia many things happened and happen
that don't and won't happen on earth.*

— CHARACTER IN A DREAM IN *Martyn Zadeka*, BY ALEKSEI REMIZOV

Given their wild history, it is hardly surprising that Russians are wild dreamers. A careful cross-cultural study of dream content, based on 1,666 dream reports from six countries, found that Russians report "exotic" dreams — with bizarre or fantastic elements, or features suggestive of paranormal experience — far more often than other populations in the test. Among the Russians, 12.7 percent of the dreams reported were categorized as "exotic"; for the Americans, the proportion was just 5.7 percent.[34]

In Russian literature — as a Russian friend puts it — dreams are "low-hanging fruit," at least they were prior to Stalin's effort to flatten and compact the imagination. The lives of Russian writers are often as wild as their dreams.

Alexander Griboyedov (1795–1829) was a character larger than any he created. You might not guess it from his picture, in which his small, round glasses and bookish expression give him the aspect of a nineteenth-century geek, or from his surname, which sounds like a joke; it means "mushroom eater." He was inspired by a dream to write his much-loved verse comedy *Woe from Wit*, still frequently performed in Russia today. The story deserves to be told just as his friend Faddey Bulgarin related it:

> This is how this comedy came into being. While in Persia, in 1821, Griboyedov longed for Petersburg, Moscow, his friends ... and for the theatre which he loved passionately. He lay down to sleep in a pavilion in a garden and saw a dream that showed him his beloved fatherland.... In his dream, he described the outline of a comedy he had written to a circle of friends, and even read them several passages from it.
>
> Upon waking, Griboyedov takes a pencil, runs into the garden, and during the same night sketches the outline of *Woe from Wit* and

composes several scenes of the first act. The comedy occupied all his free time, and he finished it in Tiflis in 1822.[35]

Bulgarin is not the most reliable source. He was a shady character, a police informer and provocateur who operated under many flags, including false flags. He also knew how to tell a good story; he produced Russia's first blockbuster novel. However, confirmation of at least one element in his account comes from a draft letter Griboyedov wrote to a friend — apparently a fellow playwright — telling him that he dreamed he promised the friend, while in Persia, that he would complete a new play within one year.[36]

In the comedy itself, the heroine tells her father a complex dream that suggests — in a way that was novel in Russian literature — that she may be a little more than a social flirt and anticipates later developments in a love triangle involving rival suitors.[37]

Griboyedov was also a hussar officer, a linguist, and a diplomat. Shortly after he married a lovely sixteen-year-old girl (and promptly got her pregnant), he was sent to Persia as the tsar's ambassador. Anti-Russian sentiment in Tehran was running strong, and it exploded when an Armenian eunuch sought sanctuary in the Russian embassy with two Armenian girls from the shah's harem. A huge Iranian mob did to the Russians what another mob did to the Americans a century and a half later: it stormed the embassy. Griboyedov fought the horde, saber in hand, at the head of his Cossack guards, but they were overwhelmed by the violent tide. The playwright was beheaded, his body was kicked to pieces in the street. When news reached his teenage widow, she miscarried.[38]

An unlikely but entirely historical Russian character strongly linked to dreaming in popular consciousness is Stepan Razin, a seventeenth-century Cossack leader and world-class brigand. Soon after Razin's execution, a folk song about the Cossack's foreboding dream began to circulate. In the song, Razin himself recounts a dream in which his horse starts prancing around nervously, "evil winds from the east" tear his cap off his head, and his weapons fall to the ground. Razin asks if anyone can interpret his dream. A "shrewd *yesaul*" (Cossack officer) tells him the worst: the dream spells doom for Razin and his band.

Razin and his dream song fired up the imaginations of many Russian writers and musicians, including Pushkin. Marina Tsvetaeva wrote a cycle of poems about Razin and his dream. In the late 1970s, singer Zhanna Bichevskaya popularized her own version of the song.

Low-Hanging Fruit

> *Young Tatiana*
> *And with her, Onegin,*
> *First appeared to me*
> *in a vague dream.*

— PUSHKIN, *Eugene Onegin*

Alexander Pushkin (1799–1837) knew that some dreams come true. In his letters and diaries, he noted a number of prophetic dreams, including a friend's report that, on the day Catherine the Great died, her former wet nurse dreamed she was holding her "little Catherine" in her lap, just as she had done sixty years before. A few months after he heard that story, Pushkin was able to test his own ability to see across time and space in a dream. He wrote to his wife that he dreamed the young Princess Polina Vyazemskaya had died, and woke in horror. A few days later, he received news that the princess had succumbed to consumption in Rome.[39] Ironically, he may have missed a precognitive message about the circumstances of his own death.

Dreams are central to the narrative structure and character development in all of Pushkin's work and were sometimes a direct source of inspiration. In *Boris Godunov*, Pushkin made a vitally important distinction between two kinds of dream: the *son*, or spontaneous dream during sleep, and the *mechta*, a daydream or fantasy. In the psychology of his stories and ballads, the spontaneous night dream is usually reliable, offering insight into the future and a corrective to people's tendencies to lose themselves in wishful or delusional thinking. The truth of the *son* versus the possible entrapment of the *mechta* becomes the key source of narrative tension in Pushkin's greatest work. The challenge is that people are confused about what is going on in their dreams, or lose them altogether and thereby condemn themselves to act out unfortunate events that the dreams could have helped them avoid, or avoid these events only at the price of tough lessons in the school of knocks.

Pushkin discloses in the penultimate stanza of his great verse novel, *Eugene Onegin*, that this tremendous work was conceived in a "vague dream." A thrilling dream by the heroine, Tatiana, is at the heart of the story. It features a bear and a Halloween fright night cast.

Before she goes to bed, Tatiana removes her "silken sash." There's a little sexual frisson in the picture of a pretty girl disrobing, but chills and thrills beyond that. The action is apparently taking place on the night of January 5–6, the time of an old pagan festival. This was — and is — a popular time for young women to practice divination by invoking the help of the dark powers, or *nechistaya sila* ("unclean forces"), commonly described simply as *nechist*. Prior to divining, people remove their baptismal crosses and belts to signal they are willing to entertain powers they would normally shun. When we hear that Tatiana removes her sash before going to bed, we are getting a hint that she is getting stripped for more than sleep or sex.

Now Tatiana is inside her dream, walking through a dark snow-covered glade. She approaches a creek, which is mysteriously free of ice. Two flimsy planks are laid over the water. Tatiana is afraid of crossing the creek over such a weak bridge. Then suddenly a large shaggy bear emerges from under the snow, offers Tatiana his paw, and helps her over the bridge. Tatiana struggles through the deep snow with the bear following her. When she collapses, the bear grabs her and carries her through the forest to a small hut, where his relative lives. The bear leaves Tatiana in the front room and disappears.

Behind the door, Tatiana hears loud voices and the clinking of glasses, as if at a "big funeral." Her curiosity overpowers her fear, and she peeks through the crack in the door. In the main room she sees a wild crowd of monsters, gnomes, witches, and skeletons, all seated around the table, with Onegin presiding. Tatiana wants to get away, but Onegin notices her and reveals her presence to the monsters. They start howling, "She's mine! She's mine!" but Onegin claims her for himself — at which point the monsters vanish. When Onegin lays Tatiana on a bench and lowers his head to her shoulder, Tatiana's sister Olga and Lensky, her fiancé, appear. A violent quarrel ensues. Onegin grabs a long knife and kills Lensky. Dark shadows gather and are pierced by a terrible scream — and Tatiana wakes up.

She tries to figure out the meaning of her dream with the help of a popular dream book, but gets nowhere with that. Maybe because she is enmeshed in superstition and magical symbols, Tatiana focuses on theatrical elements in the dream and misses its literal warning. She chooses not to share the dream with her sister Olga. If the sisters had been able to focus on the possibility that the quarrel and the killing could actually be played out, they might have been able to avoid the incident that would lead to the duel in which Onegin actually kills Lensky.

Eerily, Pushkin died under very similar circumstances, defending his young wife's honor against a nobleman who was rumored to be her lover. Life rhymes. It also seems possible that, in the dreamspace where he mined his literary creations, Pushkin, like Tatiana, had glimpsed a future death — and failed to apply the warning in his own life.

The tension between dreams and waking life is the common thread in all the fiction of Nikolai Gogol (1809–1852), another product of Cossack country whose early work featured the landscapes and legends of the Ukraine. He led a strange, marginal life. It is doubtful that he ever had sexual relations with another human being, and one of his stories centers on the protagonist's horrific dreams of the outcome of marriage; he sees himself being tormented by demonic geese and then forced to accept a "wife" in the form of a rug that is good for nothing.

The young Gogol once counseled his mother not to give credence to dreams, because they are just a "mixed salad" of waking incidents and preoccupations.[40] But his stories reflect a different and deeper understanding. In "A Terrible Vengeance," one of Gogol's Ukrainian tales, Danilo tells his wife, "You don't know even a tenth of what your soul knows."[41] However, they are unable to use the warnings in her prophetic dream to escape the series of tragedies that it foreshadows.

In a later story, "The Portrait," a physician tries to work with his patient's dreams in the cause of healing. He tries to detect "the secret relationship between the phantoms he saw in his dream and the events of his life,"[42] reflecting an appreciation that dreaming may be medicine that is both ancient and hypermodern. Once again, however, the attempt to make a bridge between dream guidance and waking life fails.

In some of Gogol's stories, the boundary between dreaming and waking becomes very porous. A character wakes with a letter in his hand that comes from his dream and was not there before.

Beyond previous Russian writers, Gogol was able to convey the fluidity and creative power of the twilight zone between sleep and waking. He gropes for a vocabulary to describe this state, playing with words like "semidream."

Gogol's literary dreams have fueled the Russian imagination, helping to generate some of the best work by Dostoyevsky, Bulgakov, and post-Soviet writers. Sadly, what worked in his writing did not work in his life. Haunted by dark dreams and inner demons, he fell under the spell of a fanatical church elder who persuaded him to burn the second volume of *Dead Souls* and took up extreme ascetic practices that contributed to his early and painful death. His torment was evoked in a Symbolist statue by Nikolai Andreyev that stood in

Moscow's Arbat Square until Stalin, who detested it, had it torn down; it survived and now stands in front of Gogol's former home.

On the day Dostoyevsky proposed to her, Anna Grigorievna noticed that the writer seemed in exceptionally good spirits. Had something special happened? "Yes, indeed! Last night I saw a wonderful dream." When Anna started to laugh, he said earnestly, "Please don't laugh. I attach great significance to dreams. My dreams are always prophetic."[43]

Long before Freud and Jung, Fyodor Dostoyevsky (1821–1881) developed a depth psychology of dreams in his novels and stories. One of the great lessons of *Crime and Punishment* — which is undoubtedly rooted in Dostoyevsky's personal dream life — is that the voice of conscience speaks clearly in dreams. If Raskolnikov had only been willing to listen to his dreams instead of the demented egomaniac in his head that kept telling him that he had the right to commit a terrible crime, he could never have gone through with the murder of the pawnbroker. While he is planning his crime, he dreams that he is a boy again, on a bridge, weeping and protesting as a brutal driver flogs his mare to death, insisting all the while that he has the right to do what he likes to the animal. Raskolnikov is shaken by the dream, which puts him in sympathy with the victim rather than the abuser. But he reverts to his plan.

After his crime and his confession, as he lies ill in a prison bed, he dreams that the world has fallen victim to a horrible plague caused by a new strain of infectious trichinae that are actually spirits with minds of their own. Plague victims become insane, yet believe themselves to be in possession of the ultimate secrets of science and life itself. In a mad world, humans feed on their own kind. Everyone will die except a few who have kept their minds and will start the human experiment all over again.

Here Dostoyevsky is improvising on one of his favorite themes: that thoughts and fantasies have a life of their own. Once born from the imagination and embodied as thought forms or elementals, they can act independently of their creator, turning against him and others. This concept is highly relevant to our contemporary condition.

Removing the Frames

Aleksei Remizov (1877–1957), a prolific Russian modernist writer, was driven by dreams. They were his creative engine, his dominant mental habitat, and his main literary vehicle. I can think of few authors, even within the dream-filled literary history of Russia, who have been so passionately involved with the dreamworld.

Remizov's youthful imagination was seized by folklore and medieval legends, and he wandered in his more forgettable writings through strange jungles of phantasmagoric forms. As a young romantic, he joined a revolutionary plot, was arrested by the tsarist secret police, and was shipped to Siberia for seven years. His experiences during the Bolshevik Revolution cured him of revolutionary sympathies. He moved to Paris in 1921 and spent the rest of his life there.

He is often compared to the Surrealists, whom he knew in Paris and who even feature in his dreams. But he despised the Surrealists' practice of automatic writing, insisting, "One has to take from the stream of words according to one's will, and not what comes automatically." He disliked the influence of both Freud and Marx in André Breton's thinking and was disgusted by the movement's embrace of Soviet communism, especially when the Surrealist review ran a fawning obituary in praise of the Soviets' brutal secret police chief, Dzherzhinsky, that opened with this line: "Alas, on a faraway sky, a star has forever ceased to shine."[44] Above all, Remizov long preceded the Surrealists in his use of dreams as literary texts, and he took dreams far more seriously.

Gogol was the writer who influenced him most. He devoted half of *The Fire of Things*, his book on Russian dream writing, to Gogol, whom he saw as the fountainhead. Turgenev's example inspired Remizov to develop his most characteristic technique, turning his own dream reports into stories or prose poems with minimal editing. When Turgenev did this, he often kept the frame, starting a story with the words "I dreamed" and ending "I woke up."

Remizov removed dreams from their frames and told them as stories of real experience. He used 340 of his own dreams in his books. He included a hundred of them in a book on dreams, *Martyn Zadeka*, whose title is borrowed from the dream interpreter in *Eugene Onegin*. Remizov's approach to dreams has nothing in common with that of psychoanalysis, which is forever hunting "latent" meanings and discarding the "manifest" content. For Remizov, writing from dreams is all about bringing through the rich, multisensory experience of the dreamworld, the smell and taste and touch and music. Working on a dream is not about laying bare some hidden meaning, but about giving a pitch-perfect voice to what is there in front of you. "To give the dream a voice is great art."[45]

Remizov often dreamed the future. He claimed his dreams gave him completely reliable weather reports. Whenever he dreamed of a professor whose name had a punning resemblance to the Russian verb *mochit* (to wet or soak), he knew it was going to rain. He noted that often his glimpses of the future involved very minor things, like seeing pretty twin girls who turned up on the Paris Metro the next day.

Remizov not only believed that dream encounters with the dead are real but also maintained that, in conversation with the dead, the living can both talk to the dead and "influence their fate."[46] Though he is not explicit, he seems to be edging here toward Yeats's affirmation that the living have the ability "to assist the imaginations of the dead."[47] Remizov's dream-based view of how afterlife situations are constructed and change is fascinating. He pictures life after death as a continuous dream whose content corresponds to ideas the dreamer had before he pushed on. What happens after these preconceived ideas fall away will depend on personal evolution, courage, and imagination. The soul may "fly like a spark into the ocean" of mystic union with the One beyond forms. Or the departed may drift back into a dreary round of familiar activities, "darning stockings" or simply "carrying on with old business."

When he was living in St. Petersburg, Remizov had a dream couch. He claimed that, as soon as he lay down on it, he saw the most vivid dreams. Throughout his life, it was his practice to keep pen and paper at his side and to write down dreams whenever he woke from sleep. He declared, "A night without a dream for me is like a day lost."[48]

He saw dreams not as a nightly escape into fantasy or the stew of the Freudian subconscious but as a realm of real experience expanding into areas that are inaccessible to the everyday mind. "Life is not limited to daytime occurrences or three-dimensional reality, but continues in the multidimensionality of dreams, which are equally existing and equally valid as the waking world."[49] Writing from dreams was not for him — as it turned out to be for the Surrealists — a passing fad. It was a lifelong and passionate calling.

The Revenge of the Imagination

The Bolshevik revolution and the rise of the totalitarian state drove dreams underground. The safe places to write about dreams — or from them — were now to be found in state-sponsored studies of folklore and folk art and in science fiction, which can put the reader inside a dream without a frame.

What happens when the imagination is driven underground?

A Russian-American writer, Olga Grushin, brilliantly depicts the revolt of the imagination in her novel *The Dream Life of Sukhanov*. The protagonist is a promising Surrealist painter who buries his art in order to get a fat paycheck and a big apartment and a chauffeured car while working as an art bureaucrat. His suppressed imagination comes after him, spawning dreamlike anomalies in his everyday world, until that world — and the false values it instilled in him — falls apart.

The Dream Kitchen and the Magic Library

For creative people, dreaming is very much about building imaginal space — a studio in the mind where ideas take form easily. The story of the Brontë sisters is a marvelous example of how this can work in the lives of creative writers. Before they could spell or even write properly, Charlotte and Emily were telling each other stories and inventing little plays they could act out together. They borrowed toy soldiers from their brother, Branwell, to create a miniature theatre in the round, where they could watch their characters grow and develop their plots. As they got better at writing, they exchanged scripts in minute handwriting designed to escape decipherment by any adult. And as they grew to adulthood, they preserved the child's ability to slip easily into a space beyond the limits of the ordinary world. They were fortunate, of course, to have each other to support and sustain them.[50]

In my night dreams, the place of creation is often a kitchen. I don't do a lot of cooking, but I love the image of the kitchen — where we are fed and nourished and we mix things together and cook things up — as the creative center. I especially like to think of the creative process as being similar to baking. You get together your startup dough, then you knead it — you stretch it and pull it apart and bring it together again. Then you stand back and let it rise (if it will). Then you get hot, and expose your project to the fire. And finally comes the test: how does it taste? I know, from the state of my dream kitchen, how a creative project is coming (or *not* coming) along.

In dreams and reverie, I often find myself slipping into the kind of Little World where the Brontës, and so many of us who are still in touch with our inner children, are at home.

Often I dream I am looking at a diorama where toy soldiers are marshaled, as I used to deploy them for Little Wars on the floor of my room when I was a boy. Then I notice that the tiny figures are alive and are moving about at their own volition. And that they are not necessarily in military uniforms. At this point, I can choose to shrink myself to their size and enter fully into their world. I can choose to be an unseen observer, or I can take on a role and become a participant in their dramas. I keep a selection of toy soldiers and miniature figures — from a knight of Agincourt to a Roman centurion to the hunting cheetahs of the nizam of Hyderabad — on my desk to please my inner boys and remind myself of the places we can go.

But my favorite imaginal space for creative inspiration and idea development is the Dream Library. You can put yourself there by the right kind of reading binge. Coleridge, for example, read an immense number of books. We have the romantic notion that Coleridge birthed his poems, word perfect, on a dream winged by opium; and this may be how "Kubla Khan" came through before the author was interrupted by "persons from Porlock."[51] But the road to Xanadu included library time; Coleridge was reading a book about Kubla Khan before he was seized by the vision that demanded to be expressed. His writing process always included reading orgies. Beyond specific borrowings — taking a scene from Schiller's "Ghost-Seer" to open the "Ancient Mariner" — there is the sense that, in his "magnificent use of his reading," Coleridge was taking in the *prima materia* for magical transformation.[52]

Works that arouse the imagination put us in a different space and into a state of mind that resembles conscious dreaming. The door to the Dream Library often opens in dreams. A woman dreamed that her house had an extra floor containing a room with her private encyclopedia, where she could look up anything she needed to know. If you have a dream like that, you have a library card and a passkey that will get you in at all hours. You can access your Dream Library by calling up the scene from your dream and willing yourself back inside that space with the intention of making further discoveries.

In the Dream Library, we can sometimes meet master teachers. We can also enter the possible workings of their imaginations. During my visits to the Dream Library, a possible Yeats showed me a method of seership previously unknown to me, and a possible Churchill showed me the science fiction novels he'd been writing — to the great satisfaction of a possible H. G. Wells — now that he is no longer required to lead nations.

If you are a writer, you can not only find great material in the Dream Library but can also sometimes read the books or stories or screenplays you have not yet written! I know a singer-songwriter who travels to her version of the Dream Library — a kind of music school — to play the CDs she has not yet recorded and get coaching from a great chanteuse from the past. I know a boat designer who redesigned the hull of a racing yacht after consulting a book in his

Dream Library, and a landscape gardener who redesigned an estate in the Hamptons after a Dream Library encounter with an architect who claimed to be Inigo Jones. For the Nobel laureate Wolfgang Pauli, a pioneer of quantum physics, the Dream Library was the "secret laboratory" where he first discovered and tested his breakthrough ideas.

CHAPTER 6

⋄⟡⋄

HOW DREAMING
GETS US THROUGH

In times when passions are beginning to take charge of the conduct of human affairs, one should pay less attention to what men of experience and common sense are thinking than to what is preoccupying the imagination of dreamers.

— ALEXIS DE TOCQUEVILLE, *Democracy in America*

The best songs are the ones that come to you in the middle of the night and you have to get up and write them down, so you can go back to sleep.

— JOHN LENNON

𝕿his chapter explores one of the key themes of this book — that over the whole course and range of history, dreaming has helped humans to get by and get through the challenges of life — through six windows. First, our contemporary political leaders may want to notice that the Founding Fathers were dreamers in several senses; John Adams and Benjamin Rush traded dreams, and a dream helped restore friendship between the second and third presidents of the United States after a political rift. Second, we'll discover that dreaming is as practical and potentially world-changing as this: a dream, assisted by the right kind of interpretation and followed up by the right kind of action, led directly to one of the biggest oil strikes in history, changing the history of the Middle East and the world. Third, we'll learn how, in one modern European country, dreams are shared in almost every household and are used by farmers to read the weather and by fishing skippers to find the fish. Fourth, we'll look at how dreams fuel the imagination of rock composers and performers. Fifth, we'll examine how athletes and sports coaches run "inner movies" to prepare for an event. Finally, we'll explore the role of dreaming — and above all the ability to enter a place of imagination — in the history of scientific creativity.

DREAMING WITH THE FOUNDING FATHERS

The friendship between Dr. Benjamin Rush of Philadelphia and John Adams, the second president of the United States, is a grand and sometimes moving example of what it means to travel through life with a true companion of mind and spirit. They were together in the Continental Congress; both of them signed the Declaration of Independence; their imaginations helped to forge a new political order; and they both weathered political storms and bitter adversity. This was also a great *epistolary* friendship. Adams and Rush corresponded with extraordinary intimacy and liveliness; the doctor's wife said they wrote to each other "like two young girls about their sweethearts."[1] Adams had "a heart formed for friendship," and he shared it with the doctor without hesitation.[2]

As a doctor and pioneer psychiatrist, Rush recorded the dreams of his patients and used them in diagnosis. Since his first travels to Europe before the American Revolution, he had been keenly interested in precognitive dreams. He developed a lifelong habit of journaling his own dreams.

During visits to the Massachusetts home of John and Abigail Adams, Rush learned that Adams, too, took a keen interest in dreams. Rush suggested that they exchange dreams, and Adams agreed to match Rush "dream for dream."[3] They proceeded to swap dreams in a way that was — and is — quite unusual for white men of power and influence in America.

Rush shared what appears to be a dream warning of ego inflation. He sees a man atop the steeple of a church, willing the weather to change — without success. He announces, in his dream, "The man is certainly mad." Then a winged figure like Mercury flies down, waving a streamer with the Latin inscription *De te fabula narrator* ("This story is being told about you") — making it impossible to miss the fact that the dream is holding up a mirror to the attitudes and behavior of the dreamer.[4]

Adams, in turn, shared a political dream that dramatized the difficulty of creating a civilized democratic system in France. In his dream, he was in front of the palace of Versailles, trying to explain the requirements of democracy to an immense crowd of wild beasts. He was howled down and in danger of being ripped apart.

Rush reported a dream in which he became president and used his power to bring in prohibition. This resulted in a storm of protest and, finally, a visit from a wise old man who counseled him that "the empire of habit" is stronger than "the empire of reason" and must be respected.[5]

This dream was another corrective to the doctor's waking assumptions. Having observed the effects of alcoholism — and having been reared in a stern Presbyterian faith — he was an early supporter of prohibition, until this dream.

Adams and Rush inspected each other's dreams for guidance on many other issues, both political and personal, including the opposition to Adams's efforts to create an American navy. The most remarkable letter in the Adams-Rush correspondence was signed by Benjamin Rush on October 16, 1809. At this point, John Adams and Thomas Jefferson, once close allies and friends, had been estranged for eleven years because of political disagreements. Rush described a dream in which his son showed him a page from a history of the United States. "I read it with great pleasure and send you a copy of it."

The page from the supposed dream history described "the renewal of the friendship and intercourse between Mr. John Adams and Mr. Jefferson, two ex-Presidents of the United States." This led to "a correspondence of several years in which they mutually reviewed the scenes of business in which they had been engaged," producing valuable lessons for posterity. "Many precious aphorisms, the result of observation, experience and profound reflection, it is said, are contained in these letters." The dream history added: "These gentlemen sunk into the grave nearly at the same time," having outlived their adversaries.[6]

We may suspect that in writing this page, Dr. Rush was attempting a dream *transfer* rather than simply forwarding a dream report, using that form to press for reconciliation between the two former presidents. The following week, Adams sent him a pleasant response: "A dream again! I wish you would dream all day and all night, for one of your dreams puts me in spirits for a month."[7] He then proceeded brusquely to make it clear that he was not ready for reconciliation, stating that (despite eleven years of noncommunication) "there has never been the smallest interruption of the personal friendship between me and Mr. Jefferson." He added, with a haughtiness that was not his usual style, that "Jefferson was but a boy to me," and that he "taught him everything that has been good and solid in his whole political conduct."[8]

Rush's dream intervention did not bring Adams and Jefferson together right away. "Of what use can it be for Jefferson and me to exchange letters?" Adams rebuffed Rush's continued efforts to play peacemaker on Christmas Day, 1811. "I have nothing to say to him, but to wish him an easy journey to heaven."[9] Yet just one week later, on New Year's Day, 1812, John Adams penned a careful overture to Jefferson, and the two former presidents moved quickly and gratefully to full reconciliation. The correspondence between them over the following years is an extraordinary gift to our understanding of the birth of democracy in America. Fourteen years later, they "sunk into the grave" on the same day, having outlived most of their enemies.

"This is the Fourth of July," Thomas Jefferson announced on his deathbed at Monticello on the evening of July 3, 1826. Informed that the day of celebration had not yet arrived, he drifted back to sleep. When he died at one o'clock in the afternoon on July 4, bells could be heard ringing in Charlottesville, Virginia, in the valley below.

A few hours later, lying on his own deathbed in Quincy, Massachusetts, with a thunderstorm raging outside, John Adams whispered, "Thomas Jefferson survives." Then his heart stopped. Whether the page from Dr. Rush's future history was dream or imagination, its prophecies were exactly fulfilled.[10]

DREAMING OIL

He lived with his large and imposing wife, Violet, in a blue-and-white house overlooking the Arabian Gulf, with a verandah on the upper level to catch the sea breezes. Under the fierce desert sun, he went shooting in gaiters and country tweeds and may have looked, in his florid bulk, the model of the type of colonial Englishman who does *not* go native. But Colonel Harold Dickson was very far from a stereotype. Born in what is now Syria, he was Bedouin as well as British — in the eyes of that desert people — from the time he suckled at the breast of a Bedouin wet nurse. As he rose high in the ranks of the colonial civil service, becoming a British political agent in Kuwait from 1929 to 1936, he hunted with the Bedouin, counseled with them over innumerable cups of cardamom-flavored coffee, and *dreamed* like them.

On at least two occasions before his retirement, he brought the sheikh of Kuwait prophetic dreams. One forewarned of a natural disaster that would destroy much of the capital but result in abundance. It was fulfilled when a storm and flood washed away thousands of mud-brick houses and then made the desert bloom. In the second dream, Dickson foresaw an attempt on the life of the king of Saudi Arabia. When the assassination attempt took place, his prowess as a prophetic dreamer was confirmed. "The Sheikh of Kuwait marveled still more, and told my story to many of his friends. The story got about and my stock went up quite appreciably in Kuwait. My dreams are still given proper weight, but I am careful not to give too much away."[11]

The sheikh urged him to stay on in Kuwait after he retired from the colonial service, and he continued to live and dream in his blue-and-white house as chief local representative of the Kuwait Oil Company.

In September 1937, the Kuwait Oil Company was drilling at a lonely place called Bahra, and work was not going well. They had probed far deeper than they had intended and found no trace of oil.

That month, Dickson dreamed that he and his wife were living in a bungalow in an oil camp in the heart of the desert. Nothing was growing in the scene except an immense ancient sidr tree standing near the house. A wild wind blew up a sandstorm of unusual violence. It shook the house, and the grains in the air made it hard to breathe. When the storm abated, Dickson went out and saw that the storm had opened a great cavity under the tree. He looked down into what appeared to be an ancient tomb. A prone figure shrouded in rotted yellow cotton cloth lay on a stone slab. When Dickson and his wife began to peel the ruined cloth away from the mummy's head, they were surprised by the beauty of the young woman's face that was revealed. Her skin was like parchment. Dickson called for his servants to dig a fresh grave, but to his amazement the mummy came alive. The parchment skin grew soft and smooth, and a lovely woman stepped free from the shroud. She told the Dicksons she was cold, after sleeping for thousands of years, and needed food and warm clothes. She gave them a very ancient copper coin. They led her by the hand into the house, where their Arab maid washed her and dressed her while they prepared food.

After eating, the woman from the tomb sat under the sidr tree. She warned that "wicked men" would try to bury her again, and that Dickson must seek the aid of the sheikh and the British government. As she spoke, a mob of angry men brandishing weapons appeared. They were led by a white-bearded man armed with a long knife "who looked like a Persian."[12] Colonel Dickson flew to her defense, killing the leader with a blow and driving off the men who were digging a fresh grave. He took the girl back inside his bungalow.

Waking in high excitement, Dickson roused his wife, Violet, and she carefully recorded all the details of his dream. This was a regular procedure in the Dickson household; he felt this one augured immense good fortune.

But it was necessary to find out exactly what was going on in the dream. For this, Dickson sought counsel from a local expert, a Bedouin woman called Umm Mubarak, who was much respected as a diviner and reader of dreams. The sand devil that opened the mummy's tomb might be a djinn — a desert demon. It might also be a drilling rig. Umm Mubarak sifted the elements of the dream and gave Dickson her judgment. The mummy that came alive and gave him treasure from the earth was showing the way to a fabulous oil field that had not yet been discovered. The ancient tree, growing alone in the desert, gave away the location. Umm Mubarak had seen this tree; it had survived alone in a waste of sand in the Burqan hills. The angry mob consisted of people in the region who would oppose Western oil operations.[13]

Dickson told his dream to the sheikh of Kuwait, who heard him with great respect. Dickson then told the managers of the Kuwait Oil Company that they should move their drilling operations to Burqan. The oil company followed his advice, and early in 1938 they hit a gusher. The find — known as Burqan Number One — was one of the richest oil discoveries in history. It was a great coup for the British in those edgy months on the eve of World War II. It turned Kuwait into a fabulously wealthy country, tempting Saddam Hussein, more than half a century later, to launch the invasion that triggered the first Gulf War.

DREAMING A WIFE — AND THE FISH

Iceland is not only a country of fire and ice. To a degree that is remarkable among modern Western societies, it is a country where people everywhere believe in dreams and follow their guidance. A Gallup survey of twelve hundred Icelanders in 2003 revealed that 72 percent found meaning in their dreams, and many reported dreaming the future and sharing dreams regularly within their families. More than half the respondents said they had experienced lucid dreaming. Over 70 percent believed that dream precognition is real, and over 40 percent reported personal experiences of precognitive dreams.[14] The Icelandic language distinguishes vital categories of significant dreams, such as dreams of the future (*berdreymi*) and dream visions (*draumspa*).

We can track Iceland's dreaming traditions back through the Eddas and the sagas. In the *Völuspá*, even the gods go to wise women for help with their dreams. The story of Thyri Haraldsdóttir, from the Icelandic sagas, is a beautiful example of how dreaming can make us wiser and opens the way of the heart. Thyri (written in Icelandic as Þyri) was the daughter of an earl in Holstein. She was a dreamer who saw far and deep into the nature of things, and her father consulted her on all important affairs.

Gormur, king of Denmark, wanted to marry Thyri and asked her father for her hand. The earl said he would leave his daughter to decide for herself, "since she is much wiser than I am." Thyri told her royal suitor to go home and build himself a new house, just big enough to sleep in, where no house had stood before. In this place he must sleep alone for three nights and pay close attention to his dreams. Then he must send a messenger to her to report on his dreams. "If you don't dream, don't bother to call on me again," Thyri told him firmly. Gormur remembered his dreams, and the content seems to have satisfied Thyri, because she consented to marry him and became the wisest of the queens of Denmark. Through dreaming, she helped the king to scout the future and read the true factors at work behind the surface of events. Decisions of state were based on these dreams.[15]

For Icelanders, some precognitive dreamers are household names. Johannes Jonsson, a farmer and shepherd who spent his life on the Langanes peninsula until his death in 1944, was nicknamed "Dream Jo" because of his ability to dream the location of lost or stolen property or of ships at sea. People traveled great distances to use him as an oracle, putting questions to him both when he was awake and when he was asleep.[16]

When smoked meat went missing from a locked loft on a farm, Jo was asked to come to the farm and allow people to ask him about the theft during his sleep. Jo gave an exact description of a man who gained entry to the loft because someone had forgotten to lock up. The thief put the meat in a bag and tied this at the back of his saddle. "So the thief came on horseback?" the questioner asked. Jo laughed, "If you could call that a horse!" When the thief was tracked down, following Jo's description, it was discovered that his "horse" was a donkey.[17]

Dreaming the fish is a skill beyond dreaming the location of stolen goods, and it is part of the mystique of the Icelandic skipper. The skipper is a dominant, sometimes heroic, figure in the Icelandic fishing industry. Generally known to his crew as The Man (*kallinn*), he is judged by his ability to find the fish by any means that work. The skipper, solely in charge of his boat and its course, must hunt the invisible with line or net in the depths of an element that often fails to offer surface clues. Some skippers talk openly about how they can dream a good catch; others, keeping an air of mystery or rough pragmatism, nonetheless carry reputations as dream pilots.[18]

A highly macho and successful skipper — a "captain of the catch" — attributed his skill in finding the fish, and his ability to weather the worst winter storms, to guidance from an elf woman who came to him in dreams and in other nocturnal trysts. His adventures with his elf lady were the subject of a popular book, *The Woman by the Waterfall*.[19]

A skipper called Eggert Gíslason did not lay claim to elvish support, but allowed that he had practiced the ability to scout the future in dreams since childhood. Sailors sought a berth on his boat because of his reputed ability to find fish when others could not. "It certainly makes life easier to know beforehand that we are going to have successful fishing." He recalled a dream that pointed him in the right direction. "It was when I was captain for the first time fishing with lines. I dreamed the course and saw the compass needle; it pointed east-north east of Gardskagi." Waking, he set the exact course he had dreamed. "We caught fish like anything. It was wonderful for me as captain in my first trip to come back to harbor with such a catch."

This skipper made dreaming the fish an exercise for the whole crew. He paid special attention to dream reports from sailors who had proved to be reliable dream scouts. One season, when most of the fishing fleet was heading west, one of Eggert's men dreamed the crew found the body of a giant cow near the village of Raufarhöfn in the east. The cow was covered with fish scales, bright and shining in a way that seemed beautiful. As soon as Skipper Eggert heard this dream, he sailed east, away from the rest of the fishing fleet. His crew proceeded to land a tremendous catch near the village of Raufarhöfn.[20]

Captain Eiríkur, of Iceland's coast guard, has given a detailed account of dream guidance at sea. The night after sailing from Reykjavik on the old coast guard cutter *Thor*, he had a dream he found "very dark and bad" that carried the sense of imminent danger. In his dream, an unfamiliar man gave him something he could not see clearly at first. When he looked closer, he realized he was holding fifteen human jawbones. They looked as if they had been weathered for a long time on shore. Horrified, the captain threw the jawbones back at the giver, yelling, "This will never be!"

The dream haunted him for the whole trip. He kept praying for the best for his ship and his men while preparing for a disaster that threatened to take fifteen lives. Before the end of the trip, the dream was played out in part, but its fatality was contained. The *Thor* was wrecked by a terrible storm. In the heaving ocean, fifteen men managed to board the lifeboats and were safely carried ashore.[21]

Eiríkur notes that, while the meaning of some of his dreams remained obscure until events caught up with them, some dreams were immediately clear — especially those involving fish. "It happened very often when I had dreams of sheep that I felt I knew almost exactly how good the fishing would be the following day. It depended on how many sheep I saw in my dreams. The more the better."[22]

The theme of contact with the "hidden people" — as in the skipper's dreams of the elf woman — is often at play in Icelandic dreams. In the following account, a sailor received a fishing advisory from a "dream guide" who made regular appearances in his dreams: "I was in the Eastfjords with our crew and boat. We had arrived some time before the fishing season started. One day before anyone had tried to go out to check if fish had already entered the fjord, we rowed out and got a hundred fish. We were extremely happy over our lot so our skipper decided we should row again the following day. For a long time I had had a dream guide, a man who used to visit me in my dreams and give me sound advice. During the following night, my dream man came to me in my sleep and said, 'It's no use fishing today.' I had no choice but to go with the others; I did not feel I could pass on the message. We caught only a couple of small fish. I understood that my dream man already had this knowledge in advance and came to alert me."[23]

The people who live closest to earth and sea continue to dream on the necessities of survival: the weather, the crops, the fish, the next volcanic eruption. While some precognitive dreams are clear, requiring no interpretation, others speak in symbolic language adapted to the dreamers' styles. Dr. Björg Bjarnadottir offers the following example from a "weather dreamer": A man dreamed he was driving white sheep into a shed in the valley; the shed had room for forty sheep. This was believed to predict snow that would last for over a month.[24]

DREAMING ROCKS

"Truth moves through us when we sleep," Roseanne Cash wrote in a song she titled "The Wheel." Many musicians and composers will recognize what she meant. Billy Joel has kept a notepad by his bed to jot down ideas and lyrics for songs that come to him in his dreams. Sleeping in an attic room in London in 1965, Paul McCartney dreamed he heard a classical string ensemble playing and woke with "a lovely tune" in his head. He played it on an upright piano in the room. "I liked the melody a lot, but because I'd dreamed it, I couldn't believe I'd written it. I thought, 'No, I've never written anything like this before.' But I had the tune, which was the most magic thing!" When fellow Beatles reassured him the tune was something new, he found the words and recorded the hit song "Yesterday."[25]

In the pop music scene, many performers have described encounters with dream visitors — often departed family members or fellow musicians — who have provided counsel and inspiration. Another popular Paul McCartney song, "Let It Be," was based on a dream visitation by his dead mother, Mary. He was run down from drug use, and the Beatles were beginning to break up. He fell into bed, deeply troubled, and dreamed his mother came to him and told him, "It's all right. It'll be all right." When he woke, he wrote down these words for a new song: "Mother Mary comes to me, speaking words of wisdom, let it be."[26]

John Lennon frequently received his inspiration in dreams or hypnagogic states. He told his biographer Frederic Seaman that he felt his "inspired" songs were usually far superior to "formula songs," as he characterized many of those that he and Paul McCartney had produced in the early years of the Beatles. "Writing formula songs is like painting by numbers." The good stuff comes to you in the middle of the night, out of a creative space, and you have to get up and write it down.[27]

How Dreams Saved Johnny Cash

Johnny Cash lost his beloved elder brother, Jack, to a horrible sawmill accident when both of them were teenagers. Throughout much of his life, Cash received dream visitations from his dead brother — who appeared to grow older from one visit to another, just as he would have done in ordinary life, and who emerged as the preacher and wise elder he had aimed to be. Cash's brother often turned up at moments of challenge, and his knowing smile would guide Johnny to consider his choices very carefully.

Cash wrote about this in his autobiography: "Jack comes to me in person. He's been showing up in my dreams every couple of months or so, sometimes more often, ever since he died, and he's been keeping pace with me." Jack always appeared to be two years older than Johnny. In the dreams, he was "a preacher, just as he intended to be," offering practical wisdom.[28]

Though Johnny Cash's rise in the country music business was meteoric, his life was dark and hard. Trapped in a loveless early marriage, lonely at home and on the road, he became addicted to amphetamines. Two things saved his life — June Carter and his dreams. June Carter was a gifted singer-songwriter. She was also a woman of profound religious beliefs, and as love between the couple grew when they toured together, she found herself thrashing in a terrible personal conflict, a choice between passion and hell. From her torment she created a song called "Ring of Fire." She was so conflicted about it that she turned it over to Johnny to record — at a time when his career was slumping and he desperately needed a hit.[29]

The night before he was set to record "Ring of Fire," Johnny dreamed he heard himself singing the song with an arrangement he had never heard before. "Mexican bullfighting trumpets"[30] framed the song with a brassy riff that added a whole new range of feeling.

Nothing like this had ever been heard in country music, which was still straitlaced into a tradition that excluded trumpets, horns, and even drums. But when Johnny shared his dream with his new producer, Jack Clement grasped at once that bringing in mariachi trumpets could give the new record a wildly exciting new edge. "Ring of Fire," with the trumpet chorus, became a monster hit and made Johnny Cash a superstar.

Cash continued to track his dreams until the end of his life. He dreamed he called on Queen Elizabeth and she told him he was "like a thorn tree in a whirlwind." The phrase haunted him, got him thinking about passages in the Bible, and eventually this gave birth to his later hit song "And the Man Comes Round."[31]

The Dream That Might Have Saved Lynyrd Skynyrd

The Southern rock band Lynyrd Skynyrd, famed for its signature hit song "Sweet Home Alabama," suffered a tragedy in October 1977. The chartered Convair plane carrying the band mysteriously ran out of fuel and crashed into a swamp not far from their destination, Baton Rouge. Six people died in the crash, including Ronnie Van Zant, the lead singer; a guitarist; and a backup singer; and twenty were badly injured.

The performers had been worried about the condition of their plane and its crew for some time. Two band members were so uneasy they made reservations on commercial flights, but then decided to stay with the group. Another group, Aerosmith, had been scheduled to use the same Convair plane during their tour early that year. But during inspection the plane was found to be unsafe, and Aerosmith's scouts spotted the pilots smoking pot and drinking whiskey just before takeoff. Aerosmith was quite familiar with the effects of intoxication on performance, and the group changed its plans.

The Lynyrd Skynyrd tragedy might have been averted had a very specific dream warning been acted upon. The warning came from JoJo Billingsley, one of the three backup vocalists for the band, known as the Honkettes. While staying at her parents' home in Mississippi shortly before the crash, JoJo dreamed that the band's plane went down. "I saw the plane smack the ground. I saw them screaming and crying, and I saw fire." She woke from this dream screaming. Her mother tried to soothe her by telling her it was "just a dream." JoJo could not shake her feelings of terror. She felt an urgent need to pass on a warning to the group. She started making frantic phone calls to musicians and managers begging them not to get on the plane.

The band took her warning seriously enough to take a vote on what to do. The majority decided, "Fly to Baton Rouge and switch to a different plane." Of course, they never reached Baton Rouge. Beset by survivor's guilt and tormented by bizarre accusations against her, JoJo did not perform for seven years after the accident. She became very religious. She did agree to perform at Lynyrd Skynyrd's induction to the Rock 'n' Roll Hall of Fame in 2006.[32]

Ironically, the members of Lynyrd Skynyrd were not strangers to dream help. Their most famous song, "Sweet Home Alabama," came to their guitarist Ed King in a dream, complete with the chords and two great guitar solos. They even used this fact to convince the producers to leave the song exactly as it was originally recorded — and succeeded, as King recalled, thanks in part to "Southern mysticism."[33] King left the band in 1975 and was replaced by Steve Gaines. They share the same birthday. Gaines was killed in the crash; King is alive and well.

Dreaming Up "Mystery Girl"

Bono of U2 has described how the song "Mystery Girl" came from a dream followed by an amazing coincidence. In jitters before a big gig at Wembley Stadium, he could not sleep and stayed up most of the night with a recording of the soundtrack to David Lynch's *Blue Velvet* set on repeat, looping around again and again to Roy Orbison's song "In Dreams."

Bono finally drifted off, and woke with a song in his head. It had something of the quality of Roy Orbison, and his first impression was that it was just another Roy Orbison song. It slowly occurred to him that the song was new, something he had composed in his sleep. It was about a "mystery girl."

He played it to the band during the sound check and they liked it. Right after the big show, he sat down with his guitar, bent on finishing the new song. At this moment, there was a knock on the door, and a bodyguard told Bono, "There is this Roy Orbison and his wife outside; they'd like to meet you." Bono and his band were incredulous. They had not known that Orbison was at the concert.

Orbison asked Bono if he had a song for him. Bono was thrilled; he loved Roy Orbison's "angel" voice. The timing, of course, was perfect: Bono had the ideal song, the gift of a dream partly programmed by Orbison's song "In Dreams." Soon after, Roy Orbison recorded "Mystery Girl," a lovely song that perfectly suited his voice and carried elements of his own signature style, together with something of the U2 edge. Orbison's album *Mystery Girl* was released posthumously and made it nearly to the top of the pop charts. Bono shared the writing credit with the Edge (the professional name of the U2 guitarist). Bono recalls that the band thought "there was a bit of voodoo in me."[34]

Rachmaninoff Gives a Piano Lesson

Leaving the rock scene, let's consider a remarkable example of dream guidance in the life of a gifted contemporary classical pianist. Olga Kern, a lovely and gifted young Russian pianist, has won many international awards. She has a remarkable musical pedigree. Her ancestor Anna Kern inspired Pushkin to write a love poem. Olga's great-great-great-grandmother was a pianist and a friend of Tchaikovsky. Her great-great-grandmother sang on stage accompanied by Rachmaninoff. Her grandfather is an oboist still active at eighty-six as a professor at Gnesyns Music Academy in Moscow. Both her parents are pianists.

At seventeen, Olga Kern was the youngest participant in the first Rachmaninoff Piano Competition in Moscow. She had a very interesting mentor. Before the second round, she dreamed that Rachmaninoff was playing a piano alone in a huge auditorium, waiting for her. He looked up at her and said, "Olga, I've been waiting for you. You should play something for me; we have a lesson scheduled." Olga was amazed, thinking, "Goodness, it's *Rachmaninoff!*" Still stunned, she sat down and played a piece from her competition program — the Barcarolle.

Rachmaninoff listened intently. When she was finished, he said, "Good. And now I'll show you how I play it." He proceeded to play the Barcarolle in his own style — "phenomenally," Olga recalled, "a bit dryly, yet impulsively, without pedals."

Olga woke up and called out, "Mama, mama, I saw Rachmaninoff in my dream!" Her mother was troubled by this. She asked Olga's father if he thought she was practicing too hard.

Inspired by her private lesson with Rachmaninoff, Olga proceeded to win the competition organized in his name. She described the rush of energy that flowed from the dream as a "hurricane" that swept her through the second and third rounds of the contest.

Prior to the dream, Olga had never heard Rachmaninoff's own rendition of the Barcarolle. This might seem surprising, given her family's musical history. But the time was 1992, post-Soviet society was a shambles, and even getting basic food was — as a Russian friend living in Petersburg at the time puts it — "an extreme sport." Recordings of Rachmaninoff were available only from private dealers at very fancy prices.

A year after winning the Rachmaninoff competition, when Olga was on tour in Japan, she was able to purchase a CD set of his complete works. When she played his rendition of the Barcarolle, she found that Rachmaninoff played it exactly as he had done in her dream.

Olga Kern went on to honor her dream tutor by playing all his piano concertos in a tour of several South African cities to great critical acclaim. Her international career took off in earnest after she won a gold medal at the Van Cliburn Competition in 2001.[35]

If John Lennon Had Been Able to Act on His Death Dreams

John Lennon's death dreams *might* have helped prevent his tragic death had he been able to do more with the urgent and specific warnings they were giving him. Late in 1979, Lennon was troubled by a dream in which he was dining out with his wife, Yoko Ono, and they were approached by a chubby, bespectacled stranger. Lennon asked the man to prove he was not "some nutcase," and the stranger became agitated. The police appeared and told Lennon the chubby man had come to the restaurant armed with a handgun. Lennon was distressed that he could not recall more details of this dream.

Then, early in 1980, Lennon had a terrifying dream in which he read his own obituary. It stated that he had been charged with his own homicide, which occurred near the Dakota on Central Park. Lennon — both perpetrator and victim in the dream — kept insisting that he was not guilty.[36]

Lennon was killed near the Dakota by a "chubby, bespectacled" man on December 8, 1980. Lennon's agitation over his inability to recall more details of the restaurant dream suggests that he intuited that it may have contained vitally important information. The Lennon obituary dream flags our need to study our dreams carefully for early warning messages. This may involve learning to read the language of our dreams. Lennon saw the murderer as himself. Many analysts, given that information, would be tempted to come up with a psychological interpretation of the dream, focused, for example, on a possible conflict within the dreamer's own psyche, or the archetypal theme of the doppelgänger. But John Lennon's second self — we can now see — was the deranged fan who wanted to *be* John Lennon. Lennon's murderer identified with his victim to the point that he married a Japanese woman, collected art as Lennon did, and signed out from work the night before the murder as "John Lennon."

Dreaming *can* get us through, but our dreams require us to learn their language and figure out what action is necessary to bring their guidance into our lives in the regular world.

ATHLETES AND INNER MOVIES

Bill Russell became a basketball superstar after he trained himself to be a movie producer and a movie star — inside his own head. His brilliantly original moves on the court were invented and practiced in his mental movies.

Russell was a gold medalist at the 1956 Olympics and won the Most Valuable Player award five times playing for the Boston Celtics. He attributed his rise to greatness as an athlete to a "mystical revelation" he experienced at sixteen while walking down a hallway at school. He was possessed by a "warm feeling" that fell on him "out of nowhere," the sense of being joined by a greater power. His sense of failure and isolation in a hostile world (he had been motherless since he was twelve) vanished. As his life went on, he often experienced the sense of a greater power coming to join him, moments when "new skills seemed to drop down out of the sky, and I felt as if I had a new eye or had tapped a new compartment of my brain."

By his own account, it was "luck" that got him picked for a California All-Star team that toured the Pacific Northwest for a month. While absorbing what he could from more experienced players, he had a breakthrough experience as he sat on the bench. When he closed his eyes, he found he could not only visualize the game move by move but also insert himself into the action as if he were the key player.

On the long bus trips, he proceeded to practice this kind of mental replay, and soon found it was effortless. "The movies I saw in my head seemed to have their own projector, and whenever I closed my eyes, it would run." He applied himself to picturing defensive moves. He saw himself as a dancing shadow, moving with whichever player he was trying to guard. He put the technique he had envisioned to work in the court and soon became famous for his innovative defensive moves.[37]

Swimmer Tracy Caulkin used imaginal rehearsal to win her third gold medal at the 1984 Olympics. Electronic touch pads had just been introduced to replace stopwatches. An electronic touch pad measures time in thousandths of seconds. It can establish whether you are ahead of or behind another swimmer by an interval of time four hundred times shorter than the blink of an eye. In Olympic relays, a swimmer is given precisely two-hundredths of a second of grace time to leave the block before the teammate ahead of her touches the pad.

A race can be won or lost by a sliver of time that simply cannot be gauged by ordinary human senses.

In the women's four-hundred-meter relay at the 1984 games, Tracy Caulkin seized the lead by diving in one-hundredth of a second before her teammate tapped the touch pad. Tracy was one of the world's greatest swimmers, but her victory in that race depended on more than the peak of fitness and hard practice; it stemmed from the fact that every night, in her head, she had rehearsed the contest, feeling the movements of her body in the water, entering the experience with all of her inner senses, living it stroke by stroke — starting with the instant she *would* leave the diving block one-hundredth of a second earlier than the swimmers in the rival relay teams.[38]

How does this work? Sports psychologists have been ahead of the field in demonstrating that the body and brain don't distinguish between a thought and a physical event. Pioneer work was done with skiers who were wired to EMG monitors (which record electrical impulses sent to the muscles) while they mentally rehearsed their downhill runs. It was discovered that their brains sent the same instructions to their bodies whether they were thinking about a jump or a turn or actually doing it. This explains why Olympic skiers can rehearse in their minds for difficult turns that can't be seen clearly with physical sight in the blur of motion on the slopes, but that can be seen and prepared for in the mind.[39]

Sports psychology is now based on the premise that the body-mind does not know the difference between an actual event and an imagined one. Mental rehearsal, or "covert conditioning" in sports, centers on seeing yourself making your moves play by play in minute detail. This is much more than vague, warm and fuzzy "positive thinking." You imagine a flawless performance, but you make the moves ahead of time.

SCIENTISTS IN THE SOLUTION STATE

Great scientists often solve problems in their sleep. It is well known that Descartes had some interesting dreams, but his work as a whole may have gained more from the "creative mood" in which he often found himself during a relaxed state after sleep. Carl Gauss said he often had his best insights immediately after awakening. John Appold, the inventor of a centrifugal pump, worked out the following routine: when faced with a problem, he would go over and over the elements in his head before going to sleep, programming his mind for the night. He generally found that he had the solution first thing in the morning.

Famously, Einstein woke up on a spring morning in 1905 with the elements of the special relativity theory in his head. He had talked to a friend the previous evening about his keen sense that he was on the edge of a tremendous breakthrough but was not yet sure what it was; the pieces came together in the secret laboratory of the night.

The role of dreaming in the history of scientific creativity is both underrated and overrated. Exaggerated claims have been made for the inspirational power of sleep dreams in scientific discovery, and when these have been exploded the reductionists have not been slow to pounce. For example, dream enthusiasts have often suggested that Einstein and Niels Bohr made their breakthroughs in dreams, but (as far as I am aware) there is no evidence that either of them was inspired by specific content from sleep dreams. However, when we do deeper research into the history of scientific discovery across time, we find evidence of something far more interesting. Many of our greatest scientists have been *dreamers* in a more expansive sense. Above all, they have known how to enter into a fluid state of consciousness — a "solution state" — where unlikely connections can be made that escape the workaday mind, and where the shapes of what was formerly inexpressible rise from the depths like creatures from the ocean bed.

To find illustrations for these statements, let's study the case of one of the most famous — and problematic — "dreams" in the history of science. This is the dream of a snake biting its tail that revealed the shape of the benzene ring to German chemist August Kekulé (1829–1896). You'll find it mentioned in almost any book that contains stories about dreams and creativity. But was it a sleep dream or an image that came during a lightly altered state of consciousness?

Kekulé wrote a personal account, reconstructing an extemporaneous speech he gave at the 1890 Benzolfest many years after his visions. Study this closely, and check the meaning of the German words, and you'll find that his dreamy perception of the "dance" of chemical elements was not a one-off affair. He described a similar experience that occurred seven years before the snake dream that gave rise to his theory of chemical structures. He made it clear that, in the years between the two visions, he had developed a *practice* of seeing or thinking in visual imagery.

In his midtwenties, when he was living near Clapham Common in London, Kekulé spent a long summer evening sharing his ideas with a friend and fellow chemist who lived in Islington, on the other side of the city. Riding home on the last bus, Kekulé drifted into a reverie (*Traumerei*) in which he saw atoms "gamboling" and dancing and forming combinations. He understood, when he analyzed their motions, that he had been given clear insights into chemical structures. Up to this time, he had been unable to grasp the nature of their motion. "Now, however, I saw how, frequently, two smaller atoms united to form a pair; how a larger one embraced the two smaller ones . . . while the whole kept whirling in a giddy dance. I saw how the larger ones formed a chain, dragging the smaller ones after them but only at the end of the chain." He stayed up late that night sketching these "dream forms." This was the origin of his theory of carbon bonding in chemical structures.

We see three conditions for creativity at work in this incident: immersion in a subject, sharing a developing idea with the right friend, and drifting or relaxing into a flow state, from which the "Eureka" moment arises spontaneously.

Seven years later, a dream or reverie during an evening nap showed Kekulé the chemical structure of the benzene ring. He was now a professor in Ghent in Belgium. Dozing by the fire in his darkened study, he again saw atoms "gamboling before my eyes." Now his inner sight, "rendered more acute by repeated visions of the kind, could distinguish larger structures of manifold conformation: long rows, sometimes more closely fitted together all twining and twisting in snake-like motion." Then he was startled to see one of the "snakes" seize hold of its own tail and whirl "mockingly" before him. He was jolted out of his languorous state "as if by a lightning bolt." The image of the whirling snake gave the chemist the clue to the structure of the benzene ring. He spent most of the night that followed working this up until he had shaped his theory.

Kekulé had become *practiced* in receiving and developing helpful images in this way. When he described the roots of his scientific creativity at the Benzolfest in his honor in 1890, Kekulé told his audience, "Let us learn to dream, gentlemen, then perhaps we shall find the truth." He added the salutary caution, "But let us beware of publishing our dreams till they have been tested by the waking understanding."[40]

The images that came to Kekulé would have been meaningless, in terms of chemistry, to someone who did not have a scientific mind that had long been working on the problems whose solutions they revealed. The imagery might have sent an artist off to paint, or sent someone with an interest in myth off to study the symbol of the ouroboros in the ancient world and in alchemy.

When Kekulé urged his audience to "dream," he was surely not talking exclusively, or primarily, about what happens in sleep. He was talking about developing the ability to enter a state of relaxed attention in which ideas take form and interact as images.

It is always exciting to know the specific ways in which a creative mind enters that imaginal space. In the 1850s, people did not travel in motorized buses. The public conveyance that carried Kekulé home to Clapham was a horse-drawn omnibus. The clatter of the hooves and the jangle of the harness and the rocking motion of the box carriage provided the soundtrack and the rhythm for Kekulé's breakthrough.

It is likely that other creative minds of his period were helped by the rhythms of a contemporary mode of transportation. For the French mathematician Jules-Henri Poincaré, it was enough to put his foot on the step of a horse-drawn omnibus. In his beautiful essay "Mathematical Creation," Poincaré recalled that he had become stuck in his efforts to formulate a new mathematical construct, when he agreed to travel to Coutances to join friends on a hike. Inspiration struck as he started to board an omnibus: "At the moment when I put my foot on the step the idea came to me, without anything in my former thoughts seeming to have paved the way for it." When he went home to Caen, Poincaré wrote up his theory of "Fuchsian functions" directly from this moment of insight.

Poincaré also received direct guidance from his night dreams. After several unsuccessful attempts to perfect an equation he had been working on, he dreamed he was giving a lecture to students on the problem and wrote the equation on the blackboard to make everything clear. After waking, Poincaré was able to hold the image of what he had chalked on the board, wrote down the equation — and found he had his solution.

Just as "chance favors the prepared mind" (Louis Pasteur), so the muses of science and creativity favor those who have done their homework. Based on a survey of recent research in creativity, we could describe the four key stages of discovery as follows:

1. Immersion — a long, in-depth engagement with a subject
2. Acquisition — collecting a wealth of data and experience relevant to the subject
3. Inspiration — the eureka moment
4. Evaluation — testing the discovery through experiment and dissemination[41]

You can't force stage three. To get to it, you may have to let go — take a walk, take a swim, take a nap, take a break.

Many leading scientists and inventors, like other creative people, have found that their best ideas come through during a stroll. The idea of a steam engine occurred to James Watt during a stroll around the outskirts of Glasgow.

Also during a stroll, the father of Russian aviation, Nikolai Zhukovsky, grasped the formula for aerodynamic lift. Another scientific stroller, William Rowan Hamilton, arrived at the solution to the problem of hypercomplex numbers while walking with his wife along a canal in Dublin. Not wishing to let the formula slip away, Hamilton pulled out a pocketknife and carved it — instead of hearts and initials — on the railing of a bridge. Russian geometrician Alexei Pogorelov said that his most original concepts came to him when he was walking to and from work every day, so he did not mind that it was a ten-mile commute.

The Russian physicist Arkady Migdal described creativity as an intermediate state "where consciousness and unconsciousness mix, when conscious reasoning continues in sleep, and subconscious work is done in waking."[42] The trick is to find your way to a state of relaxed attention or attentive relaxation. It was in this state that Einstein did his "combinatory play," weaving together "visual" and "muscular" impressions; he was a visual and kinesthetic thinker whose primary creative process was preverbal or nonverbal. He described "the psychical entities that seem to serve as elements in thought" as "certain signs and more or less clear images which can be 'voluntarily' reproduced and combined."[43]

Hermann von Helmholtz wrote that good ideas came to him in a state of "unfocused attention." For Henri Bergson, this desirable state is characterized by "effortless thinking."[44]

As I lay in bed early on a rainy Saturday morning, it occurred to me that the drifty state after waking can sometimes be — quite literally — the solution state.

That morning, I did not have narrative dream recall. Instead, I found that my mental field was like an ocean of clean, translucent oil in which many images and ideas were floating and bobbing. I could reach around and choose some of them to mix and match and to bring into clear resolution. As I did this, I was given very clear solutions to a number of specific problems and imagery sequences I could now develop — or allow to develop — into dream movies with plotlines.

It struck me that this kind of experience takes place in a kind of dream matrix that could be called a "solution," in the sense that many elements and possibilities are suspended in it — and that creative people have the ability, in that state of relaxed attention (or attentive relaxation), to enter that state to find solutions.

PART TWO

❦

MASTERS OF THE THREE "ONLY" THINGS

When a portrait painter sets out to create a likeness, he relies above all upon the face and the expression of the eyes, and pays less attention to the other parts of the body. In the same way, it is my intention to dwell upon those actions which illuminate the workings of the soul.

— PLUTARCH, *Life of Alexander*

CHAPTER 7

❧

JOAN OF ARC
AND THE TREE-SEERS

If I were in a wood, I could easily hear the Voice which came to me.

— JOAN OF ARC, ON TRIAL IN ROUEN, FEBRUARY 22, 1431

We don't know what she looked like. Although she appears in countless paintings and sculptures, they are all works of imagination. There is no surviving portrait of Joan of Arc by someone who actually saw her; the only contemporary image is by a clerk who never set eyes on her, doodling in the margin of a text.[1] We don't even know the color of her hair. While most portraitists have chosen to give her blonde or light brown hair, the French scholar Jules Quicherat, toiling over the documents in the 1840s, found a single black hair in the broken wax seal of one of her letters, which he seized as evidence she was dark haired but could mean that a scribe started losing his hair as he took dictation from this extraordinary young woman who issued decrees in the name of the King of Heaven. The black hair and the red wax have since vanished.[2] So has a portrait Joan allowed a Scotsman to paint during her campaigns, although for a number of years after she was burned at the stake it was carted around Europe and shown to the curious for a fancy ticket price.[3] One of her squires and her "gentle duke," Jean d'Alençon, reported that she had lovely breasts.[4] They also stated that her beauty aroused no carnal desires. Others said that, when Joan was around, soldiers "lost their sexual feelings"; they even stopped *talking* about sex.[5] Of all Joan's accomplishments, that effect alone is amazing, in such rough and lecherous times.

I want to call her Jehanne. That is how her name was read and spoken by her contemporaries, and how she signed herself, close to the end, when she had learned to sign her own letters. By calling her by her given name, we may gain an angle of perspective that will help us see her afresh, free from the veils of propaganda and hagiography.

She was probably born in 1412. Her parents farmed fifty acres near Dom-rémy in Lorraine, an independent-minded enclave in an area that was mostly under the sway of the Burgundians, who were allied at this time with the English in their Hundred Years' War against the French. Within three years of her birth, a French host was routed by a much smaller English army under Henry V on the field of Agincourt. The best military leaders in France were killed or captured; the young Duke Charles of Orleans was shipped off to England as a hostage, and lived there for decades while a new war was fought in his name.

From quite early in her life, Jehanne's father was haunted by dreams in which he saw her riding off with men-at-arms.[6] He was disgusted and horrified by these dreams, assuming that they meant his daughter was going to become a camp whore. Nice girls did not go away with soldiers; still less did they command them. He tried to keep her sheltered, spinning wool by the hearth in winter, minding the sheep, helping with the farm chores with her siblings, and going regularly to church. He told some confidants that, if he had believed the dreams would come true, he would rather have drowned his daughter than see her shamed.

She was a modest and dutiful child, regular in church, but she also attended a church without walls.

THE LADY TREE

She could see the great oak wood from the garden, swelling into curves of deep green above yellow gorse and gray heather and the flat wheat fields. In the night, Jehanne listened to the wind playing the forest like a harp. When she was tending the flock, she often let the sheep wander toward the oak wood on the hill. Sometimes, escaping from chores, she joined other girls in tracking one of the fevered or rheumy pilgrims who struggled up the hill in hopes of healing at the ancient spring. Daring youngsters liked to spy on the young men and women who made love nests in the woods, bedding down on heaped leaves. Sometimes the young bucks brought antlers to hang on branches, invoking the ardor of the true stag in his season.

At the heart of the oak wood, on the crest of the hill, was a grove of beeches. One beech towered above the others. Though its roots showed through the soil, like raised veins on an old woman's hand, this tree had survived wind and storm for countless generations. There were people who feared this tree and saw living serpents in the sinuous weavings of its roots.

Everyone knew it was a place of the Old Ones. It was whispered that the fairies still danced around the tree at the great turnings of the wheel of the year, especially around May Day and All Hallows. The water of the spring was the gift of an ancient power of the land. It soothed away fevers, rinsed off blemishes of the skin, and gave the gift of vision and inspiration.

Jehanne loved to touch the skin of this tree, smooth and silvery. While a nearby oak was clearly male — fierce and craggy with limbs thrown out in a boxer's stance — the great beech, rounded and silky, was plainly female. L'Arbre aux Dames, she was called in the village: the Ladies' Tree. To Jehanne, the tree herself was a lady.

The Lady Tree was loveliest in her springtime unfolding, when her reddish buds opened to release fresh soft leaves of pale and vital green. Her sex came alive on the same branches, the tasseled catkins quivering on their long stalks, the flower-balls putting up delicate tendrils that waved in the air, seeking pollen.

As spring ripened into summer, the Lady Tree dressed herself in heavier and darker greens. Under her canopy, it was cool and shady on the warmest day. Yet through the dark came bursts of brilliant light that could catch you full in the face, as if a star had leaned down to touch you. When the breeze moved among the leaves, the lights danced, the veil of perception thinned, and airy things took substance.

"If I were in a wood, I could easily hear the Voice which came to me," Jehanne told her judges.[7]

The voices that came to her, under the Lady Tree and other trees, were not merely voices. They came with bursts of light and shapes of human or more than human size, and with the scent of flowers and fresh young leaves.

Of all the imagined portraits of Jehanne, the one by the patriotic Lorraine artist Jules Bastien-Lepage most strongly evokes her experiences among the trees. It is now in the sculpture gallery of the Metropolitan Museum of Art in New York City. It shows Jehanne in her parents' garden, in her early teens, receiving one of the visions that drove her, amazingly, to claim the right to command the armies of France, to save a great city and crown a king.

In the artist's vision, the Maid's wide and beautiful blue eyes search for something above and beyond the rustic scene around her, though the scene is pulsing with magic. Her left arm is outstretched, and she is clasping something. You lean closer to the painting, to see what the girl has in her hand. Something green. Maybe fresh leaves from the tree under which she stands. She is leaning against the trunk, taking her strength from the tree.

The mottled colors of the bushes and the old stone wall behind the peasant girl in her long brown skirt are embroidery in paint. The subtle weave dissolves the planes and releases a shocking revelation.

You don't see him at first, hovering in midair behind Jehanne in golden armor. Even when you notice him, it is easy to miss his female companions. They are translucent, their forms a thin mist through which the background landscape is clearly seen. One of them appears to be carrying her own head. What kind of visitors are these?

They have assumed the forms of Catholic belief, as the archangel Michael, and Saint Catherine and Saint Margaret, all named by Jehanne later on among her voices. They may not have appeared in these guises when she first encountered them. "The first time he came," Jehanne told her judges, "I was in great doubt whether he was Saint Michael, and I was very much afraid. I saw him many times before I was certain it was Saint Michael."

The powers of the deeper world are known to produce "contact pictures," images of themselves that conform to the beliefs and expectations of a certain time. We'll return to this question, in Jehanne's own words, when she faces the men who were assembled to find an excuse to burn her.

THE SMELL OF SALT HERRING

She was sixteen when she set out to lead a war to change the history of France and the world. Her purpose burned in her with a bright clean flame. She believed she had been given a divine mission, to rally a broken and divided people against the English, who had occupied more than half the country, including Paris, in concert with their Burgundian allies. Her immediate assignments were to lead an army to the relief of the great city of Orleans then closely besieged by the English, and to escort the dauphin Charles to the northern city of Rheims to be crowned and anointed as king.

Her first step was to approach a local baron, Robert de Baudricourt. She traveled to Baudricourt's castle at Vaucouleurs under the protection of a male relative who had been seized by her mission. Her magnetism did not work on the rough soldier Baudricourt. When she informed him she had a God-given mission to liberate France, he considered handing this crazy girl to his men for recreation, but instead sent her home with a message to her father to give her a good flogging.

Yet she stirred feelings of admiration, even awe, among men-at-arms as well as rural folk. She gave people shivers. Boys and grizzled horse soldiers volunteered to fight in her service. Old prophecies were recalled, of a savior who would come from an oak wood and of a maid who would save a country destroyed by an evil woman (believed to be Isabeau of Bavaria, the queen mother). Could Jehanne be the one? The excited rumors that began to spread may have inspired the Burgundians to send a raiding party against Jehanne's village in the summer of 1428, a raid her family escaped, taking shelter in a nearby fort.

Jehanne visited Baudricourt again on February 12, 1429. The date is significant because of something else that was happening that day, many miles to the south. Visionaries are sometimes required to give practical proofs of their powers. This time the Maid was not only carrying a big vision; she came equipped to demonstrate that she was the kind of seer who could deliver military intelligence.

She told Baudricourt about a battle in which the English were cutting up the French and their Scottish auxiliaries *as they spoke*. Her voices were telling her about the rout. Maybe she could also see it and smell it. A very fishy smell. On that same day, on the road to Orleans, the French attacked an English column bringing supplies to the English garrisons along the Loire. Since it was Lent, the English vittles were fish instead of meat. The English, led by Sir John Fastolf (a colorful character immortalized by Shakespeare as Falstaff), circled their wagons, mowed down the French with arrows from their longbows, then put them utterly to flight. Because of all the fish left strewn over the field, the French defeat became known as the Battle of Herrings. When news of the battle reached Vaucouleurs a few days later, Baudricourt realized that Jehanne was a reliable seer, and he was smart enough to see this was a gift that his side could use.[8] He assigned her an escort — just four men-at-arms — to take her to the dauphin at Chinon. He took a very special precaution before he sent her on her way. He had her exorcized by a priest. A gift like Jehanne's might come from saints and angels, or the other mob.[9]

With the smell of salt herring, a pattern was established. When Jehanne could not win hard men to her cause through her numinous presence, she won them by producing military intelligence they could not obtain by other means. This helps us understand how she persuaded rough soldiers and degenerate nobles to follow her.

The next major scene in her story was played out behind the high walls of the castle at Chinon. She said to a soldier who slurred a crude insult at her as she passed through the gate, "It's a shame you deny God when you are so close to death." That same evening, the soldier drowned in the river. Word spread quickly that the Maid not only saw the future but could bring it about. This probably did not make the moody, irresolute dauphin any more eager to see this girl from Lorraine. The dauphin was shadowed by his father's madness, his country's ruin, and his own mother's assertion that he was a bastard. Yet he, too, had heard prophecies of a Maid who might save his kingdom. Another female visionary, Marie d'Avignon, had brought him a story of a woman in armor — not herself — who would lead France to victory.[10]

The dauphin's advisers counseled him to set tests. When Jehanne was admitted to his court, Charles hid himself among his courtiers after casting one of them, in gorgeous clothing, to play his part. Jehanne was not deceived. She picked him out. Then, in a private audience, she gave him a secret message. It is known as the Sign of the King. She told the dauphin something that struck him so deeply that he believed in her — at least for now — and in his own royal destiny. No one knows for certain what Jehanne said to Charles on that day in Chinon. But we can follow certain clues that both predate and postdate Jehanne's meeting with the man she made king.

THE SIGN OF THE KING

Car ung roy de France doit estre
Charles, filz de Charles, nommé,
Qui sur tous rois sera grant maistre.
Propheciez l'ont surnommé
"Le Cerf Volant."

For there will be a king of France
Called Charles, son of Charles,
Who will be grand master over all kings.
Prophecies have named him
"The Flying Stag."

— CHRISTINE DE PIZAN, *Ditié de Jehanne d'Arc*

The stag is the most important symbol of the ancient kings of France. It features in an incident in the life of the dauphin's father, Charles VI, which was preserved by the chronicler Jean Froissart. As a boy-king, Charles VI visited the royal deer park at Senlis. In the night, he dreamed he was presented with a superb hunting falcon. The king loosed it from his wrist, and was devastated when the bird, vanishing above a great forest, failed to return. Then a winged deer appeared to the king. The king mounted the flying stag, and it carried him high above the treetops. He felt a soaring delight, recovered his falcon, and was given a view across the length and breadth of the kingdom.[11]

A certain kind of shrink might say that this dream — if authentic — was "ego inflation" that prefigured Charles VI's later descent into madness. Whether or not that is correct, the dream had the quality of a shamanic soul-flight. It is possible that the chronicler invented the king's dream, but if he did this, he created it within a context of belief that is revealing in itself. A true king of France was supposed to have a deep mystical connection with the deer.[12]

This may date back to the dawn of kingship, when a true king embodied the Antlered One, joining in sacred marriage with the Goddess in the body of her chosen priestess. In this way, under the great tree whose shape the antlers reproduce, he married the land. From the union of the Deer King and the Goddess came the rightful heir to the kingdom. Here, perhaps — rather than the story from Palestine — is the truth behind the legend of holy blood running through the veins of French kings.

The dual stories converged and finally fused when, in medieval France, the stag was re-visioned as a carrier of the Christ energy. Go to Les Halles and look up at the gothic tower of the great church of Saint Eustace. Near the top, above the gargoyles, you'll see the head of a stag with the Calvary cross between his antlers, recalling a legend in which Christ converted a pagan Roman general by speaking through the form of a deer.

Notice the prophecy, recalled in verse by the great woman poet Christine de Pizan, in celebration of Jehanne and the coronation of Charles VII. "Charles, son of Charles" is the "flying stag" who will be master of kings.

There may be a clue here to what Jehanne said in private to the dauphin that persuaded him to do something all but incredible: to appoint an illiterate teenage peasant girl as his "chief of war," commanding general of the armies of France. We can be sure that whatever she said reassured him of his birthright, making up for his mother's abandonment and betrayal. To have seized his mind, it must have been something more specific than the generic picture of "an angel descending with a crown" that Jehanne — fatigued after many long days of interrogation and humiliation — later told her judges was the sign she had given.

Imagine this:

The dauphin is intrigued by the Maid. He orders his courtiers to withdraw, leaving him alone with Jehanne within the tapestry panels that provide warmth and color inside the gray stone walls of the castle.

She moves toward him. As she brushes the tapestries, the scene of a deer wood stirs and comes alive. She sits at the feet of the awkward, ill-favored prince.

"My court calls me king," he frowns at her. "Why do you call me only dauphin?"

"My dauphin, you will only be king when you find the kingdom in your heart."

"You spoke of a sign known only to me."

"You are wandering in a dark wood. You have fled here because you have been shamed and abandoned. Your own mother has denied you. You are so very young, my dauphin. You are crying for your father, but your father was lost to you long before he left this world. Your country is in the possession of evil men. Your court is full of malice and intrigue, moving like a minstrel show from one small city to another. You fear you will lose your mind, like your father. So very young. You have come into the wood to find peace, a place to dream brighter dreams."

The dauphin is sobbing. He is in the wood, deep inside the scene she is describing. He hears the wind sighing through the branches. He starts at shadows. He darts this way and that, with the fear that something is stalking him. So many enemies, even here.

There is hope. There is a horse saddled and waiting for him. He grabs for the pommel and pulls himself up. No, it's not a horse. It is a stag. It races through the undergrowth, leaping higher and higher . . . until Charles is looking down over the treetops. How can this be?

"You are coming home to the heart," a voice deeper than that of the Maid's walks through his mind. He has the impression of flying over Chinon, then swooping down through stone walls that part for him like curtains. He sees a weak, ill-favored man in the clothes of the court, slumped in a throne under a tent of tapestries.

"You must come home, Charles," the voice speaks again. "Then you can receive Him. The Maker of Kings."

The scenes stream together. He is looking through the eyes of the man in the throne.

A slender girl stands before him, holding her hands over him, palms outward. Around her, above her, is the form of a great white stag. His antlers, like tongues of white fire, seem to rise beyond the roof. Light blazes from between them, brighter than lightning.

The hands of the Maid tremble as the power that is with her moves through her, along specific pathways. Her fingers move independently. As they spread and stretch and curve, they resemble the tines of the antlers. Streams of white fire move from her fingertips to the dauphin.

"Receive his light. It is streaming to you from between his antlers, my dauphin. Receive the Christ Light. Receive the true King."

Whatever magic Jehanne wove with the dauphin, he was sufficiently impressed — and perhaps terrified — that he had her grilled for eleven days by every cleric and theologian within reach. Her intimate parts were probed, by a queen of Hungary, no less, to confirm that her hymen was intact. She was cross-examined to make sure that she held no breath of heresy. She was exorcized again. And then, having passed all tests, she was made chief of war and placed at the head of a French army charged with relieving Orleans of its English besiegers.

The dauphin offered her a sword. But she said there was only one sword that would serve, and it was hidden behind the altar of the church of Saint Catherine at Fierbois. She described this sword rather exactly. She said it had five equal-armed crosses engraved on the blade. The sword was found exactly where she said it was located, among a heap of forgotten ex-votos behind the church altar. When the rust was cleaned off, the crosses were revealed. According to legend, this same sword was carried by the hero Charles Martel. Jehanne never used it as a weapon. She wielded it as a symbol of command and an emblem of France.[13]

As she marched to war, she carried other symbols as well. The most famous was her banner. It was painted on white silk, with the figures of two angels worshipping the King of Heaven. She said the two angels represented a myriad of angels. The banner also carried the words *Jhesu Maria*. She told her judges a "clerk," that is to say, a literate man, chose those words. That man was a Scot called Powers. There were also fleurs de lys, for Orleans and for France, on her standard. She did not simply fly the flag of France, or Orleans, because she insisted her mission came from Heaven.

Another of her symbols — the hallows of Jehanne — was the ring. She was often seen to kiss the ring or hold it close to her face. It was a brass ring, not gold, befitting a peasant girl. It was engraved with a cross and those words *Jhesu Maria*.

In her march through the Loire country to relieve Orleans and, afterward, to drive the English from the castles they had occupied on either side of the river, Jehanne demonstrated again and again her ability to mobilize people to fight in her cause and to drain the morale and esprit of her adversaries. Napoleon said the most important quality in a general is luck, and Jehanne had plenty of that in this period, though she would have called it divine providence. But she also had an extraordinary ability to change the hearts and minds of men. Prior to her arrival on the field, the French had been a broken people unwilling to fight. Now they rushed to join her army. The English, who previously had had every reason for confidence, began to falter. Even the weather seemed to be on her side. Attempting a crossing of the Loire from the southern bank of the river to reach the east side of Orleans, where the English besiegers occupied only one strongpoint, the French were beaten back by a strong gale — until Jehanne appeared and the wind shifted in their favor.

In her dealings with the enemy, Jehanne sometimes appeared to be not only a clairvoyant but also a master of psychic suggestion. In the contest for Les Tourelles, the fortification commanding the bridge to Orleans, Jehanne had a sharp exchange with Glasdale, the English commander, and told him she had pity for his soul. Soon after, Glasdale fell off the bridge, fully armored, and drowned in the Loire.[14] Among her enemies, this sort of thing enhanced Jehanne's reputation as a sorceress, one who had the ability to twist the minds of her victims and drive them to self-destruction.

She again demonstrated her gifts as a seer during the siege of the English-occupied castle at Jargeau, when she saved Alençon's life by warning him that, unless he changed his position, he would be killed by an English "gunpowder machine" she pointed out on the ramparts. Alençon moved — and saw another Frenchman killed by the English cannon on that very spot.[15]

The Deer of Patay

The Earl of Suffolk was one of the English commanders Jehanne's forces made prisoner when they captured Jargeau. Two weeks later, as Jehanne led her army north on the long road to Rheims to fulfill her promise to crown the dauphin in that ancient city, Suffolk received a four-line message. It contained an old prophecy, written in Latin and attributed to Merlin. This Merlin spoke of an astrological event — *Descendit virgo dorsum sagittari*, "Virgo will ride on the back of Sagittarius" — that could also be interpreted as political prophecy. A Maid would ride the Archer.[16] The most feared archers in the known world were the English longbowmen. They were about to be mastered in the Battle of Patay accurately described by Mark Twain as "one of the few supremely great and imposing battles."[17]

The French victory at Patay, on June 18, 1429, was the gift of a stag. At the very least, the episode is a remarkable example of the importance of coincidence — or luck — in history.

There is nothing to mark the site. A dip in a wheat field may mark the intersection of the old Roman road between Paris and Blois and another old road between Chartres and Orleans. It was here, most historians agree, that the battle was fought.

Jehanne was not in the field until the battle was won, and this is highly significant, since it was her practice to put herself in the vanguard of her forces, flourishing her banner, willing her men to charge the enemy or swarm up the scaling ladders. In place of Jehanne, the deer came this day.

On the eve of the Battle of Patay, Joan of Arc's army was nervous. They had saved Orleans and driven the English from the Loire Valley. They were now facing an English relief column they outnumbered by two to one. But the French had not acquired the habit of winning. The English had been whipping them since the start of the Hundred Years' War. Numbers always favored the French but were rendered insignificant by the Englishmen's superior discipline and morale, their unity of command — and the range of their longbows.

Jehanne rallied her troops, promising them a victory that would change everything. She told Alençon that he had better wear good spurs, because he would be riding hard after the enemy to rout them all. She told her men-at-arms that, even if the English were hanging from the clouds, those who marched under her banner would take them.

It was a strange kind of engagement that was unfolding. The English commanders, Talbot and Fastolf, learned during the night that they had come too late to relieve their garrison at Beaugency, which had surrendered to the Maid. So they ordered their relief column to withdraw, stealthily and in good order, through the woods near Patay. Jehanne ordered her forces to pursue, with the mounted men-at-arms in the vanguard. But the French scouts lost track of the English in the thick woods and the thick night. And they feared, with good reason, that when they found the English they would only fall into one of the traps the English had laid successfully again and again.

Near that dip in the wheat field, five hundred select archers were driving pointed stakes in the ground. Flanked by dense bushes interspersed with dismounted knights, and with the stakes as a strong stockade in front of them and the main part of the English force, under Fastolf, on the hill behind, they were ready to mete out death to any French attackers who tried to take them head on. English longbows were the machine guns of the day; they had destroyed French armies before, and there was no reason to think they would fail now.

But they were not permitted to finish making their trap. The deer took care of that. The primary source for what happened is the narrative of the Burgundian captain Jean de Wavrin, who fought in the English ranks that day. De Wavrin described how Talbot was laying his ambush, concealed from the French, when "a stag came out of the woods, which plunged into the midst of the English battle line, whence arose a great cry, for they knew not that their enemy was so close to them."[18]

Not knowing the French were nearby, the English went into one of their hunting frenzies, raising cries and running after the stag. Hearing this commotion, the French scouts were able to locate the English positions, and sent runners back to

La Hire, one of Jehanne's most vigorous and most faithful warriors, to alert him to an opportunity. When the French cavalry galloped up, they found the formidable English longbowmen out of position, still working on their stockade. The French knights and men-at-arms plowed across the clearing, cutting and trampling the English along the whole length of their line. Panic spread through the English positions. Talbot was taken prisoner. Fastolf, at the head of a second English force, fled all the way back to Paris — where he was stripped of his Order of the Garter by the English regent, the Duke of Bedford. The casualty figures are astonishing. The English lost two thousand of their three thousand men. Three Frenchmen were killed, in an army of about six thousand.[19]

Thanks to the stag.

He was magnificent. Velvet hung in strips from his huge rack. Was he running away from the French scouts, or running in their cause?

By revealing the English positions, the deer of Patay brought the fulfillment of Jehanne's promise of a great victory. No one at the time believed that the appearance of the stag was a coincidence. The medieval mind did not allow for coincidences that were *only* coincidence. In the incidents of this world, Jehanne's contemporaries searched for the "signatures" of forces at work in a hidden reality.

None of the modern scholars has dared to pull the threads together. Nor have Joan's hagiographers, no doubt because they are afraid that to dwell too much on her connection with the deer would be to reopen the old allegations of witchcraft.

Jehanne sent the deer. Far from the front lines, slipping into one of her trances under the shade of a tree, she released him with her intent, as shamans and seers had long known how to do. Is that possible?

Before her judges, out of modesty and to avoid the witch charge, she said, "God sent us the deer to manifest his will." And the pious will recall that the stag — suitably decorated with the cross — appeared to saints of the church, such as Saint Eustace.

THE CROWN AND THE STAKE

After the Battle of Patay, Jehanne broke her sword — the sword of five crosses found behind the altar of Saint Catherine at Fierbois — when she used the flat of the blade to whack a camp woman who was servicing the soldiers. Some people thought the breaking of the sword was the moment her luck began to turn.

She rode with the dauphin to Rheims and stood in her armor, with her banner raised high, as he was crowned Charles VII, so fulfilling another of her promises. From this moment, her light and her power began to fade. She was not invited to the celebratory banquets that followed the coronation. The king's favorites did not have the stomach to pursue the war, and they guided him into deceitful diplomatic traps laid by the Duke of Burgundy.

Jehanne carried her banner to the walls of Paris, flouting the king's wishes. As she later confessed to her judges, her voices did not tell her to attack Paris. She moved because of "certain noblemen in arms," and because of her own desire "to cross the moats of Paris." Her calling was no longer clear. Famously, her assault on Paris failed. The city was huge, the walls enormous, and the presence of the Maid did not trigger a popular uprising against the Burgundian masters of the city. She threw herself into the vanguard, in her usual style, as her men tried to fill the moat in front of the St.-Honoré gate. She was wounded in the thigh by a crossbow bolt fired by a defender who called her a "cackling bawd" and was removed by Alençon — against her loud protests — from the field.

After Paris, Jehanne's road led steeply downhill. The king moved south, far away from the enemy, and she was obliged to move with the court. She was separated from her "gentle duke." After a miserable winter of loneliness and inaction, she was sent by the king's advisors along wretched muddy roads, without enough food and weapons for her men, to attack the strongholds of a robber baron east of Orleans — and suffered her first defeat, outside a walled city ironically named Charity-on-the-Loire.

Jehanne's last battle was fought defending the northern city of Compiègne against the Burgundians. This time she was facing the enemy from inside the walls. Frustrated by being cooped up, she led a sortie, ran into vastly stronger forces — and found the gate of the city barred against her when she tried to beat a necessary retreat. Historians debate whether she was betrayed by the captain of Compiègne or by her own strategy. She was taken captive by a Burgundian soldier. She had recently predicted that she would be taken prisoner, but it seems she did not know it would happen that day. If her voices and visions were no longer clear, if her power failed her, perhaps it was because since Rheims she had been deeply off mission.

Her Burgundian captors sold her to the English, who arranged a trial at Rouen, in Normandy, that was intended to discredit her and provide a pretext for her execution. There were only two judges. The principal judge, Pierre Cauchon, bishop of Beauvais, was a creature of the English. The second judge, an official of the Holy Inquisition, was so embarrassed by the barbarous unfairness of the proceedings that he absented himself from most of the court sessions. A significant number of the "assessors" engaged to question the accused and lend a veneer of dignity to the proceedings had been, quite literally, on the English payroll for some years.

Though supposedly on trial under church law as a heretic, Jehanne was confined in a secular jail, with men — dissolute, foul-mouthed English soldiers — as her jailers. She was initially confined in an iron cage, chained by the neck, hands, and feet.

The men behind the trial wanted her dead, and they stopped at nothing to see her dead. Yet at all points the notaries recording the proceedings were concerned to keep a full and honest account. They checked frequently with the prisoner to make sure she agreed with the transcript. They examined each other's versions and — when the assessors were falling over each other to interrupt and misdirect and lay traps for the accused — they were still very careful to make sure she was given full justice in the court record, though she would get it nowhere else. Thus the trial proceedings are one of the most extraordinary documentary series from the Middle Ages, and you have the sense, reading them, that you can hear the actual voice of the Maid of Orleans.

Let's listen to that voice, as she responds to her judges and assessors on the nature of her seership.

The men who want to kill her wish to know about the tree. For once, they don't need to press or repeat their question. It's the third day of the public trial, February 24, 1431.

QUESTION: *What have you to say about a certain tree which is near your village?*

She doesn't hesitate. She makes no secret of the tree. How could she?

JEHANNE: *Not far from Domrémy there is a tree they call the Ladies' Tree. Others call it the Fairies' Tree. Nearby, there is a spring where people sick with fever come to drink, as I have heard, and to seek water to restore their health.*

A note of caution comes in. She has seen pilgrims come to the tree, but will not vouch for the healing. Old folk say they have seen fairies at the tree. One of her godmothers, Jehanne Aubery, has seen them. But Jehanne will not say what she has seen. Yes, she danced and sang at the tree and hung garlands in its branches. But since she embarked on her mission to liberate France, she has given herself "as little as possible to these games and distractions."

She always avoided promising to tell her judges the *whole* truth.

What did she see at the tree, if not the fairies?

Her questioners ask her later (on March 18, 1431) what she knows about those who "travel through the air with the fairies." She says she has never done this herself, but certainly she has heard of it. She has heard that this type of flight takes place on Thursdays. This was common knowledge among country people. Jehanne tells her judges it is just a *sorcerie*, a spell, no big deal.

In a closed assize (on March 15, 1431), they asked her about her visitors.

QUESTION: *If the Devil were to put himself in the likeness of an angel, how could you tell whether it was a good or evil angel?*

JEHANNE: *I should know very well if it were Saint Michael or a counterfeit. The first time he came I was in great doubt whether he was Saint Michael, and I was very much afraid. I saw him many times before I was certain it was Saint Michael.*

That was an amazingly bold admission in the presence of men who had been engaged to send her to the stake. *I saw him many times before I was certain it was Saint Michael.* What did she think at first, before she was coached to give the names of Catholic saints to the powers of the invisible world that became visible to her?

Her judges pursue this question indirectly, by requiring her to describe Saint Michael as he appeared to her.

QUESTION (on March 17, 1431): *In what form, size, kind, and dress did Saint Michael come to you?*

JEHANNE: *In the form of a true honest man [prud'homme]; of his dress and the rest I will say nothing more.*

It was Michael, she told her judges, who named the female spirits that came to her, as Saint Margaret and Saint Catherine. These were the names of two saints depicted and worshipped at Jehanne's parish church in Domrémy. She grew up with their images, as she grew up with the Fairies' Tree in the oak wood that she and the girls crowned with flowers and the men crowned with antlers.

Modern Catholic scholars are doubtful that there ever really was a Saint Margaret or a Saint Catherine; their biographies are sketchy and crumble away under scrutiny. In 1967 the Roman Catholic Church declared the story of Catherine's martyrdom *omnia fabulosa* — completely imaginary.

I do not doubt that Jehanne's visitors were entirely real, but they may have traveled under assumed names.

They killed her for cross-dressing. When they had worn her down, they finally persuaded her to sign a document of "abjuration," confessing her crimes. The version she signed was only a few lines, and she signed it with a mark rather than the name she had learned to write, indicating to those in the know that this was not a true statement. Later her judges produced a much longer document of abjuration confessing many crimes she had not admitted; it is likely that this document was a fabrication.

The English were enraged that she had signed *anything*, since the effect was to commute her sentence from death to life imprisonment. But wait: "We will have her yet," the toad-bishop Cauchon promised Bedford, his English master. She had confessed to the "crime" of wearing men's clothes. Any relapse into so doing would constitute an act of heresy for which she could be put to death. So they sent her back to the same prison with the same brutal male jailers, who removed the female clothes she had been given, so that her only option — other than going naked in front of male brutes — was to garb herself again in the men's garments they gave her. For cross-dressing, this time involuntarily, they burned her at the stake.

OUT OF THE ASHES

She was burned three times, because her internal organs resisted the fire. After, her ashes were thrown into the Seine. Nonetheless, in 1867 part of a rib bone and other items, including the thigh bone of a cat, were found in an apothecary jar in Paris labeled "Remains found under the stake of Joan of Arc." These were held to be true relics and exhibited at Tours until forensic science proved a hoax: the rib bone was actually borrowed from an Egyptian mummy. Though found in dubious company, the French investigator noted, the cat's femur was not necessarily part of the fraud. It was not unusual in Jehanne's time for a cat ("or other sign of the devil") to be thrown on the pyre of a witch.[20]

She predicted in court that "within seven years the English would have to forfeit a bigger prize than Orleans." The French reclaimed Paris on November 12, 1437 — six years and eight months after her prophecy.

A quarter century after her murder, a trial of "nullification" convened by the pope dismissed the judgments that had been passed on her. Many of those who had known her flocked to celebrate her character and her visionary gifts.

Though it took the church until 1920 to canonize her, there is no doubt that Joan of Arc is truly a Catholic saint. She marched under the banner of Jesus and Mary. Her army was accompanied by large numbers of priests and other religious, who offered prayers and burned incense as the soldiers marched. She attended mass and made confession almost every day. She talked with Michael and with Saint Catherine and Saint Margaret. She frequently invoked Saint

Martin — "my Martin" — a patron saint of France and its royal houses since Merovingian times.[21]

Yet she was also that older thing, the *voyante*, the seer of Gallic and Celtic tradition — the *völva* of Nordic lands — who saw with the help of the trees and was considered by Caesar to be the most formidable of adversaries.[22]

We *have* to know Jehanne. We need her. What she was, what she is. In the darkest moment of World War II, Churchill understood this.

CHAPTER 8

❧

THE BEAUTIFUL DREAM SPY
OF MADRID

Inquisitor: "Why have you been arrested?"
Lucrecia de León: "Because of the dreams that are written."

— FROM THE *AUDIENCIA* AT TOLEDO, JUNE 4, 1590

He embraced her and told her, "You are so beautiful a dead man would rise up and
make you pregnant."

— TESTIMONY OF CAPTAIN IBÁÑEZ AGAINST LOPE DE MENDOZA,
OIDOR (JUDGE) OF THE INQUISITION, APRIL 4, 1591

When she lies down on her narrow bed, a man comes to her. When he touches her, all her senses come aflame, though she does not explain this to the priest who arrives every morning to steal her dreams on the pretext of hearing her confession. The same man comes to her, night after night. It is impossible not to mention something about him to her confessor, since her adventures nearly always begin with the arrival of her dream lover.

"What is his name?"

"He does not tell me."

"What does he look like?"

"He looks normal. Like any man who is strong and well made."

"What about his clothes? How much lace does he wear?"

"Nothing out of the ordinary."

The word *ordinary* was safe, dull enough to blunt suspicion. The more she used it, the less she had to turn aside questions that might remind her of the delicious pressure of her lover's touch, his nails turning arabesques along the insides of her thighs, the way he pleasured every part of her body, releasing wave after wave of delight until she was swimming through the air with him.

"And his speech? Is he of the people, or a caballero?"

"Ordinary."

So the priest wrote down, with his quill, *El Hombre Ordinario*. The Ordinary Man.[1]

Sometimes she would play with her confessor a little.

"He spoke to me of the one who is coming," she might say.

That always got Fray Lucas excited. Don Alonso, his master, would come to question her closely about the one who was coming. Was this a new king of Spain or the Messiah himself? She encouraged their speculations, which made her important and gave her the aura of prophecy. She did not reveal that the one who was most surely coming was herself. It excited her even now, with her family bowing and scraping to the clerics who roosted in the house like blackbirds, that when she slid between the covers tonight, her anything-but-ordinary man would come to her.

"Could he be John the Baptist?" Don Alonso would ask. He was a great student of scripture.

"He never tells me his name."

"That would be like Baptist John, to efface himself for the glory of the one whose coming he announces. Do you not concur, *doncella*?"

"I am no scholar, your eminence."

She could not tell how it began, even to herself. She was not sure whether he had come through a crack in the window or under the door, like a gust of wind, to stand over her bed, or had materialized out of mere air. Or whether she had stepped into his realm. This was possible, though in appearance the room remained the regular room in her parents' house, down to the crucifix above the bed and the chamber pot under it.

She wanted her dream lover to come to her in the flesh, preferably with the money and rank to satisfy her father that he would be a suitable husband for a *doncella*, a maiden of respectable family who was acquainted with the royal court. Lucrecia would be twenty soon, too old to be unmarried. She had no idea, when the dreams began, that they would become so valuable to powerful men who had little interest in her marriage prospects. On the mornings when Fray Lucas wrote down her dreams, an armed courier waited in the stench of the Calle San Salvador, his horse's nose in a bag of oats, ready to ride hard to the holy city of Toledo to bring the latest news to Don Alonso. The young scribe she had not yet met, except in dreams she did not tell the clerics, would tell her, smiling side-long under his lashes, that her dreams were the most important news in Spain.

WHEN DREAMS ARE AFFAIRS OF STATE

In the Spain of Philip II, dreams were taken very seriously. They could bring you serious power or serious trouble, sometimes in vertiginous sequence.

Lucrecia de León was a lovely young woman who really wanted to dream up a fabulous lover and husband, but who dreamed her way into the affairs of the king and the games of nations, and so eventually found herself a guest of the Inquisition (but did not end like Joan of Arc). Thanks to the men who recorded her dreams, and to the Inquisition, which seized but preserved the register, reports of 415 of Lucrecia's dreams from a three-year period (1587–1590) have survived and are now in the Archivo Histórico Nacional in Madrid. They offer an amazing window into vitally important but woefully underreported aspects of history: into the lives of women and the *experience* of dreaming in the age of the Renaissance and the Counter-Reformation.

Lucrecia was no Joan of Arc; her story begins and ends quite differently. Still less was she like Hildegard or Teresa of Avila, mystical nuns and "spiritual mothers" who yearned for spiritual marriage with Christ and the interior castle of the heart. Lucrecia was a passionate young woman who wanted the treasures and pleasures of *this* world, starting with the right husband and lover. She was beautiful and sexy, and knew it. She exercised enormous magnetism over men.

Lucrecia was a genuine *vidente*, or seer, and her main way of knowing what was going on — across time and behind closed doors — was to dream her way in. Thus she dreamed the defeat of the Spanish Armada a year before it set sail for England in 1588. She was thrust into a role in the political arena that she probably did not seek, though she may have been tempted by the power and social access it gave her. In the time and place she inhabited — except when she closed her eyes and went traveling elsewhere — a woman could have power only if she were born to it, or gained it through marriage or sex with the right man, or was recognized as a true seer.

She was treasured by a powerful faction in Madrid that tried to use the prophetic elements in her dreams to support their modernizing agenda to limit royal power and end a ruinous war and the plunder of the common people — a most interesting case of a liberalizing cause using medieval techniques of propaganda and lobbying. Paintings were made of her dreams, and an English-born duchess hosted a very chic theatrical salon where Lucrecia's dreams were turned into dramas others could witness.

Like Jehanne, Lucrecia de León manifested her gift on the edge of puberty. When she was twelve, she spoke to her family about a dream of a royal death. The location was quite specific. It was the town of Badajoz, on the road to Lisbon that the king was traveling. She described the black-draped horses and the catafalque of the royal funeral. Her father, Alonso Franco, a solicitor, was terrified. To dream of the death of the king could be interpreted as treason. And even though the girl thought the royal funeral in her dream was not for Philip, the shadow fell close enough. So Lucrecia's father beat her and ordered her not to dream again. The news came two weeks later that a royal had died in Badajoz, not Philip II but his queen, Anne of Austria. Now the family knew that Lucrecia's gift was real, but this did not improve her father's attitude.[2]

Her father did parchment work for Genoese bankers. The Genoese were almost the only people in Madrid who had a clue about money. They found the money for the endless wars of Philip II and his ridiculously expensive new palace, the Escorial, but they were not pleased with the king, because he frequently failed to pay his debts. Philip II had only recently decided to move his capital to what had previously been an insignificant town on a high, arid plateau without a navigable river flowing to the sea. It was an oddly isolated location for an empire on which the sun never set. The business of Madrid was that of the court, located in the overcrowded courtyards and offices of a refurbished Muslim fort, the Alcazar.

Lucrecia's family lived in the heart of the city in the parish of San Sebastián, later known as the Barrio of the Muses because of the celebrated artists and writers who lived there, including Cervantes. The family rented a ground-floor apartment — spacious, but sometimes shared with lodgers — in a house owned by the dowager Duchess of Feria. One of the people who boarded with the family for several years was a Moorish woman who may have imparted something of her own tradition of dreaming. There were no books in the family home. The stories Lucrecia knew, stories of Bible characters and of Spanish heroes and romances, came from what she heard, and they shaped and colored her dreams.

Let's jump to early September 1587. Lucrecia is nineteen, rather old to be unmarried in the Madrid society of those days. She is beautiful, and men find her sexually attractive, so it's not a matter of looks. No portrait of her has survived, but people who knew her spoke of her dark flashing eyes and dark brown hair, and we have a clue to her body type. One Sunday when Lucrecia visited the royal chapel with her mother Ana, a copy of the van Eycks' famous altarpiece, *The Adoration of the Lamb*, was on display, showing Eve in her naked glory. Ana exclaimed, "By Jesus, Lucrecia, her body is just like yours, from the neck down."[3] So we can picture Lucrecia, as the Dutch painters pictured Eve, with little high round breasts, a long waist, and a fertile belly that swells soft and downy as a succulent fruit.

As her later story reveals, Lucrecia was quite interested in sex and quite knowledgeable about it. So the absence of a husband was not because she was plain or because she wanted to become a nun or one of the mystical female celibates — the *beatas* — who were proliferating in Spain. She blamed her father for failing to put up an attractive dowry and to actively recruit suitors on her behalf.

Lucrecia had been recently employed at the palace as a maidservant to the governess of the Infante, the future Philip III. She may have owed this appointment to the influence of the family's landlady, the Duchess of Feria, who was a remarkable Englishwoman better known as Lady Jane Dormer, once the confidante of Queen Mary — "Bloody Mary" — the scourge of English Protestants. Working at the Alcazar, Lucrecia learned the details of court ceremonies and the layout of royal apartments, bedchambers, and "salons of lies" (*mentidoras*), which became familiar settings for her dream excursions. Presumably she caught the eye of a few minor noblemen and hangers-on. But she did not find a fiancé, and time was running on.

On her mother's side, Lucrecia's family had interesting connections. Relatives included a former governor of the Yucatán with an educated passion for astrology and divination. Another cousin, Juan de Tebes, was in the service of the Mendoza clan, whose dynastic power in Spain was second only to that of the Habsburg monarchy.

Early that month, Juan de Tebes dropped by "for a glass of water" and to trade gossip. Lucrecia was now famous in the family as a dreamer, so it was nothing out of the ordinary for Juan to ask her whether she had seen any interesting dreams. Lucrecia brushed the question away with an interesting phrase. "*Unos desvaríos diabólicos*," she shrugged. "Just some diabolical ravings."[4] The line has an undertow that could be missed by the modern reader. In Lucrecia's time, few people doubted that, in *big* dreams, it is possible to see the future and have contact with powers beyond the human. What church and state wanted to know was whether powerful dreams were the work of divine or diabolical agencies; the Inquisition issued crib sheets to help its officials decide such things.

Whether Lucrecia's dream was "diabolical" or just "ravings," Juan de Tebes pressed her to tell it. She proceeded to recount a strange story of a wild man dressed like a soldier, in half armor, spewing grain and then milk from his mouth. We can bet that she held the undivided attention of everyone present in the family *sala*. The man she described was a celebrity, a former soldier called Piedrola, who spent half his time in a madhouse and the rest of it roaming from plaza to plaza, spewing out dreams and prophecies predicting the ruin of Spain. In some versions, the enemies of Spain — the French and the English and the Turks — would fall on Spain from all sides, and the Moors would again rule the Spanish heartland. The year ahead, 1588, would be the time of apocalypse. And the "loss of Spain" would come from divine displeasure with the folly of the king.

Despite his evident instability and the treasonable content of his predictions, the Cortes (the Spanish parliament) was seriously considering a proposal to create a new position for Piedrola as the national prophet. Whatever they thought of the state of his mind, Spanish grandees opposed to Philip II's financially ruinous war in the Low Countries and the mismanagement of the economy found it expedient to encourage the dissemination of the soldier-prophet's warnings. In the absence of institutions that allowed for free debate, state policy was opposed — and sometimes affirmed — by circulating prophecies and significant dreams.[5]

And here was a young woman presenting Piedrola, in her dream, as some kind of Green Man, a male fertility figure, pouring out the gifts of the fruitful earth for those who would receive the gift of his words. Juan de Tebes finished his drink and rushed off to tell his master, Alonso de Mendoza, about the girl and her dream.

Don Alonso was a highly influential man. His brother Bernardino was a military commander and spymaster who had recently been expelled from England — where he had been posted as ambassador — for plotting the overthrow of Queen Elizabeth, and was now Spain's ambassador to France. As canon of the cathedral in Toledo, Spain's holy city, Alonso de Mendoza was one of the princes of the church. His close friends included Archbishop Quiroga, the inquisitor-general. He maintained a residence in Madrid and was deeply involved in court politics, favoring the "peace" party that wanted to end the war in the Low Countries. Don Alonso was a theologian and Bible scholar who gave lectures on scripture; he was also intensely interested in dreams and latter-day prophecy and was one of the main champions of the street prophet Piedrola.

He summoned Lucrecia to visit him and tell her story. After that he became a frequent visitor at the apartment on Calle San Salvador. Lucrecia's mother was flattered by the great man's attentions. He was avid to hear Lucrecia's dreams. To make it perfectly respectable for a man of fifty to sit alone with a lovely young woman, they would make dream-telling part of confession. Soon Don Alonso wanted more. He asked permission to keep a register of Lucrecia's dreams so nothing would be lost. This scared the family. Such writings could be dangerous. Lucrecia asked her regular confessor, a Dominican, about it, and he cautioned her to let nothing be recorded unless she wanted to be visited by the Inquisition. As a member of the order that founded the Inquisition, he could be presumed to know what he was talking about. In her dreams, Lucrecia received mixed signals about how to proceed. The danger in the situation became impossible to ignore when Piedrola was arrested by the Inquisition, despite the support of Don Alonso and other grandees. Nonetheless, Lucrecia and her family agreed to let Don Alonso keep his register. No doubt the family was influenced by the fact that he started showering them with gifts of money and finery. For her part, Lucrecia loved to be the center of attention and to have men hanging on her every word.

Because he was required to spend much of his time in Toledo, Don Alonso deputized a trusted friend, Fray Lucas de Allende, to record Lucrecia's dreams on a daily basis. Fray Lucas was another well-connected churchman, as prior of the Franciscan order in Madrid.

He was a very cautious recorder in the beginning, distancing himself from whatever the girl was saying by writing, "She said that he said," and so on.

Then the dreamer jumped out of the frame and scared him badly.

When he arrived at the Calle San Salvador to take dictation one morning, Lucrecia began, as usual, by describing the view from her window. This is the way her dreams very often began. She is looking out her window, and sees a procession in the street. Or one of her familiar dream visitors — there are three of them, all male — turns up and escorts her on a journey. Sometimes they simply go about the town. Sometimes they enter the Alcazar, the royal palace, and even see the king in his throne room or his bedchamber. Sometimes they cross the ocean and go to distant lands, even to the palace of the Great Turk.

On that morning, Lucrecia describes a very simple journey, just a short walk. She recounts, step by step, how she passes through an iron grille and along a corridor and enters a room with precious books on a shelf and the image of a tonsured man praying with birds and animals. As she begins to describe the bed in the room, and certain embarrassingly personal details, Fray Lucas shouts at her to stop. He leaves the house in haste, muttering about the devil's work. Back at the convent, he burns all the pages of the dream register he has written up to this point. Why? Because Lucrecia has described to him, in unerring detail, his cell and his circumstances at the Franciscan convent. She has never seen these things with her physical eyes, yet he is certain she has been in his space. She is a traveler, and she — or whatever travels with her — is powerful enough to fly through whatever wards Fray Lucas and his brothers have placed around their psychic space.[6]

Don Alonso found a way to calm the Franciscan's nerves, because within a few days, he took up his quill again, and now he took dictation in straightforward fashion, whether she was speaking of one of her dream guides ("The Ordinary Man said that . . ."), or describing radishes and chorizo in the market, or the length and folds of a nobleman's ruff, or otherworldly powers irrupting into the city.

Fray Lucas's night visitation was a turning point in the management of Lucrecia by her clerical handlers. They now knew that, in addition to allegorical visions, she could produce accurate intelligence on what was going on behind closed doors. If she could slip into the Franciscan convent in her dream body, she might be able to travel, undetected, to more interesting places. She had the makings of a dream spy.

For the next nineteen months, Lucas de Allende was Lucrecia's principal scribe. Then she found a new amanuensis, who was no ghost between the sheets.

LUCRECIA'S WINDOW

Lucrecia's dreams were a nightly show. "I wake up the moment my eyes are closed,"[7] she explained. Very often her dream narratives begin exactly the way a play does: the curtain goes up and the players are revealed onstage.

Typically, when she closes her eyes, she finds a familiar visitor in the room with her. This is the fellow identified by her scribes as the Ordinary Man because he won't give his name and there are no singular identifying details — at least none Lucrecia wishes to share. Typically the Ordinary Man materializes at her bedside, then draws her to her window, from which on a normal day she can watch the bustling crowds on the narrow Calle San Salvador and part of the wide Calle de Atocha. At night, the show is amazing.

She may observe a procession or performance rich in allegory. On several successive nights in early December 1587, she watched a tremendous juggernaut crushing hosts of innocents under its great bloody wheels. The wagon was pulled by giant bulls, with ruined symbols of the Habsburg dynasty on top and evil and crooked courtiers hanging on. Some of the street dramas Lucrecia observed from her window conformed to Christian and Bible imagery instilled in her by her confessors, and to popular themes in the apocalyptic prophecies that were heard all over Spain. Some seemed to draw from older, more primal sources.[8]

In addition to the Ordinary Man, she is often joined by two other male companions with extraordinary powers. They sometimes appear on a seacoast, with fishing nets. One of them likes to arrive with a lion on a leash, and so she sometimes calls him the Lion Man, and regards him as the wisest of her teachers. None of them ever gives her a personal name, though there is much discussion about this, inside and outside her dreams.[9]

Lucrecia has a gift for detailed observation and the exact description of people and locales, and this is a feature of the dream reports her sponsors search for intelligence data. Don Alonso encourages her to spy on enemies domestic and foreign, and her Ordinary Man is very willing to help.

He flies her out the window to a high tower with a view over the nations of this world. Then they swoop down to a house in England, where she observes Sir Francis Drake — who has already raided Spanish seaports and ships — plotting new attacks on Spain and writing a letter to the sultan of Turkey to enlist his support. Drake is wearing a crimson damask coat lined with fur.[10]

The Ordinary Man often takes her to the palace of Philip II to observe the condition of the king (who is frequently ill and believed to be close to death) and to witness treason in high places. In a typical visit, she goes to the king's private courtyard and witnesses a courtier who is close to Philip II engaged in treasonable correspondence. She doesn't know the conspirator's name, but she can provide identifying details: he has red hair and blue eyes, and on his breast he is wearing the cross of the Knights of Calatrava, a military order founded during the wars with the Moors.[11]

Her dreams often revealed possible future events. Some of these (such as the destruction of the Spanish Armada) came to pass; others (such as the imminent death of the king or a Moorish invasion of Spain) did not. On January 16, 1588, the Ordinary Man told her that the Marquis of Santa Cruz, the man originally appointed to command the armada, would die within weeks; the marquis died on February 9. As early as late November 1587, and again in mid-December, she saw the English defeating the Spanish Armada. When that vision was fulfilled, in the summer of 1588, a lot of people began to see Lucrecia as a prophet, and a cult began to grow around her.[12]

Some of Lucrecia's dream adventures unfold in a kind of counterpart reality that corresponds fairly closely to the physical world but exhibits anomalies. Some of her dreams are dress-up performances reminiscent of the traveling masques and morality plays that inspired the early Tarot images. Some of the reports in her dream register seem to weave together what she may have seen with what she made up and what her audience *wanted* her to say. But when the voice in these reports sounds truest and we feel that Lucrecia is telling it as it was, there comes the sense that this is a woman who could see the *understory* in the world around her: that she stepped into a reality just behind the veil of appearances, where forces behind the obvious ones are at play in a game of the world that the worldly do not see. Those forces included things older than the Christian story.

When she closed her eyes on the night of December 6, 1587, her regular dream guy — the Ordinary Man — was there at her bedside. He gave her a drink from a curious red vessel, specifying that it contained water taken from a river on Saint John's Eve. He wanted her to lean out the window. She saw an approaching parade of wildly sexy bare-breasted women in jewels and silks, followed by a magnificent giantess who had a serpent wound around one of her breasts and a headdress composed of woven and plaited snakes. This immense woman carried two great cauldrons of water with her strong arms. When she let out a cry to heaven, men of all the nations rushed to drink, and the cauldrons were never emptied.

The snake woman moved on, and a dark-skinned man of the same proportions took her place. When he cried out, his body became a living fountain, gushing from all of its parts, from which all the wild beasts and serpents of the earth came to drink.[13]

Fray Lucas may have blushed as he recorded these details. What was going on that night? The big clue is the water that was taken from a river on Saint John's Eve, better known as Midsummer's Night. That was the time of nude frolics in the Manzanares River, on the edge of the city — revels that were banned in Madrid the following year. That night was magic all across Europe. The dew of plants and herbs gathered before sunrise on Saint John's Day was believed to have healing power, to improve vision, and even to make knowing users invisible. After daybreak, the old ones said, you should no longer gather plants but rather wear them in street festivals and use them in rituals to divine the future and work love magic.[14]

Lucrecia moves from one level of dreaming into a deeper understory after drinking the water of Saint John's Eve. The Snake Goddess and the Fountaining Man are characters from the bigger drama; they can't be seen with ordinary sight, even ordinary dreamsight.

Lucrecia can't describe the woman with the cauldrons without leaving behind the Bible talk. She tells her confessor boldly that the serpent woman reminds her of the *madronas romanas*, the pagan goddesses of Roman times. My mind moves to Neil Gaiman's wondrously entertaining description, in *American Gods*, of the dramas of the old gods that continue to play behind the curtain of the world.

A medieval scholastic, trying to account for Lucrecia's time travels and her access to the understory, might say, "She stepped into the Aevum." In Thomist theology, the Aevum is an in-between realm between eternity (the divine depth beyond time) and the corrupted world where humans exist in sequential time. In the Aevum, duration is determined not by linear time but by movements of consciousness.

Don Alonso established a standard format for the dream reports. The time of each dream was noted as exactly as possible. He always wanted exact descriptions of clothing and locations, down to the length of a courtier's ruff. He made sketches from the dreams and had Lucrecia correct the details. Later, he commissioned paintings of many of her dreams, and, as these were shown at private gatherings, they helped to grow her fame.[15] He prepared an index of her dreams and cross-referenced images.

The dream is not the text. A question Lucrecia's inquisitors could not resolve was to what extent her dream reports had been "improved" by her scribes. Under examination, she said, "I cannot really remember the dreams because I forgot them after they were copied. I do remember very well some odd things, but not in the order in which they were dreamed. I do not know how to discover the difference between what I truly dreamed and what they added to the dreams."[16]

At our remove, we are even less likely to discover that difference. Yet we may sense we are close to her raw experience when the words are set down in "plain style" (*estilo llano*) and the scenes are full of details a woman, not a cleric, would notice — the chicken is in a certain type of basket, Drake's jacket is crimson damask — and above all when the *understory* is being played out beyond the imaginal world of her scribes.

Lucrecia and her growing fan club did not go unobserved. Five months after the recording of her dreams began, the royal confessor, Fray Diego de Chaves, ordered an investigation of her activities. She was briefly detained and charges of sedition were drawn up, but Don Alfonso's influence got her released. The fear generated by this episode may have contributed to the nervous illness that seized her in the spring of 1588, when she was reluctant to tell her dreams.

Then, in the summer of 1588, her prophecies of the destruction of the Spanish Armada were fulfilled. The armada was defeated by the English in July 1588 and suffered far heavier losses in westerly gales off Scotland and Ireland during the homeward journey in August. The news spread that Lucrecia was a true prophet, one who may have been sent to save Spain from the crimes and follies of its rulers. Overnight, she became the center of a cult. With all this positive attention, her appetite for telling dreams revived.

Her dreams now threatened absolute ruin for Spain, and when they looked around them, her listeners could see plenty of reasons for believing this was possible. The government was broke, most of the navy was at the bottom of the ocean, a longtime enemy of Spain had taken the throne of France, and the English sailed in and out of Spanish ports and Spanish treasure convoys, burning and looting as they pleased.

Many high-ranking people, seeking vision, wanted to see and hear the lovely *vidente*. Over the winter of 1589–1590, she became a salon celebrity. A favorite gathering place for her admirers was the palace of Lady Jane Dormer, near the Plaza Mayor. Under Lady Jane's patronage, Lucrecia told her dreams to rapt audiences. Sometimes they were turned into theatrical performances.[17]

Lucrecia not only had her own theatre but was also beginning to acquire her own army. Her supporters, including the royal architect, stockpiled food and weapons in a cave called Sopena in the hills west of Madrid, creating a huge underground bunker complex to sustain those who would survive the future calamities Lucrecia predicted. A secret order called the Holy Cross of the Restoration was founded to honor Lucrecia's dream of an army bearing white crosses to defeat the enemies and future invaders of Spain. Members of the order wore a white cross on a black scapular, small enough to conceal under their street clothes. In some of her dreams, Lucrecia now rode against the enemy on a white horse. Formerly a passive observer, she was becoming a more activist figure in her dreams, a little more like Joan of Arc. That could hardly fail to sharpen the edge of danger.[18]

In her dreams in the spring of 1590, stars fell from the sky and Moors rampaged through the royal palace. In mid-April, she saw the giant snake woman again, riding bare-breasted through Madrid on a bull, furiously brandishing a sword and hacking off heads. Lucrecia met her again in a garden. This time the goddess was in gentle, sorrowing mode. She had a bear on a leash. The words, "I am the suffering of Spain" were written on her back in blood.[19]

Lucrecia's dream reports got longer and longer, but her prophecies were now confused and contradictory and frequently proved false or self-serving. She predicted the coming of a new king-savior called Miguel, who would marry her and lead a crusade to take Jerusalem and move the Holy See to Toledo.

Whatever prompted the wedding scene in this dream, it was no longer sexual frustration. Lucrecia now had a lover, a young scholar called Diego de Vitores, who was employed to help record her dreams. He later confessed to the Inquisition that he and Lucrecia made promises of marriage to each other, "after which they treated each other as man and wife and knew each other carnally."[20]

It is surprising that her dream reporting was tolerated for so long, because her depictions of the king of Spain were becoming outrageous. She described Philip snoring and drooling in a chair, with insects scuttling in and out of his mouth, while the king held a placard that read "El Descuido" (the Negligent One) — in case anyone could fail to get the message. She even reported a dream in which the Ordinary Man fought his way into the king's bedchamber and decapitated him with a saw.[21]

We don't know whether these dreams were performed in Lady Jane's salon. But they were widely circulated in high society in Madrid and were not the kind of thing that even the most negligent of sovereigns was likely to ignore indefinitely.

The Lady Vanishes

In some of her last recorded dreams, Lucrecia saw herself giving birth in a perilous place. Those dreams were an accurate glimpse of the future. When the king authorized her arrest, the unmarried seer, now twenty-one, was pregnant. Don Alonso and Fray Lucas and Diego were arrested at the same time. The Inquisition found thirty notebooks containing the register of Lucrecia's dreams in a cupboard in Alonso de Mendoza's quarters in Toledo.

All the prisoners were taken to Toledo, the headquarters of the Holy Office. During the first months, they were treated more like guests at an inn than like convicts. Don Alonso's cell was described as a *taverna* because of the constant parties where wine flowed freely. This reflected the power of the Mendoza clan and Don Alonso's personal friendship with the inquisitor-general. It should be noted that it was the king and the royal confessor, Chaves — not the Inquisition — that had initiated the arrests. It was the king, not the church, that Lucrecia's dream prophecies directly threatened.

While receiving secret love notes from Diego, some of them larded with quotes from Petrarch, Lucrecia carried on a flirtation with a charming inquisitor called Lope de Mendoza. This Mendoza told her, "You are so beautiful a dead man would rise up and make you pregnant."[22] He arranged private trysts with her in the warden's chambers and even took her to his home. His attentions must have been interrupted by Lucrecia's growing belly. A few months after she was jailed, she gave birth to a baby girl. If this were not sufficient proof that she was of different stock than the "spiritual mothers," there is the testimony of a female cellmate that Lucrecia had impressive technical knowledge of dildoes, recommending a wooden one of a certain size sheathed in soft velvet.[23]

The good times in the Toledo jail ended with a purge that removed friendly officials. New inquisitors tortured Lucrecia until they judged her to be compliant. "She begged that for the love of God she not be tortured again, because if she dreamed those accursed black dreams and told them as she dreamed them to don Alonso de Mendoza, he made them worse, for which she is not to blame."[24]

Long years passed in jail, largely lost to the record, until in August 1595 Lucrecia appeared as a penitent with a rope around her neck and heard an official inventory of the charges against her — "that ever since she was young she began to dream, and had many dreams in which the Holy Trinity appeared, along with God himself, our Lord Jesus Christ, Moses and Ezekiel and the celestial virgins." That she had confessed to having been transported by three holy figures to "different parts of the earth and sea, to different kingdoms and provinces" where she had witnessed "visions of war and peace, of pleasure and terror, together with others of good and bad things to come."[25]

She was found guilty of blasphemy, sacrilege, falsehood, making a pact with the devil, relating her dreams to others, and allowing them to be transcribed. She was also condemned as "a mother of prophets"[26] who encouraged others to look into the future. Her sentence (by the standards of the day) was light: one hundred lashes, banishment from Madrid, and two years' seclusion in a religious house. There was difficulty in finding a suitable convent, so she was placed for a time (presumably with her daughter) in a hospital for beggars and lepers, about the worst place imaginable for a pretty woman. She begged to be relocated and was eventually transferred to the hospital of San Lorenzo. At this point she vanishes completely from recorded history.

Did she escape? Was she assisted in fleeing abroad? Did Lady Jane Dormer, her hostess and theatrical producer, get her out — maybe to England, where the nascent intelligence service may have been highly interested in her abilities as a dream spy? Lady Jane was famous as a Catholic partisan, but it is known that she kept a back channel open to Elizabeth of England. We may never know unless, like Lucrecia on her better nights, we can dream our way into the understory.

CHAPTER 9

❧

THE UNDERGROUND RAILROAD
OF DREAMS

Her imagination is warm and rich, and there is a whole region of the marvelous in her nature, which has manifested itself at times remarkably. Her dreams and visions, misgivings and forewarnings, ought not to be omitted in any life of her.

— FRANKLIN SANBORN ON HARRIET TUBMAN, 1868

Wild strawberries are out, sweet and tasting of the sun. Alice wanders away from the old folks, picking them one by one. The murmur of her mother's voice is now softer than the drone of the bees as she reads to Aunt Harriet from a book by a man who was carried across the ocean from West Africa in the belly of a great ship, as a slave.

"We had priests and magicians, or wise men. They calculated our time and foretold events. These magicians were also our doctors or physicians."[1]

Alice hopes that, later, Aunt Harriet will tell one of her own stories; they are the very best. Alice is a pretty, bright-eyed young black girl, although the Sewards, the white family who raised and educated her mother, say she is "chestnut" in color.

Alice is eating the field berries so fast that pink juice bubbles down her chin.

She freezes, because something is moving in the high grass. Gliding smoothly and soundlessly, it makes the grass ripple. Alice stays very still, though her heart is thumping. She doesn't like snakes, and she remembers when a nurse from the infirmary killed a rattler in the rocks behind the pig slurry.

The thing that is moving in the tall grass is coming toward her in zigzag, serpentine motions. Maybe she had better run. She is thinking on it when the head rises up, revealing an old woman's face. Aunt Harriet's face, often set and grim in the pictures, breaks into sunshine. With a wild riff of laughter mingled with hissing, she sets her fists in front of her chin and jabs at Alice with her fore-fingers, suggesting the fangs of a snake.

Alice's mother, Margaret Stewart Lucas, comes panting toward them from the porch, chastising the old lady for overtaxing herself. Aunt Harriet's laughter has turned to coughing, and her knees buckle when she tries to stand up straight. A nurse comes to help. Together, they half-carry Aunt Harriet back to her wheelchair on the porch.[2]

Alice is brimming with questions. She wants to know how Aunt Harriet learned to creep like a snake. She wants to hear again how Aunt Harriet flew like a bird and saw the roads she made the others walk.

Be a snake in the long grass, a leopard in the forest, a bird in the sky.

Back in her chair in the June light, the old lady is drifting away. You can see her going, the eyes unfocusing, before the eyelids come down. Soon she is away.

Where do you go? Alice would like to know.

I'm going home, child.

This confused Alice, when she first heard it. Wasn't Aunt Harriet already at home? She had lived here, on the edge of the village of Auburn, New York, for longer than many men's lives. She had brought Alice's mother here from Maryland's Eastern Shore when men in blue and gray were still fighting. *My father's people could fly.*

This scene from Harriet Tubman's last years is based on the reminiscences of Alice Lucas Brickler, who was raised as Harriet's great-niece. There is a mystery about the precise connection between Harriet and Margaret Stewart, Alice's mother. Some time before Tubman traveled to South Carolina in 1862 to serve as a scout and a spy for the first black regiments of the Union army, she brought Margaret, then aged eight or nine, from Maryland's Eastern Shore to New York and requested the family of her friend and patron William Seward — Lincoln's secretary of state — to raise and educate her. She took Margaret from her immediate family "secretly and without so much as a by-your-leave."[3] Tubman said that Margaret was the daughter of one of her many brothers, a freed man. That story does not check out. Kate Clifford Larson, in a fine recent biography of Harriet Tubman, suggests that Margaret may have been Harriet's natural daughter.[4] This would assume that Tubman remained capable of motherhood after her terrible childhood injuries, which seems doubtful. Alice's own comment was that "there is a part of the family history that is better never told."[5]

The greater mystery is in the high grass. Into her eighties, sick and infirm,

Harriet Tubman could still will her body to act in unusual ways, shifting beyond expected forms, vanishing and reappearing. The scene evokes the ancestral ways of the dream hunters of West Africa. It puts us on the trail of one of the most gifted dreamers in American history, whose dreams guided scores, possibly hundreds, of escaping slaves to freedom.

DREAMS FROM HER FATHER'S PEOPLE

Harriet Tubman (1822–1913) is an iconic figure in American history — the runaway slave from Maryland's Eastern Shore who went back to the South, braving great dangers, to free her fellow slaves. She became the most successful "conductor" of the Underground Railroad, which carried "self-liberators" to freedom before the American Civil War, and she never lost one of her "packages." Yet the secret of Harriet Tubman's achievement has rarely been told. She was a dreamer and a seer. In her dreams and visions, she could fly like a bird. Often she flew over landscapes she had never seen with her physical eyes. From her aerial maps, she was able to find the right roads and the river fords and the safe houses to get escaping slaves out.

Her gift surely owed something to her African heritage. Her ancestors came from West Africa; by tradition, some were Ashanti. The dream trackers of the Ashanti are at home with ancestral spirits and have shamanic connections with bird and animal allies.

As is often the case with seers and shamans, the fullness of Harriet Tubman's gift came at a terrible price. At about age twelve, she came between an angry overseer and a boy who was trying to run away, and she took a two-pound lead weight full in the forehead. She died and came back.

When she was back, she was changed. She had a hole in her forehead she masked later on by wearing mannish hats. And she had a frequent need to lie down and take a quick nap. Medical people might call this narcolepsy. Modern scholars speculate that she now suffered from temporal-lobe epilepsy, a condition attributed to many famous people — from Muhammad to Dostoyevsky — who have seen visions and heard voices. Whatever the medical description, it was a trigger for the visions. A window would open in her head and she would look through it — or fly through it — and see important things.

She was born on the Brodess farm in Dorchester County, on Maryland's Eastern Shore. Her given name was Araminta Ross, and she was known in early childhood as Minty. Later she adopted her mother's first name. Her parents,

Harriet ("Rit") and Ben Ross, were slaves owned by different families — Thompson and Brodess — joined by marriage but divided by frequent quarrels and wrangles over debt.

Her earliest childhood memory was of being rocked in the "gum," a cradle fashioned from a section of the trunk of the sweet gum tree. The sweet gum thrived on swampy land on the Eastern Shore and was valued for timber; Ben Ross, who knew wood, was mostly employed as a lumberjack and sawyer. In the fall, when the winged seeds of the sweet gum took off, the star-shaped leaves burst into a conflagration of reds and yellows and purples. Then you had to look out for dry gum balls lying everywhere on the ground, stabbing at bare soles and ankles with their wicked horns.

In West Africa, a skilled tracker could use his bare feet like a blind man uses his hands, to feel and read the contours of the land and the profile of what has walked a trail before him.[6] It was different on this side of the middle passage.

We won't find the story of Harriet Tubman's African ancestors in the courthouse records that allow us to trace the pedigree and shifting fortunes of Edward Brodess, the man who owned her and used her, but a few clues survive.

Franklin Sanborn, writing in 1863, described Harriet Tubman as "the grand-daughter of a slave imported from Africa" with "not a drop of white blood in her veins."[7] In 1907, a reporter for the *New York Herald* plucked this from her memories: "The old mammies to whom she told dreams were wont to nod knowingly and say, 'I reckon youse one o' dem Shantees, chile.' For they knew the tradition of the unconquerable Ashantee blood, which in a slave made him a thorn in the side of the planter or cane grower whose property he became, so that few of that race were in bondage."[8]

The "Ashantee," or Ashanti, are a matrilineal people of the forests and highlands of Ghana, known in Harriet's time as the Gold Coast. Recollections of gossip heard in childhood are not evidence that Harriet had Ashanti blood, but they suggest that the Ashanti were known where she grew up, and she was associated with them in people's minds. The Ashanti built a powerful empire in the seventeenth century under a king whose throne was a golden stool believed to embody the collective spirit of the people. The Ashanti maintained their independence until 1900, when they were defeated by the British; their territories were then incorporated into the Gold Coast colony.

Ashanti chiefs, called "masters of firepower" or simply "big men," took slaves from enemy tribes and sold them to the Europeans in the trading ports via Hausa middlemen; they boasted that no Ashanti could ever be made a slave.[9] Nonetheless, it is likely that some Ashanti — including fugitives and outcasts who had fallen out with the chiefs or violated "red taboos" — were captured and sold by their enemies.

Shipping records of the Chesapeake slave trade suggest that Harriet's ancestors were brought to America from this part of West Africa. Nearly all of the slaves carried to Maryland ports came directly from Africa, and the vast majority came on big London vessels that picked up their cargoes along the Gold Coast or from Upper Guinea.[10] Maryland planters were constantly asking for slaves from the Gold Coast; they had a reputation for strength and stamina and craftsmanship.

Harriet said she inherited special gifts — including the ability to travel outside the body and to visit the future — from her father, who "could always predict the future" and who "foretold the Mexican war."[11] Stronger than other girls, she spent a lot of time with Ben Ross in the timber gangs. In their quiet times in the woods, they may have revived something of the atmosphere of the Sacred Forest of the Ashanti and the practices of West African dream trackers, who were accustomed to operating outside the body, sometimes in the forms of animals.

We have an interesting source on Ashanti dreaming in Captain Robert S. Rattray, a British "government anthropologist" stationed in the Gold Coast before and after World War I. Rattray became a passionate student of the Ashanti, who called this Scot "Red Pepper" because of his blazing red hair. Though sometimes baffled by the mobility of consciousness among the West Africans he interviewed, he did his best to record Ashanti dream practices.

"To the Ashanti mind," Rattray explains, "dreams are caused either by the visitations of denizens of the spirit world, or by spirits, i.e., volatile souls of persons still alive, or by the journeyings of one's own soul during the hours of sleep."[12] In the Ashanti language, "to dream" is *so dae*, which literally means "to arrive at a place during sleep" — implying travel.[13]

For the Ashanti, dream incidents are real events. If you sleep with another man's wife, for example, you are held to be guilty of adultery and may be punished for it. Flying is a common experience in Ashanti dreams. "If you dream that you have been carried up to the sky . . . and that you have returned to the ground . . . that means long life."[14] This certainly held true for Harriet Tubman, who lived to be at least ninety-one.

Rattray describes an Ashanti practice for disposing of a "bad" dream by confiding it in a whisper to the village rubbish dump, which may also be the communal latrine.

One of Rattray's informants described how his dead brother guided him on the hunt. "I often dream of my brother who was a hunter, and he shows me where to go. Any antelope I kill, I give him a piece with some water." The same man's dead uncle gave him dream prescriptions. When a child was ill in the house, his deceased uncle showed him some leaves to administer as part of the medicine; "I did so and the child recovered."[15]

Ashanti hunters and trackers walked very close to their guardian animals. Shifting into the energy body of a leopard, or a nocturnal antelope, or a fish eagle, they traveled ahead of themselves to scout the land and find the game, or to locate the place where an enemy force was advancing. The Ashanti believed, like other indigenous peoples, that if you are not in touch with your dreams, you are not in touch with your soul. "If one does not dream for eighty days, it means that one will become mad."[16]

On big questions, they sought a second opinion through divination. A typical method was for the diviner to shake a set of symbolic objects — stones and bones, a hairball, a root, a seedpod, a snail shell — from a skin bag. The diviner grasped the forked end of a stick while the client held the other end, which was tipped with metal. In their hands, the wand quivered and pointed at one object after another, making a story that was then read by the diviner.[17]

How much of this traveled to Maryland with Tubman's ancestors? Maybe far more than has been generally understood. West Africans brought forcibly to North America did not lose their identity and traditional practices overnight. Recent archeology shows that key elements of West African culture survived under slavery in North America: in the miniature boats and other items placed in graves, in collections of "anomalous artifacts" that may have come from diviner's bags.[18] And in the 1820s, when Minty Ross was growing up, the Christianization of African slaves had barely begun.[19]

GIFTS IN THE WOUNDS

"God hath chosen the weak things of the world to confound the mighty," declared Zilpha Elaw, an itinerant black woman preacher who conducted camp meetings in Dorchester County when Harriet Tubman was a girl.[20] It is possible that young Minty went with her mother to hear Zilpha Elaw preach. We see, at this point in time and space, two spiritual traditions, from Africa and from a Christian revelation quite distinct from that of the slave owners, streaming together, and both are strongly at work in Harriet Tubman's life and her cause.

Zilpha Elaw learned from her own sufferings that gifts may come from our wounds. Crushed by illness, she revived after a visitation by a radiant being she believed to be Jesus Christ. The early death of her husband focused her on her cause. This free black woman was driven by dreams to take the risk of conducting "camp meetings" in the slave South, including in Maryland's Eastern Shore, where Harriet Tubman may have absorbed her message that women were the first apostles: "The first preachers of the resurrection were women."[21]

Long before she reached puberty, Minty Ross bore many wounds on her body. Her owner, perennially cash-short, hired her out, and some of her temporary masters used her brutally. A temporary mistress expected her to keep a restless, needy baby quiet by rocking her all night next to the bed. When Minty drifted off and the baby started to howl, the mother grabbed the whip she kept close by and slashed the black girl across the neck and shoulders. Minty carried the scars long afterward.

Another master sent her to service his muskrat traps in the cold swamp water in winter. Minty would stagger back chilled to the bone, her bare feet too numb to help her evade the spikes of the fallen gum pods but not too numb to feel the pain. When she was not watched too closely, she would push her ravaged feet into the ashes of the fire, willing heat and healing into her body.

She acquired a "knot" in her side where one of her abusers flogged her with a knotted rope. The sympathizers up North who later wrote her stories for her did not care to talk about rape and other sexual violence, though everyone knew these were everyday occurrences in the life of a female slave. One of the effects of abuse was that she seems to have been unable to bear children.

The definitive wound was inflicted when she was about twelve. The site where she was assaulted survives: a country store at a crossroads in Bucktown. She was in the doorway of the store when an angry white man threw a two-pound lead weight at another slave. There are differing accounts of what was going on. Some say she was trying to help a slave escape. In any event, she got between him and his master's rage. She took the blow on her head; it split her skull. She later said she was saved by her mess of woolly unbrushed hair, growing out thick, softening the blow.

She received no conventional doctoring. We may picture her mother laying a herbal poultice on the wound and her father helping to call her soul back into her body with his prayers. Among the Ashanti, when someone has suffered trauma or shock, they say the *kra* (soul) has "gone away" or "flown away."[22] It is the function of those who are spiritually alive to help bring it back.

After this, she had "trouble with her head." For the rest of her life, she suffered from "somnolence" — the sudden, urgent need to take a nap, sometimes in the most inconvenient circumstances. During these "sleeps" she had visions, some of them *big* visions. "When these turns of somnolence come upon Harriet, she imagines that her 'spirit' leaves her body, and visits other scenes and places, not only in this world, but also in the world of spirits. And her ideas of these scenes show, to say the least of it, a vividness of imagination seldom equaled in the soarings of the most cultivated minds."[23]

After her head injury, Brodess tried to sell her but "could not get sixpence for her."[24] She may have played up her disability when displayed to potential buyers; when we follow her story closely, we find craft as well as vision. In the years that followed, she applied herself to the hardest physical labor, carting and chopping and hauling wood. Her body grew as strong as a sturdy man's. By working hard as a man, hard as a pack animal, in the fields, Minty may have worked to make herself less noticeable as an object of desire while growing her muscles.

Her visions came in the midst of hard labor, as well as during her "sleeps." "We'd been carting manure all day, and the other girl and I were going home on the sides of the cart, and another boy was driving, when suddenly I heard such music as filled all the air."[25] In her dreams, she flew like a bird over green landscapes as fresh as the first day.

She took a husband, John Tubman. He was a free man, so there was a notable imbalance in their relationship. We don't know what calculations or chemistry drew them together, but we do know that she came to love him deeply. If she had been able to bear children, they would have belonged to her master. Edward Brodess, desperate for money, was not only hiring out his slaves; he was selling them to slavers from the Deep South. Harriet and her parents were powerless to block the sale of two of her sisters; she saw them marched away in a slave coffle.

She feared that Brodess was planning to sell her and her brothers as soon as he could find a buyer. She told Sarah Bradford she prayed every night, "Oh dear Lord, change that man's heart and make him a Christian." When it was plain that Brodess was not going to change, she changed her prayer. "Lord, if you ain't never going to change that man's heart, *kill him*, Lord, and take him out of de way, so he won't do no more mischief."[26]

This time, Harriet's prayer was answered — but she wished she could take it back. After the master's death, his widow, saddled with debts and lawsuits, aimed to raise money by selling off Harriet's family fast.

The slaves were promised that if they were sold it would be to local families, so they could still see each other. Harriet saw the true state of affairs in her dreams. In "visions of the night," she heard the screams of women and children being separated by force, the drumming of the slavers' horses.[27]

She prepared to follow the maps she was given in her dreams. Prior to her escape, she dreamed of "flying over fields and towns, and rivers and mountains, looking down upon them like a bird. . . . She declares that when she came North she remembered these very places as those she had seen in her dreams, and many of the ladies who befriended her were those she had been helped by in her vision."[28]

She escaped alone. Her husband flatly refused to go with her. When she confided her dreams of escape, he told her she was a fool, a stupid flapping chicken. Her brothers agreed to go, but then got cold feet. Guided by the North Star and by the aerial maps from her dreams, she walked by night and hid by day "without money and without friends."[29]

When she crossed the border into the free state of Pennsylvania, she checked to see whether she was dreaming in or out of the body. "I looked at my hands to see if I was the same person now I was free. There was such a glory over everything, the sun came like gold through the trees, and over the fields, and I felt like I was in heaven."[30]

Another great wound in Harriet Tubman's life was the loss of her husband. From this, too, she derived a great gift.

She loved John Tubman profoundly, though he never supported her or believed in her. After she escaped to the North, she spent two years struggling and saving in menial jobs in Pennsylvania before she went back to the Eastern Shore, determined to reclaim her man. She had saved up enough money to buy him a new suit of clothes. When she got to Dorchester County, she learned that John Tubman had taken a new wife. He refused even to see her. She later told sympathetic Northern audiences that she went for her husband, but all she got was his clothes.

Losing John gave her focus. She might have been overcome by her rage and pain; instead, she allowed it to power her cause. John Tubman "dropped out of her heart," as she told Ednah Cheney, "and she determined to give her life to brave deeds."[31] Deprived of her sexual identity for many years, often suppressing her femininity while in the guise of a man or an aged crone, she became wholly wedded to her cause.

THE CONDUCTOR

Bradford says Tubman returned to the South nineteen times and brought out more than three hundred fugitives.[32] Recent historians think she went back nine times and was directly involved in conducting no more than seventy slaves to freedom — although she directed other rescue operations from a distance, sometimes from a hideout in Baltimore near the waterfront.[33] Whether Harriet Tubman went back nine or nineteen times, she was taking extraordinary risks, especially after posters were circulated advising of the big reward on her head.

She brought out her brothers and eventually her parents, as well as people who knew her only as "Moses." As she approached rendezvous points in the night, she sometimes announced her coming by singing the spiritual from which she derived her nom de guerre:

> Oh go down Moses
> Way down into Egypt's land
> Tell old Pharaoh
> Let my people go.

"She seemed wholly devoid of personal fear," observed William Still, a black stationmaster for the Underground Railroad in Philadelphia. "The idea of being captured by slave-hunters or slave-holders, seemed never to enter her mind. She was apparently proof against all adversaries." To some of her charges, she seemed to be traveling in a state of trance. "Half of her time, she had the appearance of one asleep, and would actually sit down by the road-side and go fast asleep when on her errands of mercy through the South."[34]

One of her "sudden intimations" during a nap made her decide to lead a group of fugitive slaves across a river on a raw March day. As she marched her party down a country road, Harriet's head started to ache violently. She crumpled to her knees and collapsed there, in plain view, entering one of her involuntary "sleeps." When Harriet came round, she ordered the group to follow her along a completely unexpected course that seemed to be taking them deeper into the slave dominions. They came to a river that looked far too deep to wade, and nobody could swim. Harriet insisted they must all go into the river; she was sure there was a place where the water was shallow enough to wade across. Her dream had shown her that they *could* get across, and that crossing the river would mask their trail from slave hunters who were homing in on them. She had seen a cabin on the other side where they would be given food and shelter. She waded into the river, following a zigzag course. The water came up to her chin, but no higher; she had found an invisible ford. The others followed her, and they were greeted on the other side by a black family who sheltered them in their cabin. Harriet's party learned later that, had they continued on their previous road, they would have found a posse waiting for them.[35]

She drove her charges hard. "She would not suffer one of her party to whimper once, about 'giving out and going back,' however wearied they might be from hard travel day and night." She warned those who joined her that the only exit was liberty or death, and sometimes reinforced this warning by brandishing a revolver. She told them "a live runaway could do great harm by going back, but that a dead one could tell no secrets," and they heard her.[36] There were traitors and renegades on the Underground Railroad, but not on her train.

She had an inner knowing, the assurance of walking with a greater power, a God she could talk to. The presence of a soul companion made her almost impervious to fear. Sarah Bradford thought she had "direct intercourse with heaven." Bradford struggled to tell this part of the story: "I hardly know how to approach the spiritual experiences of my sable heroine. They seem so to enter into the realm of the supernatural, that I can hardly wonder that those who never knew her are ready to throw discredit upon the story. . . . Had I not known so well her deeply religious character, and her conscientious veracity, and had I not since the war, and when she was an inmate of my own house, seen such remarkable instances of what seemed to be her direct intercourse with heaven, I should not dare to risk my own character for veracity by making these things public in this manner."[37]

Abolitionist Thomas Garrett, who helped Harriet smuggle "self-liberators" into Delaware, said, "I never met with any person, of any color, who had more confidence in the voice of God, as spoken direct to her soul." She "ventured only where God sent her."[38] She gave Garrett many examples of psychic gifts. She once called on him and said, "God told me you have money for me. About twenty-three dollars." Although Harriet could not have known this by any ordinary means, that was the dollar value of a donation of five pounds sterling that Garrett had recently received from a Scottish sympathizer who wanted the money passed on to Tubman. Garrett confessed he could not tell whether it was "clairvoyance or the divine impression on her mind," but that "it was certain she had a guide within herself."[39]

She developed the power to transfer her vision. To understand this, we need to hear the thrilling timbre of her voice. She could sing courage into people's hearts. She used spirituals as coded messages, as "all clear" or "go hide" signals, or as messages that she was taking off, "bound for the promised land."

But her songs did more than speak code: they carried and revived raw energy. Words borrowed from white services were charged with a different power and identity when infused by the spirit of Africa and the yearning for the Promised Land on American soil. In her time, black churches were just beginning to be born in North America; in envisioning Tubman's day, we are present at the original fusion of Christian and African traditions and styles. Sarah Bradford often heard Harriet sing this verse:

> He whose thunders shake creation
> He who bids the planets roll
> He who rides upon the tempest
> And whose scepter sways the whole.[40]

Imagine the effect of a great voice carrying that magnificent invocation of divine power to people cowering in "potato holes" in the dark. By all accounts, Harriet's was a great voice, thrillingly different to white folks' ears. Bradford recalls, "The air sung to these words was so wild, so full of plaintive minor strains, and unexpected quavers, that I would defy any white person to learn it, and often as I heard it, it was to me a constant surprise."[41]

Another hearer said Harriet sang "baritone rather than contralto."[42] The power of the singer, and the power that rode with such words, was a key to Tubman's ability to put courage and faith into the people she helped to liberate, and to get them through the night woods and swamps.

Besides the power of song, Harriet had the gift of story. She could take you right inside a story, which might be a teaching parable, or a heart-stirring tale of heroism, or a raunchy self-mocking anecdote, or a new horizon of possibility. "She has great dramatic power," said Ednah Cheney. "The scene rises before you as she saw it, and her voice and language change with her different actors."[43]

To teach and inspire, she often spoke in parables. When she called on Lincoln to hurry up Emancipation, she liked to recount the parable of the snake on the floor: Suppose there was "an awful big snake on the floor. He bite you. Folks all scared, because you die. You send for a doctor to cut the bite; but the snake, he rolled up there, and while the doctor doing it, he bite you *again*. The doctor dug out *that* bite; but while the doctor doing it, the snake, he sprung up and bite you again; so he *keep* doing it, till you kill him. That's what master Lincoln ought to know."[44]

DREAMING WAR AND EMANCIPATION

She is in a wilderness of rocks and bushes. Something stirs among the rocks. A huge snake raises its head and turns in her direction. The head becomes that of a man with a great bristling white beard, who gazes at her "wishful like," as if he wants to speak. Two other heads rise near him, with the faces of younger men.

Then a crowd of men rush into the scene. They strike the young men's heads and then that of the old man, who continues to stare at her, "wishful."[45]

Harriet recognized the snake man from this dream a few days later, in April 1858, when John Brown visited her at her home in St. Catherine's. Fresh from fighting pro-slavery "Border Ruffians" with fire and sword in Kansas, this abolitionist zealot was now recruiting blacks for what he maintained was a God-given mission: to foment a slave rebellion in the South. Tubman and Brown hit it off. After their first meeting, Captain Brown wrote to one of his sons that she was "the most of a man, naturally, that I ever met with."[46] Soon he was calling her "General" Tubman.

Next year she was with him in Boston as he gathered cash and Springfield rifles from abolitionist supporters. But his fate in her dream may have instilled caution in Harriet. While some escaped slaves from St. Catherine's joined Brown's little army, his people could not find Tubman between July and September 1859, when they wanted to recruit her active involvement in the planned raid at Harper's Ferry.

Tubman was in New York on the night of Sunday, October 16, 1859, when Brown and his men seized the arsenal, surprising the lone guard. Across the distance, she felt the "flutter, flutter" in her heart that was one of the ways she sensed danger. She told her hostess that "it must be Captain Brown who was in trouble."[47]

For some reason, Brown and his little force holed up at the arsenal instead of making off with the weapons they could carry, and they were soon routed out by U.S. Marines under the command of Robert E. Lee. Harriet's dream of three heads struck down was played out in full when John Brown, dressed all in black, rode his own coffin to the gallows and two of his sons were hanged after him. Tubman told Ednah Cheney, "It wasn't John Brown that died on that gallows. . . . It wasn't mortal man, it was God in him."[48] A saint and martyr for many Northern abolitionists, a "terrorizer" to Southerners and moderates,[49] this strange wild man had failed in everything in his life except his effort to help incite a civil war.

Harriet Tubman had a strong vision of emancipation. She described it to a prominent New York black abolitionist, Henry Garrett, early in 1861. Garrett remarked that he did not believe they would see the emancipation of the slaves in his lifetime, or even that of his grandchildren. Tubman told him he was wrong. "You'll see it, and you'll see it soon. My people are free! My people are free."[50]

But Harriet also saw, long before the start of the Civil War, that the abolition of slavery would be accomplished only by force of arms. She believed, like

Brown and his "Secret Six" (who included her first biographer, Franklin Sanborn), that African Americans, slave and free, should be armed to take part in their own liberation.

After the Union seized the Sea Islands off the Carolina coast, Tubman went south to support the first black regiments made up of recruited former slaves. At the instigation of Governor John Andrew of Massachusetts, she was employed as a scout and a spy, as a nurse and a caterer. She walked the streets of Beaufort, South Carolina, in the sopping heat, oyster shells crunching underfoot, to meet General David Hunter, who enraged Lincoln by announcing the premature emancipation of the slaves and arming some of them. Displaying the skills of a herbalist, she brewed up a potion using local roots and herbs that cured an army doctor's dysentery; the doctor then asked her to mix up enough to treat a regiment. She accompanied fiery-whiskered Colonel James Montgomery and his "contrabands" — the former slaves of the Second South Carolina Regiment — on a raid up the Combahee River that freed eight hundred slaves and seized vast quantities of rice. Expected to interpret for the Union officers, she found she could communicate no better with Gullah-speakers than the officers could. But in a revealing incident, when desperate Sea Islanders were clutching at the rowboats of their rescuers, threatening to capsize them, Harriet burst into song and used her voice of power. "Then they threw up their hands and began to rejoice and shout Glory! And the rowboats would push off. I kept on singing until all were brought on board."[51]

She was impatient with Lincoln for delaying the emancipation she had dreamed. She urged him to hurry up, saying, "God won't let master Lincoln beat the South until he does the *right thing*."[52]

Lincoln's Emancipation Proclamation was celebrated near Beaufort, South Carolina, on January 1, 1863, with a flashy gathering in a grove of live oaks where gray moss hung low over the heads of black women in "turbans" and black soldiers in wide crimson "zouave" pants. Harriet did not join in the festivities. "I had my jubilee three years ago. I rejoiced all I could then; I can't rejoice no more."[53] In her portrait from this time, she is holding a rifle.

At the war's end, Harriet made her way back to the home in Auburn, New York, where she had settled her parents and other family members. When she showed her government pass to a racist conductor on a train from Philadelphia to New York, he was not impressed. He bawled at her that the company did not allow any "half-price niggers" to sit among white folks.[54] When he tried to evict her from the car, she grappled with him and soon had the better of him with that remarkable physical strength she had acquired in the fields and lumberyards. Other white men came to the conductor's assistance. They broke her arm and several ribs on their way to bundling her into the baggage car. This brutal homecoming did not augur well for the cause of African American rights, or Harriet's personal fortunes, in the aftermath of the Civil War.

She endured for almost half a century more, moving back and forth from fame to obscurity, always living in poverty, struggling to feed her parents and brothers and the numberless homeless people who sought sanctuary with her on her little farm in Auburn. She lobbied for many years to get a war pension, and never succeeded in getting what she deserved. She found a biographer in Sarah Bradford, a writer of children's books and Sunday school teacher who had read Bible stories to Harriet's elderly parents. Bradford, distracted by her preparations for a European tour, rushed to put together the first version of her biography, which was a blessing, since she did not have time to edit out some of the rawest material, like Harriet's discovery of her husband's infidelity. Bradford (who had been deserted by her own husband) cut this scene from the second edition. The later version of the Bradford biography was read by Queen Victoria, who invited Harriet to her birthday party. The book earned Tubman enough money to pay off the mortgage on the Auburn place.

Harriet's unfaithful husband, John Tubman, was killed soon after the end of the Civil War in a fight with a white man. She may have found comfort in her second marriage to a tall man twenty years her junior, but he suffered from tuberculosis and her role soon became that of a nursemaid.

It is not surprising that Harriet Tubman continues to inspire people today through dreams as well as popular biographies and exhibitions devoted to the Underground Railroad. In some contemporary dreams, Harriet Tubman appears as a messenger, sometimes as a mail carrier slipping letters through the door.

I first saw her as a kind of living cameo while drifting in an intermediate state in my bed in a house I once owned in Troy, New York. I later learned that Harriet had led a crowd in Troy that freed an escaped slave, Charles Nalle, who was going to be returned to the South under the infamous Fugitive Slave Act. In my favorite dream of Harriet Tubman, she is on duty in the window of a very special post office: a place where you can go pick up your lost or undelivered dreams.

CHAPTER 10

✦

MARK TWAIN'S RHYMING LIFE

History may not repeat itself, but it rhymes.

— ATTRIBUTED TO MARK TWAIN

𝕴 felt very much as if I had just awakened out of a long sleep."

This was the opening line of the very first article that a young writer called Sam Clemens signed as "Mark Twain." It was a letter to the *Territorial Enterprise* in Virginia City, Nevada — a place where Sam drank a good deal of red whisky and tried to strike it rich — dated February 3, 1863.

He would not have become Mark Twain except for a dreamlike adventure in serendipity, which was richly in play throughout his life. The episode that put Sam Clemens on the river-road to becoming Mark Twain is a marvelous example of the cardinal navigational law of serendipity: in order to find our way, we need to get lost.

While he was working as a printer in Keokuk, Iowa, Sam's reading included a book that described a certain "vegetable product with miraculous powers" that was growing in Brazil. Sam was "fired with a longing" to go up the Amazon, secure a supply of this miracle plant — and make a fortune. His enthusiasm infected a local businessman called Ward and a chemistry professor called Joseph Martin, who could be assumed to be able to make his own assessment of the claimed properties of the Brazilian plant. They agreed to mount a joint expedition. There was a slight logistical problem. No one knew how to get to Brazil. Before they figured this out, Sam's partners lost interest. He was pursuing a solo adventure when he got to Cincinnati and boarded the riverboat that took him down the Ohio River to the Mississippi, bound for New Orleans. The pilot of the packet was Horace Bixby.

When he got to New Orleans, Sam found that no ship in port was sailing for Brazil, and no one could tell him how to get there. "I couldn't get to the Amazon," he later wrote, so "I went to Horace Bixby and asked him to make a pilot out of me." When Bixby sailed upriver, Sam was on board with him as an apprentice pilot, a ticket to a good living in those days — and to a great deal more for young Sam Clemens.[1] Working on the Mississippi River, he got many of the ideas for the books that would make him famous under a pen name borrowed from the boatmen's cry "Mark Twain," meaning two fathoms, safe water.

The miracle plant Sam had set out to find was coca. Had he succeeded in his original plan, Keokuk, Iowa, would have become the cocaine capital of America. Because Sam Clemens couldn't find Brazil, he failed to become the first cocaine dealer in North American history and instead became Mark Twain.

The life on the river that brought Sam joy and creative inspiration soon delivered tragedy as well. Sam Clemens dreamed the death of his beloved younger brother Henry, in exact detail, before it took place. They took ship together on the riverboat *Pennsylvania*, Sam as apprentice pilot, Henry as lowly "mud clerk," an employee given food and sleeping space in return for helping out at places on the river where there were no proper landing sites — hence the need to thrash and wallow through the mud to deliver cargo. The night before they sailed, Sam dreamed he saw Henry as a corpse, laid out in a metal casket, dressed in one of his older brother's suits, with a huge bouquet of white roses on his chest and a single red rose at the center.

Sam woke grief-stricken, convinced this had actually happened and that Henry was laid out in the next room. He could not collect himself, or convince himself that the dream was not "real," until he had walked around outside. He had walked a whole block, he recalled, "before it suddenly flashed on me that there was nothing real about this — it was only a dream."

Family members told him it was "only a dream." Though the force of his feelings told him something else, Sam agreed to try to put the dream out of his mind.

The tragedy began to unfold soon after the two young men boarded the *Pennsylvania*. In Ron Powers's vivid phrase, the pilot of the *Pennsylvania*, William Brown, was "a seething and abusive man" with whom Sam was soon scrapping.[2] During the voyage downriver, Sam got into a full-blown fight with him. The captain sided with Sam and said they would find a new pilot when they got to New Orleans. But a new pilot could not be found, and since Sam and Brown could not coexist on the same boat, Sam was transferred to another vessel, leaving Henry on the *Pennsylvania*, which started the upriver journey first. Just before they parted company, Sam and Henry discussed how they would act in the event of a riverboat disaster such as a boiler explosion, which was a common occurrence.

The *Pennsylvania*'s boiler exploded in a hell of steam and fire, in the way they had discussed. Badly burned, Henry survived for a few days, to die in Memphis, where the injured had been carried. His handsome face was untouched, and the kindly lady volunteers were so moved by his beauty and innocence that they gave him the best casket, a metal box.

When Sam entered the "dead-room" of the Memphis Exchange on June 21, 1858, he was horrified to see the enactment of his dream: his dead brother laid out in a metal casket in a borrowed suit. Only one element was missing: the floral bouquet. As Sam watched and mourned, a lady came in with a bouquet of white roses with a single red one at the center and laid it on Henry's chest.[3]

Mark Twain kept telling and retelling the circumstances of Henry's death, in his mind and in his writing, for the rest of his life. He could never escape the thought that, had he only known how to use the information from his dream, he might have been able to prevent Henry's death.

Dreams and coincidence constantly interweave with the events and creations of Mark Twain's life. Through the weave run great bands of light and dark, grief and joy, triumph and calamity. You can't write anything worthwhile unless you have known calamity, he maintained, and he had known plenty of it. His comedy floated on an abyss of pain and was truer for that.

LIVING BY COINCIDENCE

Mark Twain lived by coincidence, and he noticed. We are able to track this in detail because, early in life, he fell into the benign habit of recording what he "noticed" in his "notebooks"; later he had special ones made with pull-off tabs so he could always find the current page easily. We also have the benefit of a splendid recent biography by Ron Powers that tracks the play of coincidence in Mark Twain's life more closely than I have seen done in any major modern biography of any important individual.

Halley's Comet appeared in the year of Sam Clemens's birth, 1835. The year before his death, he told Arthur Bigelow Paine, "I came in with Halley's Comet and will go out with it." He was pretty much right. Both Mark Twain and the comet disappeared in the same year, 1910, though not on the same day.

Samuel Langhorne Clemens arrived from the dreamworld in Florida, Missouri, on November 30, 1835, two months ahead of schedule. He was a preemie, so fragile he spent much of his first four years in bed. As his best biographer notes, "Premature babies are generally unable to sleep deeply and sometimes exist in a kind of dream world, a world of unstable boundaries."[4]

He was a floater, a sleepwalker. His sleepwalking in early childhood was a very strong indication that ordinary boundaries did not exist for him. His older brother Orion later claimed that young Sam, not yet four, came "floating" into his ailing sister Margaret's room, fast asleep, and plucked at her coverlet before drifting away. She died a few days later. This was enough to mark little Sam as a psychic prodigy in the eyes of his mother, Jane. In Kentucky — Jane Langhorne's birthplace — it was believed that someone who "plucked at the coverlet" of a person who then died had manifested psychic ability.[5]

When Sam was fourteen, a page of text flapped along the street like a fall leaf and wrapped itself around his leg. When he removed it, he found it was from a book about Joan of Arc. The few paragraphs he read kindled a vivid interest that revived in 1891, when he passed through the Maid's home village of Domrémy in the midst of a European tour.[6] He now hurled himself into the exhaustive research and imaginative odyssey that produced his *Personal Recollections of Joan of Arc*, the book he considered his most important. Based on primary documents from the Bibliothèque Nationale in Paris, the book powerfully evoked Jehanne's "battle-light" and her visionary connection with special trees; "a *white* shadow came slowly gliding along the grass towards the Tree. It reached her, flowed over her, clothed her in its awful splendor."[7]

A dream, followed by a coincidence, helped produce one of Mark Twain's more characteristic works, the story that won him fame as a humorist and launched his book-writing career. Now thirty, with exuberant whiskers and cowboy chaps, he was out in Nevada, poking around mining claims on Jackass Hill and downing quantities of whisky in the Angels Camp Hotel in nearby Calaveras County. On the first night of 1865, he dreamed of a storyteller called Jim Townsend who was widely known as "Lying Jim" because of his prowess in telling tall tales; one of these involved a frog in a jumping competition that was covertly loaded down with lead shot. In Sam's dream, Lying Jim showed him a book Sam would write. As Sam recorded in his notebook, deleting a fusillade of expletives, Lying Jim said "I could take this *** book & *** every *** in California, from San Francisco to the mountains."[8]

The dream turned a tap in Sam's head, and the brew came strong one night at the Angels Camp Hotel when he ran into another prodigious storyteller, Ben Coon. They had something in common in addition to their love of tall tales: they had both been river pilots. Ben Coon entertained Sam and his friends with his side-slapping version of the jumping frog story. Sam made some notes on the spot. "If I can tell that story the way Ben Coon told it," he said, "that frog will jump around the world." It did. Soon after his evening with Ben Coon, Mark Twain gave up prospecting for silver and gold and hit a mother lode by writing "The Jumping Frog of Calaveras County," which established his distinctive voice and launched his career as a book author.[9]

He got his first journalistic scoop, one that put him on the front pages of the world press and helped make him a lecture-circuit "rock star," all because he got saddle boils. He was visiting the Sandwich Islands, known today as Hawaii, and became intrigued by the sight of Polynesian women bathing naked. He made it his game to inspect as many as he could, and in the course of riding up and down the white sand beaches of Oahu, he developed a very painful case of saddle boils. So he was laid up in his hotel in Honolulu when the survivors of the *Hornet* washed up on one of those Oahu beaches. The fate of the men on the *Hornet* had been a subject of international speculation for months after their ship was wrecked off the Cape of Good Hope. The survivors had wandered four thousand miles on the seas before they reached dry land. The first reporter to get an interview was assured of major attention. Because he was laid up in Honolulu, Mark Twain was available — once a stretcher was provided by a friend, an American diplomat who had just returned from opening relations with the Chinese empire. Mark Twain's name was soon known in London and New York, Paris and Rome — and he would pack them in at the biggest music halls in the United States.[10] This was a fine example of one of the rules of coincidence: *For every setback, there is an opportunity.*

Coincidence guided and saved his nearly disastrous courtship of Olivia ("Livy") Langdon. He was at the Langdon manse in Elmira, New York, having little success communicating his passions to Livy. She was not immediately impressed by this cigar-smoking little man with wild carrot-red hair in a sealskin coat, whose odd rolling gait suggested that either he was used to walking a deck or was having a hard time getting home from a bar. Sam confided his love to Livy's brother Charley, who had been his drinking buddy on the amazing voyage of the *Quaker City*; their madcap exploits in Europe and the Holy Land are preserved in *Innocents Abroad*.

Charley was not entertained by the idea of his disreputable friend marrying his virginal sister. He told Sam he must leave at once and he would take him to the train station. When they got in the wagon and Charley flicked his whip at the horse, both men performed a double-backward somersault onto the cobblestone drive. The seat of the wagon had not been properly bolted in place. Sam lay on the driveway seeing stars until the Langdon women rushed to the rescue. The slapstick accident got Sam invited to stay at the Langdon house another day, and allowed him to resume his suit while enjoying the sympathy owed to an invalid.[11]

A "chance" encounter in the street on a foggy November night in New York turned Mark Twain into a book publisher and gave him his biggest financial windfall. Two men stepped out of a doorway, directly in front of him, and carried on an animated conversation that he could not avoid overhearing. One of them said, "Do you know General Grant has actually determined to write his memoirs and publish them? He has said so today, in so many words."[12] In his autobiography, Mark Twain made out the speaker was a stranger. In fact, he was R. W. Gilder, the editor of the *Century* magazine, and Mark Twain knew him perfectly well — which does not make the coincidence any less remarkable.

Mark Twain had called on General Ulysses S. Grant at his New York home several times, and had himself been urging the former president to write his memoirs. Mobilized by what he overheard in the fog, he soon discovered that the Century Company was planning to offer Grant a 10 percent royalty, which Mark Twain considered a miserable deal for a national hero. He went to Grant and made him a spectacularly higher offer: 75 percent of the profits, a deal that would make authors and publishers swoon in any era, for diverse reasons. When Grant accepted, Mark Twain became a book publisher. The Grant book was published by a new house owned by Mark Twain and named for his niece's husband, Charlie Webster, who became its first director. A remark overheard in the fog produced a runaway bestseller, a work of lasting importance that rescued Grant's family from financial distress and gave him the will to go on living and working while an excruciatingly painful illness — cancer of the throat — ate away at his life. Grant died of starvation just five days after he finished the editorial revisions of his second volume. Mark Twain's personal profit from Grant's book was two hundred thousand dollars, the equivalent of many millions today.[13]

Despite his successful maiden voyage as a publisher and the growing public appetite for his own writing and lectures, Mark Twain was no good at holding on to money. He loved to take big suites in grand hotels and order the best of everything in restaurants. Then, of course, there was the spectacular outlay on his palazzo in Hartford, Connecticut, a house he loved more than the town that marveled at it. ("If there is a man in Hartford who is not a burglar, I am not aware of it, and I am not acquainted with him."[14]) The "disorderly alarm bell" that was constantly disturbing Mark Twain's family and concentration may have been one of the warnings on which he failed to act.[15] His business investments were the biggest sinkholes. Ironically — since he so often benefited from *positive* riffs of coincidence — he might have been spared the most ruinous of his business mistakes had he noticed the symbolism of *negative* coincidence, in the shape of a recurring slip.

He was captivated by an inventor and self-promoter called James Paige. As Mark Twain ruefully recalled later, Paige "could persuade a fish to come and take a walk with him."[16] Paige was developing a new typesetting machine, and Sam — whose career started in print shops — was easily convinced that this machine was going to be the biggest thing since Gutenberg's. He became the lead investor in the Paige typesetting machine. The project was bedeviled by delay after delay, and by the time Paige had completed a working prototype, his machine was obsolete, overtaken by new and superior typesetters. Mark Twain lost most of his money in this fiasco.

Now for the slip: Mark Twain could never seem to get right the name of the inventor or the machine named after him. Again and again, in his voluminous letters and journal entries on this theme, he wrote "Page" instead of "Paige." The fact that Mark Twain could never get the name of his biggest investment straight was surely an ominous sign. With hindsight, he would no doubt have agreed to the snapper "Notice what's showing through your slip."

Mark Twain was very nearly broke when a "chance" encounter introduced him to the man who put him back on his feet. "We were strangers when we met and friends when we parted, half an hour afterward. The meeting was accidental and unforeseen but it had memorable and unforeseen consequences for me. He dragged me out of that difficulty and out of the next one."[17] The meeting took place in the lobby of the Murray Hill Hotel, where Sam's friend Dr. Rice recognized Henry Rogers of Standard Oil. Mark Twain and the forceful capitalist — sometimes called "Hell Hound" Rogers — hit it off. Rogers restructured Mark Twain's business affairs and sheltered him from his creditors until he was finally out of debt. Mark Twain joined the magnate for cruises on his yacht.

It may seem unlikely that Mark Twain invited Rogers to go very far into his dreaming mind, or that the tycoon would have been willing to go there. However, Mark Twain did write to Rogers about a dream reported by Rogers's secretary, Katherine Harrison. "Miss Harrison has had a dream which promises me a large bank account." Mark Twain advised dream reentry: "I want her to go ahead and dream it twice more, so as to make the prediction sure to be fulfilled."[18]

MENTAL TELEGRAPHY

In 1878, Mark Twain gathered some of his experiences and experiments in a most interesting article that he titled "Mental Telegraphy." He waited thirteen years to publish it, fearing ridicule or incredulity. When public interest and scientific research (notably the investigations of the young Society for Psychical Research in England) began to catch up with his own findings, he came out with the article in *Harper's* magazine. In it he wrote, "I once made a great discovery: the discovery that certain sorts of things which, from the beginning of the world, had always been regarded as merely 'curious coincidences' — that is to say, accidents — were no more accidental than is the sending and receiving of a telegram an accident."[19]

One of his favorite examples of the interplay of psyche and physics that generates coincidence is the phenomenon of "crossed letters." You write to someone (or just think about her) — maybe someone you have not been in contact with for months — and then you get a letter or a call from that person the same day or very soon after. For example, he observed in his notebook that two days after he thought of his wife's cousin Louise for the first time in three years, he received a letter from her asking for financial support.[20]

He noticed that incidences of "crossed letters" were a frequent phenomenon, and the more he thought about it, the more it seemed to occur. He concluded that it must be the effect of distant communication between minds keyed to similar wavelengths. His most amazing example is the Great Bonanza book.

One afternoon, he was seized with the passionate conviction that a great book could be written about the silver bonanza in Nevada. He felt his old newspaper colleague William Wright (better known under his pen name, Dan De Quille) was the man to do it. But Mark Twain was so possessed by the idea that, in a blue haze of cigar smoke in the billiard room of the Hartford house, he roughed out a book outline and sample chapters to get his old friend started. He was preparing to mail all this material to Wright when he received a package in the mail. Before opening the package, Mark Twain told the people with him that he was going to deliver a "prophecy": he declared that the package contained a letter from his old friend Dan De Quille, with *his* drafts for a book on the Great Bonanza. And so it did.

This incident convinced Mark Twain not only that mental telegraphy is real but also that it can be strong enough to transport the complete content of a book across a continent. When he studied the exact chronology of the crossed letters,

Mark Twain concluded that "mesmeric currents" had streamed from west to east. "It was *your* mesmeric current that flowed across the mountains & deserts three thousand miles & acted upon *me*," he told his friend.[21] Minds resonate with each other and, in doing so, transfer ideas and messages back and forth. Mark Twain was very interested in determining whether we can *pluck* the strings as well as wait for them to vibrate.

A case in point — from his personal chronicle in "Mental Telegraphy" — involved an American on the grand tour in Europe who was desperate since he had received no news from his son back in San Francisco in many months, despite sending many letters. Sam urged him to send a cable, which might sound like the merest common sense. Here's the *uncommon* sense: Sam further told the worried father that it did not matter where he sent the cable. "Send it to Peking, if you like."[22] All that mattered was that he sent a cable and, thereby, a signal to the universe. If he did that, Mark Twain promised, he would have news from his son right away. The father sent the cable and the next day received a letter from his son explaining that he had left San Francisco months before on a slow boat and was now acting on his first opportunity to post a letter. The cable did not prompt the letter, which was mailed long before; but the two communications *coincided*, just as Sam had promised.

Mark Twain developed what he was pleased to call a "superstition" about this. He decided that, if he wanted to hear from someone, he would write that person a letter and then tear the letter up. Infallibly, he claimed, he would then receive a letter from the person to whom he had written. If this was "superstition," it was fresh-minted superstition and of a most practical kind: it worked.

Certain other incidents in his life suggest not only that mind reaches to mind but also that events in the mind can influence physical events, and vice versa. In January 1870, Mark Twain was in Cambridge, New York. He had arrived exhausted in a storm of sleet and ice. He found that a local paper, the *Troy Times*, had published a transcription of his current lecture, even down to dashes and asterisks to evoke his drawl. He flew into a rage; this kind of thing deprived him of the surprise factor in front of an audience and could reduce his box office. Bouncing up and down in his fury — maybe literally hitting the ceiling (as he was known to do when his temper was up) — he saw flame and smoke burst from the nearby lecture hall where he was scheduled to speak. As the fire blazed, Mark Twain felt a wild sensation of justice and power. "My spirits came up till I felt that all I needed to be entirely happy was to see the *Troy Times* editors locked up in that burning building."[23]

He had also hoped for a night off. He was disappointed that the firemen arrived promptly and put the fire out, and that he was still obliged to deliver the leaked lecture, in a hall reeking with the stench of wet ash.

Before the Pauli Effect was named, there was a Mark Twain Effect.

THE DREAM TRICK AND THE REALITIES OF DREAMING

In a grand scene in chapter 18 of *The Adventures of Tom Sawyer*, Mary says, "Shut up, Sid! A body does just the same in a dream as he'd do if he was awake."[24] But the reader knows — as Aunt Polly and Mary and Sid will discover — that Tom's intricate account of having seen all the details of their evening life in a dream is a deception. He had actually snuck across the river from his hiding place and had concealed himself inside the house in order to eavesdrop. The trick Tom plays on the family is the inverse of the trick Mark Twain is playing on the reader.

In his later writings, Mark Twain is super clear that dreams are real experiences, even real on a physical level. We discover, through his notebooks and letters, that he not only agreed with Mary that "a body does just the same in a dream as he'd do if he was awake" but also believed that the dream self has much greater travel opportunities than the regular self.

My hunch is that he was fully aware of these things when he was writing *The Adventures of Tom Sawyer* but was not yet ready to take his readers that far, or did not believe they would be willing to go that far with him. So he switched two realities and had Tom make up a "lie" about a dream. It would be amusing to rewrite the scene and have Tom make up a "lie" about eavesdropping to explain how he had learned all the things he actually saw in a dream.

In one of his later stories, "My Platonic Sweetheart," Mark Twain wrote, "In our dreams — I know it! — we do make the journeys we seem to make, we do see the things we seem to see."[25] He also described a practice for "drilling" the memory in order to catch more dreams and use them to discover the nature of the personality and of reality itself. "Few drill the dream-memory, and no memory can be kept strong without them." The drill involves writing down dreams when they are fresh, then studying them and revisiting them and trying to figure out "what the source of dreams is, and which of the two or three separate persons inhabiting us is their architect."[26]

Mark Twain's experience was that in dreams we can find ourselves in parallel worlds where we lead a continuous life, usually forgotten after waking. In these parallel lives, we may be following a path from which we departed in ordinary life. We may find ourselves living with a lost love.

As a cub pilot, Sam had been smitten by a lovely fourteen-year-old girl in braids called Laura Wright. He spent two days as close to her as he could get, then they were forced to separate and embark on separate lives. Mark Twain's notebook entries suggest that he dreamed of Laura, and of a parallel life in which they were united, over most of his life.

He wrote enigmatically in a letter in 1893: "I dreamed I was born, and grew up, and was a pilot on the Mississippi and a miner and journalist and had a wife and children — and this dream goes on and on and *on*, and sometimes seems so real that I almost believe that it *is* real. I wonder if it is?"[27] He wished to be able to migrate to a parallel world where he could be with loved ones from whom he was cruelly separated.

He never felt that desire more strongly than after the early death of his adored daughter "Susy" — Olivia Susan Clemens — who was struck down by meningitis when she was only twenty-four. Susy was a precocious writer; she composed a biography of her father when she was fourteen. She described how she and her sister, Clara, would sit on either arm of their father's chair in the library of the Hartford home while he made up stories about the pictures on the wall. These romances had to begin with the cat in an oil painting and end with a beautiful young girl in a watercolor.[28]

The horror of her death a decade later was a violent contrast to this lovely idyll. A lethal infection had entered her system, swelling the lining of her brain and her spinal cord, driving her insane before it killed her. She roamed the Hartford house, raving and scribbling strange notes in which she identified herself with a dead Parisian singer. Shortly before she died, she clutched at one of her mother's gowns, thinking it was Livy.

Mark Twain was in England when she died. Alerted that she was gravely ill, Livy and Clara were sailing back, too late to reach her. "It is one of the mysteries of our nature," he later observed, "that a man, all unprepared, can receive a thunder-stroke like that and live."[29]

Susy's death was the most crushing of all the tragedies in Mark Twain's life. His creative work, and the "fountains of the deep" that fed it, were what got him through. Justin Kaplan may be correct in saying that, "by turning his dream life into a literary problem — into work — he saved himself from madness."[30] In "Which Was the Dream?," a story begun the year after Susy's death, Mark Twain attributes a series of terrifying dreams to a child character called "Bessie." There is good reason to think that Bessie ("all soap-bubbles and rainbows and fireworks") was modeled closely on Susy's childhood self. It is likely that Bessie's scary dreams — with the recurring theme of being pursued and eaten by bears — were also modeled on Susy's dreams. Dreams of being attacked by bears often herald illness. Since the bear, in North America, is a medicine animal, being at odds with a bear in dreams is something to investigate very carefully as a possible health advisory.

In describing Bessie's dreams, Mark Twain begins in a breezy, nonchalant fashion: "Like most people, Bessie is pestered by recurring dreams." Then he stuns us by revealing the content: "Her stock item is that she is being eaten by bears. It is the main horror of her life. Last night she had that dream again."

Then he describes Bessie thinking hard about these horrible dreams and looking up like one who feels she has not been dealt a fair hand in life, and saying, "But mamma, the trouble is, I am never the *bear* but always the *person eaten.*"

Now the author introduces a thrilling and utterly unexpected plot development. The parents are hatching a plan to turn Bessie's "persecuting dream" into something quite different. In a surprise performance to be mounted that same evening during Bessie's birthday party, her father's "high capacities in the way of invention" will be used to turn her dream into "something quite romantically and picturesquely delightful."

How would this be contrived? By putting Bessie in a bear suit and having her pursue and pretend to eat partygoers? By having a crowd of people in bear suits flee before her? Or by having her make friends with the bear and feed him birthday cake and dance with him?

We do not know, because the party is never held. A terrible fire that night destroys the house, and the father and his family are thrown into such turmoil and tragedy that their previous good fortune seems like a fading dream. Mark Twain proceeds to explore one of the favorite themes of his later years: the difficulty of distinguishing the dream of physical existence from any other dream.[31]

But in the passage relating to Bessie's dreams, he has — perhaps after examining Susy's tragedy in hindsight — taken a long step toward understanding and portraying two vital aspects of dream healing. The first is that dreams alert us to possible problems before the crisis develops. The second is that, by reworking dream imagery — if we can do this with sufficient "invention" and authenticity and drama — we can move toward resolution and healing. We can stop being the "person eaten" and claim the healing gifts of the bear. Sadly, like the characters of his story, Mark Twain was unable to apply this insight fully in the circumstances of his family life.

Mark Twain's last major work of fiction was born at Weggis, site of an ancient Celtic ferry crossing on Lake Lucerne, in the summer of 1897, after Susy's death.

Writing, as always, was his therapy for grief and disappointment. On the lake, he wrote for nine hours a day, seven days a week. A cluster of drafts emerged that he called "The Chronicles of Young Satan." The novella was published posthumously as *The Mysterious Stranger*.

On the title page, Mark Twain described it as "Being an Ancient Tale Found in a Jug, and Freely Translated from the Jug." This was another of his insider's jokes. Aside from the jesting allusion to booze, the line is echoed by a remark made by the Mysterious Stranger halfway through the story: "One cannot pour the starred and shoreless expanse of the universe into a jug."[32]

The Mysterious Stranger is set in a medieval Austrian village in the time of the witch burnings. The title character appears to boys on a wild hilltop as a handsome youth with magical powers, which he first demonstrates by lighting a pipe by pure will. He proceeds to demonstrate greater powers, creating miniature people out of clay and destroying them when he is bored with them. He can transport himself and others to distant places — China, the moon — instantly. He can fold time so that lengthy journeys in other lands occupy only instants in the ordinary environment.

He can change people's fates, and demonstrates again and again that the smallest alteration in one of the links of fate can make a radical difference in the outcome. Getting up two minutes later than was in the plan can make the difference between life and death. His interventions (such as ensuring that a boy gets up two minutes later than destined) may be anonymous and seemingly natural, or showy (as when he knocks down a whole troupe of witch-hunters at the narrator's request, breaking a rib in every person).

He is invisible unless he chooses to be seen. He can easily take possession of chosen subjects, moving over them like "transparent film" before he goes inside them. He spins moralizing stories — sometimes illustrated by grand panoramas exhibiting the whole sweep of history, from Cain and Abel on — to prove the idiocy of the "moral sense" in humans. He insists that it is humans who create right and wrong and then most often choose wrong. At the end of the tale, he contends that there is no heaven and hell, no God, no afterlife, no larger meaning — that everything we experience is "only a dream." In the last words of the story, the narrator (speaking for the author?) agrees.[33] This Satan at first identifies himself as an "angel" and says he is the nephew of the more notorious Satan. All angels, he says, are indifferent to humanity. But he is capable of doing humans a good turn — which often proves to be the gift of early death (even death by burning, as a witch) in order to avoid lengthy suffering that would otherwise ensue. He gives himself a name for the times, Philip Traum, which means Philip Dream. He is an attractive figure. Animals love him. His arrival energizes people. He seems to enjoy playing with humans, but there is an edge of cruelty to his play, like that of a boy digging into an anthill. He presents a very bleak picture of humanity and its capabilities, insisting that no human ever voluntarily changes his prearranged fate — while hinting that the slightest change could open an alternative life track in a parallel world. His circus tricks, his talking cat, and his way of producing vast effects by tiny bits of tinkering in a person's life may all have inspired Mikhail Bulgakov's version of the devil in Moscow in *The Master and Margarita*.

Playing through the novella are themes that had long haunted Mark Twain: the theme of the double, and the separate life of a dream self that travels freely outside the body. He notes "the presence in us of another *person*, not a slave of ours but . . . with a character distinctly its own."[34] Musing on Jekyll and Hyde again, he describes them as "dual persons in one body, quite distinct in nature and character and presumably each *with a conscience of his own*."[35] He speculates in his notebook that "two persons in a man have no command over each other." They "do not even *know* each other and . . . have never even suspected one another's existence."[36]

He distinguishes the double from another aspect of the self that operates independently of the ordinary personality, and which is not confined to the body. "We have a spiritualized self which can detach itself and go wandering off upon affairs of its own." This is not the double, the "partner in duality." He notes, "I am not acquainted with my double, my partner in duality . . . but I *am* acquainted (dimly) with my spiritualized self and I know that it and I are one, because we have common memory."[37] This "spiritualized self" is the dream traveler, at home in many worlds.

Waking I move slowly; but in my dreams my unhampered spiritualized body flies to the ends of the earth in a millionth of a second. Seems to — and I believe, does . . .

I do actually make immense excursions in my spiritualized person. I go into awful dangers. . . . I go to unnamable places, I do unprincipled things; and every vision is vivid, every sensation — physical as well as moral — is real.[38]

TRAVELS AMONG THE MICROBES

On lecture tour in Sydney, Australia, Mark Twain had a *big* dream. "I dreamed that the visible universe is the physical person of God; that the vast worlds that we see twinkling millions of miles apart in the fields of space are the blood corpuscles in His veins; and that we and the other creatures are the microbes that charge with multitudinous life the corpuscles."[39]

This theme plays back and forth between his dream life and his most original creative writing. In his later years, Mark Twain wrote of journeys into nanoworlds, such as a world inside a stone, or a society of microbes inside a human cell. These efforts to imagine and depict worlds inside very small things, though not widely known today, make exciting reading in the age of nanotechnology, when superstring theory suggests there may be six (or seven) dimensions of the physical universe hidden within the particles of an atom, and quantum physics speculates that, if we can enter that space, we can choose events that will manifest from the soup of possibilities.

In August 1898, Mark Twain noted a dream that gave him the idea for one of his most intriguing later stories. "Last night dreamed of a whaling cruise in a drop of water. Not by microscope but actually."[40] In "The Great Dark," he creates a world inside a drop of water on a glass slide under a microscope. The traveler gets inside it, with an appropriate ship and crew, with the aid of a person identified as the Superintendent of Dreams, who appears by his side while he is musing on a sofa. Once inside the waterworld, it becomes hard to know whether it is this world or the one with the sofa that is real; the traveler's shipmates know no other reality than the ship and the sea. Mark Twain is playing with a favorite theme, *Which is the dream?*: the world we inhabit when we think we are awake, or the one we know when we think we are dreaming? He wanted to carry his theme further. In a note on further development of this story, Mark Twain reported that the Superintendent of Dreams was not satisfied with his title: he "says his proper title is S[uperintendent] of R[ealities] and he is so-called in the other planets, but here we reverse the meanings of many words, and we wouldn't understand him."[41]

In "Three Thousand Years among the Microbes," Mark Twain goes smaller and handles the transition from human scale to microscale very briskly and effectively: "The magician's experiment miscarried . . . and the result was that he transformed me into a cholera-germ when he was trying to turn me into a bird."[42] The foundation of the story is the author's visionary experience. When Mark Twain crossed out his own name and substituted the name of his most popular character, Huck, he laid the thinnest conceivable veil over what we can read as visionary autobiography enhanced by the writer's vivid imagination.[43]

As a germ, Huck is inside a universe where everything is alive and conscious. "Nothing is ever at rest. . . . There are no vegetables; *all things are*

ANIMAL; each electron is an animal, each molecule is an animal, and each has an appointed duty to perform and a soul to be saved."[44] A week of human time is a thousand microbe years, more or less. The man-become-germ makes his adjustments — including his aesthetics — learns the local languages, and mixes comfortably in microbe society. This is a universe with commerce and political intrigues and fashions and games and science — all of which gives the author a glorious opportunity to spoof the foibles of his own society while taking us somewhere deeper.

Mark Twain shocks us by representing the germs of illness as the nobility among the microbes. The cancer cells are the very "brightest" among them; the consumption agent the most poetic. Each "noble" family has a crest that resembles the way each germ looks — to a human eye — under a microscope. Medical technology developed since Mark Twain's time suggests that this may have been more than literary invention; he may have intuited, or actually *seen*, what goes on among the cells of a body challenged by cancer. An oncology nurse with whom I shared his account made the interesting comment that cancer cells "glow" in an x-ray and are sometimes called, in hospital slang, "stars."

Sometimes our hero dreams he is back in the human world, and he wakes with the inevitable question: Which is the dream? A moment of epiphany comes when Huck decides to confide to a circle of microbe intellectuals that he comes from another world, a planet beyond the body of the drunken tramp they are all living in. They simply cannot comprehend him. They can't understand, to begin with, that they are inside the body of a larger being, and that their behavior could affect that body's health for good or ill. So how can they grasp the idea that there are similar worlds in which beings walk and eat on a planet inconceivably vast? So of course the best brains of the microbe world dismiss Huck as delusional, or at best, applaud him for his vivid and complex imagination.

Which leads our narrator to observe, "It isn't safe to sit in judgment upon another person's illusion when you are not on the inside. While you are thinking it is a dream, he may be knowing it is a planet." Mark Twain proceeds to show us microbe scientists studying the nanomicrobes who live inside their bodies. He pushes the point — hard but brilliantly — that in relation to the larger universe, we humans reading him may be of the order of microbes too, *and yet may be able to affect the state of everything*.

I discovered "Three Thousand Years among the Microbes" at the end of December 2005. Leafing through one of my old journals shortly afterward, I was excited to discover that I had apparently received Mark Twain's invitation to explore the worlds within very small objects nearly four years earlier. Here's the dream, just as I recorded it in my journal:

Worldstones [June 27, 2002]

I am training people to journey into very small objects, especially stones. Some of these are Worldstones; you find a whole world within them. Some contain universes generated by books. I enjoy my adventures inside a stone that contains the world of Huck Finn.

That's the mark of a world-class dreamer: that he can extend an invitation to join him in a tramp through the Dreamlands — in a dream. Mark Twain worked with dreams, coincidence, and imagination through the best years of his immensely creative and productive life, and lived deeper and deeper in their play as he matured. He also understood the importance of nurturing and following a *life* dream: "Twenty years from now you will be more disappointed by the things that you didn't do than by the ones you did do. So throw off the bowlines. Sail away from the safe harbor. Catch the trade winds in your sails. Explore. Dream. Discover."

CHAPTER 11

❧

THE MAN WHO
BLEW THINGS UP

This was a kind of spell he was supposed to cast on people or objects in his neighborhood, particularly in physics laboratories, causing accidents of all sorts. Machines would stop running when he arrived in a laboratory, a glass apparatus would suddenly break, a leak would appear in a vacuum system, but none of these accidents would ever hurt or inconvenience Pauli himself.

— NUCLEAR PHYSICIST RUDOLF PEIERLS ON THE PAULI EFFECT

We do not know whether what we on the empirical plane regard as physical may not, in the Unknown beyond our experience, be identical with what on this side of the border we distinguish from the physical as psychic.... They may be identical somewhere beyond our present experience.

— C.G. JUNG, *"The Tavistock Lectures:
On the Theory and Practice of Psychoanalysis,"* 1935

Over a quarter of a century, the psychologist Carl Jung and the physicist Wolfgang Pauli shared dreams and coincidences and wild imaginings, groping together toward a unified theory to explain the interplay of mind and matter at all levels of the multidimensional universe. It was the friendship of intellectual giants, and we can track it through their letters. In this long dialogue, we see both of these brilliant minds growing and goading each other to reach further, beyond their disciplines and any kind of comfort zone. As Jungian analyst Beverley Zabriskie observes, "Each had the humility essential to look for precedents from the past, as well as the arrogance necessary to risk speculation about the future."[1] In their encounter, physics met psychology, erasing facile past distinctions between objective and subjective and opening the way to understanding the *unus mundus*, the underlying unity.

Pauli was probably the only person in Jung's life from whom the great psychologist tolerated challenging feedback and criticism on the matters most precious to him for a period of time anywhere near this long. This, in itself, is amazing, since many people found Pauli's rudeness and incinerating criticism unbearable.

In 1930, when they first met, their minds were moving on parallel tracks in their separate explorations of the I Ching, in their close attention to dreams, in their fascination with the pre-Newtonian worldviews of the alchemists and the Renaissance magicians, and in their quest for the common ground of mind and matter. They were both at the peak of their creativity and professional status. Several years earlier, still in his twenties, Pauli had made the key scientific discoveries for which he was later awarded the Nobel Prize in Physics. Though Jung's greatest books came after death knocked on his heart in 1944, he had, by 1930, founded his own school of analytical psychology and introduced original theories on the structure and dynamics of the psyche, the collective unconscious, and the archetypes, and on the "compensation" function of dreams.

Jung was groping his way toward an exposition of the phenomenon he called "synchronicity" — a term he first tried out in front of an audience in 1929, the year before he met Pauli. He needed a second mind, one with complementary skills and equal brilliance, to help him bring through a coherent theory. Pauli was that mind.

Both men had tremendous energy. Laurens van der Post attributes Jung's extraordinary "spontaneous generation" of ever-renewing creative energy to the fact that "he was somehow always following the mainstream of himself."[2] Jung thought that one mainspring of his life was that he had discovered *the* Work — the work to which you give your all, for its own sake — quite early. "From my eleventh year," Jung wrote of himself, "I have been launched upon a single enterprise which is my 'main business.'"[3]

Pauli too was a driven man, on a quest to grasp and explain the fabric of reality, yearning for the harmonies. But his energy had a volatile, explosive quality. It produced wild and shocking effects not only on people but also on the physical environment around him. When, at age thirty, he came to see Jung, Pauli did not come as a scientific colleague. He came as a patient desperately in need of help, a man at the end of his tether.

DEMONS OF VIENNA

Wolfgang Pauli was born in Vienna, Freud's city, in the centennial year 1900, when Freud published his book on dreams. Pauli's last name might have been Pascheles, which was the name of his grandfather, the well-respected rabbi in Prague who performed the bar mitzvah for Franz Kafka, but his father decided to change the family name and convert to Roman Catholicism, a politic move made by other Viennese Jews in the effort to avoid the antisemitism that flowed in their city's gutters like raw sewage. Pauli's mother, née Bertha Schütz, was Catholic on *her* mother's side, but her father was a well-known Jewish writer, which made Wolfgang three parts Jewish. Nobody explained this to him until he was in his teens. It was the source of one of the many identity problems that bedeviled his life.

Vienna has been described as a two-room apartment: the front room, where visitors come, is gay and frivolous and flirty; but the back room is dark and brooding, strange and unfathomable.[4] This was certainly Pauli's family situation.

He was a boy who did not like fairy tales; they made him uneasy.[5] Beneath his precocious brilliance was an edgy sense of an abyss beneath the obvious that deepened when his closest friend killed himself.

After graduating with high honors from the Döblinger-Gymnasium in Vienna, Pauli studied in Munich under Arnold Sommerfeld, who introduced him to the mysteries of the fine-structure constant. Sommerfeld asked him to write a review of Einstein's relativity theory for the German *Encyclopedia of Mathematical Scientists*. Pauli's review, completed two months after he received his doctorate, at age twenty-one, ran to 237 pages. When Einstein read it, he made an extraordinarily generous comment: "No one studying this mature, grandly conceived work could believe that the author is a man of twenty-one. One wonders what to admire most, the psychological understanding for the development of ideas, the sureness of mathematical deduction, the profound physical insight, the capacity for lucid systematic presentation, the complete treatment of the subject matter, or the sureness of critical appraisal."[6] Pauli's reputation was made.

When he was just twenty-four, he formulated what would become known as the Pauli exclusion principle, the achievement for which he was awarded the Nobel Prize, on Einstein's recommendation, in 1945. Briefly stated, the principle is that no two identical electrons can share the same quantum state.

While Pauli was now known in the scientific world as a master of spin theory, his family and personal life were spinning wildly. In 1927, his mother committed suicide after learning that his father was having an affair. Pauli's father proceeded to marry a young woman his son's age.

The following year, Pauli moved to Zurich to take up a professorship at the Federal Polytechnic Institute. Although the Viennese sniffed that Zurich was "twice the size of the Vienna cemetery, but half as entertaining," Pauli remained a resident of Zurich for the rest of his life, apart from his time at Princeton during World War II.

He left the church in 1929 and married a cabaret dancer, Käthe Deppner. She was involved with another man — a chemist — when they met, and Pauli came to suspect she continued to see him on the side. They divorced in less than a year, and she promptly married the chemist; Pauli said he would have preferred her to run off with a bullfighter.

The savage drama of his collapsing marriage may have fueled an extraordinary new burst of scientific creativity. Creative people are sometimes able to take the raw energy of "negative" emotions like grief and jealousy and anger, all of which were raging in Pauli, and use them to power fresh production. It was in this period that Pauli invented the neutrino. He "made it up" out of thin air in an attempt to salvage laws of conservation that were threatened by experimental findings about beta decay. When he introduced the idea to the scientific community, in a celebrated communiqué that began "Dear radioactive colleagues," some were dazzled and some were incredulous.[7] It took more than thirty years before experiments proved that what Pauli made up was also real.

But his heart and his head were exploding with the stress and the constant work. His bulging eyes may indicate a hyperactive thyroid, which would certainly not contribute to emotional balance. He was drinking hard for relief, but not holding it well. He was thrown out of bars and restaurants, and once was left bleeding on the sidewalk after a brawl in the street. Fearing that he was headed for a complete nervous breakdown, his father insisted that he seek help and recommended an analyst called Jung, who had once worked with Freud and who lived nearby.

THE FOX AND THE GARDEN

Jung is walking in his garden at Küsnacht, on Lake Zurich, with a woman patient. He likes to observe the play of natural phenomena as he talks with a client. He finds significance in every shift in the environment — a sudden wind whipping up the lake water, the shape of a cloud, the cry of a bird.

In the gentle sunlight, they walk beyond the garden, into a little wood. The woman is talking about the first dream of her life that had a huge impact on her; she calls this an "everlasting" impression. "I am in my childhood home," she recalls, "and a spectral fox is coming down the stairs." She stops and puts her hand on Jung's arm, because in this moment a real fox trots out of the trees, less than forty yards in front of them. The fox proceeds to walk quietly along the path in front of them for several minutes. "The animal behaves as if it were a partner in the human situation."[8]

Jung had long been in the habit of reading signs from the world, together with dreams, and drawing counsel from the convergences as he counseled his patients. He had been encouraged to do this in his celebrated breakthrough work with a female patient who had been seriously blocked until she dreamed of a scarab, the dung beetle of the Nile Valley. Despite its lowly origins, the scarab was one of the most important Egyptian symbols of rebirth and transformation; it had been deified as Khepri and was placed over the heart of the soul traveler to guide journeys beyond the body and beyond death. As the woman discussed her dream, a flying beetle known as a rose chafer appeared at the window. It was the nearest match for the Egyptian scarab you could hope to find in Europe, and as the patient's eyes widened in recognition, she experienced a sense of confirmation of her dream and the work she was doing with Jung that carried her to deep healing.

When he saw patients inside the house, he liked to sit so that they both faced the garden, the poplars at the edge of the lake, and the water beyond, noticing what the world was saying. He was impressed by other cases in which animals or birds seemed to participate in a human exchange. Another woman patient told him she noticed birds massing around her house whenever there was a death in the family. While treating this woman's husband, Jung felt the man was exhibiting symptoms of a heart condition and insisted that he consult a physician. He did this, and was given a clean bill of health — but died of a massive heart attack on his way home from the doctor. His wife was prepared for this event, she told Jung afterward, by a new massing of the birds around her home.[9]

A woman doctor told him she felt she had been tormented by the strange behavior of animals she loved as a punishment for a terrible crime she had succeeded in concealing for many years. She confessed to Jung that she had poisoned her best friend in order to steal her husband. In revenge, as she told it, the horses she loved had taken to shying away from her, and one of them had thrown her out of the saddle. And her favorite wolfhound had been stricken by paralysis in a way the veterinarian could not understand. Jung commented, "Sometimes it seems as if even animals and plants 'know' it."[10]

It is not recorded whether Jung walked with Pauli in his garden, or why he decided he would not be Pauli's analyst. Jung passed the troubled physicist on to a relatively inexperienced female analyst.

Why did Jung decline to work personally with Pauli? He wrote enigmatically that it was because Pauli's psyche was "chock-full of archaic material"[11] — but Jung loved hunting down archaic references. Perhaps he felt personal resistance to working with Pauli, who was an odd-looking, roly-poly figure given to shaking and even rocking his whole upper body when he was thinking hard, and capable of blurting out *anything*. Maybe Jung felt that Pauli, so troubled in his relations with women, could be helped by a female therapist. Sensing that the stream of Pauli's consciousness would contain treasures, Jung may have chosen a junior apprentice to work with him on the calculation that she would not interrupt the flow. Recognizing Pauli's genius, Jung may have grasped the potential for a productive collaboration with one of the pioneers of the new physics, and may have wanted to avoid burdening that with a clinical history.

It's not beyond imagining that the notorious Pauli Effect — the way things seemed to blow up around him — came into play on his first visit to Jung's house and made the psychologist cautious. Jung was not unaccustomed to special effects during times of charged emotion. He often recalled the loud crack that had emanated from a piece of furniture when he was breaking up with Freud. And his whole household had been bedeviled by poltergeist-type phenomena in the period before he wrote *Seven Sermons of the Dead*. But there was no one like Pauli for blowing things up.

THE SECRET LABORATORY OF DR. PAULI

Jung did not altogether absent himself from Pauli's case. When Pauli proceeded to deliver a torrent of dream reports — some thirteen hundred over an eighteen-month period — the junior analyst passed the cream of the crop on to Jung, who drew on four hundred of them (with Pauli's permission and the promise of anonymity) for a major essay that was included in his book *Psychology and Alchemy*. Here's a sampling:

Pauli dreams of a treasure in the deep. To reach it, he has to dive through a narrow opening. This is dangerous, but down below he will find a companion.

The dreamer takes the plunge into the dark and discovers a beautiful garden in the depths, symmetrically laid out, with a fountain in the center.[12]

In another dream, he is falling, not diving, into the abyss. At the bottom is a bear whose eyes glow alternately in four colors — red, yellow, green, and blue. Looking more closely, he sees it has four eyes that change into four lights. The bear disappears, and Pauli goes through a long, dark tunnel. Beyond it, in the light, is a pile of treasure with a diamond ring on top. Pauli is told the ring will lead him on a long journey to the east.[13]

In a dream that surely resonated with Jung, the son of a disillusioned minister, Pauli comes to a strange, solemn house — the House of the Gathering. The doorkeeper says of the people who are entering, "When they come out again, they are cleansed." When Pauli goes inside, he hears these words: "Woe unto them who use religion as a substitute for another side of the soul's life; they are in error and will be accursed. Religion is no substitute; it is to be added to the other activities of the soul as the ultimate completion. Out of the fullness of life shall you bring forth your religion; only then shall you be blessed!"[14]

In addition to goading him to pursue a dangerous quest for a secret treasure — perhaps the secret of the universe — beyond any maps, Pauli's dreams were now confirming that religion is no substitute for the work of the soul and "the fullness of life." Hearing this, Jung's mind may have gone back to one of the indelible *big* dreams of his childhood in which he looked up into the sky above the cathedral in Basel, all the way to the high throne of God — and saw a colossal turd dumped from the divine throne that fell on the cathedral and crushed it. This had brought him a blessed sense of relief.[15]

Pauli and Jung both felt that his adventures in dreaming and dream sharing had brought him to some kind of balance when he reported a dream of exquisite harmony, the dream of the World Clock. He saw a vertical blue disk and a horizontal disk of four colors, both turning from a common center and supported by a great bird. This was the World Clock, and it had three rhythms or pulses: a complete revolution of the vertical disk turned the horizontal disk by a fraction; a revolution of the horizontal disk moved the golden ring. This vision gave Pauli a sense of "the most sublime harmony." Jung was fascinated by the image of a multidimensional mandala displaying the interplay of time and times and eternity.[16]

For more than twenty years after his analysis was concluded, Pauli shared dreams with Jung directly, especially in long and thoughtful letters. Pauli did not essentially offer dreams for interpretation, though he welcomed the feedback Jung offered, characteristically through "amplification" in which he associated

Pauli's dream symbols with images drawn from his encyclopedic knowledge of the world's history, mythology, and religions. As Pauli later explained to Jung's wife, Emma, "I am quite skeptical about interpretations of dreams. . . . What has worked best for me has been on the one hand 'shedding as broad a light' as possible into the context, and reflecting on the general problems to be found in this context, and on the other hand observing the dreams over periods of several years."[17]

For Pauli as a scientist and intellectual explorer, dreams were, as he put it, a "secret laboratory" where he received and tested some of his best ideas and where he was constantly encouraged to move beyond existing paradigms.[18] Thus in 1934 a dream figure who seemed to be Einstein appeared and told Pauli his quantum theory was a "one-dimensional section of a two-dimensional, more meaningful world, the second dimension of which could be only the unconscious and the archetypes."[19] Pauli understood from this that he must deepen his engagement with depth psychology and work toward the unification of physics and psychology.

Pauli's dream guides appeared and reappeared in guises adapted to his growing understanding, sometimes with the faces of familiar colleagues or departed family members, sometimes as exotic strangers, such as a "Persian," a "light-dark stranger," and an attractive "Chinese woman" who can move like a snake dancer and who takes Pauli to unfamiliar places and audiences. While Pauli and Jung often tried to tag the dreams with Jungian labels (the "anima," the "shadow"), the dream figures eluded such confinement, as in the dream where an enigmatic dream character tells Pauli, "You are *my* shadow."[20] The Chinese woman stepped out of the dream space altogether and into the world, in a way that presented Pauli with the greatest intellectual challenge of his life.

THE PAULI EFFECT ON THE PAULI EFFECT

Beyond their shared fascination with dreams, Jung and Pauli shared a consuming interest in meaningful coincidence. Each of them was, in his own way, a magnet for coincidence. With Jung, this was often evident by means of natural phenomena, like the fox on the path and the "scarab" at the window. With Pauli, coincidence became manifest explosively through the Pauli Effect.

Both men had studied their precursors in this field. Jung, who was a great classical scholar and read Latin and Greek with gusto to the end of his life, was familiar with the Stoic doctrine that all things resonate through a cosmic sympathy. He liked to quote the Latin tag *Omnia plena diis esse* — "All things are full of gods." He was thoroughly familiar with the medieval worldview, in which everything is connected and speaks of everything else through correspondences: as within, so without; as above, so below. He especially enjoyed the language of Synesius, our Bishop of Dreams, when he spoke of signs and correspondences as "symbolic enticements."[21]

Both Jung and Pauli had experimented in depth with the I Ching. Jung first read James Legge's literary translation — almost unusable for a practitioner — and then had the good fortune to meet, and receive personal instruction in casting the Chinese oracle from, Richard Wilhelm, the great German sinologist whose translation first made it truly accessible in the West. "If I understand anything of the I Ching," Jung wrote to a correspondent in 1935, "then I should say it is *the* book that teaches you your way and the all-importance of it."[22]

Pauli had come to the I Ching via Leibniz (who studied it as a mathematical model of the universe) and Schopenhauer. He used it to get a second opinion on his dreams and as "a mathematical textbook." Pauli strongly identified with hexagram 51 of the I Ching, Chen ("Arousing"). He thought this evoked the force and the challenge of his own personality. The hexagram depicts a yang line pushing up forcibly against two yin lines so violently that it arouses terror. The image is doubled. The name of the hexagram means "shock" as well as "arousing." The "judgment" on the hexagram, as rendered by Wilhelm, reads:

SHOCK brings success.
Shock comes — oh, oh!
Laughing words — ha, ha!
The shock terrifies for a hundred miles.
And he does not let fall the sacrificial spoon and chalice.[23]

It's easy to see why this appealed to Pauli. He loved to shock people. Sometimes he rendered colleagues speechless with his rudeness. He not only struck people like a lightning bolt but also had this effect on his physical environment, especially on expensive scientific equipment. Most of us think we know someone who pops lightbulbs, stops watches, or makes computers crash. We may have observed such phenomena multiplying around ourselves in a time of conflicted emotions. Blowing up a computer was far beneath Pauli.

The *Pauli Effect* was a term invented to describe the way his presence in the vicinity tended to cause things, especially physics experiments and equipment, to blow up, without damage to Pauli himself. At least one experimental physicist (Otto Stern) banned Pauli from coming anywhere near his laboratory.

Pauli's friend and colleague Rudolf Peierls (a German-born physicist who moved to England and later worked on the Manhattan Project) described the Pauli Effect as follows: "This was a kind of spell he was supposed to cast on people or objects in his neighborhood, particularly in physics laboratories, causing accidents of all sorts. Machines would stop running when he arrived in a laboratory, a glass apparatus would suddenly break, a leak would appear in a vacuum system, but none of these accidents would ever hurt or inconvenience Pauli himself."[24]

When important experimental equipment in Professor James Frank's laboratory at the Physics Institute at the University of Gottingen blew up for no apparent reason, someone remarked that this could be the Pauli Effect. However, Pauli was nowhere in the area; he was on a train, traveling to Denmark. It was later discovered that, at the time of the lab explosion, the train carrying Pauli from Zurich to Copenhagen was making a stop at Gottingen station.

When he arrived at Princeton in 1950, an expensive new cyclotron that had recently been installed burned for no obvious reason, and there was again speculation about the Pauli Effect.

Such phenomena happened outside the laboratory as well. When the Jung Institute was inaugurated in Zurich in 1948, Pauli attended the opening ceremony, since Jung had asked him to become a "scientific patron" and so represent the convergence of physics and psychology. At the time, Pauli's mind was turning on the tension between two earlier approaches to knowledge represented by the alchemist Robert Fludd and the scientist Johannes Kepler. When Pauli entered the reception room for the Jung party, a large Chinese vase inexplicably slid off a table, creating a flood that drenched some of the distinguished guests. Pauli saw huge symbolic significance because of the echo of "Fludd" in the phenomenon of the spontaneous "flood." This incident inspired him to write his paper "Background Physics."

On another occasion, Pauli was sitting at a table in the window of the Café Odeon, thinking intently about the color red and its feeling tones. While thinking "red," he was unable to take his eyes off a large, unoccupied car parked in front of the restaurant. As he watched, the car burst into flames, and his field of vision was filled with fiery red.[25]

Erwin Panofsky, the famous art historian, recounted that as a young man he had met with Pauli and a friend for lunch at a restaurant in Hamburg. After a long and animated session ending with dessert and postprandial drinks, they rose from the table to find that two of the men had been sitting — inexplicably — in whipped cream, now smeared over their trousered rumps. The only one unscathed was, of course, Pauli.[26]

According to his close colleague Marcus Fierz, "Pauli believed thoroughly in his effect."[27] He experienced an unpleasant inner tension before things blew up. After the event, he felt relief and release from tension, even moments of euphoria. No doubt he enjoyed his ever-growing reputation for producing wickedly strange phenomena. This was, after all, the man who dressed up as Mephistopheles for a skit in front of Niels Bohr's circle in Copenhagen.

The best story on the Pauli Effect is from Rudolf Peierls. Some of Pauli's fellow scientists plotted to spoof the effect attributed to him at a reception. They carefully suspended a chandelier by a rope that they intended to release when Pauli entered the room, causing the chandelier to crash down. "But when Pauli came, the rope became wedged on a pulley and nothing happened — a typical example of the Pauli Effect."[28]

What would account for the Pauli Effect? It is hard not to suspect psychokinesis, the spilling over of mental and emotional forces roiling within the man into the physical world around him. Some of his colleagues joked, uneasily, that the Pauli Effect was an extreme example of the permanent hostility of theoretical physicists toward experimenters.

Jung may have understood the Pauli Effect in terms of his beloved books on alchemy and Renaissance magic. One of Jung's favorite quotations, used in his synchronicity essay, was from a treatise attributed to Albertus Magnus, the Dominican teacher of Aquinas (but probably, in this case, the pseudonym of an unidentified magus of the type of Cornelius Agrippa). The passage speaks of the tremendous power of the passions, when running at their height, to effect changes in the environment:

> A certain power to alter things indwells in the human soul and subordinates the other things to her, particularly when she is swept into a great excess of love or hate or the like. When therefore the soul of a man falls into a great excess of any passion, it can be proved by experiment that it binds things and alters them in the way that it wants, and for a long time I did not believe it. . . . But I found that the emotionality of the human soul is the chief cause of all these things. . . . Whoever would learn the secret of doing and undoing these things must know that everyone can influence everything magically if he falls into a great excess . . . and he must do it at that hour when the excess befalls him, and operate with the things which the soul prescribes.[29]

Perhaps the Pauli Effect was a (generally) unconscious example of such forces at work. Given his shocking relationship with the world around him, it is not surprising that Pauli dedicated himself to studying and explaining the interplay of mind and matter. In this sense, certainly, he fulfilled the judgment on the hexagram of the I Ching with which he identified, and did not let fall the sacred tools.

THE KNOCK AT THE HEART

Pauli was at Princeton during the war years, but unlike many of his colleagues at the Institute for Advanced Study, he was not invited to participate in the Manhattan Project. It has been suggested that the reason he was not approached was that Oppenheimer and other key figures were well aware of the Pauli Effect and were worried he would trigger a nuclear explosion at the wrong place and time.[30]

In Switzerland, to whose mountains and woods he so deeply belonged, Jung slipped on the snow during his daily constitutional in February 1944, and then sought medical help for his injured leg. While in the hospital, he suffered a heart attack and nearly died. His recovery was long, painful, and often reluctant. In a vision near death, Jung felt he was leaving the earth, which he could see far below as if from a thousand miles above. He was content to let "the whole phantasmagoria of earthly existence" fall away. He was about to enter a temple when his heart specialist floated up and told him there was a protest on earth about his departure; he must return.[31] When the cardiologist died not long after Jung's recovery, Jung felt that in some way their lives had been traded.

Synchronicities and overlapping dreams involving his students and circle abounded during and after Jung's medical crisis, as is often the case when life and death are being experienced most passionately. One of Jung's students succumbed to a terrible case of flu and nearly died. She recovered after Jung appeared to her in a vision and told her urgently, "I have decided to go back to the earth; get back into your own body as quickly as you can."[32]

Toward the end of his illness, Jung found a deep affirmation welling from within him: "an unconditional 'yes' to that which is" and a willingness to pursue his calling without being detoured by guilt and regret over past mistakes. He now announced, ringingly: "Anyone who takes the sure road is as good as dead."[33]

After his heart attack, Jung brought out his greatest works, including *Mysterium Coniunctionis*, which he and Pauli both saw as his magnum opus, and also the definitive version of his synchronicity theory. To clear the way, he had to deal with something that certainly weighed heavily on his heart: the psychic evil that had claimed Germany, and his own responsibilities in relation to that.

Jung firmly maintained at the end of World War II, as he had done all along, that work for positive change has to focus on the individual because "the psychopathology of the masses is rooted in the psychology of the individual."[34] Nonetheless, he was drawn to deeper reflection on group-thought forms and the possibility that a whole collective can be possessed by them. He recalled that as early as 1918 he had noticed in the dreams and preoccupations of his many German patients "peculiar disturbances... which could not be ascribed to their personal psychology." He became aware that "there was a disturbance of the collective unconscious in every one of my German patients." He saw that Hitler's rise was made possible by "an upheaval of forces lying dormant in the unconscious, ready to break through all moral barriers.[35]

As the full horror of Nazism unfolded, he came to believe not only that Hitler was possessed by a dark force but also that the collective mind of the German people had been possessed. His first sustained attempt to explain the phenomenon of *Ergriffenheit* — the state of being "seized" or possessed — was in a 1936 essay titled "Wotan." He brings out of Teutonic mythology the wild and furious figure of a wandering hunter-god who seizes the minds of men and drives them to crazy and violent excess. "Wotan is an *Ergreiffer* [possessor] of men, and, unless one wishes to deify Hitler — which has indeed actually happened — he is really the only explanation" for him.[36]

As he tries to grasp the nature of the psychic evil that took possession of Germany, Jung withdraws his abstract language of the archetypes and falls back on a more primal understanding, that there are forces at work in history that have been identified as gods or demons, and that these may be friendly, hostile, or inimical to humans who have transactions with them.

You Are *My* Shadow

Pauli did not have a vocation for happiness. When he returned to Zurich and his work at the Polytechnic after Hitler had been beaten, he was unhappier than usual, frustrated in his second marriage and his relations with other women, alienated from his work in physics, feeling driven to pursue *the* Work — the unification of physics and psychology — yet unable to find the ways.

Advisers came to him in dreams, in various guises: as an exotic Chinese woman, as a dark-skinned man, as a man both dark and blond, as a piano teacher. Pauli tried to sort them out according to Jung's taxonomy (the anima, the shadow, and so on), but they would not wear the labels.

In one of his *big* dreams, Pauli arrives at his old home and finds a dark-skinned young man pushing letters and a round piece of wood *into* the house through a window. Pauli knows this young man from previous dreams and thinks of him as Persian. The Persian has been refused entry to the place where Pauli lives and works.

Pauli: "You are not allowed to study?"

"No, therefore I study in secret."

"What subject are you studying?"

"*You!*"

Pauli is shocked. "Are you my shadow?"

"I am between you and the Light, so you are my shadow, not the other way round."

"Are you studying physics?"

"There your language is too difficult for me, but in my language you do not understand physics."

"What are you doing here?"

"I am here to help you." The Persian gives Pauli some personal advice: "You think you are involved with several women, but there is only one." He concludes by observing that Pauli doesn't have a chair in his study; he will bring one.[37]

In another dream, Pauli is with colleagues on the upper floors of a house where a conference on physics and math is taking place. He sees that he is scheduled to conduct a cooking course. A fire breaks out in an adjoining room; he scrambles down the staircase in panic. Looking back, he sees that the floors of the house where his colleagues were gathered have been totally consumed by the fire.

He walks to a garage where a taxi is waiting for him. As the driver fills the tank with gas, Pauli realizes he is familiar — he is "the light-dark stranger." With this recognition, Pauli feels secure, even though he suspects the driver set the fire in the physics building. The cab driver says softly, "Now we can refuel, because upstairs there has been a fire. I will take you where you belong!"[38]

Pauli woke with feelings of "great relief." He later commented on the taxi driver who may also be the arsonist: "He is not an Antichrist, but in a certain sense an 'Antiscientist'" who will set fire to "the scientific way of thinking nowadays taught at colleges and universities. If you take too little notice of him, he draws attention to himself by any means, for instance through synchronistic phenomena (which he, however, calls 'radioactivity') or depressive states or incomprehensible emotions."[39]

While in ordinary life Pauli's contemporaries regarded him as a genius in his field, the mysterious stranger in his dreams considers him uneducated in the things that matter most. Pauli came to feel that this stranger was operating not only in his dreams but also in the play of coincidence around him. The stranger was often pushing him toward new studies and a new public role. Again and again, he was invited in dreams to a new chair, a new professorship, a new course of lectures to a new audience.

Even more intriguing than the Persian and the dark-and-light taxi driver was the "dark woman" who frequently came to Pauli in his dreams, offering a selection of "symbolic enticements." In her most alluring form, she seems to be Chinese and moves with the sinuous, sensual grace of a snake dancer. In a *big* dream, she takes a ring from her finger and lets it float in the air. She calls it "the ring i." In mathematics, *i* denotes the imaginary unit, or square root of minus one.[40]

ACTS OF CREATION IN TIME

It took Jung more than twenty years to bring his synchronicity theory into a form he was willing to publish. While he was working on the final draft of his paper, he was simultaneously carving the face of a laughing trickster on the west wall of his tower at Bollingen.[41]

In an outstanding recent study, Suzanne Gieser calls his synchronicity theory Jung's "spiritual testament" and defines it as follows: "the principle of synchronicity is an attempt to pinpoint, alongside the law of causality, another factor ordering the world of our experience — a factor which builds on relatively simultaneously occurring constellations of a certain quality or significance."[42]

Jung's coinage of "synchronicity" puts the emphasis on simultaneity in time. When he gave his memorial address for Richard Wilhelm, back in 1930, Jung actually promoted time into the engine of synchronicity: he described time as "a concrete continuum which possesses qualities or basic conditions capable of manifesting themselves simultaneously in different places by means of an acausal parallelism."[43]

Pauli thought (as did Arthur Koestler) that Jung was mistaken in featuring an aspect of coincidence that applies only to certain cases and is not the key element. For me, meaningful coincidence has to do with the intersection of timeless forces with the world of time, with the "understory" beneath and behind the surface events of our lives irrupting into our field of perception. This most certainly produces synchronous experiences. But it can also generate "rhyming" sequences played out, in dream and in waking, over days, weeks, or years.

As Jung worked on draft after draft of his synchronicity theory, Pauli goaded and cajoled like the laughing trickster on the wall at Bollingen. From the start, Pauli had a very clear personal idea of what is involved in meaningful coincidence. It is the convergence of an internal condition — for example, you think of someone or recall a dream — with an external event that is related to that condition. The inner condition and the external event are related by meaning. Sometimes it feels like the world is mirroring back your thought or commenting on it.

Pauli waged a long campaign to persuade Jung to drop the word *synchronicity* in favor of one that suggested connection through *meaning* rather than *simultaneity*. He would have been content to go back to the old medieval *correspondentia*. Why not speak of "meaningful correspondence" or "connection through meaning"?[44]

In Pauli's dreams, which often brought scientific terms alive as living symbols, he was encouraged to substitute modern terms for "synchronicity." How about *isomorphy*? Pauli tried that on Jung after he was told in a dream that "cathedrals should be built for isomorphy."[45] In a nonmathematical context, *isomorphy* would refer to the same form reappearing in different structures or materials. Jung did not buy it, and it is unlikely to catch on today.

Pauli was constantly after Jung to clarify the distinction between the spontaneous phenomenon of coincidence and the *induced* phenomenon, as produced through methods of divination such as the I Ching.[46] This distinction was central to the ancients, as Jung knew well.

Throughout their discussions of synchronicity, Pauli exhibited qualities for which many of his colleagues were willing to forgive his abrasiveness and which even led some of them to call him "the conscience of physics": scientific integrity, a disinclination to put up with BS from anyone, his requirement that one clear the fog. Such people are vital to progress in science, and Pauli was vital to Jung. He grilled Jung over every term and definition. It is astonishing that Jung put up with this.

Pauli expressed satisfaction, after reading a near-final version of Jung's synchronicity paper, that they were in full agreement on "the necessity of a further principle of interpretation of nature other than the causal principle."[47] The emerging consensus was this: in our perception of the world, we encounter events that are connected by causation and those that are connected by meaning. The duality may resemble the wave/particle complementary observed in quantum physics. If you don't look, it's a wave; if you look, it's a particle.

Pauli subscribed to the quantum uncertainty position — the presence of the observer changes what is observed — and added this: in order to know "which aspect of nature we want to make visible . . . we simultaneously make a sacrifice." In selecting one event, we sacrifice another.[48]

Thus at quantum levels, the act of observation is held to pull one event into manifestation out of a soup of limitless possibilities. Suppose this "observer effect" worked on a human scale, not merely on the level of tiny bundles of energy we can't see? What would that be like? Maybe it's going on all the time, and we notice only when we remark on an "amazing coincidence": things coming together in a way that is meaningful but cannot be explained, except through the act of observation.

The phenomenon of synchronicity depends on "an excited archetypal situation in the observer," says Beverley Zabriskie. It centers on the coming together of inner and outer events. It may bring the felt sense of participating in "acts of creation in time."[49] It is interesting to speculate whether the experience of meaningful coincidence can also be part of an "act of creation in time" in the outer world as well as the inner one, plucking a particular event out of the quantum wave of possibility and manifesting it.

PAULI'S CHINESE WOMAN

She's an exotic, sexy woman of mystery who may be Chinese. She entices and prods Pauli to go beyond the circuit of his customary attitudes. She is both psychic and physical, he tells Jung; she first comes into his dreams as "the bearer of psychophysical secrets, ranging from sexuality to subtle ESP phenomena."[50] She "sees connections other than those of conventional time."

She is vitally alive. He dares to hope for the *hieros gamos*, the sacred marriage.[51] But nothing will come of this unless he moves beyond his regular mind-set.

In a 1952 dream, the Chinese woman walks ahead and beckons for him to follow. She opens a trapdoor and walks down the steps, leaving the door open. She moves like a dancer; her meanings are in her movements. Pauli follows her and finds that the steps lead into an auditorium where a crowd of unknown people is waiting for him. The woman motions for him to get up on the rostrum and speak. "She dances rhythmically back up the steps, through the open door into the open air, and then back down again. . . . The difference between the two floors seems to diminish 'magically.'"[52] When she returns, she keeps her left arm and left index finger pointing upward, right arm and index finger pointing down. She keeps moving rhythmically, circling round and round. Pauli decides that in this circling movement, she brings the union of psyche and physis that he is seeking.

He wonders whether she is the spirit of the I Ching. For Jung, predictably, she is the dreamer's anima. She may also be a Chinese woman at Columbia University whose brilliant experiments, several years later, would blow apart one of Pauli's articles of scientific faith.

In November 1954 Pauli dreamed he was in a room with the "dark woman." Experiments were being conducted in which "reflections" were generated. While others regarded these reflections as real objects, Pauli and the Dark Woman knew they were only mirror images. This became "a sort of secret" between them — but a secret that filled him with apprehension and dread.[53] Two months later, he dreamed that the "Chinese woman" had a child, "but 'the people' refused to acknowledge it."[54]

This dream of the mirror experiments may have been preparing Pauli for a scientific discovery that shook him to his core. The discovery involved a challenge to the principle of parity conservation, which Pauli preferred to call Spiegelung — "mirroring" or "mirror symmetry." It had been generally accepted that the laws of nature show exact symmetry — for example, when left turns to right, as in a mirror image, or when a positive charge changes to a negative one. Pauli had long been a fierce defender of this symmetry. Significantly, it was a team of *Chinese* scientists who created the experiments that demonstrated that the universe is not perfectly symmetrical; it has a slight tendency to favor the left.

The experiments were proposed in 1956 by two young theoretical physicists, Chen Ning Yang and Tsung-Dao Lee, who had come to the United States during the Japanese occupation of China. At a luncheon at the White Rose Café in New York, they recruited a brilliant woman physicist based at Columbia to design an experiment to test their theory. Her name was Chien Shiung Wu, and she was an expert in beta decay. She was so excited by the project that she cancelled a sentimental journey to China she had planned to take with her husband on the twentieth anniversary of their emigration, even though they had already booked their cabin on the *Queen Elizabeth*.[55] She constructed an experiment involving the beta decay of cobalt 60 that demonstrated early in 1957 that parity — the behavior of a physical system in response to spatial inversion, or reversal of spatial coordinates — is not conserved in weak interactions, the forces associated with radioactive decay. Parity is conserved in gravity, electromagnetism, and strong interactions (which hold nuclei together), but not here.

The Pauli Effect was played out on a human level at Princeton when Pauli interrupted a talk by Chen Ning Yang, demanding, "What is the mass of this particle?" Yang responded that he did not yet have a definitive answer (nothing unusual in particle physics). Pauli thundered, "That is not a sufficient excuse!"

Stunned by this blast, Yang had to stop his talk and sit down to steady himself. The next day, Yang found this note from Pauli in his mailbox: "I regret that you made it almost impossible for me to talk to you after the seminar."[56]

Pauli came to accept that the "Chinese revolution" in physics had succeeded; the universe was not perfectly symmetrical. In his last surviving letter to Jung, in the summer of 1957, he stated, "God is a weak left-hander after all." Pauli confessed that this discovery had come as a tremendous "shock"; he had been "very upset and behaved irrationally for quite a while." Pauli could not bear to be trumped in a scientific debate. But there was something deeper at work here. His revulsion at the violation of parity is reminiscent of Einstein's allergic reaction to some aspects of quantum mechanics (which prompted Einstein to cry out, "God does not play dice with the universe"). The wild imbalance of Pauli's emotional and psychic life may help explain how desperately he clung to the vision of a perfectly balanced universe, where yin and yang, dark and light, both dance and alternate in harmony. "Your anima already had a scent of asymmetry" before it was proven, Jung suggested to him.[57] But Pauli was about to discover that the "Chinese woman" in his dreams was more than a Jungian anima figure from his personal unconscious. She had a physical body and a name, and she was now known as one of the world's greatest experimental physicists.

Pauli's dream that the "Chinese woman" had an unacknowledged baby was played out at the end of November 1957, when Yang and Lee accepted the Nobel Prize in Physics for their work on parity nonconversion. The Chinese woman who had created the experiments that confirmed their theories was ignored by the Nobel committee. Her baby went unacknowledged. Like the woman in Pauli's dreams, she was very attractive; indeed, when she had first arrived at an American university (University of California, Berkeley) from Shanghai, "she was one of the most ardently pursued coeds on campus."[58] Clearly Pauli had previewed an event three years before it took place.

The Pauli-Jung correspondence ended abruptly before that event. It may have led Pauli to reappraise quite carefully the strengths and failings of the approach to dreams that Jung had encouraged him to follow. Had Pauli realized that his Chinese woman was more than an anima figure, he might have been better prepared for the new revolution in physics.

The story of Pauli's Chinese woman is, as Mark Twain might have said, an "astonisher." The sense of a dream spilling over into waking life is enhanced by names and places in the literal story: the White Rose Café, a slow boat to China, and so on. The episode casts a clear cold light on a fatal flaw in Jung's approach to dreams: the decision to disregard literal and precognitive dream content. Jung formulated this doctrine early on, and — even in its revised version — one can still sense the influence of Freud: "One of the basic principles of analytical psychology is that dream-images are to be understood symbolically; that is to say, one must not take them literally, but must surmise a hidden meaning in them."[59]

What about the ancients Jung loved and read so deeply, for whom dream interpretation was *mostly* about reading the future? "For modern man," he went on, "it is hardly conceivable that a God existing outside ourselves should cause us to dream, or that the dream foretells the future prophetically. But if we translate this into the language of psychology, the ancient idea becomes much more comprehensible. The dream, we would say, originates in an unknown part of the psyche and prepares the dreamer for the events of the following day."[60] There is an acknowledgment in the last sentence that dreams can rehearse us for future events, but it's grudging and very limited.

Jung's position had shifted a bit when he wrote in a 1947 letter, "Precognitive dreams can be recognized and verified as such only when the precognized event has actually happened. Otherwise the greatest uncertainty prevails. Also, such dreams are relatively rare. It is therefore not worth looking at dreams for their future significance. One usually gets it wrong."[61] Now he acknowledges that dream precognition is a reality, but says we should forget about it because it's "rare" and people generally get it wrong. We can only speculate how many messages about the future that Jung — and Pauli, to the extent that he conformed to Jung's approach — may have missed by taking this line. The disease that killed Pauli was diagnosed less than two weeks before he died. Is it not possible that his dreams were warning him long before?[62]

DEATH'S CONSTANTS AND CORRESPONDENCES

In 1958, Pauli developed pancreatic cancer and was admitted to the Red Cross Hospital in Zurich on December 5, 1958. He was struck by the number of the room he was assigned: 137. Since his postgraduate work with Sommerfeld in Munich, Pauli had been preoccupied with the question of why the fine-structure constant, a dimensionless fundamental constant characterizing the strength of the electromagnetic interaction, has a value nearly equal to $1/137$. His friend Werner Heisenberg said that the problems of quantum theory would disappear only when 137 was explained.

There was a story about Pauli and the number 137 that had been circulating among his fellow scientists for years. Pauli goes through the pearly gates, and God wants to see him. God tells him that the questions Pauli failed to solve can now be answered. Pauli wants to know why the fine-structure constant has the value $^1/_{137.036}$. God manifests a blackboard and starts scribbling equations at a furious pace. Pauli watches for a bit, then starts mumbling and shaking his upper body. God pauses, and Pauli barks, "*Ganz falsch!*" "Utterly wrong!"[63]

Ten days after checking into Room 137, Pauli entered a dimensionless constant.

After Pauli's death, and as he neared his own, Jung returned to reflecting on the I Ching as a way of modeling the universe of synchronicity and of evoking and entering a sensory dream: "The I Ching consists of readable archetypes, and it very often presents not only a picture of the actual situation but also of the future, exactly like dreams. One could even define the I Ching oracle as an experiential dream, just as one can define a dream as an experiment of a four-dimensional nature. I have never tried even to describe this aspect of dreams, not to speak of the hexagrams, because I have found that our public today is incapable of understanding."[64] We realize, with these words, how much Jung felt he had left unsaid about the nature of reality, for all his voluminous published works.

Jung was no stranger to death's correspondences. In a cold snap after his wife, Emma, died, the vine over the front door of his tower at Bollingen oozed a strange red sap that ran down over his crest. He felt the vine was weeping tears of blood.[65]

Shortly before his death, Jung dreamed of the "other Bollingen," the counterpart in another world to the sanctuary he had helped to build with his own hands. The place was suffused with sourceless light. The deep voice he had come to trust told him his new home had been completed and was now ready for him to move in. Far below the tower, he saw a mother wolverine teaching her child to dive and swim in shining water.[66]

Jung died at a quarter to four in the afternoon on June 6, 1961. Two hours after his death, an old poplar in the garden where he had watched the changing moods of the lake was struck by lightning in a sudden storm. The tree still stood, but its death was coming, since it had been completely skinned; great strips of bark covered the garden. Those who knew felt the strong play of synchronicity in the lightning-struck tree.[67] Jung might have seen a deeper level of symbolism. In his last recorded dream, he saw a grove of trees, "all fibrous roots, coming up from the ground and surrounding him," and gold threads gleaming among the roots.[68] He had written that our true life is "invisible, hidden in the rhizome"; what we see in the leaf and bark and blossom passes. Beneath the flux of our surface lives, the rhizome remains.[69] Lightning stripped the bark from the tree, and death stripped away Jung's body; life continued, rooted in an unseen world.

CHAPTER 12

✦❦✦

WINSTON CHURCHILL'S TIME MACHINES

Churchill's dominant category, the single, central organizing principle of his moral and intellectual universe, is a historical imagination so strong, so comprehensive, as to encase the whole of the present and the whole of the future in a framework of a rich and multicolored past.

— ISAIAH BERLIN, *Mr. Churchill in 1940*

It is not enough to do your best. We must do what is necessary.

— WINSTON CHURCHILL

Wells is a seer. His Time Machine *is a wonderful book. . . . It is one of the books I would take with me to Purgatory.*

— WINSTON S. CHURCHILL, DECEMBER 7, 1947, AS REPORTED IN THE DIARY OF HIS PERSONAL PHYSICIAN, LORD MORAN

It's bleak November, and a dirty gray fog hangs over the gardens like cold washing on the line. The painter is working at his easel under a strong day lamp that also casts light on his subject, a damaged portrait of his father originally commissioned by a political club in Ireland. The original picture has been torn, or slashed.

The painter is making a copy.

Painting faces is not his métier, and in his effort to get this right he has neglected the large cigar between his teeth, which has gone out. There is something missing in the picture he is copying. There is bound to be, in any portrait. What is it? The flash of brilliance, edged with madness, in his father's eyes? No,

233

not madness. The painter wills that unkind thought away. He chooses to remember his father's good days, when he sparkled with wit and love of life. Especially a certain day, long ago, when his father got down on the floor and helped him deploy his model armies in the battle lines of a field in Flanders.

The painter's eyes move between the copy and the original portrait. Then he turns, palette in hand, to contemplate the double. This appears in a tall looking glass set up behind him. If he stands just so, he sees the uncertain copy of his father emerging through the gobbets of wet paint. If he moves a little to one side, he can see the scarred original, features reversed.

But the painter does not move, because his father is watching him and preparing to light up. With easy, practiced motions, Lord Randolph tamps a little pad of cotton wool into his amber cigarette holder. The painter recalls, in this moment, that his father believed he could exclude the evil element in nicotine by creating a filter in this way.

Lord Randolph looks young and dashing.

It's the moustache that's wrong in the portrait, the painter realizes. The hired artist missed the debonair flourish. The painter turns back to his canvas and brushes in the correct twirl.

It is not until he smells Virginia tobacco — so different from the humid depth of his Havana cigar smoke — that it fully dawns on him that this new image of his father is not a fancy born of his work.

He turns again. This Lord Randolph is not a trick of the mirror. If he was in the mirror, he has passed through it. He is seated in the red upholstered armchair on the near side of the looking glass.

"Is that you, Winston? Good heavens, boy, how did you get to be so old and fat?"

"It's called time, father."

"What year is it now?"

"Nineteen forty-seven."

"Of the Christian era, I presume."

"Yes, Papa. That all goes on. At least they still count that way."

"I don't remember anything since — let me see — 'ninety four. I was very confused then. Now it seems I have mislaid more than fifty years. You must bring me up to date immediately. There must be business to attend to. But wait — what on earth are you doing, Winston?" Lord Randolph has noticed the palette and easel.

"I'm copying your portrait, Papa, the one you had done when you went over to Ulster."

"You are a painter? I would never have believed it."

"I only do it for amusement."

"Then how do you earn your living?"

"Oh, I write articles for the newspapers — they pay quite well — and the odd book or two."

"There is no shame in that, Winston."

By his own account (which this version closely follows), Winston Churchill received a visitation from his dead father, Lord Randolph Churchill, in 1947, more than half a century after Randolph's death. Winston himself was in his early seventies. He had been rewarded for his stunning wartime leadership by an overwhelming defeat for his party and his policies in the first postwar general election. In the conversation with his father that followed, he proceeded to give a rather sardonic account of how democracy works in the midst of great historical convulsions, reflecting his view that "democracy is the worst of all political systems, except for all the others." When Lord Randolph asked if there had been war, Winston responded, "We have had nothing else but wars since democracy took charge." He never revealed, in this dialogue, that he had played more than an observer's role in great events.

The literary device of presenting a moral (or for that matter, an immoral) tale within the frame of an invented dream was ancient, as Churchill certainly knew. We might conclude that the dream of his father was a writer's trick of this kind, except for the very special atmosphere that surrounds this little-known essay. Churchill titled it "Private Article" and gave strict orders to his secretary that it was not to be shown or published until after his death. Retitled "The Dream," it was first published one year after his death in the *Sunday Telegraph*.[1]

Winston's son, Randolph, told the newspaper that he first heard the story at the family dinner table, when his sister asked who Churchill would most like to see sitting in the chair opposite. Churchill replied, without hesitation, "My father, of course." He proceeded to describe Lord Randolph's visitation. "It was not plain whether he was recalling a dream or elaborating on some fanciful idea that had struck him earlier. But this was the genesis of the story."[2]

It carries a deep personal undertow; Lord Randolph, who died tragically young, consistently underrated his son's abilities. This was not Churchill's only conversation with someone from the past, though it is the only one he described at length. He dreamed of his ancestor John Churchill, the Duke of Marlborough, who won a famous victory over the French at Blenheim in 1704. In 1955, he told his physician that he had had "an interesting dream" in which he was talking to Sir Edward Grey, who was British foreign minister from 1906 to 1915, "forty years ago"; "it was a long conversation."[3]

In the painter's studio, Lord Randolph takes the silver matchbox clipped to his watch chain to light his cigarette. Winston notices that it is the same watch chain *he* is wearing. He feels a sense of awe. He rubs his brush in the paint on his palette to make sure that everything is real. "All the same I shivered."[4]

Truth comes with goose bumps. In this instant, any suspicion that Churchill's account of the visitation is merely a fanciful idea is shivered away. The pocket watch at the end of the chain is a clue to much more: the elasticity and doubling of time, the possibility of time travel and of alternate worlds, in parallel times, all of which fascinated Churchill. After the visitation, he told his longtime confidant and private secretary, Sir John ("Jock") Colville, that he would die on the same day as his father, January 24 — a prediction that came true many years later, in 1965.

The Churchill who deletes himself from world history in a moving conversation with his dead father is very different from the man of action, driven by colossal ambition, whose adventures thrilled his admirers and dismayed his critics for more than half of the twentieth century. This is certainly not the Churchill described by Liberal journalist Alan Gardiner, on the eve of the First World War, as "the man of action simply, the soldier of fortune who lives for adventure, loves the fight more than the cause."[5] Of course, the Churchill of "The Dream" is a much older man grimly aware of his own mortality and his failing body. Yet he is still driven, as he was from his earliest years, by the need to know the father who neglected him and left him, through early death, before Winston had made his first marks on the world. And the late story hints at an understory running through Churchill's life. Beneath all the action and drama, there is a mind entirely at home in the realm of imagination and capable of bringing extraordinary gifts from it.

THE SHARP AGATE POINTS OF DESTINY

As Paul Addison observes, Churchill's was "a career of many snakes and ladders."[6] The longest downward slide came with the tragic error of the Gallipoli campaign in 1915; the longest lift in his fortunes came with his appointment as wartime prime minister at age sixty-five. Churchill spent long periods in the wilderness and was written off, again and again, as a failure and a has-been, a relic of the dead Victorian era. But again and again, events looped back to him. In times of crisis, elements in his character that had been seen as flaws or anachronisms were transformed into unique and essential strengths. When his country was challenged to do impossible things, the man dismissed as an "impossibilist" was precisely the one for the job.

Churchill wrote about "the tiny things, the sharp agate points" on which the fate of a battle or the fortunes of a life depend.[7] He noticed "the decisive part which accident and chance play at every moment" in events large and small.[8] When we examine the agate points in Churchill's own life, we find that chance — or luck — plays a tremendous role. He was fully alive to this and reveled, as a betting man, when he succeeded at something at long odds thanks to an improbable coincidence or an error that turned out to be providential. Sometimes we may feel that his "agate points" were the corners of dice, recklessly shot across life's table.

Notoriously, Churchill was not a good student, and his army examinations cost him "very special effort." But on at least one notable occasion, he was assisted by good luck. He knew that he would be required to draw a map of some country from memory in the topography exam. He decided, for no particular reason, that he would memorize the map of New Zealand. In the exam room, the first question on the paper was, "Draw a map of New Zealand." Churchill later observed that if he had been at Monte Carlo, this was the kind of bet that would have earned him thirty-five times his stake.

Churchill's luck as a correspondent during the Boer War made him a celebrity, secured his independent income, and launched his political career. In 1899, at the start of hostilities in South Africa, the *Morning Post* hired Churchill as a war correspondent. Soon after landing at Cape Town on the first available steamer, Churchill rushed north to cover the fighting in northern Natal Province, where the Boers had a large British force encircled and besieged at Ladysmith.

Thanks to an army friend, he was able to get close to the action on board an armored train sent on a scout. The train was attacked and derailed by Boer commandos. Never content with a spectator's role, Churchill took it on himself to supervise the clearing of the line, dodging a hail of fire. He found it awkward to clamber in and out the engine window wearing his Mauser pistol in its holster — not part of a regular reporter's kit, but this was Churchill — so he unstrapped it and left the gun in the cabin.

A mounted Boer in a long flapping coat and a weather-beaten slouch hat rode down and leveled a rifle at him. "I thought I could kill this man," Churchill recalled, "and I earnestly desired to do so. I put my hand to my belt, the pistol was not there." So Churchill surrendered, on Napoleon's principle that, "when one is alone and unarmed, a surrender may be pardoned."[9]

He was treated well by his Boer captors, who were impressed that they had bagged "a lord's son." He managed to escape from the POW camp by climbing out a latrine window and walking directly out the gate. He jumped a coal train and concealed himself among the sacks. After a time, he realized the train was going the wrong way — toward Pretoria, deeper inside Boer territory. He jumped off, wandered about for a while, then chanced knocking on the door of the first house he encountered. The man who opened the door happened to be the only Englishman in the territory, a coal mine manager called John Howard, who helped Churchill to safety.

Churchill reflected that he was remarkably lucky not only in his escape but also in the circumstances of his capture. He wrote that it "laid the foundations of my later life." The reputation it gave him opened the door to national politics, with party agents pressing him to become a candidate for several constituencies, and the demand for his books and articles guaranteed a good income.[10]

There was a further aspect to the luck involved in the Boer adventure. Three years later, at a luncheon for South African generals in London, Churchill was introduced to General Louis Botha. Churchill did not immediately recognize this distinguished figure in a frock coat as the mounted commando who had taken him prisoner at rifle point. After Botha reminded him of their first meeting, "an almost unbelievable introduction ripened into a friendship which I greatly valued." Botha returned to London as the first prime minister of the Transvaal a few years later, and remarked to Churchill's mother, "He and I have been out in all weathers."[11]

As history unfolded, Churchill came to realize that — by leaving his pistol behind — he had avoided pulling the trigger on an alternate version of World War I. General Botha became a staunch friend of Britain, helping to head off a second Boer rebellion encouraged by the Germans. "Chance and romance continued to weave our fortunes together in a strange way."[12] Thus a message from Churchill got through to Botha at a remote location in the northern Transvaal in an improbable way — just in time to stop him boarding a German ship on the day the Great War began. If Botha had not received Churchill's warning, he would have been a guest of the Germans at the start of the war, unable to direct events in his country.

For much of his life, Churchill was fascinated by the "what ifs" involved. If he had shot Botha in 1899, or if his message in 1914 had failed to get through, a new Boer war would probably have begun. This would have obliged the British to divert Australian and New Zealand troops bound for Suez to South Africa. That would have been bad for the British — but good for the Australians and New Zealanders who might have avoided dying on the beaches of Gallipoli.[13]

Churchill was very proud of his role in creating the Royal Air Force. Long before other politicians or the military high command, he saw that air power would be crucial in the future of warfare. For the whole period from 1911 to 1921 (with the exception of 1916, when he was forced to stay on the sidelines), he was directly in charge of Britain's nascent air force.

Coincidence and luck came royally into play in this period. The Royal Air Force began at Eastchurch in Kent, on farmland leased for use as an airstrip. Local farmers were skeptical. They looked on the early fliers as if they had strapped on wings and announced they were going to the moon. They wagered pints in the local pubs on how long it would be before the next crash. One pilot who was often there was Lieutenant J. W. Dunne, who helped design and build the first "swept wing" aircraft in 1910, on principles that are still in use with stealth planes. Another frequent flyer from Eastchurch was Winston Churchill, who was thrilled by the air and thought it would be a "stimulus to progress" for the First Lord of the Admiralty to be seen at the controls of experimental aircraft.

Dunne was a very interesting character. In outward appearance, he was the model Anglo-Irish military gentleman; his first book was on fly-fishing. But he was also a world-class dreamer. His dreams helped to inspire his successful aircraft design. And his frequent experience of dream precognition led him to write a series of provocative books on the relativity of time that may have helped to fire Churchill's imagination.

In his ventures into the air, Churchill was often close to death, and death tagged those who flew with him. The young pilot instructor who gave him his first lesson at Eastchurch was killed the day after they flew together. A few weeks later, Churchill joined the test flight of an experimental seaplane. No sooner had he sailed off on the Admiralty yacht *Enchantress* than the seaplane nose-dived into the ocean, killing the three officers on board. He was prevented by the press of government business from going up in a new dual-control machine; during the flight he had intended to copilot, the machine went down "in a spin of a kind then quite unknown," gravely injuring the two pilots on board.[14]

A dream of Churchill's wife, Clementine, persuaded him to give up flying lessons the summer before the Great War began.[15] Churchill was guided by his own sense of when luck was running or about to give out. At a banquet in 1919, he counseled John Alcock, one of the pilots who had just successfully flown across the Atlantic, "You ought to stop now and leave a winner; you must have used up all your luck."[16] Churchill's instinct was correct; a few months later, Alcock was killed flying a new Vickers seaplane to the Paris air show.

An army chief of staff complained, after Churchill became prime minister, that Churchill was unlucky. "He was throughout the last war; and that is a real thing and a bad and dangerous failing."[17] Certainly, Churchill made decisions that ended in disaster, then and later. Yet his luck held when it came to personal survival. He recalled an instance in a Flanders field: "If I had not turned back to get that matchbox which I left behind in my dug-out in Flanders, might I not just have walked into the shell which pitched so harmlessly a hundred yards ahead?"[18]

IMAGINATION AND HISTORY

In his valedictory lecture at Oxford, Hugh Trevor-Roper observed that "the historian's function is to discern alternatives, and that, surely, is the function of imagination." He added, "History is not merely what happened: it is what happened in the context of what might have happened. Therefore it must incorporate, as a necessary element, the alternatives, the might-have-beens."[19] As we have seen in the selective chronicle of the play of coincidence and luck in his early life, Churchill had excellent reason to look at history this way, his mind always turning on alternatives, on the ghost trails of roads not taken.

Another English historian, J. H. Plumb, observed that, for Churchill, history was not a subject; it was "a part of his temperament" that "permeated everything that he touched, and it was the mainspring of his politics and the secret of his immense mastery." Isaiah Berlin, studying Churchill in his "finest hour," concluded that "Churchill's dominant category, the single, central organizing principle of his moral and intellectual universe, is a historical imagination so strong, so comprehensive, as to encase the whole of the present and the whole of the future in a framework of a rich and multicolored past."[20]

Churchill was a time traveler, at least in imagination, and his ability to read the tides of human events and the workings of character across the ages enabled him to see the patterns of the present — through the fog of war and the incredible proliferation of pressure and detail — and to grasp the history of the *future*.

In his time travels into the past, Churchill may have gained most from his ability to enter — fully — into the mind and situation of his great ancestor John Churchill, Duke of Marlborough, who led the (uneasily) allied armies of the

Grand Alliance to victory against the French in the early eighteenth century. Churchill's four-volume biography of Marlborough, written during his "wilderness years" when he was out of office in the 1930s, is widely regarded as his greatest literary work. Churchill announced that his intent was to unravel "the unfathomable mystery which Marlborough's character represents."[21]

He learned from Marlborough's steady resolve in adversity; early in his command, Marlborough had announced, "The issue in this matter is liberty or death." He studied with Marlborough how to exercise leadership within an alliance, in a war involving much of the world and therefore offering multiple choices and rival priorities. Marlborough "never ceased to think of the war as a whole"; Churchill too was always looking for the big picture. Churchill noted that Marlborough's success in command was related to his ability to enter the mind of his adversary: "The mental process of a general should lead him first to put himself faithfully in the position of the enemy, and to credit that enemy with the readiness to do what he himself would most dread. . . . The safe course is to assume that the enemy will do his worst — i.e., what is most unwelcome."[22]

Churchill concluded from Marlborough's example that contrarians win when they are guided by accurate intuition. Marlborough made many command decisions that baffled or terrified generals with more conventional minds. On the eve of the crucial battle of Blenheim in August 1704, he divided his forces by sending an allied commander, the margrave of Baden, off on a secondary mission far from the main field of battle. With the margrave's forces gone, Marlborough had yielded numerical superiority to the French. Churchill noted, "We know of no similar defiance of the principle of gathering all forces together for a battle by any of the successful captains of history."[23] Marlborough felt he would be stronger, not weaker, by shedding the unreliable soldiers and shaky generalship of the margrave. And events in the field proved him correct; he won a great victory at Blenheim.

In the darkest period of World War II, with Britain at imminent risk of invasion, Churchill decided to divide his forces by shipping off a large battle contingent to Cairo to defend the Suez Canal against a possible Italian offensive.

Churchill was able to roam the past without being lost in it. His command of history helped him see the broad lines of a situation; he was able to swim through details without drowning in them.

He pulled off a remarkable double act in his career, both fighting and writing. He was a prime mover in events he rushed to write up as history. He said of controversy, "I shall leave it to history, but remember I shall be one of the historians." He confided to Eisenhower, shortly before Ike became president, "I think you and I are agreed that it is not only important to discover the truth but to know how to present the truth."[24]

Churchill's works of history were participatory. He wrote about events in which he or ancestors with whom he felt a close affinity had taken part, and about causes he had espoused. There is no pretense of standing at the margins of the action as an impartial scholar. He said that his method was borrowed from Defoe's *Memoirs of a Cavalier*, in which the author "hangs the chronicle" of great events "upon the thread of the personal experiences of an individual."[25]

The production of his massive six-volume history *The Second World War* was an example of the principle — often at play in Churchill's life — that for every setback there's an opportunity. He was able to find time for this history (written with the aid of a "syndicate" of helpers) when he lost the elections of July 1945. He published the two-million-word *Second World War* (a third of which was serialized in the *New York Times*) between 1948 and 1954; by contrast, it took de Gaulle a decade to publish his memoirs. The book deal (with subsidiary rights) earned Churchill $2.25 million, the largest advance for a work of nonfiction in American publishing history up till that time, worth perhaps $50 million in today's money.[26]

IMAGINING THE FUTURE

Churchill seemed as adept at entering the history of the future as that of previous times. At age fourteen, he told a friend at Harrow that he dreamed of the future. "I tell you I shall be in command of the defenses of London.... In the high position I shall occupy, it will fall to me to save the Capital and save the Empire."[27] On several occasions before he won his first parliamentary seat, he predicted he would become prime minister.

His prescience extended far beyond his personal fortunes. In the war rooms after 1940, his grasp of future developments — his ability to scan a naval map and foresee where German U-boats would be in a few weeks, for example — seemed uncanny to those around him. They credited him with second sight.

Just as he grasped the coming importance of air power, he foresaw that "land ironclads" — better known as tanks — would transform the nature of war on land and one day release the infantry from "chewing barbed wire." Decades before the manufacture of the atom bomb, he predicted that "a bomb no bigger than an orange" would be developed with "a secret power to concentrate the force of a thousand tons of cordite and blast a township at a stroke."[28] In the

1920s, he forecast that "wireless telephones and television" would allow their owner "to connect up with any room similarly installed, and hear and take part in the conversation as if he put his head in through the window."[29] He saw the rising danger in Germany and the evil of Hitler when most of the British and American establishments refused to look.

Having seen the depth of Muslim faith among Afghan tribesmen in the North-West Frontier Province — something that baffled military intelligence officers with a secular outlook back in the 1890s — Churchill was able to grasp, when he observed the Wahhabis in Saudi Arabia in 1921, that Islamic fundamentalism would emerge as a major threat to the Western democracies.[30]

He predicted both the cold war and the collapse of communism in eastern Europe.

Early in the twentieth century, he warned that mankind had now developed the ability to destroy its planetary environment. "The story of the human race is War."[31] But a terrible change was taking place in the nature of war, because humanity "had got into its hands for the first time the tools by which it can unfailingly accomplish its own destruction."[32]

He declared the need for moral and spiritual progress that would enable humanity to contain the possible effects of new technologies used in the cause of raw power and fanatical beliefs: "It is above all things important that the moral philosophy and spiritual conceptions of men and nations should hold their own amid these formidable scientific evolutions. It would be much better to call a halt in material progress and discovery rather than to be mastered by our own apparatus and the forces which it directs."[33]

Churchill was capable of monumental errors, yet on this and many other issues he proved an accurate prophet. He observed that "every prophet has to come from civilization, but every prophet has to go into the wilderness. He must have a strong impression of a complex society and all that it has to give, and then he must serve periods of isolation and meditation. This is the process by which psychic dynamite is made."[34]

Certainly there were plenty of combustible materials available in Churchill's life to make "psychic dynamite." But his prescience was also mentored. In his years in the wilderness between the two world wars, he was coached on the impact of new technologies on warfare by a remarkable Anglo-German physicist and tennis star called Frederick Lindemann, and fed secret intelligence by his extraordinary neighbor Major Desmond Morton.[35] Above all, the futurist element in his imagination was honed by H. G. Wells and his science fiction.

As early as 1901, Wells's publishers sent Churchill a copy of his latest book, which at that time was *Anticipations*, a book of predictions advocating the creation of a new society on scientific principles. Churchill responded with a personal note to the author saying, "I read everything you write." Churchill and Wells first met the following year and kept in touch until Wells's death, in 1946. Churchill's Glasgow speech of 1906, in which he referred to the "left-out millions" deserving government help, was influenced by Wells's book *A Modern Utopia*. Churchill's vision of tank warfare was greatly influenced by Wells's story "The Land Ironclads," though Wells gave his tanks wheels instead of caterpillar treads. Churchill may even have borrowed his phrase "the gathering storm" — used in the title of the first volume of his history of the Second World War — from Wells's *War of the Worlds*, in which Martians are the attackers.[36]

Wells fired up the imaginations of physicists as well as politicians in ways that shaped world history. In 1932, the Hungarian physicist Leo Szilard read H. G. Wells's novel *The World Set Free* (originally published in 1914). The novel describes a device that accelerates the process of radioactive decay, producing "atomic bombs." When Hitler took power the following year, Szilard moved to London. He was irritated by an article in the *Times* dismissing the possibility that atomic power could be developed for any useful purpose. Still seething over this piece as he waited for a traffic light to change in Bloomsbury, Szilard had a eureka moment: he saw how a nuclear chain reaction like the one described in Wells's science fiction could provide the fuel for an atomic weapon.[37]

CHURCHILL'S BLACK DOG

Churchill has been a favorite study for psychohistorians who want to link greatness to abnormalities such as bipolar disorder. The defect of such approaches is that there are plenty of people who are bipolar but precious few who accomplish anything, in any field, comparable to what Churchill achieved in several. The term *cyclothymic* — denoting strong and recurring mood swings — probably defines his condition better than *manic-depressive*. But certainly he was no stranger to depression. He called it his "Black Dog." And in his upbeat moods, better described as "elation" rather than "mania," he was capable of marvels of production.

He overcame his Black Dog through work, work, work. It nearly mastered him when he was sidelined, removed from the centers of power where he knew he belonged. Painting helped. All the research and composition required for his mammoth histories probably helped even more. But it was incessant, unremitting work that helped most. He could not stay still; he could not afford to stop.

When the narrowing of his cerebral arteries in his mideighties finally compelled him to slow down and then stop, his Black Dog overcame him. He sat staring into space, immobilized by a dreadful melancholia over which his physician, Sir Charles Wilson, better known as Lord Moran (so revealing of Churchill's earlier life in his diaries and memoirs), chose to draw a veil. But then, who would have supposed that a man who lived all-out like Churchill would survive until he was ninety?

His life is a wonderful example of the principle that great gifts are in our wounds. He was born two months premature — which may have given him the preemie's mobility of consciousness noted in Mark Twain. He grew up in the body of an undersized weakling. When he entered Sandhurst, his chest still measured only thirty-one inches, narrower by far than his abdomen. He wrote from Sandhurst in 1893, "I am cursed with so feeble a body that I can scarcely support the fatigues of the day."[38] He had soft, smooth, sensitive skin that required special silk underwear (and later pink silk pjs he designed for himself). He was bullied at Harrow and had bitter memories of a day when he was forced to hide behind a tree from bullies lobbing cricket balls at him. He had been grossly neglected by both his parents; his main emotional nourishment came — famously — from his nanny, Mrs. Everest, whom he called "Womany" and whose photograph hung in his room until the end of his life.

So he had something to prove, to himself and the world. Certainly his loneliness in early boyhood must have been an inducement to hurl himself into adventures in the inner world of imagination. But he soon hurled himself into the adventures of the world, putting himself at the center of the battles he had imagined as he deployed his miniature armies of toy soldiers. He needed to prove that, despite his inferior physique, he was capable of any action, and his life became a study in courage. He took unthinkable risks in the air and at the front in the Great War. He came to develop a sense of invulnerability. He lost his belief in God early on, yet later in life he speculated that a superior power — call it God — had spared him for the job he took on when he became prime minister at sixty-five. "This cannot be accident, it must be design. I was kept for this job," he told his physician.[39]

This was a specimen of his magical thinking. It did not always serve him or the world well; his critics count at least fifteen monumental errors in his political career, starting with Gallipoli. Yet during World War II, what he was able to imagine carried Britain through its time of perilous isolation.

Moran wrote of "the inner world of make-believe in which Winston found reality."[40] British psychiatrist Anthony Storr builds on this statement: "It is probable that England owed her survival in 1940 to this inner world of make-believe. The kind of inspiration with which Churchill sustained the nation was not based on judgment, but on an irrational conviction independent of factual reality.... We do not know, and we shall never know, the details of Churchill's world of make-believe. But that it was there, and that he played an heroic part in it, cannot be gainsaid."[41] "In 1940, his inner world of make-believe coincided with the facts of external reality in a way which very rarely happens to any man. It is an experience not unlike that of passionate love when, for a time, the object of a man's desire seems to coincide exactly with the image of woman he carries within him."[42]

Storr provides a vital corrective to the often-claimed connection between great creativity and abnormal psychology: "Creative powers are to some extent protective against mental illness.... It has been demonstrated that creative people exhibit more neurotic traits than the average person, but are also better equipped than most people to deal with their neurotic problems."[43]

TRANSFERRING VISION

Winston Churchill liked to start the day by lighting a cigar and sipping a whiskey and soda while propped up in bed with the newspapers. This is not an image that would come to many people when the word *visionary* is mentioned. Yet as John Lukacs argues decisively, we must recognize Churchill as a visionary in the positive sense.[44] He could certainly call on the gifts of vision in two of the senses defined by the *Oxford English Dictionary*: he possessed the ability to see "something which is apparently seen otherwise than by ordinary sight" and to engage in "a mental concept of a distinct and vivid kind: a highly imaginative scheme or anticipation."

Churchill not only could call on the power of vision but also could transfer it to others. It was the ability to transfer a vision that he most admired in Joan of Arc, and this was the secret of how he rallied the British people to defy Hitler in 1940, when all was so nearly lost. Let's recall what he accomplished in his greatest and most decisive speech.

On June 18, 1940, after he had been prime minister for just over a month, Churchill warned the British people about the stakes involved in the battle with Hitler. If they failed to resist, the world would be plunged "into the abyss of a new Dark Age made more sinister, and perhaps more protracted, by the lights of perverted science."

But defeatism was prevalent. It had paralyzed the British establishment and kept America on the sidelines. How could Churchill fire up his people to believe in the possibility of victory against seemingly impossible odds? He delivered his most famous sentence: "Let us therefore brace ourselves to our duties and so bear ourselves that, if the British Empire and its Commonwealth last for a thousand years, men will still say, 'This was their finest hour.' "[45]

These words seized the imagination of a people. They transferred moral courage and confidence. We want to pay close attention to two distinctive elements in Churchill's vision transfer that helped it to take root in the minds of many.

The first was the *time shift*. He carried his listeners with him into the far future, beyond current dangers into a time where everything has long been resolved. He persuaded his audience that victory over Hitler was not only inevitable but had been won long ago — so brilliantly that anything that has followed looks like an anticlimax.

Second, he engineered a *shift to the witness perspective*. He stirs us to do our duty now ("brace ourselves to our duties"). But at the same time he lifts us, with his words, to a place above, a place of eagles. We look down on our current struggles from a higher level. The bigger self looks down on the smaller self and says with admiration, "This was *their* finest hour."

Churchill brought his audience inside his tremendous imagination, where the war was already won.

THE FULL MOON OF RUDOLF HESS

The first anniversary of Churchill's premiership, May 10, 1941, was the night of a full moon and of the Luftwaffe's most devastating attack on London so far. In a rain of bombs, fifteen hundred civilians were killed and many buildings were destroyed, including the chamber of the House of Commons. That same night, a strange visitor landed by parachute on a farm near Glasgow.

Jock Colville's first knowledge of him came in a stray thought he found in his mind on waking. It may well have been the legacy of a dream, but the dream itself was gone. Churchill's private secretary recorded his impression this way in his diary on Sunday, May 11: "Awoke thinking unaccountably of Peter Fleming's book *Flying Visit* and day-dreaming of what would happen if we captured Göring during one of his alleged flights over London."[46]

Flying Visit was a humorous fantasy, illustrated by the popular cartoonist David Low, that had been published the year before. The action centered on Hitler's improbable and unheralded arrival in London by parachute. The author, Peter Fleming, was a well-known travel writer and adventurer now working for Military Intelligence (Research) to build resistance networks in Britain that would fight a Nazi invasion; his younger brother, Ian Fleming, employed by Naval Intelligence, was to become famous as the creator of James Bond.

Colville walked from Downing Street to morning service at Westminster Abbey. Churchill was away from London at Ditchley Park, where he usually repaired at the time of the full moon. The sky over London was blue, but smoke from smoldering fires obscured the sun, and charred papers from a burning mill flew about like leaves on an autumn day. Colville found there were no services at the abbey, because a bomb had fallen on the roof. A policeman on duty pointed at Big Ben; the face of the clock was pocked and scarred. "After no previous raid has London looked so wounded."[47]

Colville strolled over to the Foreign Office to chat with a friend who was on duty that weekend. He found his friend on the phone. Seeing Colville, the friend said to his caller, "Hold on a minute, I think this is your man." The Duke of Hamilton, a Conservative member of Parliament whose family seat was near Glasgow, was on the line, wanting to talk to the prime minister's private secretary. When Colville took the phone, the duke told him a "fantastic" story that sounded like the plot of a spy novel. A top Nazi had landed in Scotland on a secret mission. "At that moment I vividly remembered my early waking thoughts on Peter Fleming's book and I felt sure that either Hitler or Göring had arrived."[48]

In fact, the Nazi who had landed was Rudolf Hess, the deputy führer. He had flown himself to Scotland in a Messerschmitt 110, leaving the plane to crash when he dropped by parachute near the estate of the Duke of Hamilton, whom he had met at the 1936 Berlin Olympics and hoped would take him to King George VI.

When Colville reached Churchill by phone, the prime minister told him to send the duke to see him — as long as he was certain he was dealing with the Duke of Hamilton "and not a lunatic."[49] When the duke reached Ditchley Park, he found Churchill relaxing with a Marx Brothers movie. "Hess or no Hess," Churchill declared, "I am going to see the Marx Brothers."[50]

Under interrogation, Hess explained that his mission was to negotiate peace, with the aim of creating a British-German alliance against the Soviet Union; this would require the removal of Churchill.

The British public was not informed about Hess until 11:20 PM on Monday, May 12, when a statement drafted by Churchill himself was read over the BBC.

The news gave an important boost to British morale after the terrible bombings. Churchill told Parliament that Hess's flight was a case where "imagination is sometimes baffled by the facts as they present themselves." He ordered that Hess be kept in solitary confinement. The bizarre circumstances of the Hess affair have generated many conspiracy theories, fueled by the British government's long delay in releasing relevant documents and Hess's 1987 suicide in Spandau Prison in Berlin, where he was sentenced to life as a war criminal in the Nuremberg trials. Given the novelistic elements in the story, it's appropriate that some of the tales center on the creator of James Bond.

Ian Fleming was in contact with the flamboyant British occultist Aleister Crowley, whom he later used as a model for the character of Le Chiffre in his novel *Casino Royale*. Knowing Hess's keen interest in astrology and esoteric theories, Fleming hatched a scheme involving Crowley to trick Hess into making contact with a fake network of anti-Churchill occultists. This plan became obsolete when Hess decided to fly himself to Scotland. It has been claimed that Ian Fleming was again involved, using other channels, in a deception operation that took in Hess, but the evidence (so far) is not solid.[51] Churchill, who loved "funny operations," would have relished a deception operation that played on the credulity and occult beliefs of a Nazi leader, but Jock Colville's diary strongly suggests that, if Hess was the victim of such a plot, Churchill was not in on it.

"CAN THESE DREAMS DO ANY HARM?"

Among all the Churchill documents, there is little information on his sleep dreams. He does not seem to have kept a dream journal, and he said little about his dream life to his confidants until his later years. He did speak of a terrifying visionary experience in 1938, after Anthony Eden resigned from the government in protest against Chamberlain's policy of appeasement. During a restless, sleepless night, Churchill saw a brave young man struggling alone against immense forces of darkness. Then, as gray dawn broke, the figure of Death loomed in triumph over a ghastly field.

By contrast, the night after Churchill became prime minister — on May 10, 1940 — he slept peacefully, despite the immense responsibilities he was shouldering. He said genially that he had no need of "cheering dreams" that night; "facts are better than dreams."[52] Throughout his wartime premiership, he kept up the bluff facade, at least, of being an effortless sleeper, ready on waking to attack whatever the day's "boxes" of official business might bring. He spoke of his "happy gift of falling almost immediately into deep sleep."⁵³ We may suspect that his celebrated naps brought him dream inspiration; certainly he often bounced out of them with clarity on a problem as well as renewed energy.

He may have set himself up to solve problems in his sleep — while clearing his mental desk — by a nightly practice he described as follows, in the late summer of 1940: "Every night I try myself by court martial to see if I have done anything effective during the day. I don't mean just pawing the ground; anyone can go through the motions; but something really effective."⁵⁴ We can picture him prowling in his golden dragon dressing gown, interrogating himself before going to sleep.

The best place to track Churchill's sleep dreams is in the postwar diaries of his personal physician, Lord Moran. These dreams were shared over the period when his health was deteriorating — one of them may have prepared him for a stroke — and he was engaged in waging cold war against the Soviets. For example, Churchill woke with a start in the late morning in his cabin on the *Queen Elizabeth* early in 1952 and said he had dreamed "he could not walk straight or see straight." He immediately tested this by walking around the space.⁵⁵

At the end of that year, he told his doctor, "I dream a lot. Why do I do that? The dreams are always pleasant, so that I am sorry when I wake. I want them to go on. They are extremely complicated. I dreamt last night about ten cigars. They were of enormous size and each had attached to it a piece of paper with the history of that particular cigar." We are not told whether either man thought of trying to read the histories of the oversized cigars, or whether it occurred to either that there might be a health advisory in this dream. Moran simply noted in his diary that Churchill was displaying "the unmistakable signs of old age" though he had "no intention of giving up."⁵⁶

Early in 1953, full of energy, acting as if he could handle the work of half the cabinet before breakfast, Churchill gave credit to his dreams for contributing to his vitality and good spirits. "I get the most agreeable dreams — the detail is beautifully done. I get the sense of being in a scene or situation."⁵⁷

On September 2, 1953, Churchill shared a dream with his doctor that may have been a long-range prophecy: "Last night I dreamed of a large woman of the Eleanor Roosevelt type, and this woman was President of the United States. It was all extremely vivid but I want to know what it means."⁵⁸ Moran does not tell us whether they discussed the possibility that a woman would one day become the American president. He merely recorded that, as on numerous other occasions, Churchill was eager for informed guidance on his dreams. "Do you know anything about dreams, Charles, and their meaning? I have curious, elaborate, complicated dreams. I wake, but when I go to sleep again they go on."[59] His dreams, he insisted, were "enjoyable."

Nine days after meeting a woman president of the United States, Churchill dreamed he helped to eliminate much of the Soviet leadership: "I dreamed we were on a train in Russia with all the Russian Bolsheviks, Molotov, Malenkov, Zhukov, Voroshilov; the relationship between us was so vivid and so correct. There was a counter-revolution. We had some special bombs, none of them larger than a matchbox, with a very local effect. With them we destroyed the Russians, all of them. There was no one left. The counter-revolution was entirely successful. The dream went on for a long time." He asked his doctor, "Can these dreams do any harm, Charles?"[60] Once again, the doctor left his response unrecorded, if there was one.

On July 20, 1955, Moran recorded this lapidary statement by Churchill: "I had an interesting dream. I was talking to Edward Grey, forty years ago. It was a long conversation." As Churchill spoke to his doctor, a budgerigar alighted in his hand. Moran noted, sweetly, that Churchill "held it to his lips." Churchill could not recall anything more from the dream except that he had been talking to a dead statesman a long time ago. He drifted into complaining about all the work involved in correcting three volumes of his monumental history of the English-speaking peoples, and the difficulty of keeping the different periods separate in his mind. It seemed that different times were streaming together in his thoughts and imaginings, the dead crossing into realms of the living, and the living into those of the dead. "I must not do too much of it," Churchill sighed. "I can only die."[61] When Moran returned to Chartwell a few days later, he found Churchill sitting by the lake, contemplating the black swans.[62] If Churchill told him any more dreams, they went unrecorded. His dream recall may have been reduced by the sleeping pills the doctor was now prescribing.

PAINTING ON THE OTHER SIDE

In Churchill's later years, the immensity of his achievement often palled in his mind in comparison to what he had left undone. Ever since the Bolshevik Revolution, he had wanted to defeat Soviet communism, yet in 1945 he saw an "iron curtain" (in the phrase he coined) come down over eastern Europe. This is why he titled the last volume of his history of the Second World War *Triumph and Tragedy*. On New Year's Day, 1953, he nevertheless predicted to Jock Colville that, if the younger man lived his "normal span," he would "assuredly see Eastern Europe free of communism."[63] This was exactly right, and the prediction is a further demonstration of Churchill's gifts as a seer; it is hard to think of another Western statesman who could have seen so clearly so far into the future.

Churchill, sneered at by early opponents as a "half-breed American" because of his beautiful American mother, Jenny Jerome, yearned for a reunion of Britain and America in a grand alliance of the English-speaking peoples. This was another vision that was unfulfilled, except in the pages of his alternate history. On one of his birthdays, well into his seventies, he responded to his daughter Diana's expressions of wonderment over all he had done in his life, "I have achieved a great deal to achieve nothing in the end."[64]

Until close to the end, he found solace in his painting. He once observed that, for most people, work is work and pleasure is pleasure. But for some, "work and pleasure are one. . . . Fortune's favored children belong to the second class. For them the working hours are never long enough. Each day is a holiday."[65] Still, change and alternation are necessary, and painting in oils gave Churchill balance and that necessary "alternation." He took up painting at forty, in the depths of personal despair after the tragic Gallipoli disaster in 1915. Relegated to the sidelines in the midst of a war, he was "like a sea-beast fished up from the depths, or a diver too suddenly hoisted . . . my veins threatened to burst from the pressure."[66] In painting, he found release. He started with a child's paint box. Then he bought a complete outfit for painting in oils and never stopped until his body and brain gave up.

"When I get to heaven," he declared, "I mean to spend a considerable portion of my first million years in painting, and so get to the bottom of the subject. But then I shall require a still gayer palette than I get here below. I expect orange and vermilion will be the darkest, dullest colors upon it, and beyond them there will be a whole range of wonderful new colors which will delight the celestial eye."[67]

Though from his early years he was an agnostic about the claims of religion, Churchill's encounters with the departed left him in no doubt that there is an afterlife. His longtime private secretary observed that "he unquestionably developed in his later years a conviction that this life was not an end."[68] While he imagined himself a painter in heaven, he told his doctor that, if he had to go to purgatory first, he was going to take a time machine with him — to be specific, a copy of H. G. Wells's *Time Machine*.[69] It is amusing to picture Winston traveling through time, inspecting people and events from the perspective of someone released from the rules of ordinary reality. Given his fascination with alternate history, he would no doubt go one better than Wells (whose vision of time travel was confined to movement along a single track) by examining ever-forking alternate event tracks. Since he loved to write up his adventures, it's not hard to imagine this master of make-believe crafting amazing stories that we would read, if we could, as science fiction. It's even easier to see him painting with colors beyond the earthly spectrum, in a world made up on the Other Side.

❧

THE FUTURE HISTORY
OF DREAMING

In my dream, the Angel shrugged and said, "If we fail this time, it will be a failure of imagination." And then she placed the world gently in the palm of my hand.

— ERICA JONG

While I was working on this book, I found myself on a plane sitting next to a round-faced little girl in pink. Her mother called her "Mouse" and wasn't interested in talking to her, but the girl was full of curiosity about everything from the ventilation system to the creation of the world, so she plied me with questions and stories for the whole flight.

She gazed out the window as we skimmed the cloudbanks, and observed, "It looks like we're flying on glass."

I was struck by the freshness of that expression.

She asked me, "Have you ever landed from the sky in water?"

"Not in this body."

"But can people do that?"

"Oh, sure. There's a kind of plane called a floatplane, or a seaplane, that lands on pontoons that keep it afloat. And then there are rocket ships that splash down and are fished out."

"Have you ever touched the sun?"

"Not with my hand."

"Sometimes I feel the sun is following me, real close."

I could feel its warmth. I started keeping mental notes. This girl was a fountain of fresh words.

She frowned and asked me, point-blank: "How was the world invented?"

I did my best. "Some people say God made the world. Others say it began with a Big Bang and the star-stuff has been expanding ever since."

She told me, "I know a boy who says the world was made by God blowing sand."

She glanced up at the air vent and asked me to show her how it worked. I demonstrated how if you turned the knob to the left, counterclockwise, the air came out. If you turned it the other way, it shut off.

"Maybe that's how the universe was made," said the girl in pink. "God turned everything counterclockwise."

She laughed, delighted by her theory. Her mother looked sullen; Mouse wasn't supposed to laugh.

The conversation with Mouse illustrates something fundamental about imagination. Children are the natural princes and princesses of the imagination, unless the adult world crushes their curiosity and their sense of wonder. If our imagination fails us, it is because we have lost touch with that wonder-child within us, the one who can picture God making the world by giving everything a twist to the left.

Luly Yang, one of America's most original and sought-after dress designers, consciously creates with the child-self who knows she can fly. Luly based her fall 2007 collection on her recurring childhood dreams of flying. In her Seattle studio, she told me, "My dreams of flying were liberating."

As a very young girl, when she dreamed of being chased, she was the one who could fly, so she could always get away and go somewhere more fun. She grew up in Taiwan and lived in Japan. She had friends in other countries and kept in touch by flying to see them in her dreams. "It was a very efficient way to keep in touch — and no jet lag."

In February 2007, when Luly was planning her annual fashion show, she dreamed of flying and woke charged with the magic of her childhood dreams. She told her staff that she wanted to call her show "Dreams Take Flight," even though preparations based on a different theme were well advanced. The new theme seemed especially relevant since the show was conceived as a benefit for the Children's Hospital, whose logo is a hot air balloon.

Luly describes her experience of dream flight this way: "I'm in my own body. I feel air currents. I am flying over the ocean and through cities, at different speeds. Sometimes I fly very fast and it's hard to regulate my speed. I fly from a mountain peak down to a still body of water, tropical blue. The surface is glassy smooth, and the water is so clear I can see all the way to the bottom. I'm curious about what's down there, and decide to fly down into the water. I find I can breathe underwater, so I am free to explore. I could be in the water, in the air, or in-between."

Her Dreams Take Flight collection was divided into five segments, each expressing a part of her dream. A silver-white dress of crisp fabrics, folded in unusual ways, evoked paper airplanes. Another was airy, icy blue and silver, while "Aurora Borealis" had brighter hues borrowed from a photograph of mountains at sunset, enlarged so that only the bands and flow of color remained. Other creations evoked the sparkles of the moon reflected on the ocean and the moon's glow in deep space, the sense of skimming the ocean and plunging into the depths.

Dreams are part of Luly's design for creative work and creative living. "Dreams help me realize things. I go to sleep with a question, and my dream solves a problem or gives me a new perspective. When you dream, your mind isn't distracted by your senses, and you can really focus in on something."

A young Australian schoolteacher, Nick Cumbo, flew from Melbourne to attend a weekend workshop called "Dreaming from the Heart" that I was leading in the foothills of the Sierra Nevada — in the original California gold rush country — in the summer of 2007. I knew the weekend was going to be very interesting when an older American couple explained why they had decided to attend. The husband had received a flyer for the workshop, which featured the image of a hummingbird. He had recently undergone open heart surgery, and he was struck by the title of the workshop and the suggestion in the flyer that the hummingbird is "medicine for the heart." He was still undecided about coming when he opened the door of his car, flyer in hand, and found a hummingbird fluttering about inside the vehicle. He shut the door in a hurry, and went to fetch his wife, feeling she wouldn't believe this unless she saw it for herself. When he led her back to the car and opened the door, *two* hummingbirds flew out. "So we decided we *both* needed to come to the hummingbird workshop," he told us.

The greatest gift of that weekend, for me, was the dream my young fellow-Australian, Nick, reported on Sunday morning. In the first scene, he was in a rough neighborhood in Melbourne among refugees from the fighting in the Indonesian-controlled part of New Guinea, people he has tried to support in regular life. Then, in the dream, he bit into a superhot pepper and was blown into a scene of vivid colors. I'll let Nick tell this part of the adventure for himself:

> I arrive at a large building. It looks like a well-known university build-
> ing, but now it's faced with brilliant multicolored tiles, bold oranges, reds,

yellows, and greens. Beyond the facade, I see a huge glasshouse. It is full of young schoolchildren. They are having a grand time playing games involved with dreaming. They are shaking, wriggling, dancing, moving — embodying and performing their dreams, relating to the dreaming process through the movements of their bodies. They are having such fun!

Toward the other end of the building, I see the familiar face of a ten-year-old I know. The older children here are sharing their dreams, making stories out of them and giving each other feedback and suggestions. Some of them are beginners at this. One of the girls seems to be frothing at the mouth, finding it very difficult to be upfront about her experiences. But she'll learn!

I'm thoroughly enchanted by what I see. It dawns on me that I'm being shown ways of making dreamwork with children a reality, of bringing dreaming into our school system at every level. I get a real *Aha* feeling about this.

I wonder what made the change. Suddenly, I find myself in a car with four of the ten-year-olds. They are all very bubbly and happy, talking to me about their dreams and what they are doing with them. They all keep dream journals and get credit for that in class. They start singing a song recorded by a famous female pop star. The song is titled *My Secret Diary*. It's about the treasures you find in your dream journal. It seems that everything changed in the culture when this pop star discovered the magic of dreams and put that into her song.

Whether the change comes in the way that Nick dreamed, or in some other way, it needs to come. We want to support and encourage our children, from the earliest grades in our schools, to share their dreams, perform them, write and create from them, and transfer energy and visions of possibility from the dreamworld into regular life. Then they can teach their parents and elders to stop making the magical children within them play mouse.

THE REVENGE ON MONTEZUMA

Let's consider another episode from history as a cautionary tale about what happens when a culture silences its dreamers.

Years before the Aztecs ever laid eyes on a European or heard the sound of a firearm, people in Mexico were dreaming strange and terrible things. They saw temples being burned and cities destroyed. They saw things the Nahuatl language had no words to describe. Trying to explain their visions, dreamers spoke of mountains moving on the waters, and serpents of bright metal spewing fire.

Coming in the wake of ominous portents like Halley's Comet, which the diviners held to be a terrible sign heralding a world turned upside down, word of all these evil dreams, seen by people who were respected as powerful dreamers, spread deep alarm. The Aztec emperor, Moctezuma II — better known in the Anglo world as Montezuma — summoned some of the leading dreamers to tell him in person what they were seeing.

Here is what Fray Diego de Durán was able to glean from the memories of the old ones, after the conquest: Montezuma was notified that "certain old people had dreamed strange things," and he had them brought before him. One old man told him, "These last nights the Lords of Sleep have shown us the temple of Huitzilopochtli burning with fearful flames, the stones falling one by one until it was totally destroyed." Another dreamer, a grandmother, told the Aztec emperor, "In our dreams we, your mothers, saw a mighty river enter the door of your royal palace, smashing the walls in its fury. It ripped up the walls from their foundations, carrying beams and stones with it until nothing was left standing."[1]

These truth tellers must have been brave, to deliver their unwelcome dreams to a tyrant who had ordered that "if any common man dared to lift his eyes to look at him," he should be executed on the spot. Montezuma was not going to tolerate bad dreams. On top of the falling star and other evil portents, news of such dreams could encourage vassal states and intriguers in the capital to believe that he was an unlucky ruler whose time was over. He rewarded the dreamers by having them cast into jail. He ordered that they be given very small portions of food, so they would starve to death with exquisite slowness.

Some of the dreamers managed to escape, possibly assisted by guards who believed in their powers. Montezuma ordered his soldiers to go into the towns of all those who had prophesied evil things. "Tear down their houses. Kill their wives and children and dig in the places where the houses had been, until you reach water. All their possessions are to be destroyed. And if any one of them is ever seen in a temple, he is to be stoned and his body throne to the wild beasts."

"After that," Durán reported, "no one wished to tell his dreams to Montezuma."[2]

Montezuma succeeded in blinding his empire. When the mountains moving on the waters turned out to be the ships of the conquistadors, the Aztecs were completely unprepared. Montezuma was stunned by the appearance of the invaders the dreamers had struggled to describe. They were formidable hairy men who wore metal armor and had serpents that spat fire, mounted on strange four-legged beasts. Trying to explain what had happened, Montezuma's courtiers grasped at an old prophecy about the return of a god from across the water — a superstition that helped paralyze the will to action.

Many factors contributed to the fall of the Aztec empire. But a critical element was that the emperor — though he "believed in a thousand omens and signs"[3] — would not listen to dreams he did not want to hear.

"Those who die are those who do not understand; those who live will understand it," runs the Mayan book of prophecies, the *Chilam Balam*.[4] Not long after the conquest, that hard-edged student of history and power Machiavelli observed that "the occurrence of important events in any city or country is generally preceded by signs or portents, or by men who predict them" (*Discorsi* 1:56). There is a message for us in Montezuma's mistake, and we need to hear it today.

THE RETURN OF THE SEER: A NECESSARY FUTURE

Confident of our technology — which can find a nickel using a satellite in space, or make a sixty-year-old woman look twenty, with a twenty-year-old's body parts — we trust only what can be measured and manufactured. We have consigned our health to doctors, cosmeticians, and pill pushers. We are at some risk of caging our imaginations with consumer entertainment and virtual reality and mass role-playing games.

We leave reading the future to so-called professionals: futurists, mathematicians, spies, and consultants. We go on paying them when they fail us again and again.

In the West, despite all our technology, we are constantly being blindsided by major new events that shatter our previous view of the possible. Few people involved with security thought an event like 9/11 was possible until it happened.

We need to revive and nurture the true art of seership. We have seen how Joan of Arc did it. Let's get clear now about what genuine seership, in the present and the future, will involve. There are three kinds of seer: the receivers, the travelers, and the far-seers.

Receivers know things because they come to them or come *through* them, in the way of the medium. They receive visitations, both waking and sleeping. They may be "speakers for the dead," passing on messages from the departed. This type of receiver is in great demand because there are so many people on the other side who are *desperate* to communicate with the living. Receivers may also be empaths who pick up what is going on in other people's bodies and energy fields. The very first kind of training receivers need is instruction in shielding and screening and, above all, in discernment. They must learn how to pick up things useful to know without being swamped by someone else's feelings and psychic litter. They need help in establishing healthy psychic boundaries. They need fully functional BS detectors that help them screen out false or misleading information.

The traveler learns things by going to the places where knowledge is to be found, in this world or in other dimensions of reality. This is the shaman's way, and the journeys beyond the body may be assisted by drumming or other forms of "sonic driving." Some indigenous cultures use hallucinogens to facilitate astral travel, and there is a lively New Age tourist traffic that involves going into the jungle to ingest rather nasty stuff like ayahuasca. Drugs are not recommended for Western journeyers, and they are not required. A practiced traveler requires only two things to embark on a journey, once the body is relaxed in a quiet and protected space: a mental picture and an intention. Essential training for the traveler includes learning to recognize the nature and the needs of the different energy vehicles that can operate outside the physical body. And it involves developing a strong working relationship with guardians who can protect the dreamers and guide the journeys. As young children and shamans know, there is no better escort for these journeys than an animal guardian.

The far-seer knows by expanding his or her sight to include whatever he or she needs to know. This may be like turning on an inner light and directing it — like a searchlight with x-ray properties — on a target that may be on the other side of the world, or inside the molecular structures of the body, or in another dimension. Or far-seeing may be a process of mental expansion, in which the field of consciousness grows until everything necessary to know is inside it. This is profoundly simple once we understand that, if we think of something or someone, we are with the object of our thoughts. Thought travels faster than light, so the connection is instantaneous. The trick is to get out of our own way — to sideline the clutter and confusion of the trivial everyday mind — so we can see and operate in the larger field.

Seers may also be *skryers*. Skrying means using an object — or a series of objects — as a focusing device. We may recall how, as children, we used to stare at a certain spot on the surface of a creek or a lake, where the light struck just so, and would stare and stare until pictures came to us in the mirror-bright surface of the water. Or we found shapes inside a rough rock crystal, or while peering through a hole in a stone, and saw the Other Side as well as the other side.

In our time, as in other times, the core training of the seer comes from paying the closest attention to dreams, coincidence, and the symbolic language of the world.

THE FUTURE OF IMAGINAL HEALING

As we reclaim the skills of dreaming, imagery for healing will become central to our medicine. Advances in hard scientific research, especially in the fast-expanding field of psychoneuroimmunology, have helped provide the mandate, because they supply overwhelming evidence that the body believes in images, and that our thoughts and feelings can make us sick or make us well.

According to molecular biologist Candace Pert, there is a "psychosomatic communications network" that operates not only in the brain but also in all parts of the body. Our conscious or unconscious thoughts and feelings are constantly affecting our health by sending directives to a pharmaceuticals factory inside the body. Pert's work is helping to overthrow the long reign of the Cartesian dogma that mind and body are separate. Our mind, she maintains, is in every cell of our bodies.[5]

Physician Larry Dossey, a leader in mind-body medicine since the 1980s, observes that "the body responds to mental input as if it were physically real. Images create bodily changes, just as if the experience were really happening. For example, if you imagine yourself lying on a beach in the sun, you become relaxed, your peripheral blood vessels dilate, and your hands become warm, as in the real thing."[6]

Our feelings determine whether we are open or closed to a viral housebreaker. Candace Pert explains that "viruses use the same receptors as neuropeptides to enter a cell, and depending on how much of the natural peptide for a particular receptor is around and available to bind, the virus that fits that receptor will have an easier or harder time getting into the cell." For example, the rheovirus, held to be a cause of the common cold, uses the receptor for norepinephrine, a feel-good natural chemical, to enter the cell. If you're happy — it would seem — the cold virus can't get in.[7]

In Latin, *placebo* means, "I shall please." In health care, the term "placebo effect" is used to describe an improvement in health due to the patient's belief that he or she is receiving treatment when in fact the patient is not. A placebo might be a sugar pill or the pretense that a patient has received surgery or an IV treatment that was actually not administered. Not that long ago, some American hospital dispensaries contained bottles of sugar and starch pills labeled "Obecalp" — "placebo" spelled backward.

There is a vast amount of new research confirming the placebo effect. Parkinson's patients given fake surgery or fake drug treatments produce dopamine (a chemical their bodies lack) in quantities similar to those they might have received in a genuine intervention.[8]

In 2006 a Johns Hopkins team led by Dr. James Campbell conducted what I like to call the Red Hot Chili Pepper Test. Campbell's team injected capsaicin — the fiery element in chili peppers — into subjects, and then injected a harmless inactive saline solution the subjects were told would ease the pain. PET scans showed the midbrain area in placebo responders then released a class of natural painkillers known as endogenous opioids, rapidly easing their perception of pain.[9]

Studies of clinically depressed patients suggest that placebos can encourage dramatic changes in activity in the same parts of the brain that respond to antidepressants: the prefrontal cortex and the cingulated cortex. Some of the big pharmaceutical companies were shaken by a 2002 study that reevaluated FDA data on six widely prescribed antidepressants and found that 80 percent of their effect was duplicated in placebo control groups.[10]

French psychiatrist Patrick Lemoine maintains that 35–40 percent of official prescriptions are "impure placebos" — "pharmacologically inactive substances contaminated with a tiny amount of active ingredient" that is "not enough to have a clinical effect, but enough for doctors to claim that it does."[11]

As ancient healers well understood, the role of personality, drama, and ritual in promoting the placebo effect is huge. From the moment a pilgrim entered an Asklepian temple, he was given constant encouragement to believe that healing was available and to abandon old mental habits and self-defeating attitudes. In a society where we find authority in white coats and medical degrees, the placebo effect is stronger in patients who meet face-to-face with practitioners.

We are often unaware of our shifting thoughts and feelings. We may be wholly unaware of memories and images held in the body that bring us down. The decision to bring unrecognized thoughts and feelings into consciousness is an essential step toward self-healing. Starting from here, we can develop the practice of investing the energy of our attention in images that make us well.

We can make it our choice, for example, to increase blood flow to a certain body part, giving it the strength to flush out toxins and the nutrients required to heal. Norman Cousins got over a broken elbow and returned to the tennis court in record time because he spent twenty minutes a day focusing on his intention to increase blood flow through the injured joint, after his doctor explained that elbow injuries often healed slowly because of poor blood supply.

Herbert Benson maintains that all stress-related disorders, from high blood pressure to depression, from migraine headaches to arthritis, can be alleviated by what he calls the "relaxation response," a simple technique for calming the body and quieting the mind that centers on breathing and the repetition of a simple word or phrase for ten to twenty minutes a day.[12]

For mind-body researcher Lyn Freeman, imagery is "the foundation of mind-body medicine." It is "the thought process that invokes and uses the senses." It draws on our lived experience, "an experience that can be vividly recalled and modified."[13]

There is clinical evidence that imagery is beneficial in treating skin disease, diabetes, breast cancer, arthritis, migraine and tension headaches, and severe burns. Imagery has also been used as effective treatment for improving lactation in mothers of premature babies, pain management, and improving immune function. When imagery is used as a clinical tool, it involves the deliberate focusing of attention on specific images to bring about desired changes. The different modes of healing imagery recognized in the health care community are well explained by the authors of *Rituals of Healing*.[14]

A study conducted in the summer of 2007 captured the attention of the health insurance industry by proving that imagery not only works but cuts costs. Insurance giant Blue Shield of California decided to test the effect of guided imagery on 905 health plan members who were scheduled to undergo surgery. Researchers did this by playing a simple guided-imagery tape designed to allay fears about the procedure and promote recovery. The results of the study were very alluring for number crunchers. Seventy-four percent of patients "adopted" the imagery regardless of upbringing or prior attitudes. The general effect was to relieve anxiety, speed recovery, and reduce time spent in the hospital after surgery — and this cut the average cost of total treatment, per patient, by $2,003. This was a powerful inducement for the insurance industry to reappraise the value of funding guided imagery programs whose cost is trivial compared to most medical procedures.[15]

Guided imagery tapes, like the one used in the California study, are now widely available. Hospitals are giving CDs to patients to help them marshal inner forces to attack cancer cells or to establish and visit a healing place in the imagination.

As we become a dreaming society, we can do much better. In my dream, "pre-need" clinics will be established in health care and community centers. People will come together to share dreams according to the Lightning Dreamwork protocol,[16] and will help each other to recognize and act on diagnostic and "management" advisories.

Imagery harvesting will be a central part of an integrated approach to health care. This will involve helping patients — and anyone who chooses to stay well — to harvest positive imagery from life experiences and dream material.

We can learn to grow and gift a dream — a healing image, a vision of possibility — to someone in need of a dream. In our dreaming society, nurses, therapists, and community guides will be trained in *vision transfer* techniques for producing fresh, customized images for healing that can be gifted to someone in need.[17]

The new approach to health care will feature the healing power of story. In the clear understanding that finding *meaning* in any life passage may be at the heart of healing, our healers — declared or undeclared — will help people use the power of dreaming to move beyond personal history into a bigger story that contains the juice and sense of purpose to get them through.

In all of this, we will be guided by Mark Twain's insight (in *Christian Science*) that "the power which a man's imagination has over his body to heal it or make it sick is a force which none of us is born without. The first man had it; the last one will possess it."[18]

THE FUTURE OF DREAM ARCHEOLOGY

To help us remember the importance of all of this, we will need many dream archeologists to bring to light more of the workings of the secret engine of dreaming in evolution and history. Some, like historian John Lukacs in his studies of the "duel" between Churchill and Hitler, will help us to understand that coincidence is not a side issue and may point to a hidden logic of events.[19] Some, like Ron Powers in a magnificent recent biography of Mark Twain, will show us that the play of dreams and coincidence can drive a life story, year by year. Others will bridge disciplines and mix materials. A multidisciplinary team may be required to expose the full story of Pauli's dreams and the interplay with a parallel chain of coincidence involved in the "Chinese revolution"; they'll start by going through the immense scientific correspondence that Pauli's widow, Franca, gifted to the archives of CERN (the European Organization for Nuclear Research) in Switzerland.

The dream archeologist, like the other kind, will dig in places where there are no written texts to be found. Some of the discoveries that result will be published as fiction, until publishers agree to recognize a new genre. The good historical novelist has always had the ability to transport us to another time and place from which we can return measurably enlightened. Joan Grant, in her "far memories" of Egypt, and Scottish novelist Manda Scott, in her splendid quartet of novels about Boudica the ancient British warrior-queen, take us even further, into the *experience* of dreaming in cultures that have left us few relevant documents.

The dreamers in Manda Scott's novels of ancient Britain are druids and shamans. They are scouts and trackers for warriors, and conscience for leaders. They mediate between the living and the ancestors. They fly with the birds and run with the hound or the deer. They enter each other's psychic space, travel at will into other times and other dimensions. We won't find much about them in ancient texts. The druids of Britain wrote in Greek but chose not to keep written records, so we have nothing from their point of view.

I asked Manda Scott for her sources. She told me she had gleaned everything possible from the Roman sources, including Caesar's account (in *De bello gallico*) of "a people who live forever in the eyes of their gods," and from the archeology of the midden remains of Boudica's people in East Anglia. She read the old Irish and Welsh sagas for evidence of women as warriors and engaged in battle reenactments where she thrust and parried with sword and spear to enter the lives of her characters kinesthetically.

Her dreams guided her "massively, continually and through every sentence of the writing." She explains, "My intent with the first book was that every part of the dreaming, from Breaca's vision quest through to the end where Macha and the dreamers call down the mist to confound the legions, was something I had either done personally, or had seen done — mostly the former." In bringing through the books, she journeyed into Boudica's world with the aid of shamanic drumming.

The genesis of the books was a moving experience that reflects Manda Scott's deep love and knowledge of animals. She had just finished writing her crime thriller *No Good Dead*. She had contracted to write a sequel and was out walking with her dogs — a pair of lurchers — thinking about that. The dogs caught and killed a lactating hare. "I was devastated. Hares are sacred and she had young, which meant if I couldn't find them, they would die. I couldn't find them, though I did spend a long time looking. I sat down and decided that if something had to die to show me that I was walking along with my brain in neutral going in the wrong direction, then I had better pay attention."

She went back into the woods alone and asked the natural world around her, "What do you want of me?" She felt the answer move through her. She was to write the Boudica story. She had made a personal commitment to do this years before, but had weakened the intention by adding the caveat "when I am a good enough writer." In the truth of that moment, all the excuses for delay fell away.[20]

LIFE CATCHER

Copenhagen, June 2004

I am spinning a web from my solar plexus. It expands outward like an immense spider web until it covers a large community.

What is going on? Am I becoming a spider?

I realize I have generated a huge dreamcatcher, except I want to call it a Life Catcher. Its mesh will screen out negative energies and projections while welcoming positive, life-supporting influences and visitations.

Within the safety of the web, the community can grow shared visions of life and possibility and find ways to manifest them.

Scouts can move across the skeins of the web, spying out things that are developing at a distance.

I wake excited from this dream, rolling out of the narrow bed in my closet-sized room in the Copenhagen hotel.

The web reminds me — as in the dream itself — of the Native American dreamcatchers. The original dreamcatchers, an Onondaga friend once told me, were actual spiderwebs. The modern ones, whether made in China or Arizona, are imitation spiderwebs, and the idea is that they'll catch the bad dreams and let only the good ones through.

But the web in my Copenhagen dream is something more. In the bathroom, I remember hearing that there are some indigenous peoples who practice a form of group dreaming that involves growing a kind of communal energy web. On a remote island chain (I can't remember where), a people of fierce hunter-gatherers sleep together in big houses. As they approach sleep, they chant together, synchronizing their takeoff into the dream lands. While they dream together, they create a web that allows them to travel safely wherever they need to go. They move across it like human spiders, tracking game animals or shoals of fish, scanning their environment for possible dangers.

"Did you remember any dreams?" my friend Wanda Burch asks me when we meet for breakfast in the hotel dining room. We never ask, "Did you dream?" We are dreamers, and we know that — even in the view of the hardheads of cognitive neuroscience, some of whom will be at our conference — nearly everyone dreams every night. Anyone who says, "I don't dream," is really saying, "I don't remember."

I tell her my dream of spinning the web as I wield the cheese cutter on the buffet. Cold cuts for breakfast is the Danish way. I don't mind a bit, since my body hasn't really known the time since we flew in yesterday.

"Maybe you should get in touch with the Spider-Man script writers," someone else from the conference quips, listening in on our conversation. "Spidey hasn't gone that far yet."

"How did you feel when you woke up?" Wanda asks.

"Juiced. Full of energy. Almost high."

"Could anything like this happen in the future?"

I look at her doubtfully.

"Is there some way you could spin a web like that for others? What did you call it, a Life Catcher?"

"Oh, I'd love that."

"What do you want to know?"

She was asking the questions we always ask about dreams in our everyday dream-sharing game.

What I want to know is: did I dream the way back into an ancient way of dreaming? Is there a clue here to bringing back something we need?

We fast-walk along the Esplanade in the summer rain. Around us, umbrellas are sprouting everywhere like giant mushrooms. Water trickles down the back of my neck, inside my collar. From the boat dock, we take the yellow water bus, the *toldbot*, across the canal to the Holmen district, where the conference of the International Association for the Study of Dreams (IASD) is taking place in the School of Architecture. The IASD is a wonderful and singular entity, bringing together the world's top experts and devotees of dreaming from many disciplines, from psychiatrists to filmmakers.

The presenters range from neuroscientists who describe dreams as "delirium" to anthropologists who have broken the glass and lived with tribal peoples who dream the hunt and communicate with gods and spirits. Patricia Garfield is giving a lecture on the dreams of Hans Christian Andersen, newly translated from old Danish, and how he may have tried to play therapist for his unhappy life by writing happy endings for the dreams that most troubled him.

The keynote speaker, that soggy morning, is a Finnish psychology professor, Antti Revonsuo. His white hair shines like a tight cluster of icicles. His talk has an ambitious title — "Towards a Unified Science of Dreaming and Consciousness" — and a promising graphic to open.

At a click of a mouse, the big screen fills with a scene of two pretty young men, dozing side by side on a canopied bed. One is clutching poppies; the other has an abandoned lyre near at hand. They look like they are sleeping off an antique bender. The style is unmistakable. This has to be the work of J. W. Waterhouse, the dreamiest of the pre-Raphaelite painters, famed for his mermaids and nymphs. The title of this canvas is *Sleep and His Half-Brother Death*. It draws from the classical understanding that there is a close affinity between sleep and death because in both states we leave the body and travel to other realms, including those where the dead are alive and at home.

My attention drifts toward the blurry background of the painting. Behind the droopy ephebes and a brazier that may be smoking, there is a portico with Corinthian columns, and indistinct shapes in the dark beyond. I can imagine leaning forward and traveling through that gate.

Professor Revonsuo pulls me back. He has a very generous view of dream content, for a cognitive scientist — a breed notorious for trashing dream content — but he is not here to talk about traveling to realms of the dead. I like the pragmatic thrust of his remarks. What goes on in dreaming, he tells us, is a process of "world simulation." I wonder if he is going to compare these environments in the dreaming brain to online role-playing games like Second Life. He's going somewhere else. This is about evolution more than entertainment.

Revonsuo offers a bold thesis: dreaming is central to human evolution — maybe to human survival — because in the "simulated world" of the dreamspace, we practice "threat simulation." This has been going on since the Pleistocene era, and it helped get humans through life when we were just "bipedal hominids" being stalked for breakfast by vastly more efficient predators. Threat simulation has two aspects. It improves our ability to *identify* threats, and it sharpens our ability to *respond* quickly and effectively when a threat appears. Revonsuo believes we are all engaged in threat simulation, inside our personal dreamspace, every night. It is going on even when we don't remember our dreams. Indeed, as he tells it, whether or not we remember dreams is of almost incidental importance. What is of primary importance is the practice we are getting, every night. We get the benefits even if we have no recollection of what we were doing through the sleep hours.

I like all of this, though "threat simulation" theory stops far short of what ancient and indigenous dreamers — and active dreamers today — know: that dreaming is traveling. We are not confined to a "simulated world" inside our own heads. We can travel across time and space and scout out the possible future. We not only rehearse for generic threats; we can identify specific threats, to ourselves and our communities, and bring home information that can inspire specific and effective action.

My mind goes back to the Life Catcher dream.

More is possible, on the dream web, than the scientists of sleep and dreaming are generally willing to recognize. We must go outside the sleep labs, into the lived experience of people everywhere whose dreams help them to get through life, in order to understand.

After the Copenhagen conference, the IASD journal *Dreaming* published a fascinating account of how the Andamans — a hunter-gatherer people who live on islands in the Bay of Bengal — grow a nightly web of dreams to produce life-supporting information for the community. In their communal big houses, they enter dreaming together with a shared story or intention. They may want to scout out where the best supply of jackfruit, or wild pigs, or a shoal of fish can be found to feed the people the next day. They spin a shared web and venture out on its skeins, like human spiders.[21]

This account reminded me of my Life Catcher dream.

At the end of that same year, the terrible Asian tsunami triggered by an earthquake off Sumatra on December 26, 2004, brought home just how vital to life the web of dreaming can be.

The aftershocks of the earthquake hurled great waves across the Andaman islands. At that time of year, the Andamans were usually to be found in their seasonal fishing settlements along the coast. When the ocean calmed, their shelters were gone. The Indian government, which claims possession of the islands, assumed that the Andamans along the coast had been drowned, as nearly 250,000 people had been throughout the region. Then the Andamans reappeared on their forested hills, shooting arrows at an Indian government helicopter that was scouting the terrain. They *knew* the tsunami was coming, and got out of its way by quietly abandoning their fishing huts and taking to the hills. They knew because they observed the movements of animals and listened to the voices of wind and water, and because they travel on the web of dreams.

The dream web can truly be a Life Catcher.

ACKNOWLEDGMENTS

$\mathfrak{I}$ begin by thanking the teachers in my native Australia who first encouraged and helped me to grow my love of history: K. C. Masterman, Geoffrey Fairbairn, and Manning Clark, who insisted that his honors history students immerse themselves in Dostoyevsky and Freud, Faulkner and Goethe, Gibbon and the King James Bible, to know "the ditch where we are digged." They left historical time many years ago, but they are not dead to me in my dreams.

I am grateful to many fine scholars and dream researchers who generously shared the fruits of their investigations into the history, anthropology, and psychology of dreaming, including Stanley Krippner, Patricia Garfield, Deidre Barrett, Kelly Bulkeley, Iain Edgar, Barbara Tedlock, Charles Stewart, Richard Wilkerson, Rita Dwyer, and Bob Hoss. Larry Dossey and Lyn Freeman helped to deepen my understanding of the ancient and now (thankfully) renewing field of imagery in medicine and healing.

I owe a profound intellectual debt to two great French scholars of *l'imaginaire*: Henry Corbin and Jacques LeGoff.

My sense of the importance of dreaming in helping us navigate life's passages and bring new things into our world has been constantly strengthened and educated by thousands of dreamers who have shared their experiences with me in my workshops and seminars, and online. I am grateful to the adventurers in consciousness who have joined me since 1996 in the retreats on a mountain in the New York Adirondacks and in other advanced programs, where we have test-flown new Active Dreaming techniques and traveled together, as dream archeologists, to uncover the buried cities of imagination. I am especially grateful to the wonderful volunteer coordinators who have helped to bring my workshops into many communities; they include Donna Katsuranis, Karen Silverstein, Irene D'Alessio, Carol Davis, Karen McKean, Nancy Friedman, Jane E. Carleton, Steffani LaZier, Suzette Rios-Scheurer, and Jeni Hogenson.

Several creative friends gave me very special help and encouragement through the nights and days when I was writing this book. Louisa Bokacheva goaded me to go on a wild *droshky* ride through the dreaming history of Russian literature, made a valiant attempt to bring me up to speed on physics, and shared her amazing knowledge of pop music. Robyn Johnson gave the kind of creative feedback that keeps the mind fired up while making sure that the sparks don't fly all over the house. Jamie Jamison kept me thinking about what vision means in leadership and joined me in making up "snappers" we hope Mark Twain would have enjoyed. Janie Carleton, a marvelous host and dreamkeeper in the San Francisco Bay Area, prompted me to investigate the unlikely dreamer who struck oil in Kuwait and confirmed that dreamers can be time travelers and soul healers.

I met Wanda Burch in the Mohawk Valley in the late 1980s, when I embarked on a dream-inspired quest to explore the life of an Anglo-Irishman who lived among the Iroquois before the American Revolution. I found her managing the historic site that had been his last home. From our shared love of history and dreaming, and our shared need to understand how to use the imagination in healing, a friendship grew that constantly fed and nurtured this book.

I have written about coincidence as "a secret handshake from the universe," and I have no doubt that something of this kind brought me to my present editor, Georgia Hughes, and her wonderful colleagues at New World Library. Georgia is a magnificent editor; she seeks out the best and truest work that a writer can bring through, and attends and supports the birthing in every way.

My daughters have helped me remember that, to claim the power of imagination, all we really need do is let the child inside us out to play. My greatest debt is to my wife, Marcia, an extraordinary friend and counselor in all seasons, who saw the shape and nature of this book twenty years before I sat down to write it, at an unusual desk — a desk that is literally a door — she created for me after I told her a certain dream.

NOTES

INTRODUCTION

1   Kasia Maria Szpakowska, "The Perception of Dreams and Nightmares in Ancient Egypt: Old Kingdom to Third Intermediate Period" (PhD diss., University of California, Los Angeles, 2000), pp. 23–26.

2   Petru Popescu, *Amazon Beaming* (New York: Viking, 1991), p. 60.

3   T. J. Knab, *A War of Witches: A Journey into the Underworld of the Contemporary Aztecs* (New York: HarperCollins, 1995).

4   Roger Ivar Lohmann, *Dream Travelers: Sleep Experiences and Culture in the Western Pacific* (New York: Palgrave Macmillan, 2003), p. 6.

5   Robert Moss, *Dreamways of the Iroquois: Honoring the Secret Wishes of the Soul* (Rochester, VT: Destiny Books, 2005), pp. v, 105–106.

6   "My Platonic Sweetheart," in *Tales of Wonder*, ed. David Ketterer (Lincoln: University of Nebraska Press, 2003), pp. 117–126.

7   Winston Churchill, *Thoughts and Adventures* (1932; reprint, London: Odhams Press, 1949), p. 189.

8   Natalie Angier, "Modern Life Suppresses Ancient Body Rhythm," *New York Times,* March 14, 1995.

9   A. Roger Ekirch, "Sleep We Have Lost: Pre-Industrial Slumber in the British Isles," *American Historical Review* 106, no. 2 (April 2001): 343–386.

10   Paul Bohannan, "Concepts of Time among the Tiv of Nigeria," *Southwestern Journal of Anthropology,* no. 9 (Autumn 1953): 253.

11   *London Gazetteer and New Daily Advertiser*, February 11, 1769, cited in Ekirch, "Sleep We Have Lost," p. 373.

12   Thomas Middleton, "The Black Book," in *The Works of Thomas Middleton*, ed. A. H. Bullen (New York: AMS Press, 1964), 8:14.

13   British researcher Mark Solms, in his work with brain trauma patients, has supplied evidence that dreaming also takes place in other phases of sleep, when the higher visual centers and the emotional centers of the brain are activated. According to Solms, even someone who has suffered major damage to the brainstem or the visual cortex will continue to dream. See G. W. Domhoff, "Refocusing the Neurocognitive Approach to Dreams: A Critique of the Hobson versus Solms debate," *Dreaming* 15 (2005): 3–20.

14   Charles J. Limb and Allen R. Braun, "Neural Substrates of Spontaneous Musical Performance: An fMRI Study of Jazz Improvisation," *Public Library of Science Journal* 3, no. 2 (February 2008): 1–9.

15 Tore A. Nielsen and Philippe Stenstrom, "What Are the Memory Sources of Dreaming?" *Nature* 437, no. 27 (October 2005): 1287.

16 Ibid., p. 1287.

17 Roger M. Knudson and Gillian M. Finocan, "What I Learned Teaching Dreams 101 — a Cautionary Tale," *Dream Time* (Fall 2007): 13. *Dream Time* is published by the International Association for the Study of Dreams.

18 Edward Hallett Carr, *What Is History?* (New York: Random House, 1961), 9.

1. EARTH SPEAKERS AND DREAM TRAVELERS

1 Marina Roseman, *Healing Sounds from the Malaysian Rainforest: Temiar Music and Medicine* (Berkeley: University of California Press, 1993), pp. 52–53.

2 Jürgen Riester, "Curanderos y brujos de los indios chiquitanos," *Revista de la Universidad Boliviana "Gabriel René Moreno"* 16, no. 31–32 (1972): 5–17. "Chiquitanos" (little people) was a name imposed on a number of peoples of eastern Bolivia and Mato Grosso amalgamated by the Jesuit missions in the seventeenth century.

3 Norman E. Whitten Jr., *Sacha Runa: Ethnicity and Adaptation of Ecuadorian Jungle Quichua* (Urbana: University of Illinois Press, 1976), pp. 58–59.

4 Nancy Connor and Bradford Keeney, eds., *Shamans of the World* (Boulder, CO: Sounds True, 2008), p. 46.

5 Walter Bogoras, "Ideas of Space and Time in the Conception of Primitive Religion," *American Anthropologist*, n.s., 27, no. 2 (April 1925): 208–209.

6 Michael F. Brown, "Ropes of Sand: Order and Imagery in Aguaruna Dreams," in *Dreaming: Anthropological and Psychological Interpretations*, ed. Barbara Tedlock (Santa Fe, NM: School of American Research Press, 1992), p. 157.

7 Irving A. Hallowell, *Culture and Experience* (Philadelphia: University of Pennsylvania Press, 1955), p. 178.

8 Sigmund Freud, *Introductory Lectures on Psychoanalysis,* trans. Sydney Walker (London: Penguin Books, 1991), p. 231.

9 Sylvie Poirier, "This Is Good Country, We Are Good Dreamers: Dreams and Dreaming in the Australian Western Desert," in *Dream Travelers: Sleep Experiences and Culture in the Western Pacific*, ed. Roger Ivar Lohmann (New York: Palgrave Macmillan, 2003), pp. 112, 115.

10 Howard Morphy, *Journey to the Crocodile's Nest* (Canberra: Australian Institute of Aboriginal Studies, 1984).

11 Fiona Magowan, "Syncretism or Synchronicity? Remapping the Yolngu Feel of Place," *Australian Journal of Anthropology* (December 2001).

12 Jeremy Naydler, *Shamanic Wisdom in the Pyramid Texts* (Rochester, VT: Inner Traditions, 2005).

13 Robert Moss, *Dreamgates: An Explorer's Guide to the Worlds of Soul, Imagination, and Life beyond Death* (New York: Three Rivers Press, 1998), pp. 284–290.

14 E. A. Wallis Budge, *Osiris: The Egyptian Religion of Resurrection* (New Hyde Park, NY: University Books, 1961).

15 Michel Chauveau, *Egypt in the Age of Cleopatra*, trans. David Lorton (Ithaca, NY: Cornell University Press, 2000), pp. 123–126.

16 John Ray, *Reflections of Osiris: Lives from Ancient Egypt* (Oxford: Oxford University Press, 2002), pp. 148–152.

17 Joan Grant, *Far Memory* (Columbus, OH: Ariel Press, 1988).

18 George Seferis, *Collected Poems,* trans. Edmund Keeley and Philip Sherrard (London: Anvil Press Poetry, 1982).

19 Joan Grant, *Winged Pharaoh* (Columbus, OH: Ariel Press, 1986).

20 Robert Moss, *Dreamways of the Iroquois: Honoring the Secret Wishes of the Soul* (Rochester, VT: Destiny Books, 2005), and "Missionaries and Magicians," in *Wonders of the Invisible World: 1600–1900,* ed. Peter Benes (Boston: Boston University Press, 1995).

21 Reuben Gold Thwaites, ed., *Jesuit Relations and Allied Documents: Travels and Explorations of the Jesuit Missionaries in New France, 1610–1791* (Cleveland, OH: Burrows Brothers, 1896–1901), 23:121–123.

22 Ibid., 33:191.

23 Harriet Maxwell Converse, *Myths and Legends of the New York State Iroquois* (Albany, NY: New York State Museum, 1908), p. 94.

24 Thwaites, *Jesuit Relations,* 33:195.

25 This narrative interweaves (1) the Manchu version translated in Margaret Nowak and Stephen W. Durrant, *The Tale of the Nishan Shamaness: A Manchu Folk Epic* (Seattle: University of Washington Press, 1977), with (2) oral traditions, especially a Daur Mongol version transcribed in Caroline Humphrey and Urgunge Onon, *Shamans and Elders: Experience, Knowledge, and Power among the Daur Mongols* (Oxford: Clarendon Press, 1996).

26 M. A. Czaplica, *Aboriginal Siberia, a Study in Social Anthropology* (Oxford: Clarendon Press, 1914), p. 243.

27 Barbara Tedlock, *The Woman in the Shaman's Body* (New York: Bantam, 2005).

28 Stephen W. Durrant, "The Nišan Shaman Caught in Cultural Contradiction," *Signs* 5, no. 2 (Winter 1979): 338–347.

29 Cornelius Tacitus, *Annals,* trans. J. Jackson (Cambridge, MA: Loeb Classical Library, 1937), bk. 14, chap. 30.

30 Ibid.

31 Chesca Potter's image of Elen is in John Matthews, *The Celtic Shaman's Pack* (Shaftesbury, England: Element, 1995).

32 *The Mabinogion,* trans. Jeffrey Gantz (London: Penguin Books, 1976), pp. 118–127.

33 Caitlín Matthews, *King Arthur and the Goddess of the Land: The Divine Feminine in the Mabinogion* (Rochester, VT: Inner Traditions, 2002), pp. 57–82.

2. INTERPRETERS AND DIVINERS

1 Plutarch, "Caesar," in *Fall of the Roman Republic: Six Lives,* trans. Rex Warner (London: Penguin Books, 1962), p. 233.

2 Cicero, *De divinatione* 1.12. For discussion see Malcolm Schofield, "Cicero for and against Divination," *Journal of Roman Studies* 76 (1986): 47–65.

3 Aristotle, "On Prophesying by Dreams."

4 Artemidorus, *Oneirocritica: The Interpretation of Dreams,* trans. Robert J. White (Torrance, CA: Original Books, 1990), pp. 224, 117.

5 The oldest "questioners" (*ensi* in Sumerian, *sha'ilu* in Akkadian) are goddesses, embodied by priestesses. Gilgamesh takes his dreams to his mother, the goddess Nin-sun, Lady Wild Cow, "she who knows all." Dumuzi takes his terrifying dream to his sister Geshtin-anna, goddess of dreams and wine (see chapter 5).

6 The "woman as tall as the sky" is Inanna in the dream of Sargon. See Jerrold S. Cooper and Wolfgang Heimpel, "The Sumerian Sargon Legend," *Journal of the American Oriental Society* 103 (1983): 67–82.

7 Scott B. Noegel, "Dreams and Dream Interpreters in Mesopotamia and in the Hebrew Bible," in *Dreams*, ed. Kelly Bulkeley (New York: Palgrave Macmillan, 2001), pp. 45–72.

8 Lionel Casson, *Libraries in the Ancient World* (New Haven, CT: Yale University Press, 2001), pp. 11–12.

9 O. R. Gurney, "Babylonians and Hittites," in *Oracles and Divination*, ed. Michael Loewe and Carmen Blacker (Boulder: Shambhala, 1981), p. 158.

10 *The New Jerusalem Bible* (New York: Doubleday, 1990), p. 67, note e.

11 Kasia Maria Szpakowska, "The Perception of Dreams and Nightmares in Ancient Egypt: Old Kingdom to Third Intermediate Period" (PhD diss., University of California, Los Angeles, 2000), p. 273.

12 A. Leo Oppenheim, *The Interpretation of Dreams in the Ancient Near East* (Philadelphia: American Philosophical Society, 1956), pp. 302–303.

13 John L. Strong, *The Legend of King Asoka* (Princeton, NJ: Princeton University Press, 1989), pp. 274–275.

14 Antonella Crescenzi and Fabrizio Torricelli, "A Tun-huang Text on Dreams: MsPelliot tibetan 55–IX," *Tibet Journal* 20, no. 2 (Summer 1995): 3–17.

15 Artemidorus, *Oneirocritica*, pp. 82–85.

16 Sophocles, "King Oedipus," in *The Theban Plays*, trans. E. F. Watling (London: Penguin Books, 1967), p. 52.

17 Artemidorus, *Oneirocritica*, p. 83.

18 Ibid.

19 Ibid., p. 84.

20 Ibid., p. 85.

21 Plutarch, "Caesar," p. 245.

22 George Devereux, *Dreams in Greek Tragedy: An Ethno-Psycho-Analytical Study* (Berkeley: University of California Press, 1976), pp. xxii, xxvi.

23 G. W. Bowerstock, *Fiction as History: Nero to Julian* (Berkeley: University of California Press, 1997), p. 84.

24 Artemidorus, *Oneirocritica*, pp. 21–22.

25 Ibid., p. 158.

26 Ibid., pp. 22–24.

27 Ibid., p. 24.

28 Ibid., p. 23.

29 Ibid., p. 224.

30 S. R. F. Price, "The Future of Dreams: From Freud to Artemidorus," *Past and Present*, no. 113 (November 1986): 29.

31 Artemidorus, *Oneirocritica*, pp. 217–218.

32 Ibid., p. 57.

33 Ibid., p. 204.

34 Ibid., p. 164.

35 Christine Walde, "Dream Interpretation in a Prosperous Age? Artemidorus, the Greek Interpreter of Dreams," in *Dream Cultures: Explorations in the Comparative History of Dreaming*, ed. David Shulman and Guy G. Stroumsa (New York: Oxford University Press, 1999), pp. 126, 128.

36 Plutarch, "Alexander," in *The Lives of the Noble Greeks and Romans*, trans. John Dryden, rev. Arthur Hugh Clough (New York: Modern Library, 1960), p. 802.

37 Ibid., p. 810.

38 Arrian, *Anabasis of Alexander*, 1.25, trans. E. J. Chinook, 1893, online at www.alexander-sources.org.

39 Ibid., 2.18.

40 Plutarch, "Alexander," p. 818.

41 Ibid., p. 824.

42 Ibid., p. 825.

43 Arrian, *Anabasis of Alexander*, 4.15, 7–8.

44 Richard Wilhelm and Cary F. Baynes, trans., *The I Ching, or Book of Changes* (Princeton, NJ: Princeton University Press, 1990), p. 294.

45 *I Ching: The Classic of Changes* [Mawangdui text], trans. Edward L. Shaughnessy (New York: Ballantine Books, 1997), pp. 203, 201.

46 Ibid., p. 191.

47 Ibid., p. 199.

48 *Suma Ch'ien's Historical Records*, trans. Herbert J. Allen (London: Journal of the Royal Asiatic Society, 1895), chap. 3.

49 *Shu Jing*, trans. James Legge (Hong Kong: Hong Kong University Press, 1960), 3:281–283.

50 Jonathan D. Spence, *Emperor of China: Self-Portrait of K'ang-hsi* (New York: Vintage Books, 1975), pp. 47–48.

51 Ibid., p. 45.

52 Spence, *Emperor of China*, p. 29.

53 Ibid., p. 58.

54 Ibid.

55 Ibid., p. 59.

56 Wilhelm and Baynes, *The I Ching, or Book of Changes*, p. 294.

57 Kristofer Schipper, *The Taoist Body* (Berkeley: University of California Press, 1993), p. 37.

58 G. Willoughby-Meade, *Chinese Ghosts and Goblins* (London: Constable, 1928).

59 Beverley Zabriskie, "Synchronicity and the *I Ching*: Jung, Pauli, and the Chinese Woman," *Journal of Analytical Psychology* 50 (2005): 224.

60 The chapter added to the 1914 edition is titled "Representation by Symbols in Dreams — Some Further Typical Dreams," in *The Interpretation of Dreams*, trans. John Strachey (New York: Avon, 1965), pp. 385–439.

61 Ibid., p. 405.

62 C. G. Jung, *Memories, Dreams, Reflections*, ed. Aniela Jaffé (New York: Vintage, 1965), pp. 161–162.

63 Freud, *Interpretation*, pp. 138–151.

64 Freud described the inscription he wanted in a 1900 letter to Wilhelm Fliess (who implored him to give up smoking). See Louis Breger, *Freud: Darkness in the Midst of Vision* (New York: John Wiley & Sons, 2000), p. 143.

65 Freud, *Interpretation*, p. 139.

66 The descriptions of Freud's dream in the preceding three paragraphs, ibid., pp. 139–140.

67 Ibid., p. 141.

68 Ibid., p. 144.

69 The prime source on the symptoms and treatment of Freud's cancer are the medical notes of his oral surgeon, H. Pichler (Case History of Prof. Sigmund Freud), trans. L. Levy, in the Max Schur Papers (3–85R–13), in the Library of Congress. So far as I am aware, the first person to detail the connection between the Irma Dream and Freud's mouth cancer was the Argentine cancer surgeon and psychoanalyst José Schavelzon, in his monograph *Freud, un paciente con cancer* (Buenos Aires: Editorial Paidos, 1983).

70 Ibid.

71 For a thorough and helpful discussion of the tumor marker hypothesis, see Thomas R. Hersh, "How Might We Explain the Parallels between Freud's 1985 Irma Dream and His 1923 Cancer?" *Dreaming* 5, no. 4 (December 1995): 267–287.

3. DIVINE DREAMING

1 Alain Daniélou, *Hindu Polytheism* (London: Routledge & Kegan Paul, 1964), p. 150.

2 Lawrence C. Watson, "Dreaming as World View and Action in Guajiro Culture," *Journal of Latin American Lore* 7, no. 2 (1981): 239–254.

3 Marc de Civrieux, *Watunna: An Orinoco Creation Cycle*, trans. David M. Guss (San Francisco: North Point Press, 1980), p. 23.

4 On the sexual issue in rival versions of the Buddha's conception, see Serinity Young, *Courtesans and Tantric Escorts: Sexualities in Buddhist Narrative, Iconography, and Ritual* (London: Routledge, 2004), pp. 67–72.

5 T. S. Eliot, "Burnt Norton," in *Four Quartets*; Exodus 24:17.

6 Tacitus, *Histories*, trans. Alfred John Church and William Jackson Brodribb, bk. 4, pp. 83–84, online at http://classics.mit.edu/Tacitus/histories.html.

7 The name *Serapis* is derived from the Egyptian Asar-Hapi, which combines the names of Osiris and the Apis bull.

8 Michel Chauveau, *Egypt in the Age of Cleopatra*, trans. David Lorton (Ithaca, NY: Cornell University Press, 2000), pp. 123–126.

9 Tacitus, *Histories*, bk. 4, p. 81.

10 Ibid., bk. 4, p. 82.

11 Aelius Aristides, Oration 45, in *Complete Works*, trans. Charles A. Behr (Leiden, Netherlands: E. J. Brill, 1981), 2:264.

12 Ibid., 2:266.

13 *The Rig Veda: An Anthology*, trans. Wendy Doniger O'Flaherty (New York: Penguin Books, 1986), p. 228.

14 Wendy Doniger O'Flaherty, *Dreams, Illusion, and Other Realities* (Chicago: University of Chicago Press, 1984), p. 15.

15 Brhadaranyaka Upanishad, 4.3, 9–10, in S. Radhakrishnan, trans., *The Principal Upanishads* (New Delhi: Indus, 1995), p. 257.

16 Ibid., 4.3.11–12, pp. 258–259.

17 Ibid., 4.3.13, p. 259.

18 O'Flaherty, *Dreams, Illusion*, pp. 141–143.

19 Ibid., pp. 143–146.

20 Sudhir Kakar, *Shamans, Mystics, and Doctors: A Psychological Inquiry into India and Its Healing Traditions* (Boston: Beacon Press, 1983), p. 246.

21 Serinity Young, *Dreaming in the Lotus: Buddhist Dream Narrative, Imagery, and Practice* (Boston: Wisdom Publications, 1999), p. xi.

22 Mircea Eliade, *Yoga: Immortality and Freedom*, trans. Willard R. Trask (Princeton, NJ: Princeton University Press, 1973), p. 181.

23 Serinity Young, "Dream Practices in Medieval Tibet," *Dreaming* 9, no. 1 (March 1999): 34, 38n41.

24 Ibid., p. 35.

25 Garma C. C. Chang, trans., *The Hundred Thousand Songs of Milarepa* (Boston: Shambhala, 1989), p. 489.

26 Ibid., p. 484.

27 Ibid., p. 496.

28 Francesca Fremantle, *Luminous Emptiness: Understanding the Tibetan Book of the Dead* (Boston: Shambhala, 2001).

29 Aleida Assmann, "Engendering Dreams: The Dreams of Adam and Eve in Milton's *Paradise Lost*," in *Dream Cultures: Explorations in the Comparative History of Dreaming*, ed. David Shulman and Guy G. Stroumsa (New York: Oxford University Press, 1999), p. 291.

30 "The Apocalypse of Adam," trans. George W. MacRae, in *The Nag Hammadi Library*, ed. James M. Robinson (New York: Harper & Row, 1977), pp. 256–264.

31 Josephus, *Jewish Antiquities*, trans. H. St. J. Thackeray (Cambridge, MA: Harvard University Press, 1967), p. 205.

32 Isabel Moreira, *Dreams, Visions, and Spiritual Authority in Merovingian Gaul* (Ithaca, NY: Cornell University Press, 2000), p. 42.

33 Joel Covitz, *Visions of the Night: A Study of Jewish Dream Interpretation* (Boston: Shambhala, 1990), p. 58.

34 Freely adapted from A. J. Arberry, *Tales from the Masnavi* (London: Curzon Press, 1994), pp. 267–268.

35 Richard C. Trexler, *The Journey of the Magi: Meanings in History of a Christian Story* (Princeton, NJ: Princeton University Press, 1997), p. 37.

36 Amir Harrak, trans., *Chronicle of Zuqnin, AD 488–775* (Toronto: Pontifical Institute of Mediaeval Studies, 1999).

37 John J. Rousseau and Rami Arav, *Jesus and His World: An Archeological and Cultural Dictionary* (Minneapolis: Fortress Press, 1995), p. 33.

38 N. H. Baynes, *Constantine the Great and the Christian Church* (Oxford: Oxford University Press, 1972), p. 3.

39 Robin Lane Fox, *Pagans and Christians* (New York: Albert A. Knopf, 1989), pp. 613–614.

40 *Eusebius' Life of Constantine*, trans. and ed. Averil Cameron and Stuart G. Hall (Oxford: Clarendon Press, 1999).

41 Ibid.

42 George Pitt-Rivers, *The Riddle of the "Labarum," and the Origin of Christian Symbols* (London: George Allen & Unwin, 1966), pp. 28–29.

43 *Eusebius' Life of Constantine*.

44 Lane Fox, *Pagans and Christians*, p. 618.

45 Ibid., pp. 642–653.

46 Jay Bregman, *Synesius of Cyrene, Philosopher-Bishop* (Berkeley: University of California Press, 1982), p. 148.

47 Ibid., p. 76.

48 Synesius, Letter 137 in Augustine FitzGerald, ed. and trans., *The Essays and Hymns of Synesius of Cyrene* (Oxford: Oxford University Press, 1930); Bregman, *Synesius*, pp. 26, 32–33.

49 Bregman, *Synesius*, pp. 60–61.

50 All quotations from Synesius's treatise on dreams are from FitzGerald, *Essays and Hymns of Synesius*.

51 A. A. Nock, *Conversion* (Oxford: Oxford University Press, 1933).

52 Synesius, *On Providence*; Bregman, *Synesius*, pp. 66–72.

53 Socrates Scholasticus, "The Murder of Hypatia," in *A Treasury of Early Christianity*, ed. Anne Fremantle (New York: Viking, 1953), pp. 379–380.

54 Bregman, *Synesius*, p. 148.

55 E. R. Dodds, *Pagan and Christian in an Age of Anxiety: Some Aspects of Religious Experience from Marcus Aurelius to Constantine* (Cambridge: Cambridge University Press, 1965), p. 67.

56 Ambrose, Epistle 51; quoted in Isabel Moreira, *Dreams, Visions, and Spiritual Authority*, p. 16.

57 Moreira, *Dreams, Visions, and Spiritual Authority*; Peter Brown, *The Making of Late Antiquity* (Cambridge, MA: Harvard University Press, 1978).

58 Gregory related a drunkard's vision in his *Historia Francorum*; see Moreira, *Dreams, Visions, and Spiritual Authority*, p. 16.

59 Sulpicius Severus, *Vita Martini*, quoted in Moreira, *Dreams, Visions, and Spiritual Authority*, p. 58.

60 The vision of Anselm in Matthew's *Flowers of History* is cited in Frank Seafield, *The Literature and Curiosities of Dreams* (London: Lockwood, 1869), pp. 108–109. The monk's dream is in Raphael Holinshed's *Chronicles of England, Scotland, and Ireland*, ed. Henry Ellis (1577; reprint, New York: AMS Press, 1965), 3:44. See Frank Barlow, *William Rufus* (Berkeley: University of California Press, 1983); and C. Warren Hollister, "The Strange Death of William Rufus," *Speculum: A Journal of Medieval Studies* 48, no. 4 (October 1973).

61 Jean-Claude Schmitt, "The Liminality and Centrality of Dreams in the Medieval West," in *Dream Cultures: Explorations in the Comparative History of Dreaming*, ed. David Shulman and Guy G. Stroumsa (New York: Oxford University Press, 1999), p. 275.

62   Paul Edward Dutton, *The Politics of Dreaming in the Carolingian Era* (Lincoln: University of Nebraska Press, 1994), p. 63.

63   Al-Khallal's massive *Tabaqat al-mu'abbirim* (The Classes of the Dream Interpreters) has not survived, but we have a reliable guide to its content in a later enormous work on dream interpretation by al-Dinawari. See John C. Lamoreaux, *The Early Muslim Tradition of Dream Interpretation* (Albany: State University of New York Press, 2002), pp. 17–19.

64   Ibn Khaldun, *The Muqaddimah: An Introduction to History*, trans. Franz Rosenthal (Princeton, NJ: Princeton University Press, 1967), p. 75.

65   Ibid., p. 70.

66   Ibid., pp. 81, 83.

67   Ibid., pp. 75–79; see also Muhsin Mahdi, *Ibn Khaldun's Philosophy of History* (London: George Allen and Unwin, 1957), pp. 202, 259n.

68   Ibn Khaldun, *Muqaddimah*, p. 84.

69   Bukhari, *The Translations of the Meanings of Sahihal-Bukhari*, trans. M. M. Khan (Lahore, Pakistan: Kazi Publications, 1979), 9:96.

70   Shahabuddin Suhrawardi, *A Dervish Textbook* [*'Awariful-Ma'arif*], trans. H. Wilberforce Clarke (London: Octagon Press, 1990), p. 53.

71   Bukhari, *Translations of the Meanings of Sahihal-Bukhari*, 9:92.

72   Suhrawardi, *Dervish Textbook*, p. 53.

73   Ibid., p. 50.

74   Bukhari, *Translations of the Meanings of Sahihal-Bukhari*, 9:104.

75   Amira Mittermaier, "The Book of Visions: Dreams, Poetry, and Prophecy in Contemporary Egypt," *International Journal of Middle East Studies* 39 (2007): 229–247.

76   The dream hadiths quoted are from Marcia Hermansen, "Dreams and Dreaming in Islam," in *Dreams: A Reader in the Religious, Cultural, and Psychological Dimensions of Dreaming*, ed. Kelly Bulkeley (New York: Palgrave Macmillan, 2001), pp. 73–92.

77   Leah Kinberg, "Interaction between this World and the Afterworld in Early Islamic Tradition," *Oriens* 29 (1986): 296.

78   The practice of dream incubation at a tomb is called *tawadjdjuh*. Fritz Meier, "Quelques aspects de l'inspiration par les démons en Islam," in *Le rêve et les sociétés humaines*, ed. G. E. Von Grünebaum and Roger Caillois (Paris: Editions Gallimard, 1967), pp. 418–419.

79   Kinberg, "Interaction," pp. 300–303.

80   William C. Chittick, *The Sufi Path of Knowledge: Ibn al-'Arabi's Metaphysics of Imagination* (Albany: State University of New York Press, 1989), p. 119.

81   Henry Corbin, *Creative Imagination in the Sufism of Ibn 'Arabi*, trans. Ralph Mannheim (Princeton, NJ: Bollingen, 1981), p. 179.

82   Ibid., pp. 189–90.

83   Henry Corbin, *Spiritual Body and Celestial Earth*, trans. Nancy Pearson (Princeton, NJ: Bollingen, 1989), pp. 118–119.

84   Ibid., p. 124.

85   Chittick, *Sufi Path of Knowledge*, p. 43.

86   Ibid., pp. 116, 117, 396n4.

87   Ibn 'Arabi, *al-Futuhat al-makkiyya* [The Meccan Openings], quoted in Chittick, *Sufi Path of Knowledge*, p. 119.

88   Ibid., p. 116.

89   Ibid., p. 113.

90   Ibid., p. 105.

91   Corbin, *Creative Imagination*, p. 223.

92   Ibid., pp. 238–239.

93   Tom Cheetham, *The World Turned Inside Out: Henry Corbin and Islamic Mysticism* (Woodstock, CT: Spring Journal Books, 2003), pp. x–xi. The Corbin translation mentioned is Shihaboddin Yahya Sohravardi, *Le livre de la sagesse orientale*, trans. Henri Corbin (Paris: Editions Verdier, 1986). There is a recent critical edition of the *Hikmat al-Ishraq*: Suhrawardi, *The Philosophy of Illumination*, trans. John Walbridge and Hossein Ziai (Provo, UT: Brigham Young University Press, 1999).

94   Henry Corbin, *The Voyage and the Messenger: Islam and Philosophy*, trans. Joseph Rowe (Berkeley: North Atlantic Books, 1998), p. 140.

4. THE ANGEL THAT TROUBLES THE WATERS

1   Cotton Mather, *The Angel of Bethesda*, ed. Gordon Jones (Worcester, MA: American Antiquarian Society, 1972).

2   Antoine Duprez, *Jésus et les dieux guérisseurs: A propos de Jean, V* (Paris: Gabalda, 1970).

3   Aelius Aristides, Oration 45 in *Complete Works*, trans. Charles A. Behr (Leiden, Netherlands: E. J. Brill, 1981), 2:266. (Henceforth "Aristides." All references in this chapter are to vol. 2 of Behr's translation.)

4   Ibid.

5   E. R. Dodds, *The Greeks and the Irrational* (Berkeley: University of California Press, 1951), p. 119.

6   Rufus of Ephesus, *Medical Questions*, in Steven M. Oberhelman, "Galen, *On Diagnosis from Dreams*," *Journal of the History of Medicine and Allied Sciences* 38 (January 1983): 41–42.

7   Ibid.

8   Ibid.

9   Ibid., p. 37.

10   Emma J. Edelstein and Ludwig Edelstein, *Asclepius: Collection and Interpretation of the Testimonies* (Baltimore: Johns Hopkins University Press, 1998), p. 263. (Henceforth "*Asclepius*").

11   Georg Misch, *A History of Autobiography in Antiquity* (Cambridge, MA: Harvard University Press, 1951), 2:499.

12   Oberhelman, "Galen," p. 38.

13   Ibid., p. 45.

14   Jody Rubin Pinault, *Hippocratic Lives and Legends* (Leiden, Netherlands: E. J. Brill, 1997), pp. 67–68.

15   Galen, *Three Treatises on the Nature of Science*, trans. Richard Walzer and Michael Frede (Indianapolis: Hakket, 1985), p. 41.

16   *Asclepius*, p. 202.

17   Ibid., pp. 208–209.

18   Edward Tick, *The Practice of Dream Healing: Bringing Ancient Greek Mysteries into Modern Medicine* (Wheaton, IL: Quest Books, 2001), pp. 121–123.

19   Aristides, p. 237.

20   Galen, "Of Antidotes," in *Asclepius*, p. 331, my free translation.

21   *Asclepius*, pp. 163–164.

22   Ibid., p. 239.

23   Pamela Cox Miller, *Dreams in Late Antiquity: Studies in the Imagination of a Culture* (Princeton, NJ: Princeton University Press, 1994), p. 113.

24   *Asclepius*, p. 196.

25   Ibid., p. 333.

26   Aristides, p. 234, freely translated.

27   Ibid., pp. 297–298.

28   Ibid., p. 316.

29   Lynn R. LiDonnici, "Compositional Background of the Epidaurian 'Iamata," *American Journal of Philology* 113, no. 1 (Spring 1992): 33–34.

30   Ibid., p. 31.

31   Aristides, p. 238.

32   LiDonnici, "Compositional Background," p. 25.

33   Aristides, p. 278.

34   Ibid., p. 290.

35   Ibid., pp. 295–296.

36   Dr. John Scarborough, professor of pharmacy and classics at the University of Wisconsin-Madison, offers this diagnosis of Aristides's tumor: "Initially, one suspects an inguinal hernia, fairly common (then and now), among men (as opposed to women, although childbirth can bring this on, too), but the self-professed cure with the resultant flaps of skin suggest an omental hernia, which on occasion will fade away on its own." Personal communication.

37   *Asclepius*, p. 176.

38   Ibid., p. 177.

39   Morton Smith, *Jesus the Magician* (New York: HarperCollins, 1981).

40   Miller, *Dreams in Late Antiquity*, p. 117.

41   G. Dagron, ed. and trans., *Vie et miracles de sainte Thècle* (Brussels: Societé des Bollandistes, 1978).

42   Aristides, pp. 316–317.

43   Thornton Wilder, *The Angel That Troubled the Waters*, in *The Collected Short Plays of Thornton Wilder: Volume II* (New York: Theatre Communications Group, 1998), p. 74.

5. FROM THE DREAM LIBRARY

1   In colloquializing the story of Dumuzi's dream, I have glossed over a major element in the cycle that is not in the dream poem itself. As the price for her own return from the Underworld, Inanna has to deliver another soul. She travels from city to city, with the *galla* demons in tow, trying to determine which of her many consorts — the kings — deserves this fate. She picks Dumuzi because he has gone on a bender and, hungover, fails to give her the treatment she thinks she deserves.

This translation of the Dream of Dumuzi is in Diane Wolkstein and Samuel Noah Kramer, *Inanna, Queen of Heaven: Her Stories and Hymns from Sumer* (New York: Harper & Row, 1983), pp. 74–84.

In support of my rendition of the name of Geshtin-anna's consort, see Curtis Hoffman, "Dumuzi's Dream: Dream Analysis in Ancient Mesopotamia," *Dreaming* 14, no. 4 (December 2004): 249.

Dumuzi (later called Tammuz) is a Mystery god who dies and is reborn, and the cycle of his ever-recurring death and resurrection is also the cycle of the crops in what is now southern Iraq. He dies in the spring at the time that Iraqi farmers, in their hot country, harvest their wheat and barley; he is resurrected when they put seeds in the earth. In the Christian calendar, this is Easter time. The Shia ritual mourning for the martyred Imam Hussein at the site of the battle of Karbala — a rite Saddam tried to suppress — takes place at the same time. Life rhymes, and so do the life cycles of gods. See E. W. Fernea, *Guests of the Sheikh* (Garden City, NY: Doubleday, 1969).

2   Bert O. States, *Dreaming and Storytelling* (Ithaca, NY: Cornell University Press, 1993), p. 3.

3   Bert O. States, "Authorship in Dreams and Fictions," *Dreaming* 4, no. 4 (December 1994): 239.

4   Ibid., p. 240.

5   Samuel Beckett, *Proust* (New York: Grove, 1931), p. 56.

6   Stefania Pandolfo, *Impasse of the Angels: Scenes from a Moroccan Space of Memory* (Chicago: University of Chicago Press, 1997), p. 259.

7   Ibid., p. 265.

8   Charles Dickens, letter to Dr. Stone, February 2, 1851; see Warrington Winters, "Dickens and the Psychology of Dreams," *PMLA* 63, no. 3 (September 1948): 984–1006.

9   C. S. Lewis, "It All Began with a Picture," *Junior Radio Times* 68 (July 15, 1960), reprinted in *Of Other Worlds* (San Diego: Harcourt Brace, 1975), p. 42.

10   W. B. Yeats, "Per Amica Silentia Lunae," in *Mythologies* (New York: Macmillan, 1959), p. 346.

11   Helen Darbishire, ed., *The Early Lives of Milton* (London: Constable, 1932), p. 33.

12   G. E. Von Grünebaum and Roger Caillois, eds., *Le rêve et les sociétés humaines* (Paris: Editions Gallimard, 1967).

13   Ibid.

14   Graham Greene, *A Sort of Life* (New York: Simon and Schuster, 1971), p. 32. In his memoir, Greene says he was five at the time.

15   Ibid., p. 98.

16   Ibid., pp. 32–33.

17   Letter from Greene to his fiancé, Vivien Dayrell-Browning, December 11, 1925, quoted in Norman Sherry, *The Life of Graham Greene: Volume 1, 1904–1939* (New York: Viking, 1989), p. 106.

18   Graham Greene, *Ways of Escape* (London: Penguin Books, 1982), p. 210.

19   Greene, *Sort of Life*, p. 101.

20   Norman Sherry, *The Life of Graham Greene: Volume 3, 1955–1991* (New York: Viking, 2004), p. 477.

21   Greene, *Ways of Escape*, p. 210; the story was published in the collection *A Sense of Reality*.

22   Ibid., p. 211.

23   Ibid.

24   Sherry, *Life of Graham Greene: Volume 3*, p. 103.

25   Graham Greene, *A World of My Own: A Dream Diary* (London: Reinhardt Books/ Penguin, 1992), pp. 59–60.

26   Yvonne Cloetta, *In Search of a Beginning: My Life with Graham Greene*, as told to Marie-Francoise Allain., trans. Euan Cameron (London: Bloomsbury, 2004), p. 45.

27   Greene's Shakespeare Prize acceptance speech, "The Virtue of Disloyalty," delivered in Hamburg in 1969; cited in Cloetta, *In Search of a Beginning*, p. 101.

28   *Sort of Life*, p. 27.

29   *World of My Own*, pp. 115–116.

30   Cloetta, *In Search of a Beginning*, p. 185.

31   Ibid., p. 186n.

32   Ibid., p. 204.

33   Graham Greene, *The Confidential Agent* (London: Heineman, 1954).

34   Stanley Krippner and Laura Faith, "Exotic Dreams: A Cross-Cultural Study," *Dreaming* 11, no. 2 (June 2001): 73–82.

35   Faddey Venediktovich Bulgarin, *Memoirs of the Unforgettable Alexander Sergeyevich Griboyedov* (1830; reprint, Moscow: Sovremennik, 1990).

36   The draft letter in French is available online at http://feb-web.ru/feb/griboed/TEXTS/ FOM88/PS88_29.htm.

37   Michael R. Katz, *Dreams and the Unconscious in Nineteenth-Century Russian Fiction* (Hanover, NH: University Press of New England, 1984), pp. 28–35, 157–158.

38   Peter Hopkirk, *The Great Game: The Struggle for Empire in Central Asia* (New York: Kodansha Globe, 1997), pp. 113, 122. See also Laurence Kelly, *Diplomacy and Murder in Tehran: Alexander Griboyedov and the Tsar's Mission to the Shah of Persia* (London: I. B. Tauris, 2002).

39   Katz, *Dreams and the Unconscious*, p. 38.

40   Ibid., p. 67.

41   Nikolai Gogol, "A Terrible Vengeance," in *The Complete Tales of Nikolai Gogol*, vol. 1, ed. Leonard J. Kent (Chicago: University of Chicago Press, 1985), p. 151.

42   Nikolai Gogol, "The Portrait," in *The Complete Tales of Nikolai Gogol*, trans. Richard Pevear and Larissa Volokhonsky (New York: Vintage, 1999), p. 354.

43   Katz, *Dreams and the Unconscious*, p. 84.

44   *La Révolution Surréaliste* 8 (1925): 15.

45   Natalia Kodrianskaya, *Aleksei Remizov* (Paris, n.p., 1959), p. 41.

46   Ibid.

47   W. B. Yeats, *A Vision* (London: Macmillan, 1937), p. 221.

48   Aleksei Remizov, *Martyn Zadeka: Sonnik* (Paris: Opleshnik, 1954), p. 3. Quoted in Adrian Wanner, "Aleksei Remizov's Dreams," *Russian Review* 58 (October 1999): 599–614.

49   Ibid., p. 98, quoted in Wanner, "Aleksei Remizov's Dreams."

50   Juliet Barker, *The Brontës* (New York: St. Martin's Press, 1995).

51   Samuel Taylor Coleridge, *The Major Works* (Oxford: Oxford University Press, 1985), p. 102.

52   Norman Fruman, *Coleridge, the Damaged Archangel* (New York: George Braziller, 1971).

6. HOW DREAMING GETS US THROUGH

1   Miriam Elson, "John Adams and Benjamin Rush Exchange Dreams," *Progress in Self Psychology* 19 (2003): 272.

2   David McCullough, *John Adams* (New York: Simon & Schuster, 2001), p. 47.

3   Joseph J. Ellis, *Passionate Sage: The Character and Legacy of John Adams* (New York: Norton, 1993), p. 214.

4   Benjamin Rush, *Letters of Benjamin Rush*, ed. L. H. Butterfield (Princeton, NJ: American Philosophical Society, 1951), 2:893–894.

5   Ibid., 2:978–979.

6   John Adams and Abigail Adams, *Letters of John and Abigail Adams*, ed. William J. Bennett (Rochester, NY: Westvaco [private edition], 2001), pp. 104–106.

7   Ibid., p. 107.

8   Ibid.

9   Ibid., p. 111.

10 McCullough, *John Adams*, p. 64.

11 H. R. P. Dickson, *The Arab of the Desert: A Glimpse into Badawin Life in Kuwait and Sau'di Arabia* (London: George Allen & Unwin, 1949), p. 332.

12 Ibid.

13 Ibid., pp. 332–335. There is a photograph of Colonel Dickson — appearing to be half Churchillian Brit, half Bedouin — at the *sidr* tree he dreamed in his later book *Kuwait and Her Neighbors* (London: George Allen & Unwin, 1956). The *sidr* is a sacred tree for Muslims because it is mentioned in the Koran four times, and it is also known for its medicinal uses. It is not related to American cedars, which are actually members of the cypress family.

14 The 2003 Gallup survey, which posed forty questions about dreams, was designed by Dr. Björg Bjarnadóttir and her team at the Skuggsjá Dream Center in Akureyri, Iceland. Full details at http://skuggsja.is.

15 The story of Thyri Haraldsdóttir is in the version of *Ólafs Saga Tryggvasónar* in the fourteenth-century Icelandic *Flateyjarbók*. While Thyri is from Holstein in Germany, her story comes to us through Icelandic tradition. I am indebted to Valgerður Hjördis Bjarnadóttir for bringing this wonderful story to my attention, and for the translation on which this summary is based.

16 Loftur Gissurarson and William H. Swatos, *Icelandic Spiritualism: Mediumship and Modernity in Iceland* (New York: Transaction Publishers, 1997), pp. 197–200.

17 Águst H. Bjarnason, *Drauma-Jói* (Reykjavik, n.p., 1915), pp. 113–114. I am grateful to Dr. Björg Bjarnadóttir for her generous help in locating and translating this and other accounts in Icelandic of modern dreamers cited in notes 19–23.

18 E. Paul Durrenberger and Gísli Pálsson, "Finding Fish: The Tactics of Icelandic Skippers," *American Ethnologist* 13, no. 2 (May 1986): 213–229.

19 Magnus Sveinsson, *The Woman by the Waterfall: The Life of Skipper Jon Danielsson and His Relationship with an Elf Woman* [in Icelandic] (Reykjavik: Bokautgafan Þjodsaga, 1978).

20 "I Am Nothing But a Sailor," *Faxi* (Keflavik), no. 5 (1976): 9.

21 G. M. Magnúss, *Eiríkur Skipherra* (Reykjavik, n.p., 1967).

22 Ibid.

23   O. Clausen, *Draumspakir Íslendingar* (Reykjavík: Iðunnarútgáfan, 1950), p. 96.

24   Björg Bjarnadóttir, *Draumalandið* (Akureyri: Skuggsjá, 2003), p. 105.

25   Barry Miles, *Paul McCartney: Many Years from Now* (New York: Henry Holt, 1997).

26   Ibid., p. 20. Also Bob Spitz, *The Beatles* (New York: Little, Brown, 2005), pp. 73–76.

27   Frederic Seaman, *The Last Days of John Lennon* (New York: Random House, 1996), p. 171.

28   Johnny Cash, *Cash: The Autobiography* (New York: HarperOne, 2003), p. 29.

29   Steve Turner, *The Man Called Cash* (New York: Thomas Nelson, 2004), p. 99.

30   Ibid.

31   Larry King interview at www.cnn.com/TRANSCRIPTS/0211/26/lkl.oo.html.

32   Rich Everitt, *Falling Stars: Air Crashes That Filled Rock and Roll Heaven* (Boyne City, MI: Harbor House, 2004); JoJo Billingsley interviews at www.swampland.com/ articles/view/swampland90 and www.downsouthjukin.com/jojo_billingsley _interview_with.htm.

33   See www.gibson.com/en-us/Lifestyle/Features/LynyrdSkynyrdsEdKing/.

34   Bono interview in the 1999 TV movie *In Dreams: The Roy Orbison* story, directed by Mark Hall.

35   Olga Kern interview with Sergey Elkin (in Russian): www.eurochicago.com/ modules/weblog/details.php?blog_id=7.

36   Geoffrey Giuliano, *Lennon in America* (New York: Cooper Square Press, 2000), pp. 103, 205.

37   William F. Russell, *Second Wind: The Memoirs of an Opinionated Man* (New York: Simon & Schuster, 1991).

38   Lynne McTaggart, *The Intention Experiment* (New York: Free Press, 2007), p. 130.

39   R. M. Suinn, "Imagery Rehearsal Applications in Performance Enhancement," *Behavioral Therapist* 8 (1985): 155–159.

40   Kekulé's written version of the 1890 speech is translated in O. T. Benfey, "August Kekulé and the Birth of the Structural Theory of Organic Chemistry," *Journal of Chemical Education*, no. 35 (1958): 21–23. For alternative translations and the original German text, see Albert Rothenberg, "Creative Cognitive Processes in Kekulé's Discovery of the Structure of the Benzene Molecule," *American Journal of Psychology* 108, no. 3 (Fall 1995): 419–438.

41   I have borrowed from an excellent article by Stanley Krippner, "Access to Hidden Reserves of the Unconscious through Dreams in Creative Problem Solving," *Journal of Creative Behavior*, no. 15 (1981): 11–22.

42   N. V. Zhilkina, "The Extreme Component in Idea Generation" [in Russian], *Analytical Culturology* 2, no. 6 (2006).

43   Jacques Hadamard, *The Psychology of Invention in the Mathematical Field* (Princeton, NJ: Princeton University Press, 1945), p. 142.

44   Henri Bergson, "Le rêve," *Bulletin de l'Institut Psychologique International*, no. 1 (1901): 103–122.

7. JOAN OF ARC AND THE TREE-SEERS

1   On May 10, 1429, Clement de Fauquemberge, clerk to the Parliament of Paris, penned a little drawing of a woman in the margin of the register where he had recorded a report

of "a Maid alone bearing a banner" in the Relief of Orleans. He had never set eyes on Joan of Arc.

2 Régine Pernoud and Marie-Véronique Clin, *Joan of Arc: Her Story*, trans. Jeremy du Quesnay Adams (New York: St. Martin's Griffin, 1999), p. 256.

3 Joan of Arc told her prosecutors she had seen a portrait of herself at Arras by a "Scottish painter"; she suggested that it was a faithful likeness and said that no portrait from life had been made since. It's a good guess that the Scottish artist was Hamish Power, who lived in Tours and had gone sufficiently native in France to have a French version of his name, "Hauves Pourlnois." He painted Jehanne's famous standard and her pennon, a small triangular flag used to signal and deploy her archers.

4 Alençon in Pierre Duparc, *Procès en nullité de la condemnation de Jeanne d'Arc* (Paris: Société de l'Histoire de France, 1977–89), 1:387.

5 Gobert Thibault, the royal esquire, in ibid., 1:370.

6 Régine Pernoud, *Joan of Arc by Herself and Her Witnesses*, trans. Edward Hyams (Lanham, NH: Scarborough Press, 1982), p. 23.

7 February 22, 1431. Unless otherwise noted, quoted testimony from Joan of Arc's trial at Rouen, which unfolded over five months, from January to May 30, 1431, is from the W. P. Barrett translation of the French and Latin documents from the Trial of Condemnation, which are available through the Yale Law School Avalon Project at www.yale.edu/lawweb/avalon/treatise/jean_darc/jeanne.htm.

8 Kelly DeVries, *Joan of Arc: A Military Leader* (Stroud, England: Sutton Publishing, 2003), pp. 62–63.

9 Pernoud, *Joan of Arc*, p. 39.

10 Jean Barbin, lawyer, in Duparc, *Procès en nullité*, 1:375.

11 Anne Lombard-Jourdan, *Aux origines de Carnaval* (Paris: Odile Jacob, 2005), pp. 139–141.

12 In the grand hall of the Palais de la Cité in Paris (known today as the Salle des Pas Perdu), a wall painting of a great antlered stag, presiding over images of the kings of France since Faramond, recalls the giant wooden statue of a stag that dominated the space until a fire in 1618.

13 Pernoud, *Joan of Arc*, pp. 61–62.

14 Friar Jean Pasquerel, Jehanne's confessor, in Duparc, *Procès en nullité*, 1:395.

15 Pernoud, *Joan of Arc*, p. 114.

16 The Merlin prophecy is in MS. 7301 of the Bibliothèque Nationale in Paris. The account of the message that reached Suffolk is in the testimony of Jean, Bastard of Orleans, at the trial of nullification.

17 Mark Twain, *Personal Recollections of Joan of Arc* (New York: Gramercy, 2000).

18 DeVries, *Joan of Arc*, pp. 113–114.

19 Ibid., pp. 114, 215–216.

20 Christian Panvert, "Mystery of Joan of Arc Is Solved," *The Independent*, December 17, 2006, quoting Dr. Philippe Charlier.

21 It is ironic that Jehanne invoked Saint Martin of Tours, because he was a celebrated tree-cutter while bishop of Tours after 371. Sulpicius Severus, who wrote his first life history and knew him personally, reported that the locals did not resist when Martin pulled

down ancient pagan temples, but they opposed him bitterly when he attacked the sacred groves in his efforts to root out druidic practices. Severus, *On the Life of St. Martin*, trans. Alexander Roberts (1894), available online at www.users.csbsju.edu/~eknuth/ npnf2-11/sulpitiu/lifemart.html.

22 The importance of trees in early European seership and spiritual practice can hardly be overstated. Robert Graves takes us into these realms with his inspired poetic exploration of the Celtic Battle of the Trees in *The White Goddess*. There are treasures awaiting future dream archeologists in this field.

8. THE BEAUTIFUL DREAM SPY OF MADRID

1 The dialogue here is paraphrased. The transcripts of Lucrecia's dreams frequently begin: "The Ordinary Man [*Hombre Ordinario*] appeared in my bedroom," or "I saw the Ordinary Man." The registers of Lucrecia's dreams are in the Archivo Histórico Nacional, Sección de Inquisición, in Madrid. Richard L. Kagan supplies an index of the 415 dreams in his excellent study *Lucrecia's Dreams: Politics and Prophecy in Sixteenth-Century Spain* (Berkeley: University of California Press, 1990), pp. 167–174. Kagan rightly observes that "the registers of Lucrecia's dreams represent a source without parallel in the annals of European history" (p. 56).

2 Kagan, *Lucrecia's Dreams*, p. 44.

3 Ibid., p. 19.

4 "*Unos desvaríos diabólicos*": Kagan translates this as "only some diabolical rubbish" (p. 45).

5 On Miguel de Piedrola, see Vicente Beltrán de Heredia, "Un grupo de visionarios y pseudoprofetas durante los últimos años de Felipe II," *Revista Española de Teología* 7 (1947): 373–397; also Richard L. Kagan, "Politics, Prophecy and the Inquisition in Late Sixteenth-Century Spain," in *The Impact of the Inquisition in Spain and the New World*, ed. Mary Elizabeth Perry and Anne J. Cruz (Berkeley: University of California Press, 1991), pp. 111–115. On the character of prophecy in Lucrecia's era, see Keith Thomas, *Religion and the Decline of Magic* (London: Weidenfeld and Nicolson, 1971), pp. 389–432.

6 Kagan, *Lucrecia's Dreams*, p. 51. In his terror, Allende destroyed all the dream reports in his possession.

7 This is the author's translation of a Spanish transcript.

8 Juggernaut dream of December 1, 1587: translated in Roger Osborne, *The Dreamer of the Calle San Salvador: Visions of Sedition and Sacrilege in Sixteenth-Century Spain* (London: Pimlico, 2002), p. 1.

9 A "professor" asked her in a dream, "Who has been your master?" Lucrecia responded, in the dream, "The Lion Man"; Kagan, *Lucrecia's Dreams*, p. 63.

10 Ibid., pp. 67, 75.

11 Osborne, *Dreamer of the Calle San Salvador*, pp. 39–40; note that this version renders the name of the Order of Calatrava as "Culutrava," perhaps a misreading of sixteenth-century orthography. It was an order of warrior monks that took its name from a fortress captured from the Moors. Its badge was a Greek cross in gules with lilies at the ends. See "Military Order of Calatrava," in *Catholic Encyclopedia*, online at www.newadvent.org.

12   Kagan, *Lucrecia's Dreams*, pp. 71, 75–76, 80, 118, 151; Osborne, *Dreamer of the Calle San Salvador*, pp. 23–25.

13   Dream of December 6, 1587; translation in Osborne, *Dreamer of the Calle San Salvador*, pp. 27–29.

14   The old custom in Madrid was to bathe naked in the Manzanares River on Saint John's Eve (June 23). This was a time of bawdy abandon. The custom was banned by the church in 1588, not long after Lucrecia's dream of the bare-breasted snake woman and the fountaining man.

15   Kagan, *Lucrecia's Dreams*, p. 53.

16   Ibid., p. 153.

17   Ibid., pp. 125–127. On the House of Feria's dramatic interests, see Anne E. Wiltrout, *A Patron and Playwright in Renaissance Spain: The House of Feria and Diego Sánchez de Badajoz* (Melton, England: Tamesis Books, 1987).

18   A black scapular with a white cross, inspired by Lucrecia's dreams and worn by her followers in the Cofradía of the Restoration under their regular clothes, is in the Archivo Histórico Nacional in Madrid. One of those who wore this scapular was Hernando de Toledo, the prior of the military order of St. John of Jerusalem and a member of Philip II's council of state, which gives some idea of how high Lucrecia's influence had reached.

19   Kagan, *Lucrecia's Dreams*, p. 77.

20   Ibid., p. 21.

21   Ibid., pp. 80–81.

22   Ibáñez de Ochandia testified on April 4, 1591, that Mendoza told Lucrecia, *"Que hermosa estáis a que un muerto la podía empreñar."* Kagan, *Lucrecia's Dreams*, p. 206n26.

23   Lucrecia's cellmate in Toledo, Marí de Vega, had been charged as a *judizante* (one who secretly practiced Judaism); Kagan, *Lucrecia's Dreams*, p. 141. After hearing Marí describe a dildo made of sheepskin, Lucrecia allegedly commented that she preferred one fashioned from "a special kind of wood, with hinges, and a cover of satin or velvet," and that she had a friend in Madrid who owned one of these items. Ibid., p. 185n72, quoting AHN Inq 2105/1, fol. 205.

24   Kagan, *Lucrecia's Dreams*, p. 145.

25   Ibid., pp. 154–155.

26   Ibid.

9. THE UNDERGROUND RAILROAD OF DREAMS

1   *The Interesting Narrative of the Life of Olaudah Equiano* (1789), online at www.digitalhistory.uh.edu/modules/slavery/documents.html.

2   Alice Lucas Brixler to Earl Conrad Brixler to Conrad, July 28, 1939, in Kate Clifford Larson, *Bound for the Promised Land: Harriet Tubman, Portrait of an American Hero* (New York: Ballantine Books, 2004), p. 288.

3   Brixler to Conrad, July 19, 1939.

4   Larson, *Bound for the Promised Land*, pp. 196–202.

5   Brixler to Conrad, November 26, 1940.

6   R. S. Rattray, *The Leopard Priestess* (London: Thornton Butterworth, 1934), pp. 168–169.

7   Franklin Sanborn, "Harriet Tubman," *Boston Commonwealth*, July 16, 1863.

8   Frank C. Drake, "The Moses of Her People," *New York Herald*, September 2, 1907.

9   Marcus Rediker, *The Slave Ship: A Human History* (New York: Viking, 2007).

10   Lorena S. Walsh, "The Chesapeake Slave Trade: Regional Patterns, African Origins, and Some Implications," *William and Mary Quarterly* 58, no. 1 (January 2001): 148.

11   Sanborn, "Harriet Tubman"; Sarah Hopkins Bradford, *Scenes in the Life of Harriet Tubman* (Auburn, NY: W. J. Moses, 1869), pp. 79–80.

12   R. S. Rattray, *Religion and Art in Ashanti* (Oxford: Clarendon Press, 1927), p. 192.

13   Ibid., p. 193.

14   Ibid., p. 195.

15   Ibid., p. 194.

16   Ibid., p. 196.

17   Rattray, *Leopard Priestess*, pp. 107–109.

18   Walsh, "Chesapeake Slave Trade," pp. 162–163.

19   Michael A. Gomez, *Exchanging Our Country Marks: The Transformation of African Identities in the Colonial and Antebellum South* (Chapel Hill: University of North Carolina Press, 1998).

20   William L. Andrews, ed., *Sisters of the Spirit: Three Black Women's Autobiographies of the Nineteenth Century* (Bloomington: Indiana University Press, 1986), p. 92.

21   Ibid.

22   Eva L. R. Meyerowitz, "Concepts of the Soul among the Akan of the Gold Coast," *Africa: Journal of the International African Institute* 21, no. 1 (January 1951): 24.

23   Bradford, *Scenes*, p. 56.

24   Larson, *Bound for the Promised Land*, p. 42.

25   Ednah Dow Cheney, quoted in Jean M. Humez, *Harriet Tubman: The Life and the Life Stories* (Madison: University of Wisconsin Press, 2003), p. 180.

26   Sarah Hopkins Bradford, *Harriet, the Moses of Her People* (New York: George R. Lockwood & Son, 1886), p. 24.

27   Ibid., p. 26.

28   Sanborn, "Harriet Tubman."

29   Bradford, *Harriet*, p. 29.

30   Ibid., p. 30 (dialect removed).

31   Humez, *Harriet Tubman*, p. 183.

32   Bradford, *Harriet*, p. 6.

33   Compare Larson, *Bound for the Promised Land*.

34   William Still, *The Underground Railroad: A Record of Facts, Authentic Narratives, Letters, &c* (Philadelphia: Porter & Coates, 1872). Project Gutenberg Ebook 15263.

35   Bradford, *Harriet*, pp. 73–74.

36   Still, *Underground Railroad*.

37   Bradford, *Harriet*, pp. 75–76.

38   Thomas Garrett, 1868 testimonial letter in Bradford, *Harriet*, pp. 83–84.

39   Ibid., pp. 86–87.

40   Bradford, *Harriet,* p. 36.

41   Ibid., p. 37.

42   Humez, *Harriet Tubman,* p. 137.

43   Larson, *Bound for the Promised Land,* p. 169.

44   Lydia Marie Child to John Greenleaf Whittier, January 21, 1862, in Larson, *Bound for the Promised Land,* p. 206.

45   Sanborn, "Harriet Tubman."

46   Letter to John Brown Jr., April 8, 1858, in Franklin B. Sanborn, *Life and Letters of John Brown* (1885; reprint, New York: Negro Universities Press, 1969), p. 452.

47   Bradford, *Harriet,* p. 119.

48   Humez, *Harriet Tubman,* p. 40.

49   Ken Chowder, "The Father of American Terrorism," *American Heritage* 51, no. 1 (February–March 2000).

50   Bradford, *Harriet,* p. 93.

51   Humez, *Harriet Tubman,* p. 191.

52   Lydia Maria Child to John G. Whittier, January 21, 1862, in Larson, *Bound for the Promised Land,* p. 206.

53   Bradford, *Harriet,* p. 93.

54   Martha Coffin Wright to Marianna Pelham Wright, November 7, 1865, in Larson, *Bound for the Promised Land,* p. 232.

10. MARK TWAIN'S RHYMING LIFE

Epigraph: Mark Twain scholars agree that this snapper is something he may very well have said, but no source has been found. His closest sourced statement on this theme is much less fun: "It is not worth while to try to keep history from repeating itself, for man's character will always make the preventing of the repetitions impossible." See Bernard DeVoto, ed., *Mark Twain in Eruption: Hitherto Unpublished Pages about Men and Events* (New York: Harper & Brothers, 1940).

1   Mark Twain, "The Turning-Point of My Life," in *What Is Man? And Other Philosophical Writings,* ed. Paul Baender (Berkeley: University of California Press, 1973).

2   Ron Powers, *Mark Twain: A Life* (New York: Free Press, 2005), p. 84.

3   *The Autobiography of Mark Twain,* ed. Charles Neider (New York: Perennial Classics, 1990), p. 130.

4   Powers, *Mark Twain,* p. 9.

5   Ibid., pp. 20–21.

6   Ibid., p. 541.

7   Mark Twain, *Personal Recollections of Joan of Arc* (New York: Gramercy, 2000), p. 50.

8   Mark Twain, *Notebooks & Journals,* ed. Frederick Anderson et al. (Berkeley: University of California Press, 1975–1979), 1:69.

9   Powers, *Mark Twain,* pp. 151–152.

10   Ibid., pp. 162–164.

11   Ibid., p. 250.

12   Twain, *Autobiography,* p. 310.

13   Ibid., pp. 310–311; Mark Perry, *Grant and Twain: The Story of a Friendship That Changed America* (New York: Random House, 2004), pp. 85–89.

14 Twain, *Notebooks & Journals*, 2:412.

15 Ibid., p. 402.

16 Powers, *Mark Twain*, p. 545.

17 Twain, *Autobiography*, p. 339.

18 Mark Twain, *Which Was the Dream? And Other Symbolic Writings of the Later Years*, ed. John S. Tuckey (Berkeley: University of California Press, 1968), p. 4.

19 Mark Twain, "Mental Telegraphy," in *Tales of Wonder*, ed. David Ketterer (Lincoln: University of Nebraska Press, 2003), pp. 96–111. See also "Mental Telegraphy Again," in ibid., pp. 112–116.

20 Twain, *Notebooks & Journals*, 2:402.

21 Letter to Dan De Quille, March 29, 1875; Mark Twain, *Letters*, ed. Michael B. Frank et al. (Berkeley: University of California Press, 1988–2002), 6:434.

22 Twain, "Mental Telegraphy."

23 Twain, *Letters*, 4:25.

24 *The Adventures of Tom Sawyer*, chap. 18, in Mark Twain, *Mississippi Writings* (New York: Library of America, 1982), p. 120.

25 "My Platonic Sweetheart," in *Tales of Wonder*, ed. David Ketterer (Lincoln: University of Nebraska Press, 2003), pp. 117–126.

26 Ibid.

27 Letter to Susan Crane in Mark Twain, *Letters*, 2:581.

28 Twain, *Autobiography*, p. 267.

29 Ibid., p. 422.

30 Justin Kaplan, *Mr. Clemens and Mark Twain* (New York: Simon & Schuster, 1966), p. 343.

31 Twain, *Which Was the Dream?* pp. 46–47.

32 Mark Twain, *No. 44, The Mysterious Stranger* (Berkeley: University of California Press, 1982), p. 144.

33 Ibid., p. 187.

34 Albert Bigelow Paine, ed., *Mark Twain's Notebook* (New York: Harper & Bros., 1935), p. 348.

35 Ibid.

36 Ibid., p.250.

37 Ibid., pp. 349–50.

38 Ibid., pp. 350–351.

39 Twain, *The Equator: A Journey around the World*, chap. 12.

40 Paine, *Mark Twain's Notebook*, p. 365.

41 John S. Tuckey, ed., *The Devil's Race-Track: Mark Twain's "Great Dark" Writings* (Berkeley: University of California Press, 2005), p. 109n.

42 Twain, *Which Was the Dream?* p. 434.

43 Mark Twain wrote his own name on page 111 of his manuscript, then substituted "Huck." Tuckey, *Devil's Race-Track*, p. xvii. He identified the Huck of the story — a character inside another character — as "Huxley Bishop," to distinguish him from the famous boy hero of earlier adventures, but any reader's mind would still go to Huck Finn.

44 Mark Twain, "Three Thousand Years among the Microbes," in John S. Tuckey, ed., *The Devil's Race-Track: Mark Twain's "Great Dark" Writings* (Berkeley: University of California Press, 2005), p. 162.

11. THE MAN WHO BLEW THINGS UP

1 Beverley Zabriskie, "Jung and Pauli: A Meeting of Rare Minds," in *Atom and Archetype: The Pauli/Jung Letters, 1932–1958*, ed. C. A. Meier, trans. David Roscoe (Princeton, NJ: Princeton University Press, 2001), p. xxviii.

2 Laurens Van der Post, *Jung and the Story of Our Time* (New York: Vintage Books, 1977), p. 94.

3 C. G. Jung, *Memories, Dreams, Reflections*, ed. Aniela Jaffé (New York: Vintage, 1965), p. 206.

4 Paul Hoffmann, *The Viennese: Splendor, Twilight, and Exile* (New York: Doubleday, 1988), p. 1.

5 R. E. Peierls, "Wolfgang Ernest Pauli, 1900–1958," *Biographical Memoirs of Fellows of the Royal Society* 5 (February 1960): 174.

6 David Lindorff, *Pauli and Jung: The Meeting of Two Great Minds* (Wheaton, IL: Quest Books, 2004), p. 11.

7 Quotation from Wolfgang Pauli, *Writings on Physics and Philosophy* (New York: Springer Verlag, 1992), p. 18.

8 The date of this incident is not known. Jung described it in a letter to J. B. Rhine in November 1945, citing it as an example of "the synchronicity of archetypal events." C. G. Jung, *Letters*, ed. Gerhard Adler and Aniela Jaffé, trans. R. F. C. Hull (Princeton, NJ: Princeton University Press, 1973), 1:395.

9 Jung, "Synchronicity," in *Collected Works* (hereafter CW), vol. 8, par. 844.

10 Jung, *Memories, Dreams, Reflections*, p. 123. Jung's brief reference to this case was the inspiration for Morris West's novel *The World is Made of Glass*.

11 Jung, "The Tavistock Lectures: On the Theory and Practice of Analytical Psychology," in CW 18, par. 402.

12 Jung, "Individual Dream Symbolism in Relation to Alchemy," in CW 12, par. 117.

13 Jung, CW 12, par. 262.

14 Jung, "House of the Gathering," in CW 12, par. 293.

15 Jung, *Memories, Dreams, Reflections*, pp. 39–40.

16 Jung, "World Clock," in CW 12, par. 307.

17 Pauli to Emma Jung, November 16, 1950, in C. A. Meier, ed., *Atom and Archetype: The Pauli/Jung Letters, 1932–1958*, trans. David Roscoe (Princeton, NJ: Princeton University Press, 2001), pp. 52–53.

18 Pauli, "Statements by the Psyche," in Meier, *Atom and Archetype*, p. 134.

19 Meier, *Atom and Archetype*, p. 122.

20 Herbert van Erkelens, "Wolfgang Pauli's Dialogue with the Spirit of Matter," *Psychological Perspectives*, no. 24 (1991): 38.

21 Jung, CW 8, par. 77.

22 Jung, *Letters*, 1:201.

23 Richard Wilhelm and Cary F. Baynes, trans., *The I Ching, or Book of Changes* (Princeton, NJ: Princeton University Press, 1990), p. 197.

24 Peierls, "Wolfgang Ernest Pauli," p. 185.

25 Maier, prefatory material in *Atom and Archetype*.

26 Lindorff, *Pauli and Jung*, p. 13.

27 Charles Enz, *No Time to Be Brief: A Scientific Biography of Wolfgang Pauli* (New York: Oxford University Press, 2002), p. 150.

28 Peierls, "Wolfgang Ernest Pauli," p. 185.

29 Albertus Magnus [attr.], *De mirabilibus*. Found by Jung in the Zentralbibliothek, Zurich. Quoted in Jung, "Synchronicity," in CW 8, par. 859.

30 Suzanne Gieser, *The Innermost Kernel: Depth Psychology and Quantum Physics* (Berlin: Springer Verlag, 2005), p. 21.

31 Jung, *Memories, Dreams, Reflections*, pp. 289–290.

32 Barbara Hannah, *Jung, His Life and Work: A Biographical Memoir* (Boston: Shambhala, 1991), p. 278.

33 Jung, *Memories, Dreams, Reflections*, p. 297.

34 Broadcast talk, 1946; published as an introduction in Jung, *Essays on Contemporary Events*, trans. R. F. C. Hull (Princeton, NJ: Princeton University Press, 1989), p. 1.

35 Ibid., p. 2.

36 Ibid., pp. 15–16.

37 Pauli dream of December 1947 in the archive of Aniela Jaffé at the Federal Polytechnic Institute, Zurich. Translation in van Erkelens, "Wolfgang Pauli's Dialogue with the Spirit of Matter," pp. 36–37.

38 Van Erkelens, "Wolfgang Pauli's Dialogue," p. 39.

39 Ibid., p. 40.

40 Ibid., pp. 47–52.

41 Marie-Louise von Franz, *C. G. Jung: His Myth in Our Time* (New York: G. P. Putnam's Sons, 1975).

42 Gieser, *Innermost Kernel*, p. 274.

43 Jung, CW 15, par. 81.

44 Meier, *Atom and Archetype*, p. 44.

45 Ibid., p. 69.

46 Ibid., p. 44.

47 Ibid., p. 53.

48 Werner Heisenberg, *Across the Frontiers*, trans. Peter Heath (New York: Harper, 1974), pp. 35–36.

49 Zabriskie, "Jung and Pauli," p. xxxix.

50 Meier, *Atom and Archetype*, p. 88.

51 Ibid., p. 91.

52 Ibid., p. 89.

53 Ibid., p. 162.

54 "Afterward (January 1955), I dreamed that 'the Chinese woman had a child' but 'the people' refused to acknowledge it." Ibid., p. 163.

55 Andrzej K. Wroblewski, "The Downfall of Parity — the Revolution that Happened Fifty Years Ago," *Acta Physica Polonica* 39, no. 2 (2008): 257.

56 Ed Regis, *Who Got Einstein's Office?* (Cambridge, MA: Perseus Publishing, 1987), p. 196.

57   Meier, *Atom and Archetype*, p. 168.

58   Krishna Myneni, "Symmetry Destroyed: The Failure of Parity" (1984), online at http://ccreweb. org/documents/parity/parity.html#Madame%20Wu.

59   Jung, "Two Kinds of Thinking," in CW 5, par. 7.

60   Ibid.

61   Jung, *Letters*, 1:460–461.

62   To answer this question, it would be necessary to examine the mine of unpublished Pauli correspondence and papers in the archives of CERN (European Organization for Nuclear Research) and the Federal Polytechnic Institute, Zurich, from an angle different from that of investigators who have focused on Pauli's science or the Jungian approach.

63   G. E. Brown and Chang-Hwan Lee, eds., *Hans Bethe and His Physics* (Singapore: World Scientific, 2006), pp. 107–108.

64   Jung, *Letters*, 2:584.

65   Hannah, *Jung, His Life and Work*, p. 329.

66   Ibid., p. 344.

67   Ibid., p. 348.

68   Miguel Serrano, *C. G. Jung and Hermann Hesse: A Record of Two Friendships* (New York: Schocken Books, 1966), pp. 105–106.

69   Jung, *Memories, Dreams, Reflections*, p. 314.

12. WINSTON CHURCHILL'S TIME MACHINES

1   "The Dream," was first published in the *Sunday Telegraph*, January 30, 1966. It was reprinted in *The Collected Essays of Sir Winston Churchill*, ed. Michael Wolff (London: Library of Imperial History, 1976), 4:504–11. A handsome stand-alone edition was published in 2005 by Levenger Press.

2   Randolph Churchill, "How He Came to Write It," *Sunday Telegraph*, January 30, 1966.

3   Lord [Charles] Moran, *Churchill: Taken from the Diaries of Lord Moran* (Boston: Houghton Mifflin, 1966), p. 723.

4   *The Dream* (Delray Beach, FL: Levenger Press, 2005), p. 47.

5   A. G. Gardiner, *Pillars of Society* (London: James Nisbert, 1913), p. 63.

6   Paul Addison, "The Three Careers of Winston Churchill," *Transactions of the Royal Historical Society* 11 (2001): 184.

7   Winston Churchill, "If Lee Had Not Won the Battle of Gettysburg" (1930), in *The Great Republic* (New York: Random House, 1999), p. 247.

8   Winston Churchill, "Mass Effects in Modern Life," in *Thoughts and Adventures* (1932; reprint, London: Odhams Press, 1949), p. 192.

9   Winston Churchill, *My Early Life* (1930; reprint, New York: Charles Scribner's Sons, 1987), p. 252.

10   Ibid., p. 257.

11   Ibid., p. 254.

12   Ibid., p. 255.

13   Winston Churchill, "A Second Chance," in *Thoughts and Adventures* (1932; reprint, London: Odhams Press, 1949).

14 Winston Churchill, "In the Air," in *Thoughts and Adventures* (1932; reprint, London: Odhams Press, 1949), pp. 135–136.

15 Robert Moss, *The Three "Only" Things* (Novato, CA: New World Library, 2007), pp. 89–92.

16 Churchill, "In the Air," p. 135.

17 John Lukacs, *Five Days in London: May 1940* (New Haven, CT: Yale University Press, 2001), p. 24, quoting General Pownall.

18 Churchill, *Thoughts and Adventures*, p. 5.

19 Hugh Trevor-Roper, "History and Imagination," *Times Literary Supplement*, July 25, 1980, pp. 333–335.

20 J. H. Plumb, "Churchill the Historian," in *Churchill Revised: A Critical Assessment*, ed. A. J. P. Taylor et al. (New York: Dial Press, 1969), pp. 133–169; Isaiah Berlin, *Mr. Churchill in 1940* (Boston: Houghton Mifflin, 1949), p. 12.

21 Winston Churchill, *Marlborough, His Life and Times* (London: Sphere, 1987), 2:270.

22 Ibid., 3:94.

23 Ibid., page number not available.

24 Churchill-Eisenhower conversation on January 5, 1953, reported in John ("Jock") Colville, *The Fringes of Power* (Guilford, CT: Lyons Press, 2002), p. 660.

25 John Lukacs, *Churchill: Visionary. Statesman. Historian* (New Haven, CT: Yale University Press, 2002), p. 106.

26 David Reynolds, *In Command of History: Churchill Fighting and Writing the Second World War* (New York: Random House, 2005).

27 Douglas S. Russell, "Lt. Churchill: 4th Queen's Own Hussars," *Proceedings of the International Churchill Societies* (1994–95); the school friend was Murland Evans.

28 Churchill, *Thoughts and Adventures*, p. 189.

29 Ibid., p. 209.

30 Churchill's speech warning against Wahhabi fundamentalism was delivered to the House of Commons on June 14, 1921.

31 Churchill, *Thoughts and Adventures*, p. 184.

32 Ibid., p. 187.

33 Ibid., p. 213.

34 Winston Churchill, "Moses," in *Thoughts and Adventures* (1932; reprint, London: Odhams Press, 1949), p. 219.

35 Desmond Morton was born at 9 Hyde Park Gate in the house that was later Churchill's London home. He purchased a country estate (Earlylands) three miles from Churchill's beloved Chartwell within a year of the Churchills' moving in. Despite a careful recent biography, his role in the Churchill adventure has yet to be fully disinterred; see Gill Bennett, *Churchill's Man of Mystery: Desmond Morton and the World of Intelligence* (London: Routledge, 2007).

36 Sarah Cassidy, "Churchill Borrowed Famous Lines from Books by H. G. Wells," *The Independent*, November 27, 2006.

37 When he moved to the United States, Szilard made it his cause to mobilize the Roosevelt administration to get ahead of the Nazis in the race to produce nuclear weapons — a race people in Washington did not realize was under way — and recruited Einstein to

cosign the famous letter that led to the Manhattan Project. Ironically, Szilard later lobbied passionately, humanist that he was, against the use of the atomic bomb on humans (as opposed to a demo on an unpopulated atoll). One of his last works was a visionary fable in which the dolphins — presented as a species wiser than humans — try to educate humans about their responsibilities to each other and the planet.

38   Randolph S. Churchill, *Winston S. Churchill* (London: Heinemann, 1966), 1:212.

39   Lord [Charles] Moran, *Churchill: The Struggle for Survival* (London: Constable, 1966), p. 776.

40   Ibid., p. 778.

41   Anthony Storr, "Churchill the Man," in *Churchill's Black Dog, Kafka's Mice, and Other Phenomena of the Human Mind* (New York: Ballantine Books, 1990), p. 27.

42   Ibid., p. 49.

43   Anthony Storr, "Sanity of True Genius," in *Churchill's Black Dog, Kafka's Mice, and Other Phenomena of the Human Mind* (New York: Ballantine Books, 1990), p. 264.

44   Lukacs, *Churchill*, p. 2.

45   Churchill's "Finest Hour" speech was delivered to the House of Commons and then broadcast, on June 18, 1940.

46   Colville, *Fringes of Power*, p. 385.

47   Ibid., p. 386.

48   Ibid., p. 387.

49   Ibid.

50   David Stafford, *Churchill and Secret Service* (Woodstock: Overlook Press, 1997), p. 219.

51   See Anthony Masters, *The Man Who Was M: The Life of Charles Henry Maxwell Knight* (Oxford: Basil Blackwell, 1987).

52   Winston Churchill, *The Gathering Storm* (Cambridge, MA: Houghton Mifflin, 1948), pp. 522–523.

53   Ibid., p. 325.

54   Colville, *Fringes of Power*, p. 231.

55   Moran, *Churchill: Taken from the Diaries*, p. 395.

56   Ibid., p. 420.

57   Ibid., p. 429.

58   Ibid., p. 496.

59   Ibid.

60   Ibid., p. 501.

61   Ibid., p. 723. Sir Edward Grey was British foreign minister from 1906 to 1915.

62   Ibid., pp. 723–724.

63   Colville, *Fringes of Power*, p. 658.

64   Sarah Churchill, *A Thread in the Tapestry* (London: Andre Deutsch, 1967), p. 17.

65   Winston Churchill, "Hobbies," in *Thoughts and Adventures* (1932; reprint, London: Odhams Press, 1949), p. 228.

66   Winston Churchill, "Painting as a Pastime," in *Thoughts and Adventures* (1932; reprint, London: Odhams Press, 1949), p. 234.

67   Ibid., p. 240.

68   Colville, *Fringes of Power*, p. 128.

69   December 7, 1947; Moran, *Churchill: Taken from the Diaries*, p. 352.

EPILOGUE

1 Diego de Durán, *The Aztecs: The History of the Indies of New Spain*, trans. Doris Heyden and Fernanda Horcasitas (New York: Orion Press, 1964), p. 246.

2 Ibid., pp. 247–271.

3 Motolinia, "Carta de Chihuahua" (1554), quoted in Tzvetan Todorov, *The Conquest of America*, trans. Richard Howard (New York: Harper & Row, 1984), p. 64.

4 Todorov, *Conquest of America*, p. 77.

5 Candace Pert interview, in Bill Moyers, *Healing and the Mind* (New York: Doubleday, 1993).

6 Larry Dossey, MD, personal communication.

7 Candace Pert, *Molecules of Emotion: Why You Feel the Way You Feel* (New York: Scribner, 1997), p. 190.

8 Raúl de la Fuente-Fernández et al., "Expectation and Dopamine Release: Mechanism of the Placebo Effect in Parkinson's Disease," *Science* 293, no. 5332 (August 10, 2001): 1164–1166.

9 *Baltimore Sun*, December 6, 2006.

10 Alun Anderson, "Physician, Fool Thyself," *Fortune* (September 18, 2006).

11 Patrick Lemoine interview in Laura Spinney, "Purveyors of Mystery," *New Scientist*, no. 2582 (December 16, 2006).

12 Herbert Benson, MD, personal communication.

13 Lyn Freeman, personal communication.

14 Jeanne Achterberg, Barbara Dossey, and Leslie Kolkmeier, *Rituals of Healing: Using Imagery for Health and Wellness* (New York: Bantam Books, 1994).

15 Deborah Schwab et al., "A Study of Efficacy and Cost-Effectiveness of Guided Imagery as a Portable, Self-Administered, Presurgical Intervention Delivered by a Health Plan," *Advances in Mind-Body Medicine* 22, no. 1 (Summer 2007).

16 See Robert Moss, *The Three "Only" Things* (Novato, CA: New World Library, 2007), pp. 82–94.

17 Ibid., pp. 201–208.

18 Mark Twain, *Christian Science* (New York: Harper & Bros., 1907), p. 51.

19 John Lukacs, *The Duel: The Eighty-Day Struggle between Churchill and Hitler* (New Haven: Yale University Press, 2001).

20 The full text of the interview with Manda Scott is online at www.mossdreams.com.

21 Vishvajit Pandya, "Forest Smells and Spider Webs: Ritualized Dream Interpretation among Andaman Islanders," *Dreaming* 14, nos. 2–3 (June–September 2004): 136–150.

BIBLIOGRAPHY

Achterberg, Jeanne. *Imagery in Healing: Shamanism and Modern Medicine*. Boston: Shambhala, 1985.

Achterberg, Jeanne, with Barbara Dossey and Leslie Kolkmeier. *Rituals of Healing: Using Imagery for Health and Wellness*. New York: Bantam Books, 1994.

Adamnan. *Life of Saint Columba, Founder of Hy*. Llanerch, Wales: Llanerch Enterprises, 1988.

Adams, John, and Abigail Adams. *Letters of John and Abigail Adams*. Ed. William J. Bennett. Rochester, NY: Westvaco Corporation, 2001.

Addison, Paul. "The Three Careers of Winston Churchill." *Transactions of the Royal Historical Society* 11 (2001): 183–199.

Alkon, Paul L. *Winston Churchill's Imagination*. Lewisburg, PA: Bucknell University Press, 2006.

Andrews, William L., ed. *Sisters of the Spirit: Three Black Women's Autobiographies of the Nineteenth Century*. Bloomington: Indiana University Press, 1986.

Arden, Harvey. *Dreamkeepers: A Spirit-Journey into Aboriginal Australia*. New York: HarperCollins, 1994.

Aristides, P. Aelius. *Complete Works*. Trans. Charles A. Behr. 2 vols. Leiden, Netherlands: E. J. Brill, 1981.

Arrian. *Anabasis of Alexander*. Trans. E. J. Chinook. 1893. Online at www.alexander-sources .org.

Artemidorus of Daldis. *Oneirocritica: The Interpretation of Dreams*. Trans. Robert J. White. Torrance, CA: Original Books, 1990.

As I Crossed a Bridge of Dreams: Recollections of a Woman in Eleventh-Century Japan. Trans. Ivan Morris. London: Penguin, 1975.

Augustine. *Confessions*. Trans. R. S. Pine-Coffin. London: Penguin Books, 1961.

Ball, Philip. *The Devil's Doctor: Paracelsus and the World of Renaissance Magic and Science*. New York: Farrar, Straus and Giroux, 2006.

Barfield, Owen. *Poetic Diction: A Study in Meaning*. Middletown, CT: Wesleyan University Press, 1973.

Barker, Juliet. *The Brontës*. New York: St. Martin's Press, 1995.

Barrett, Deirdre. *The Committee of Sleep*. New York: Crown, 2001.

———. "In Dreams Begin Technologies." *Invention and Technology Magazine* 17, no. 2 (Fall 2001).

Barrett, Deirdre, and Patrick McNamara, eds. *The New Science of Dreaming*. 3 vols. Westport, CT: Praeger, 2007.

Bascom, William R. "The Relationship of Yoruba Folklore to Divining." *Journal of American Folklore* 56, no. 220 (April–June 1943): 127–131.

———. "The Sanctions of Ifa Divination." *Journal of the Royal Anthropological Institute* 71, nos. 1–2 (1941): 43–54.

Beard, Mary, John North, and Simon Price. *Religions of Rome.* 2 vols. Cambridge: Cambridge University Press, 2006.

Becker, Raymond de. *The Understanding of Dreams and Their Influence on the History of Man.* New York: Bell, 1968.

Beckwith, Martha. *Hawaiian Mythology.* 1940. Reprint, Honolulu: University of Hawaii Press, 1976.

Béguin, Albert. *L'Ame Romantique et le Rêve: Essai sur le Romantisme Allemand et la Poésie Française.* Paris: Librairie José Corti, 1960.

Bennett, Gill. *Churchill's Man of Mystery: Desmond Morton and the World of Intelligence.* London: Routledge, 2007.

Beradt, Charlotte. *The Third Reich of Dreams.* Trans. Adriane Gottwald. Chicago: Quadrangle Books, 1966.

Berkun, Scott. *The Myths of Innovation.* Sebastopol, CA: O'Reilly, 2007.

Berlin, Isaiah. *Mr. Churchill in 1940.* Boston: Houghton Mifflin, 1949.

Berndt, Ronald M., and Catherine H. Berndt. *The Speaking Land: Myth and Story in Aboriginal Australia.* Rochester, VT: Inner Traditions, 1994.

Binger, Carl A. L. "The Dreams of Benjamin Rush." *American Journal of Psychiatry* 125, no. 12 (June 1969): 1653–1659.

Bogoras, Waldemar. "Ideas of Space and Time in the Conception of Primitive Religion." *American Anthropologist,* n.s., 27, no. 2 (April 1925): 205–266.

Borges, Jorge Luis. *Labyrinths.* New York: New Directions, 1964.

———. *Other Inquisitions, 1937–1952.* Trans. Ruth L. C. Simmons. London: Souvenir Press, 1973.

Borges, Jorge Luis, with Silvina Ocampo and A. Bioy Casares, eds. *The Book of Fantasy.* New York: Viking, 1988.

Boss, Medard. *The Analysis of Dreams.* New York: Philosophical Library, 1958.

Bradford, Sarah H. *Harriet, the Moses of Her People.* New York: George R. Lockwood & Son, 1886.

———. *Scenes in the Life of Harriet Tubman.* Auburn, NY: W. J. Moses, 1869.

Breger, Louis. *Freud: Darkness in the Midst of Vision.* New York: John Wiley & Sons, 2000.

Bregman, Jay. *Synesius of Cyrene, Philosopher-Bishop.* Berkeley: University of California Press, 1982.

Brenk, Frederick E. *In Mist Apparelled: Religious Themes in Plutarch's Moralia and Lives.* Leiden, Netherlands: E. J. Brill, 1977.

———. "In the Light of the Moon: Demonology in the Early Imperial Period." *Aufstieg und Niedergang der römischen Welt* 16, no. 3 (1986): 2068–2145.

Brown, Michael F. "Ropes of Sand: Order and Imagery in Aguaruna Dreams." In *Dreaming: Anthropological and Psychological Interpretations,* ed. Barbara Tedlock, pp. 154–170. Santa Fe, NM: School of American Research Press, 1992.

Brown, Peter. *The Making of Late Antiquity.* Cambridge, MA: Harvard University Press, 1978.

Budge, E. A. Wallis. *Osiris: The Egyptian Religion of Resurrection*. New Hyde Park, NY: University Books, 1961.

Bulkeley, Kelly. "Sacred Sleep: Contributions to the Study of Religiously Significant Dreaming." In *The New Science of Dreaming*, ed. Deirdre Barrett and Patrick McNamara, 3:71–94. Westport, CT: Praeger, 2007.

———. *The Wilderness of Dreams: Exploring the Religious Meanings of Dreams in Modern Western Culture*. Albany: State University of New York Press, 1994.

Burch, Wanda Easter. *She Who Dreams: A Journey into Healing through Dreamwork*. Novato, CA: New World Library, 2003.

Burkert, Walter. *Ancient Mystery Cults*. Cambridge, MA: Harvard University Press, 1987.

Busch, Briton Cooper. "Divine Intervention in the *Muqaddimah* of Ibn Khaldūn." *History of Religions* 7, no. 4 (May 1968): 317–329.

Caillois, Roger, ed. *The Dream Adventure*. New York: Orion Press, 1963.

Calaprice, Alice, and Trevor Lipscombe. *Albert Einstein: A Biography*. Westport, CT: Greenwood Press, 2005.

Calderón de la Barca, Pedro. *La vida es sueño*. Madrid: Espasa-Calpe, 1969.

Campbell, Joseph. *The Way of the Animal Powers*. San Francisco: Alfred van der Marck/Harper & Row, 1983.

Carrington, Dorothy. *The Dream-Hunters of Corsica*. London: Weidenfeld & Nicolson, 1995.

Cashford, Jules. *The Moon: Myth and Image*. New York: Four Walls Eight Windows, 2003.

Castronova, Edward. *Synthetic Worlds: The Business and Culture of Online Games*. Chicago: University of Chicago Press, 2005.

Chauveau, Michel. *Egypt in the Age of Cleopatra*. Trans. David Lorton. Ithaca, NY: Cornell University Press, 2000.

Chittick, William C. *The Sufi Path of Knowledge: Ibn al-'Arabi's Metaphysics of Imagination*. Albany: State University of New York Press, 1989.

Churchill, Winston S. *The Dream*. Delray Beach, FL: Levenger Press, 2005.

———. *The Gathering Storm*. Cambridge, MA: Houghton Mifflin, 1948.

———. "If Lee Had Not Won the Battle of Gettysburg" (1930). In *The Great Republic*, ed. Winston S. Churchill, pp. 246–256. New York: Random House, 1999.

———. *Marlborough, His Life and Times*. 4 vols. London: Sphere, 1987.

———. *My Early Life*. 1930. Reprint, New York: Charles Scribner's Sons, 1987.

———. *Thoughts and Adventures*. 1932. Reprint, London: Odhams Press, 1949.

———. *The World Crisis, 1911–1918*. 2 vols. London: Odhams Press, 1938.

Civrieux, Marc de. *Watunna: An Orinoco Creation Cycle*. Trans. David M. Guss. San Francisco: North Point Press, 1980.

Clarke, J. D. "Ifa Divination." *Journal of the Royal Anthropological Institute* 69, no. 2 (1939): 235–256.

Clinton, Catherine. *Harriet Tubman: The Road to Freedom*. New York: Little, Brown, 2004.

Cloetta, Yvonne. *In Search of a Beginning: My Life with Graham Greene*. As told to Marie-Francoise Allain. Trans. Euan Cameron. London: Bloomsbury, 2004.

Colville, John. *The Fringes of Power*. Guilford, CT: Lyons Press, 2002.

Connor, Nancy, and Bradford Keeney, eds. *Shamans of the World*. Boulder, CO: Sounds True, 2008.

Cooper, Andrew. *Playing in the Zone: Exploring the Spiritual Dimensions of Sports.* Boston: Shambhala, 1998.

Cooper, Jerrold S., and Wolfgang Heimpel. "The Sumerian Sargon Legend." *Journal of the American Oriental Society* 103 (1983): 67–82.

Corbin, Henry. *Avicenna and the Visionary Recital.* Trans. Willard R. Trask. Princeton, NJ: Bollingen, 1990.

———. *Creative Imagination in the Sufism of Ibn 'Arabi.* Trans. Ralph Mannheim. Princeton, NJ: Bollingen, 1981.

———. *Spiritual Body and Celestial Earth.* Trans. Nancy Pearson. Princeton, NJ: Bollingen, 1989.

———. *Swedenborg and Esoteric Islam.* Trans. Leonard Fox. West Chester, PA: Swedenborg Foundation, 1995.

Couliano, I. P. *Out of This World: Otherworld Journeys from Gilgamesh to Einstein.* Boston: Shambhala, 1991.

Covitz, Joel. *Visions of the Night: A Study of Jewish Dream Interpretation.* Boston: Shambhala, 1990.

Cowan, James. *Letters from a Wild State.* Shaftesbury, Dorset: Element, 1991.

Csikszentmihalyi, Mihaly. *Creativity: Flow and the Psychology of Discovery and Invention.* New York: HarperCollins, 1996.

———. *Flow: The Psychology of Optimal Experience.* New York: Harper & Row, 1990.

Curti, Merle. "The American Exploration of Dreams and Dreamers." *Journal of the History of Ideas* 27, no. 3 (July–September 1966): 391–416.

Dante Alighieri. *Divine Comedy.* Bilingual ed. Trans. John D. Sinclair. 3 vols. New York: Oxford University Press, 1961.

———. *Purgatorio.* Trans W. S. Merwin. New York: Alfred A. Knopf, 2000.

Davidson, H. R. Ellis. *Gods and Myths of the Viking Age.* New York: Barnes & Noble Books, 1996.

———. *Myths and Symbols of Pagan Europe.* Manchester, England: Manchester University Press, 1988.

Davis, Patricia M. "Dreams and Visions in the Anglo-Saxon Conversion to Christianity." *Dreaming* 12, no. 2 (June 2005): 75–88.

Delaney, Gayle. *Sexual Dreams.* New York: Fawcett Columbine, 1994.

Dentan, Robert Knox. "Butterflies and Big Hunters: Reality and Dreams, Dreams and Reality." *Psychiatric Journal of the University of Ottawa* 13, no. 2 (1988): 51–59.

Devries, Kelly. *Joan of Arc, a Military Leader.* Stroud, England: Sutton Publishing, 2003.

Dickson, Harold R. P. *The Arab of the Desert.* London: George Allen and Unwin, 1949.

———. *Kuwait and Her Neighbors.* London: George Allen and Unwin, 1956.

Dickson, Violet. *Forty Years in Kuwait.* London: George Allen and Unwin, 1971.

Dodds, E. R. *The Greeks and the Irrational.* Berkeley: University of California Press, 1951.

———. *Pagan and Christian in an Age of Anxiety: Some Aspects of Religious Experience from Marcus Aurelius to Constantine.* Cambridge: Cambridge University Press, 1965.

Dossey, Larry. *Reinventing Medicine: Beyond Mind-Body to a New Era of Healing.* San Francisco: HarperSanFrancisco, 1999.

Dunne, J. W. *An Experiment with Time.* London: Faber and Faber, 1934.

the SECRET HISTORY of DREAMING

————. *Intrusions?* London: Faber and Faber, 1955.

————. *The Serial Universe.* New York: Macmillan, 1938.

Duprez, Antoine. *Jésus et les dieux guérisseurs: A propos de Jean, V.* Paris: Gabalda, 1970.

Durán, Diego de. *The Aztecs: The History of the Indies of New Spain.* Trans. Doris Heyden and Fernanda Horcasitas. New York: Orion Press, 1964.

Durrant, Stephen W. "The Nišan Shaman Caught in Cultural Contradiction." *Signs* 5, no. 2 (Winter 1979): 338–347.

Edelstein, Emma J., and Ludwig Edelstein. *Asclepius: Collection and Interpretation of the Testimonies.* Baltimore: Johns Hopkins University Press, 1998.

Edgar, Iain. "Comparison of Islamic Dream Theory and Western Psychological Theories of the Dream." In *Dreaming in Christianity and Islam: Culture, Conflict, and Creativity*, ed. Kelly Bulkeley and Kate Adams. Piscataway, NJ: Rutgers University Press, forthcoming.

————. *Guide to Imagework.* London: Routledge, 2004.

Eitrem, Samson. "Dreams and Divination in Magical Ritual." In *Magika Hiera: Ancient Greek Magic and Religion*, ed. Christopher A. Faraone and Dirk Obbink, pp. 175–187. New York: Oxford University Press, 1991.

Ekirch, A. Roger. "Sleep We Have Lost: Pre-Industrial Slumber in the British Isles." *American Historical Review* 106, no. 2 (April 2001): 343–386.

Eliade, Mircea. *Myths, Dreams, and Mysteries.* Trans. Philip Mairet. New York: Harper Torchbooks, 1960.

————. *Shamanism: Archaic Techniques of Ecstasy.* Princeton, NJ: Princeton University Press, 1974.

————. *Yoga: Immortality and Freedom.* Trans. Willard R. Trask. Princeton, NJ: Princeton University Press, 1973.

Elkin, A. P. *Aboriginal Men of High Degree.* New York: St. Martin's Press, 1978.

Enz, Charles. *No Time to Be Brief: A Scientific Biography of Wolfgang Pauli.* New York: Oxford University Press, 2002.

Eusebius of Caesarea. *The Life of the Blessed Emperor Constantine*, in P. Schaff and H. Wace, eds., *Nicene and Post-Nicene Fathers.* Grand Rapids: Eerdmans, 1955.

Evans-Wentz, W. Y. *The Fairy Faith in Celtic Countries.* New York: Citadel, 1990.

————. *The Tibetan Book of the Dead.* London: Oxford University Press, 1990.

————. *Tibetan Yoga and Secret Doctrines.* London: Oxford University Press, 1967.

Faraone, Christopher A., and Dirk Obbink, eds. *Magika Hiera: Ancient Greek Magic and Religion.* New York: Oxford University Press, 1997.

Faulkner, R. O. *The Ancient Egyptian Pyramid Texts.* Oxford: Oxford University Press, 1969.

FitzGerald, Augustine, ed. and trans. *The Essays and Hymns of Synesius of Cyrene.* 2 vols. Oxford: Oxford University Press, 1930.

Ford, Patrick K., trans. and ed. *The Mabinogi and other Medieval Welsh Tales.* Berkeley: University of California Press, 1977.

Forrester, John. *Dispatches from the Freud Wars: Psychoanalysis and Its Passions.* Cambridge, MA: Harvard University Press, 1997.

Fortune, Dion. *The Magical Battle of Britain.* Bradford-on-Avon, England: Golden Gates, 1993.

Freud, Sigmund. *The Interpretation of Dreams.* Trans. John Strachey. 1899–1900. Reprint, New York: Avon, 1965.

————. *Leonardo da Vinci and a Memory of His Childhood*. Trans. Alan Tyson. 1910. Reprint, New York: Norton, 1989.

Gaiman, Neil. *Adventures in the Dream Trade*. Framingham, MA: NEFSA Press, 2002.

Galan, José M. "The Ancient Egyptian Sed-Festival and the Exemption from Corvée." *Journal of Near Eastern Studies* 59, no. 4 (October 2000): 255–264.

Galen. *Three Treatises on the Nature of Science*. Trans. Richard Walzer and Michael Frede. Indianapolis: Hakket, 1985.

George, Marianne. "Dreams, Reality, and the Desire and Intent of Dreamers as Experienced by a Fieldworker." *Anthropology of Consciousness* 6, no. 3 (1995): 17–33.

Gieser, Suzanne. *The Innermost Kernel: Depth Psychology and Quantum Physics*. Berlin: Springer Verlag, 2005.

Gilbert, Adrian G. *Magi: The Quest for a Secret Tradition*. London: Bloomsbury, 1996.

Gilbert, Martin. *Churchill: A Life*. New York: Henry Holt, 1991.

Giles, Cynthia. *The Tarot: History, Mystery, and Lore*. New York: Simon and Schuster, 1994.

Ginzberg, Louis. *The Legends of the Jews*. 7 vols. Baltimore: Johns Hopkins University Press, 1998.

Giskin, Howard. "Dreaming the Seven-Colored Flower: Eastern and Western Approaches to Dreams in Chinese Literature." *Asian Folklore Studies* 63 (2004): 79–94.

Gogol, Nikolai. *The Collected Tales of Nikolai Gogol*. Trans. Richard Pevear and Larissa Volokhonsky. New York: Vintage, 1999.

Gollnick, James. *The Religious Dreamworld of Apuleius' Metamorphoses*. Waterloo, Ontario: Wilfred Laurier University Press, 1999.

Gottesmann, Claude. "A Neurobiological History of Dreaming." In *The New Science of Dreaming*, ed. Deirdre Barrett and Patrick McNamara, 1:1–52. Westport, CT: Praeger, 2007.

Grant, Joan. *Winged Pharaoh*. Columbus, OH: Ariel Press, 1986.

Green, Miranda. *Celtic Goddesses: Warriors, Virgins, and Mothers*. New York: George Braziller, 1996.

Greene, Graham. *A Burnt-Out Case*. London: William Heinemann, 1960.

————. *The Confidential Agent*. London: Heineman, 1954.

————. *A Sort of Life*. New York: Simon and Schuster, 1971.

————. *Ways of Escape*. 1980. Reprint, Harmondsworth: Penguin Books, 1982.

————. *A World of My Own: A Dream Diary*. London: Reinhardt Books/Penguin, 1992.

Grushin, Olga. *The Dream Life of Sukhanov*. New York: Penguin Books, 2005.

Guss, David M. *Language of the Birds: Tales, Text, and Poems of Interspecies Communication*. San Francisco: North Point Press, 1985.

Hallowell, Irving A. *Culture and Experience*. Philadelphia: University of Pennsylvania Press, 1955.

Hannah, Barbara. *Jung, His Life and Work: A Biographical Memoir*. Boston: Shambhala, 1991.

Harper, George Mills, et al., eds. *Yeats's "Vision" Papers, Volume 3: Sleep and Dream Notebooks, "Vision" Notebooks 1 and 2, Card File*. Iowa City: University of Iowa Press, 1992.

Harrison, Jane Ellen. *Epilegomena to the Study of Greek Religion*. 1921. Reprint, New Hyde Park, NY: University Books, 1966.

————. *Prolegomena to the Study of Greek Religion*. 1903. Reprint. London: Merlin Press, 1980.

Harrison, S. J. "Apuleius, Aelius Aristides, and Religious Autobiography." *Ancient Narrative* 1 (2000–2001): 245–259.

Hartmann, Ernest. "Making Connections in a Safe Place: Is Dreaming Psychotherapy?" *Dreaming* 5 (1995): 213–238.

Hazarika, Anjali. *Daring to Dream: Cultivating Corporate Creativity through Dreamwork.* New Delhi: Response Books, 1997.

Hermansen, Marcia. "Dreams and Dreaming in Islam." In *Dreams: A Reader in the Religious, Cultural, and Psychological Dimensions of Dreaming*, ed. Kelly Bulkeley, pp. 73–92. New York: Palgrave, 2001.

Hersh, Thomas R. "How Might We Explain the Parallels between Freud's 1895 Irma Dream and His 1923 Cancer?" *Dreaming* 5, no. 4 (December 1995): 267–287.

Heschel, Abraham J. *The Prophets.* New York: Harper & Row, 1969.

Hewitt, J. N. B. "The Iroquoian Concept of the Soul." *Journal of American Folk-Lore* 8 (1895): 107–116.

Hillman, James. *The Dream and the Underworld.* New York: Harper & Row, 1979.

———, ed. *Facing the Gods.* Dallas: Spring Publications, 1988.

Hoffman, Curtis. "Dumuzi's Dream: Dream Analysis in Ancient Mesopotamia." *Dreaming* 14, no. 4 (December 2004): 240–251.

Hoffman, Valerie J. "The Role of Visions in Contemporary Egyptian Religious Life." *Religion* 27 (1997): 45–64.

Holowchak, M. Andrew. "Diagnostic Dreams in Greco-Roman Medicine." *Journal of the History of Medicine and Allied Sciences* 56 (October 2001): 382–399.

Homer. *The Iliad.* Trans. E. V. Rieu. London: Penguin Books, 1961.

———. *The Odyssey.* Trans. E. V. Rieu. London: Penguin Books, 2003.

Horowitz, Mardi Jon. *Image Formation and Cognition.* New York: Appleton-Century-Crofts, 1970.

Houston, Jean. *The Hero and the Goddess.* New York: Ballantine, 1992.

———. *The Passion of Isis and Osiris.* New York: Ballantine, 1995.

Howe, Michael J. A. *Explaining Genius.* Cambridge: Cambridge University Press, 2001.

Howells, William Dean. *My Mark Twain.* 1910. Reprint, Mineola, NY: Dover, 1997.

Hultkrantz, Åke. *Conceptions of the Soul among North American Indians.* Stockholm: Statens Etnografiska Museum, 1953.

Humez, Jean M. *Harriet Tubman: The Life and the Life Stories.* Madison, WI: University of Wisconsin Press, 2003.

———. "In Search of Harriet Tubman's Spiritual Autobiography." In *This Far by Faith: Readings in African-American Women's Religious Biography*, ed. Judith Weisenfeld and Richard Newman, pp. 239–261. New York: Routledge, 1996.

Humphrey, Caroline, with Urgunge Onon. *Shamans and Elders: Experience, Knowledge and Power among the Daur Mongols.* Oxford: Clarendon Press, 1996.

Hunt, Harry T. *The Multiplicity of Dreams.* New Haven, CT: Yale University Press, 1989.

Huson, Paul. *Mystical Origins of the Tarot.* Rochester, VT: Destiny Books, 2004.

Ibn Khaldun. *The Muqaddimah: An Introduction to History.* Trans. Franz Rosenthal, ed. N. J. Dawood. Princeton, NJ: Princeton University Press, 1967.

Jackson, Susan A., and Mihaly Csikszentmihalyi. *Flow in Sports.* Champaign, IL: Human Kinetics, 1999.

Jaffé, Aniela, ed. *C. G. Jung: Word and Image*. Trans. Krishna Winston. Princeton, NJ: Princeton University Press, 1979.

Josephus. *Jewish Antiquities*. Trans. H. St. J. Thackeray. Cambridge, MA: Harvard University Press, 1967.

————. *The Jewish War*. Trans. G. A. Williamson. London: Penguin, 1959.

Jung, C. G. *Collected Works*. Trans. R. F. C. Hull. 19 vols. Princeton, NJ: Princeton University Press, 1957–67.

————. *Essays on Contemporary Events*. Trans. R. F. C. Hull. 1947. Reprint, Princeton: Princeton University Press, 1989.

————. *Letters*. Ed. Gerhard Adler and Aniela Jaffé, trans. R. F. C. Hull. 2 vols. Princeton: Princeton University Press, 1973.

————. *Memories, Dreams, Reflections*. Ed. Aniela Jaffé. 1961. Reprint, New York: Vintage, 1965.

————. *Modern Man in Search of a Soul*. Trans. W. S. Dell and Cary F. Baynes. New York: Harcourt Brace Jovanovich, 1933.

Kagan, Richard L. *Lucrecia's Dreams: Politics and Prophecy in Sixteenth-Century Spain*. Berkeley: University of California Press, 1990.

Kakar, Sudhir. *Shamans, Mystics, and Doctors: A Psychological Inquiry into India and Its Healing Traditions*. Boston: Beacon Press, 1983.

Kalweit, Holger. *Dreamtime and Inner Space: The World of the Shaman*. Boston: Shambhala, 1988.

Kaplan, Aryeh. *Innerspace: Introduction to Kabbalah, Meditation, and Prophecy*. Ed. Abraham Sutton. Jerusalem: Moznaim, 1990.

————. *Meditation and the Bible*. York Beach, ME: Weiser, 1988.

Kaplan, Justin. *Mr. Clemens and Mark Twain*. New York: Simon & Schuster, 1966.

Karlinsky, Simon. *The Sexual Labyrinth of Nikolai Gogol*. Chicago: University of Chicago Press, 1992.

Katz, Michael R. *Dreams and the Unconscious in Nineteenth-Century Russian Fiction*. Hanover, NH: University Press of New England, 1984.

Kearns, Doris. *Lyndon Johnson and the American Dream*. New York: Harper & Row, 1976.

Kelly, Laurence. *Diplomacy and Murder in Tehran: Alexander Griboyedov and the Tsar's Mission to the Shah of Persia*. London: I. B. Tauris, 2002.

Kelsey, Morton T. *God, Dreams, and Revelation: A Christian Interpretation of Dreams*. Rev. ed. Minneapolis, MN: Augsburg, 1991.

Kennedy, Angus J., and Kenneth Varty, eds. *Ditié de Jehanne d'Arc*. Oxford: Society for the Study of Mediæval Languages and Literature, 1977. Online version at www.smu.edu/ijas/cdepisan/index.html.

Kharitidi, Olga. *Entering the Circle*. New York: HarperSanFrancisco, 1996.

Kingsley, Peter. *Ancient Philosophy, Mystery, and Magic: Empedocles and Pythagorean Tradition*. Oxford: Oxford University Press, 1995.

Kirk, Robert. *The Secret Commonwealth of Elves, Fauns, Fairies*, with commentary by Andrew Lang. 1691. Reprint, London: David Nutt, 1893.

Kirsch, James. *Reluctant Prophet: An Exploration of Prophecy and Dreams*. Los Angeles: Sherbourne Press, 1973.

Knab, T. J. *A War of Witches: A Journey into the Underworld of the Contemporary Aztecs*. New York: HarperCollins, 1995.

Koortbojian, Michael. *Myth, Memory, and Meaning on Roman Sarcophagi*. Berkeley: University of California Press, 1995.

Kracke, Waud. "Encounter with Other Cultures: Psychological and Epistemological Aspects." *Ethos* 15, no. 1 (1987): 58–81.

Krageluld, Patrick. "Dreams, Religion, and Politics in Republican Rome." *Historia* 50 (2001): 53–95.

Krippner, Stanley. "Anomalous Experiences and Dreams." In *The New Science of Dreaming*, ed. Deirdre Barrett and Patrick McNamara, 2:285–306. Westport, CT: Praeger, 2007.

Krippner, Stanley, and Laura Faith. "Exotic Dreams: A Cross-Cultural Study." *Dreaming* 11, no. 2 (June 2001): 73–82.

Krippner, Stanley, and Patrick Welch. *Spiritual Dimensions of Healing*. New York: Irvington, 1992.

Lafitau, Joseph-François. *Customs of the American Indians Compared with the Customs of Primitive Times*. Ed. and trans. William N. Fenton and Elizabeth L. Moore. 2 vols. Toronto: Champlain Society, 1974, 1977.

Lake, Medicine Grizzlybear. *Native Healer: Initiation into an Ancient Art*. Wheaton, IL: Quest Books, 1991.

Lamoreaux, John C. *The Early Muslim Tradition of Dream Interpretation*. Albany: State University of New York Press, 2002.

Lang, Andrew. *Dreams and Ghosts*. Hollywood, CA: Newcastle Publishing, 1972.

Larsen, Stephen. *The Shaman's Doorway*. Barrytown, NY: Station Hill Press, 1988.

Larson, Kate Clifford. *Bound for the Promised Land: Harriet Tubman, Portrait of an American Hero*. New York: Ballantine Books, 2004.

Lateiner, Donald. "Signifying Names and Other Ominous Accidental Utterances in Classical Historiography." *Greek, Roman, and Byzantine Studies* 45 (2006): 35–57.

Lawlor, Robert. *Voices of the First Day: Awakening in the Aboriginal Dreamtime*. Rochester, VT: Inner Traditions, 1991.

Lawrence, Lauren. *Private Dreams of Public People*. New York: Assouline, 2002.

Le Goff, Jacques. *The Birth of Purgatory*. Trans. Arthur Goldhammer. Chicago: University of Chicago Press, 1984.

———. *The Medieval Imagination*. Trans. Arthur Goldhammer. Chicago: University of Chicago Press, 1992.

Lester, Toby. "What Is the Koran?" *Atlantic Monthly* (January 1999).

Lewis, Bernard. *The Assassins: A Radical Sect in Islam*. New York: Basic Books, 2003.

Lewis, C. S. *The Discarded Image: An Introduction to Medieval and Renaissance Literature*. Cambridge: Cambridge University Press, 2003.

Lewis, Naphtali. *The Interpretation of Dreams and Portents in Antiquity*. Wauconda, IL: Bolchazy-Carducci, 1996.

LiDonnici, Lynn R. *The Epidaurian Miracle Inscriptions*. Atlanta: Scholar's Press, 1995.

Lindorff, David. *Pauli and Jung: The Meeting of Two Great Minds*. Wheaton, IL: Quest Books, 2004.

Loehle, Craig S. "A Guide to Increased Creativity in Research — Inspiration or Perspiration?" *BioScience* 40, no. 2 (1990): 123–129.

Loewe, Michael, and Carmen Blacker, eds. *Oracles and Divination*. Boulder: Shambhala, 1981.

Lohmann, Roger Ivar, ed. *Dream Travelers: Sleep Experiences and Culture in the Western Pacific*. New York: Palgrave Macmillan, 2003.

Lombard-Jourdan, Anne. *Aux origines de Carnaval*. Paris: Odile Jacob, 2005.

Long, Max Freedom. *The Secret Science behind Miracles*. Marina del Rey, CA: DeVorss, 1976.

Lowie, Robert. "Scholars as People: Dreams, Idle Dreams." *Current Anthropology* 7, no. 3 (1966): 378–382.

Lowry, Beverly. *Harriet Tubman: Imagining a Life*. New York: Doubleday, 2007.

Loyola, Ignatius. *The Spiritual Exercises*. Trans. Thomas Corbishley. Wheathampsted, England: Anthony Clarke, 1987.

Lukacs, John. *Churchill: Visionary. Statesman. Historian*. New Haven, CT: Yale University Press, 2002.

———. *The Duel: The Eighty-Day Struggle between Churchill and Hitler*. New Haven, CT: Yale University Press, 1990.

———. *Five Days in London: May 1940*. New Haven, CT: Yale University Press, 2001.

Lunenfeld, Marvin. " 'Everything Shall Become a Desert': Amerindian Premonitions of the Coming of the White Man." *Proteus* 9, no. 1 (1992): 18–25.

The Mabinogion. Trans. Jeffrey Gantz. London: Penguin Books, 1976.

MacCormack, Sabine. "Roma, Constantinopolis, the Emperor, and His Genius." *Classical Quarterly* 25, no. 1 (May 1975): 131–150.

Macleod, Fiona [William Sharp]. *Iona*. Edinburgh: Floris Books, 1996.

Macrobius. *Commentary on the Dream of Scipio*. Trans. and ed. William Harris Stahl. New York: Columbia University Press, 1990.

Mahdi, Muhsin. *Ibn Khaldun's Philosophy of History*. London: George Allen and Unwin, 1957.

Mainemelis, Charalampos. "Time and Timelessness: Creativity in (and out of) the Temporal Dimension." *Creativity Research Journal* 14, no. 2 (2002): 227–238.

Manaceine [Manasetna], Marie de. *Sleep: Its Physiology, Pathology, Hygiene, and Psychology*. London: Walter Scott, 1897.

Mansfield, Victor. *Synchronicity, Science and Soul-Making*. Chicago: Open Court, 1998.

Marshall, S. J. *The Mandate of Heaven: Hidden History in the I Ching*. New York: Columbia University Press, 2001.

Martin, Geoffrey T. *The Hidden Tombs of Memphis*. London: Thames and Hudson, 1992.

Matthews, Caitlín. *King Arthur and the Goddess of the Land: The Divine Feminine in the Mabinogion*. Rochester, VT: Inner Traditions, 2002.

Matthews, Caitlín, and John Matthews. *The Encyclopaedia of Celtic Wisdom*. Shaftesbury, England: Element, 1994.

Mavromatis, Andres. *Hypnagogia*. London: Routledge, 1991.

McCullough, David. *John Adams*. New York: Simon & Schuster, 2001.

McGill, T. O. "Dreams: Some Instances of the Prophetic, the Revelative and the Sequential." *New York Times*, September 21, 1901.

McTaggart, Lynne. *The Intention Experiment*. New York: Free Press, 2007.

Meier, C. A., ed. *Atom and Archetype: The Pauli/Jung Letters, 1932–1958*. Trans. David Roscoe. Princeton, NJ: Princeton University Press, 2001.

Merridale, Catherine. *Night of Stone: Death and Memory in Twentieth-Century Russia*. New York: Viking, 2001.

Metzner, Ralph. *The Well of Remembrance: Rediscovering the Earth Wisdom Myths of Northern Europe*. Boston: Shambhala, 1994.

Meuleman, Johan H. "La causalité dans la *Muqaddimah* d'Ibn Khaldūn." *Studia Islamica*, no. 74 (1991): 105–142.

Middleton, John, ed. *Magic, Witchcraft, and Curing*. Garden City, NY: Natural History Press, 1967.

Milarepa. *The Hundred Thousand Songs of Milarepa*. Trans. Garma C. C. Chang. 2 vols. Boston: Shambhala, 1989.

Miller, Arthur I. *Insights of Genius: Imagery and Creativity in Science and Art*. New York: Copernicus/Springer-Verlag, 1996.

Miller, Pamela Cox. *Dreams in Late Antiquity: Studies in the Imagination of a Culture*. Princeton, NJ: Princeton University Press, 1994.

Misch, Georg. *A History of Autobiography in Antiquity*. 2 vols. Cambridge, MA: Harvard University Press, 1951.

Mittermaier, Amira. "The Book of Visions: Dreams, Poetry, and Prophecy in Contemporary Egypt." *International Journal of Middle East Studies* 39 (2007): 229–247.

Modesto, Ruby, and Guy Mount. *Not for Innocent Ears: Spiritual Traditions of a Desert Cahuilla Medicine Woman*. Arcata, CA: Sweetlight Books, 2000.

Moran, Lord. *Churchill: The Struggle for Survival*. London: Constable, 1966.

———. *Churchill: Taken from the Diaries of Lord Moran*. Boston: Houghton Mifflin, 1966.

Moreira, Isabel. *Dreams, Visions, and Spiritual Authority in Merovingian Gaul*. Ithaca, NY: Cornell University Press, 2000.

Morphy, Howard. "Art and Religion in Eastern Arnhem Land." In *The Inspired Dream: Life as Art in Aboriginal Australia*, ed. Margie K. C. West, pp. 30–33. Brisbane: Queensland Art Gallery, 1988.

Moses, Stéphane. "The Cultural Index of Freud's *Interpretation of Dreams*." In *Dream Cultures: Explorations in the Comparative History of Dreaming*, ed. David Shulman and Guy G. Stroumsa, pp. 303–314. New York: Oxford University Press, 1999.

Moss, Robert. "Blackrobes and Dreamers: Jesuit Reports on the Shamanic Dream Practices of the Northern Iroquoians." *Shaman's Drum*, no. 28 (1998): 30–39.

———. *Conscious Dreaming*. New York: Crown, 1996.

———. *The Dreamer's Book of the Dead*. Rochester, VT: Destiny Books, 2005.

———. *Dreamgates: An Explorer's Guide to the Worlds of Soul, Imagination, and Life beyond Death*. New York: Three Rivers Press, 1998.

———. *Dreaming True*. New York: Pocket Books, 2000.

———. *Dreamways of the Iroquois*. Rochester, VT: Destiny Books, 2005.

———. *The Firekeeper*. New York: Tom Doherty Associates, 1995.

———. "Missionaries and Magicians." In *Wonders of the Invisible World: 1600–1900*, ed. Peter Benes. Boston: Boston University Press, 1995.

———. *Moscow Rules*. New York: Villard, 1985.

———. *The Three "Only" Things: Tapping the Power of Dreams, Coincidence, and Imagination*. Novato, CA: New World Library, 2007.

Moyers, Bill. *Healing and the Mind*. New York: Doubleday, 1993.

Myers, F. W. H. *Human Personality and Its Survival of Bodily Death*. 2 vols. London: Longmans, Green, 1903.

Nahin, Paul J. *Time Machines: Time Travel in Physics, Metaphysics, and Science Fiction*. New York: Springer Verlag, 1999.

Naydler, Jeremy. *Shamanic Wisdom in the Pyramid Texts*. Rochester, VT: Inner Traditions, 2005.

Needham, Joseph. *Science and Civilisation in China*. 2 vols. Cambridge: Cambridge University Press, 1956.

Nerval, Gérard de. *Aurélia*. Trans. Geoffrey Wagner. Boston: Exact Change, 1996.

Nicholl, Charles. *Leonardo da Vinci: Flights of the Mind*. New York: Penguin, 2004.

Nielsen, Tore A., and Stenstrom, Philippe. "What Are the Memory Sources of Dreaming?" *Nature* 437, no. 27 (October 2005): 1286–89.

Nock, Arthur Darby. *Conversion*. Oxford: Oxford University Press, 1933.

Noegel, Scott B. "Dreams and Dream Interpreters in Mesopotamia and in the Hebrew Bible." In *Dreams: A Reader in the Religious, Cultural, and Psychological Dimensions of Dreaming*, ed. Kelly Bulkeley, pp. 45–72. New York: Palgrave, 2001.

Nowak, Margaret, and Stephen W. Durrant, eds. and trans. *The Tale of the Nišan Shamaness: A Manchu Folk Epic*. Seattle: University of Washington Press, 1977.

Oberhelman, Steven M. "Galen, *On Diagnosis from Dreams*." *Journal of the History of Medicine and Allied Sciences* 38 (January 1983): 36–47.

O'Flaherty, Wendy Doniger. *Dreams, Illusion, and Other Realities*. Chicago: University of Chicago Press, 1984.

———, trans. *The Rig Veda: An Anthology*. New York: Penguin Books, 1986.

Oppenheim, A. Leo. *The Interpretation of Dreams in the Ancient Near East*. Philadelphia: American Philosophical Society, 1956.

Osborne, Roger. *The Dreamer of the Calle San Salvador: Visions of Sedition and Sacrilege in Sixteenth-Century Spain*. London: Pimlico, 2002.

Pandolfo, Stefania. *Impasse of the Angels: Scenes from a Moroccan Space of Memory*. Chicago: University of Chicago Press, 1997.

Pandya, Vishvajit, "Forest Smells and Spider Webs: Ritualized Dream Interpretation among Andaman Islanders." *Dreaming* 14, nos. 2–3 (June–September 2004): 136–150.

Paracelsus. *Selected Writings*. Trans. Norbert Guterman. Princeton, NJ: Princeton University Press, 1995.

Park, George K. "Divination and Its Social Contexts." *Journal of the Royal Anthropological Institute* 93, no. 2 (1963): 195–209.

Paterson, Jacqueline Memory. *Tree Wisdom*. London: Thorsons, 1996.

Pauli, Wolfgang. *Writings on Physics and Philosophy*. Ed. Charles P. Enz and Karl von Meyenn, trans. Robert Schlapp. Heidelberg: Springer-Verlag, 1994.

Pearcy, Lee T. "Diagnosis as Narrative in Ancient Literature." *American Journal of Philology* 113, no. 4 (Winter 1992): 595–616.

Peek, Philip M. *African Divination Systems*. Bloomington: Indiana University Press, 1991.

Peierls, R. E. "Wolfgang Ernest Pauli, 1900–1958." *Biographical Memoirs of Fellows of the Royal Society* 5 (February 1960): 174–192.

Pernoud, Régine. *Joan of Arc by Herself and Her Witnesses.* Trans. Edward Hyams. Lanham, NH: Scarborough Press, 1982.

Pernoud, Régine, and Marie-Véronique Clin. *Joan of Arc: Her Story.* Trans. Jeremy du Quesnay Adams. New York: St. Martin's Griffin, 1999.

Perry, Mark. *Grant and Twain: The Story of a Friendship That Changed America.* New York: Random House, 2004.

Pert, Candace. *Molecules of Emotion: Why You Feel the Way You Feel.* New York: Scribner, 1997.

Philo. "On Dreams, That They Are God-Sent." In *The Works of Philo,* trans. C. D. Yonge, pp. 365–410. Peabody, MA: Hendrickson Publishers, 1993.

Pinney, Christopher. *"Photos of the Gods": The Printed Image and Political Struggle in India.* London: Reaktion Books, 2004.

Pisan, Christine de. *The Writings of Christine de Pisan.* Ed. Charity Cannon Willard. New York: Persea Books, 1993.

Plato. *Collected Dialogues.* Ed. Edith Hamilton and Huntington Cairnes. Princeton, NJ: Bollingen, 1989.

Plutarch. "Concerning the Face Which Appears in the Orb of the Moon." In *Moralia.* Vol. 12, trans. Harold Cherniss and William Helmbold. Cambridge, MA: Harvard University Press, 1995.

———. "Isis and Osiris." In *Moralia.* Vol. 5, trans. F. C. Babbitt. Cambridge, MA: Harvard University Press, 1993.

———. *The Lives of the Noble Greeks and Romans.* Trans. John Dryden, rev. Arthur Hugh Clough. New York: Modern Library, 1960.

———. "The Obsolescence of Oracles." In *Moralia.* Vol. 5, trans. F. C. Babbitt. Cambridge, MA: Harvard University Press, 1993.

———. "On the Delays of the Divine Vengeance." In *Moralia.* Vol. 7, trans. Philip H. DeLacy and Benedict Einarson. Cambridge, MA: Harvard University Press, 1959.

Poirier, Sylvie. "This Is Good Country, We Are Good Dreamers": Dreams and Dreaming in the Australian Western Desert." In *Dream Travelers: Sleep Experiences and Culture in the Western Pacific,* ed. Roger Ivar Lohmann, pp. 107–126. New York: Palgrave Macmillan, 2003.

Popescu, Petru. *Amazon Beaming.* New York: Viking, 1991.

Porteous, Alexander. *The Forest in Folklore and Mythology.* Mineola, NY: Dover, 2002.

Powers, Ron. *Mark Twain: A Life.* New York: Free Press, 2005.

Price, S. R. F. "The Future of Dreams: From Freud to Artemidorus." *Past and Present,* no. 113 (November 1986): 3–37.

Priestley, J. B. *Man and Time.* London: Aldus Books, 1964.

Pushkin, Alexander. *Eugene Onegin.* Trans. Walter Arndt. New York: E. P. Dutton, 1963.

Radhakrishnan, S., trans. *The Principal Upaniṣads.* New Delhi: Indus, 1995.

Rattray, Captain R. S. *Religion and Art in Ashanti.* Oxford: Clarendon Press, 1927.

Ray, John. *Reflections of Osiris: Lives from Ancient Egypt.* Oxford: Oxford University Press, 2002.

Reardon, B. P., ed. *Collected Ancient Greek Novels.* Berkeley: University of California Press, 1989.

Reid, Janice. *Sorcerers and Healing Spirits: Continuity and Change in an Aboriginal Medical System*. Rushcutters Bay: Australian National University Press, 1983.

Richardson, Slan, ed. *Dancers to the Gods: The Magical Records of Charles Seymour and Christine Hartley, 1937–1939*. Wellingborough, England: Aquarian Press, 1985.

Richey, Stephen W. *Joan of Arc: The Warrior Saint*. Westport, CT: Praeger, 2003.

Rock, Andrea. *The Mind at Night: The New Science of How and Why We Dream*. New York: Basic Books, 2004.

Roheim, Geza. *The Gates of the Dream*. New York: International Universities Press, 1970.

Roseman, Marina. *Healing Sounds from the Malaysian Rainforest: Temiar Music and Medicine*. Berkeley: University of California Press, 1993.

Ross, Anne. *The Folklore of the Scottish Highlands*. New York: Barnes & Noble, 1993.

Ross, Anne, and Don Robins. *The Life and Death of a Druid Prince*. New York: Summit, 1989.

Rothenberg, Albert. "Creative Cognitive Processes in Kekulé's Discovery of the Structure of the Benzene Molecule." *American Journal of Psychology* 108, no. 3 (Fall 1995): 419–38.

Ruderman, David B. *A Valley of Vision: The Heavenly Journey of Abraham ben Hananiah Yagel*. Philadelphia: University of Pennsylvania Press, 1990.

Rumi, Jalal al-Din. *Tales from the Masnavi*. Trans. A. J. Arberry. Richmond, England: Curzon Press, 1994.

Rush, Benjamin. *Letters of Benjamin Rush*. Ed. L. H. Butterfield. 2 vols. Princeton, NJ: American Philosophical Society, 1951.

Russo, Richard, ed. *Dreams Are Wiser Than Men*. Berkeley: North Atlantic Books, 1987.

Savary, Louis, with Patricia H. Berne and Strephon Kaplan Williams. *Dreams and Spiritual Growth*. Mahwah, NJ: Paulist Press, 1984.

Schmitt, Jean-Claude. *Ghosts in the Middle Ages: The Living and the Dead in Medieval Society*. Trans. Teresa Lavender Fagan. Chicago: University of Chicago Press, 1998.

———. "The Liminality and Centrality of Dreams in the Medieval West." In *Dream Cultures: Explorations in the Comparative History of Dreaming*, ed. David Shulman and Guy G. Stroumsa, pp. 274–287. New York: Oxford University Press, 1999.

Schubert, Gotthilf Heinrich von. *Die Symbolik des Träumes*. 1814. Reprint, Leipzig: Brodhaus, 1862.

Schutz, John A., and Douglass Adair. *The Spur of Fame: Dialogues of John Adams and Benjamin Rush*. San Marino, CA: Huntington Library, 1966.

Seferis, George. "The Angel." In *Mythistorema*, in *Collected Poems*, trans. Edmund Keeley and Philip Sherrard, p. 3. London: Anvil Press Poetry, 1982.

Shafton, Anthony, ed. *Dream Reader: Contemporary Approaches to the Understanding of Dreams*. Albany: State University of New York Press, 1995.

Shainberg, Catherine. *Kabbalah and the Power of Dreaming*. Rochester, VT: Inner Traditions, 2005.

Shaughnessy, Edward L., trans. *I Ching, the Classic of Changes*. New York: Ballantine, 1997.

Shelden, Michael. *Graham Greene: The Enemy Within*. New York: Random House, 1994.

Sherry, Norman. *The Life of Graham Greene: Volume 1, 1904–1939*. New York: Viking, 1989.

———. *The Life of Graham Greene: Volume 2, 1939–1955*. New York: Viking, 1994.

———. *The Life of Graham Greene: Volume 3, 1955–1991*. New York: Viking, 2004.

Shlain, Leonard. *Art and Physics: Parallel Visions in Space, Time, and Light*. New York: Quill, 1991.

Shulman, David, and Guy G. Stroumsa, eds. *Dream Cultures: Explorations in the Comparative History of Dreaming.* New York: Oxford University Press, 1999.

Sireen, Allamah Muhammad bin. *Dreams and Interpretations.* Trans. Muhammad Hathurani. New Delhi: Islamic Book Service, 2007.

Snow, C. P. *Variety of Men.* London: Macmillan, 1967.

Soames, Mary, ed. *Winston and Clementine: The Personal Letters of the Churchills.* Boston: Houghton Mifflin, 1999.

Sobel, Mechal. *Teach Me Dreams: The Search for Self in the Revolutionary Era.* Princeton, NJ: Princeton University Press, 2000.

Stafford, David. *Churchill and Secret Service.* Woodstock: Overlook Press, 1997.

States, Bert O. "Authorship in Dreams and Fictions." *Dreaming* 4, no. 4 (December 1994): 237–254.

———. *Dreaming and Storytelling.* Ithaca, NY: Cornell University Press, 1993.

Steiner, George. "The Historicity of Dreams." In *No Passion Spent: Essays, 1978–1996,* pp. 207–223. New Haven, CT: Yale University Press, 1996.

Stephen, Michele. *A'aisa's Gifts: A Study of Magic and the Self.* Berkeley: University of California Press, 1995.

Still, William. *The Underground Railroad: A Record of Facts, Authentic Narratives, Letters, &c.* Philadelphia: Porter & Coates, 1872. Project Gutenberg Ebook 15263.

Storr, Anthony. *Churchill's Black Dog, Kafka's Mice, and Other Phenomena of the Human Mind.* New York: Ballantine Books, 1990.

Suhrawardi, Shahabuddin. *A Dervish Textbook* ['*Awariful-Ma'arif*]. Trans. H. Wilberforce Clarke. London: Octagon Press, 1990.

Sullivan, Lawrence E. *Icanchu's Drum: An Orientation to Meaning in South American Religions.* New York: Macmillan, 1988.

Szpakowska, Kasia Maria. "The Perception of Dreams and Nightmares in Ancient Egypt: Old Kingdom to Third Intermediate Period." PhD diss., University of California, Los Angeles, 2000.

Tedlock, Barbara. "Bicultural Dreaming as an Intersubjective Communicative Practice." *Dreaming* 17, no. 2 (2007): 57–72.

———, ed. *Dreaming: Anthropological and Psychological Interpretations.* Santa Fe, NM: School of American Research Press, 1992.

———. "The New Anthropology of Dreaming." *Dreaming* 1, no. 2 (1991).

———. *The Woman in the Shaman's Body.* New York: Bantam, 2005.

Temple, Robert K. G. *The Sirius Mystery.* Rochester, VT: Destiny Books, 1987.

Thomas, Ronald R. *Dreams of Authority: Freud and the Fictions of the Unconscious.* Ithaca, NY: Cornell University Press, 1990.

Thwaites, Reuben Gold, ed. *Jesuit Relations and Allied Documents: Travels and Explorations of the Jesuit Missionaries in New France, 1610–1791.* 73 vols. Cleveland, OH: Burrows Brothers, 1896–1901.

Tick, Edward. *The Practice of Dream Healing: Bringing Ancient Greek Mysteries into Modern Medicine.* Wheaton, IL: Quest Books, 2001.

Todorov, Tzvetan. *The Conquest of America.* Trans. Richard Howard. New York: Harper & Row, 1984.

Trachtenberg, Joshua. *Jewish Magic and Superstition: A Study in Folk Religion.* New York: Atheneum, 1974.

Tsao Hsueh-chin. *Dream of the Red Chamber*. Trans. and adapted by Chichen Wang. 1754. Reprint, New York: Anchor Books, 1989.

Twain, Mark. *The Autobiography of Mark Twain*. Ed. Charles Neider. New York: Perennial Classics, 1990.

———. *A Connecticut Yankee in King Arthur's Court*. Berkeley: University of California Press, 1984.

———. *The Devil's Race-Track: Mark Twain's "Great Dark" Writings*. Ed. John S. Tuckey. Berkeley: University of California Press, 2005.

———. *The Innocents Abroad*. New York: New American Library, 1980.

———. *Letters*. Ed. Michael B. Frank et al. 6 vols. Berkeley: University of California Press, 1988–2002.

———. *Letters from the Earth*. Ed. Bernard DeVoto. New York: HarperCollins, 1991.

———. *Mark Twain's Notebook*. Ed. Albert Bigelow Paine. New York: Harper & Bros., 1935.

———. *Mississippi Writings: The Adventures of Tom Sawyer, Life on the Mississippi, Adventures of Huckleberry Finn, Pudd'nhead Wilson*. New York: Library of America, 1982.

———. *No. 44, The Mysterious Stranger*. Berkeley: University of California Press, 1982.

———. *Notebooks & Journals*. Ed. Frederick Anderson et al. 3 vols. Berkeley: University of California Press, 1975–1979.

———. *Personal Recollections of Joan of Arc*. New York: Gramercy, 2000.

———. *Tales of Wonder*. Ed. David Ketterer. Lincoln: University of Nebraska Press, 2003.

———. *What Is Man? And Other Philosophical Writings*. Ed. Paul Baender. Berkeley: University of California Press, 1973.

———. *Which Was the Dream? And Other Symbolic Writings of the Later Years*. Ed. John S. Tuckey. Berkeley: University of California Press, 1968.

Ullman, Montague, and Nan Zimmerman. *Working with Dreams*. New York: Delacorte Press, 1979.

Uphill, Eric. "The Egyptian Sed-Festival Rites." *Journal of Near Eastern Studies* 24 (1965): 365–83.

Valli, Katja, and Antti Revonsuo. "Evolutionary Psychological Approaches to Dream Content." In *The New Science of Dreaming*, ed. Deirdre Barrett and Patrick McNamara, 3:95–116. Westport, CT: Praeger, 2007.

Van de Castle, Robert L. *Our Dreaming Mind*. New York: Ballantine, 1994.

Van der Post, Laurens. *Jung and the Story of Our Time*. New York: Vintage Books, 1977.

Van Erkelens, Herbert. "Wolfgang Pauli's Dialogue with the Spirit of Matter." *Psychological Perspectives*, no. 24 (1991): 34–53.

Vasilevic, G. M. "The Acquisition of Shamanic Ability among the Evenki Tungus." In *Popular Beliefs and Folklore in Siberia*, ed. V. Dioszegi. Bloomington: Indiana University Press, 1968.

von Franz, Marie-Louise. *Dreams*. Boston: Shambhala, 1991.

———. *The Golden Ass of Apuleius*. Boston: Shambhala, 1992.

———. *On Divination and Synchronicity: The Psychology of Meaningful Chance*. Toronto: Inner City Books, 1980.

———. *On Dreams and Death*. Boston: Shambhala, 1987.

———. *Projection and Re-Collection in Jungian Psychology*. La Salle, IL: Open Court, 1980.

Von Grünebaum, G. E., and Roger Caillois, eds. *The Dream and Human Societies*. Los Angeles: University of California Press, 1966.

Walde, Christine. "Dream Interpretation in a Prosperous Age? Artemidorus, the Greek

Interpreter of Dreams." In *Dream Cultures: Explorations in the Comparative History of Dreaming*, ed. David Shulman and Guy G. Stroumsa, pp. 121–142. New York: Oxford University Press, 1999.

Walsh, Lorena S. "The Chesapeake Slave Trade: Regional Patterns, African Origins, and Some Implications." *William and Mary Quarterly* 58, no. 1 (January 2001): 139–170.

Wells, H. G. *Selected Stories*. New York: Modern Library, 2004.

Wilhelm, Richard, and Cary F. Baynes, trans. *The I Ching, or Book of Changes*. Princeton, NJ: Princeton University Press, 1990.

Wilhelm, Richard, with C. G. Jung. *The Secret of the Golden Flower*. Trans. Richard Wilhelm. 1931. Reprint, San Diego: Harcourt Brace Jovanovich, 1962.

Winkler, Gershon. *Magic of the Ordinary: Recovering the Shamanic in Judaism*. Berkeley: North Atlantic Books, 2003.

Winters, Warrington. "Dickens and the Psychology of Dreams." *PMLA* 63, no. 3 (September 1948): 984–1006.

Wolfson, Boris. "Escape from Literature: Constructing the Soviet Self in Yuri Olesha's Diary of the 1930s." *Russian Review* 63, no. 4 (October 2004): 609–620.

Wolkstein, Diane, and Samuel Noah Kramer. *Inanna, Queen of Heaven: Her Stories and Hymns from Sumer*. New York: Harper & Row, 1983.

Wroblewski, Andrzej K. "The Downfall of Parity — the Revolution That Happened Fifty Years Ago." *Acta Physica Polonica* 39, no. 2 (2008): 251–264.

Yeats, W. B. *Autobiography*. New York: Collier Books, 1965.

———. *Essays and Introductions*. New York: Collier Books, 1977.

———. *Mythologies*. New York: Macmillan, 1959.

———. "Swedenborg, Mediums, and Desolate Places." In *Visions and Beliefs in the West of Ireland*, ed. Lady Gregory. Gerrards Cross, England: Colin Smythe, 1992.

———. *A Vision*. New York: Collier Books, 1966.

———. "Witches and Wizards and Irish Folk-Lore." In *Visions and Beliefs in the West of Ireland*, ed. Lady Gregory. Gerrards Cross, England: Colin Smythe, 1992.

Young, Serinity. *Dreaming in the Lotus: Buddhist Dream Narrative, Imagery, and Practice*. Boston: Wisdom Publications, 1999.

———. "Dream Practices in Medieval Tibet." *Dreaming* 9, no. 1 (March 1999): 23–42.

Zabriskie, Beverley. "Synchronicity and the *I Ching*: Jung, Pauli, and the Chinese Woman." *Journal of Analytical Psychology* 50 (2005): 223–235.

Zajaczowski, Henry. "Tchaikovsky: The Missing Piece of the Jigsaw Puzzle." *Musical Times* 131, no. 1767 (1990): 238–242.

Zambrano, Maria, with Edison Simons and Juan Blazquez. *Sueños y procesos de Lucrecia de León*. Madrid: Editorial Tecnos, 1987.

Zeitlin, Solomon. "Dreams and Their Interpretation from the Biblical Period to the Tannaitic Time: An Historical Study." *Jewish Quarterly Review* 66, no. 1 (July 1975): 1–18.

Zhilkina, N. V. "The Extreme Component in Idea Generation." *Analytical Culturology* 2, no. 6 (2006).

Zohar: The Book of Enlightenment. Trans. and ed. Daniel Chanan Matt. New York: Paulist Press, 1993.

INDEX

ABOUT THE AUTHOR

Robert Moss was born in Australia, and his fascination with the dreamworlds dates from his childhood, when he had three near-death experiences and first learned the ways of a traditional dreaming people through his friendship with Aborigines. He is the pioneer of Active Dreaming, an original synthesis of modern dreamwork and shamanic practices for journeying and healing, and leads seminars and trainings all over the world. He is also a novelist, journalist, and independent scholar. He has been a professor of ancient history at the Australian National University, a syndicated columnist, and a magazine editor. His many books include *Conscious Dreaming*, *Dreamgates*, and *The Three "Only" Things: Tapping the Power of Dreams, Coincidence, and Imagination*. He hosts the *Way of the Dreamer* radio show and leads a very active online dream school. He lives in upstate New York. His website is www.mossdreams.com.

NEW WORLD LIBRARY is dedicated to publishing books and other media that inspire and challenge us to improve the quality of our lives and the world.

We are a socially and environmentally aware company, and we strive to embody the ideals presented in our publications. We recognize that we have an ethical responsibility to our customers, our staff members, and our planet.

We serve our customers by creating the finest publications possible on personal growth, creativity, spirituality, wellness, and other areas of emerging importance. We serve New World Library employees with generous benefits, significant profit sharing, and constant encouragement to pursue their most expansive dreams.

As a member of the Green Press Initiative, we print an increasing number of books with soy-based ink on 100 percent postconsumer-waste recycled paper. Also, we power our offices with solar energy and contribute to nonprofit organizations working to make the world a better place for us all.

Our products are available
in bookstores everywhere.
For our catalog, please contact:

New World Library
14 Pamaron Way
Novato, California 94949

Phone: 415-884-2100 or 800-972-6657
Catalog requests: Ext. 50
Orders: Ext. 52
Fax: 415-884-2199
Email: escort@newworldlibrary.com

To subscribe to our electronic newsletter, visit
www.newworldlibrary.com